DIARY OF
THE REAL
SOUL CREW
THE COMPLETE
CHRONICLES

DIARY OF THE REAL SOUL CREW

THE COMPLETE CHRONICLES

ANNIS ABRAHAM JNR.

Pennant Books

First published in paperback 2010 by Pennant Books.

Text copyright © 2008/2009/2010 by Annis Abraham Jnr.

The moral right of the author has been asserted.

Pictures reproduced with kind permission of the author.

Cover photos © Press Association Photos.

British Library Cataloguing-in-Publication Data:
A catalogue record for this book is available on request from
The British Library

ISBN 978-1-906015-53-4

Design & Typeset by Envy Design Ltd.

Printed and bound in Great Britain by Cox & Wyman

Pennant Books
PO Box 5675
London W1A 3FB

www.pennantbooks.com

Best wishes

his F.
CCFC

ABOUT THE AUTHOR

Annis Abraham Jnr. is a lifelong Cardiff City FC supporter, with deep-rooted connections to his club. The son of a self-made millionaire of direct Egyptian descent, he has not merely been a football fan or (allegedly) a hooligan, but also an entrepreneur who has sponsored Cardiff City's players, kits, vehicles, match balls and programmes. As a successful businessman, Annis stresses that he has long since moved on from any personal association with football hooliganism. *Diary of the Real Soul Crew* is his compendium of testimony from Cardiff City's hooligan era, and a monumental work of 'hooli-lit'.

www.annisabraham.co.uk

CONTENTS

ACKNOWLEDGEMENTS

Once again, a big thank-you and love to my wife Joanne for typing it all up and being patient with me. (I did manage to learn to type a few lines. Hee hee!) Special love to my children Annaise and Alexandra, who are both true Bluebirds, and to baby Tilly Annis.

A big thank-you to all the lads who helped put the book together, for all their stories: Pat Dolan (Chelsea); Jonathan Evans (Cardiff); Mikey Dye (Ely Trendy, Cardiff); Viking (Cardiff); Little Collin (Cardiff); Frankie D (Cardiff); Jeff Marsh (Cardiff); Simon Neads (Neath Punk); Dave Sugarman (Cardiff); John Simmonds ('Simmo', Cardiff); Glenn V (Cardiff); Lee 'Tonto' Davies (Cardiff); Dave Chappell (Crystal Palace); Con (Cardiff); Paul Corkery (Valleys Cardiff); Mallo (Cardiff); Mac (Cardiff); Simon Williams (Cardiff); Big Sam (Valleys Cardiff); Gwyn Davies (Valleys Cardiff); Alex Mannings (Cardiff Youth); Mac (Cardiff); 'Little Pete' Lintern (Cardiff); Joe (Cardiff); Taffy Anton (Cardiff); Tony Ridgeway ('Guff', PVM, Port Talbot); Stefan (Offenbach FC); Mark Gregory (QPR); Diddy (Boro); Hicky (Chelsea); Danny (Plymouth); Nicky Muff (Leeds Utd); Ginger Bob (Millwall); Sooty Jason and J (Zulus, Birmingham City); Barnsley Five-0; Mick (Man Utd).

Special thanks to a good friend, Warren Feeney (ex-Luton and Cardiff/Northern Ireland International).

Thanks to my godsons, Connor Sullivan and Daniel Evans, for being Bluebirds.

Thank you to all the following who gave me photos: Alun Griffiths ('Jaffa', Bridgend); Steve Wilson (Llanrumney); Darren Williams (Bridgend); Paul Williams (Canton); Tim (Lawnmower MB); Richard Sandham (Skewen); Jerry (Gazza Llantrisant);

Steve Williams (Suggs); Kev Ederle (Holyhead); Gareth Rogers; Wayne and Morgan Anderson; Pam, Lee and Jermaine Simmonds; Sean Canton (for promoting my books); Steve Evans (Wolf MB); Martin (Cardiff 74 MB); Glenn Villis; Damian (Feedback MB); Nick Fish (MB); Chunky (Pontypridd); Callum (MB); Peter Thomas (photos); Dave, Rob and Angie (Express Imaging, City Road, Cardiff); Mike Williams (Press to Print, City Road, Cardiff); Simon Insole, Wayne and Mario.

To the following persons and shops, who have helped me and have sold my books: Matthew Stern Clothing (Pontypridd); Matt at Loft Clothing (Barry); Sam; A2 Clothing (Victoria Street, Merthyr); Paul; Mojo King (Wellfield Road, Cardiff); Nick; Original Footwear (Barnsley); Mark; Dudden Newsagents (80 Albany Road, Cardiff); Sean (Cardiff market); Billy (the Badge Man); Here's News newsagents (32 Albany Road, Cardiff); www.casualsclobber.co.uk (WBA).

Thanks also to: Geraint Handley (Cheggers); Jamie Sullivan; Chippy, Milly and Clare; Frankie Dimodica; Viking (Nils); Dave Bennett; Lyndon Cushing; Bradley Ashford; Conrad; Paul Corky (Valley Rams); Big Sam's wife Debbie and daughter Kate Murphy; Jamie Francis; Dai Thomas; Ginger Jones; the Clemo brothers (Bridgend); A. Rawlings; Darryl; Julian Jenks; Richard E; Paul Williams (Willie); Ian Thomas; Kersy; Shep; Terry; Staples; Wally; Joff; James; Wayne Critchon; Neil MacInnes; Andrew Jones; P. Gregson; C. Beer; Chris (Jelly Head); Paul Santos; Richard Cordle; Weller; Big Foot; Maxwell; Ivor; Oggy; Gary S; Ginger Nick; Jason (TGI); Neil Davey; Ritchie (the Mod); Gabbsnewt (MB); Wilts Blue (MB); Steven (Brummy); Keith (the King's Castle pub); Webber; Gonk; Simon; Julian Kelly; Toddy; Tongy; Kenny (Aberdare); Alistar; G. Price; Mojo; Dayo; Wilts; Fisher; Marksy; Stud; Jaffa (Valleys); Ketty; Peter Morgan (Moggs); Mr Williams; Sticky; Chris Smith (Snibs); Peter Morgan; Gareth Davies; Paul Morgan (Sect A, and all the other lads who sit in there); Big Tec; Little Tec; Chris Price; Craig McGowan; Vince and Matthew Alm; Leighton; Thomas; Christian; Dean; Wilbur; Carl and Jammo Curtis; Lug; Chongo; Dobbo; Wilo; Gabby; Jacko; Sam Hammam and Steve Borley;

Carl Curtis; Baz; Greg Davies; Milly; Chippy; Jamie Curtis; Ian Shepherd; Claire; Jez; Ben; Papa; Thomas; Steve Davies; Gwyn Davies; Paul Humphries; Ian Derby Bluebird; John Smith; Fishy; Steff; Clarkie (Welsh Guards); Taunton Blue; Pete (under the spotlight); Matt (cage fighter); Skunky; Bobby; Billy; Anne and Mark (Scotch Corner Santa Ponsa).

To the following Ely Trendies: Peter Mannings, R. Moorie, Smiler, Nick, Penny, Baggers, Pip, Dean, Young Ant, Morgan, Justin, Glen J, Andrew, Ben, Jayo S, Jammo, Zub, Ernie Gee, Harry, Pie Face, Cissy, Mexi, Dulla, Derym and the main lad again, Dyo.

To the following for their support: Dean (Roath); M Lyons; Chuggy; Big and Little Bubble; Mark (Penarth); Harvey; Nathan; Rob (Merthyr); McGrath (Australia); Nick and Dave (*Bluebirds Fly* fanzine); Marco; Jock; Nigel Lancastle; Dixie and Willie (Penarth); the Brownhills Dirty 30; Dave Allan (Topman); Jason; Catherine D; Helen Thomas; Nadia; Joseph and Sarah; Tony Dai H; Jonah (Brighton); Pocock; Spud; Richie (Blackwood); Johnny Bywater; Ben and Chris Griffiths; Karl and Ashley (Hereford); Stan (Pontypool); Deacon; Glenn Waife; Ian Charles; Anthony Rivers (Lakey); Dave Jones; Foster; Keith; Mark; Granville; Ginger John; Paul and Rob; Stanley; Sully; the Valley Commandoes; the Rhondda Lads; Woody; Nigel; Quinny; Rotters; Kenny H; Wilbur (Canton's); Jerky; H (Thailand); Dibble; Wally; Matty (USA); Scouse; Nigel; Gary J; AP; Phyllis (Port Talbot); Tony Jeffries; Allun Williams; Mike Flynn; Lee Beames; Chris Price; Newt; Beefy; Bevan; Blond Simmo; Chris (Caerphilly); Wilbur's (Roath); Carlton; Dafyd; Wurzel (Gloucester); Ian (Older Blue); Jesse; Hugh Boy; Rhys (Magor); Paul (Fairwater); Robert Maggs; Emlyn and Patrick (Bridgwater); Brian Edge; Pigeon; Ching; Frankie Humphries; Ray Pill Blue; Leon and Harley Phipps; John – a true blue in Jackland; Gazza and Peter, Bridgend; Joe Mullins; Beachy; Ducky; PVM (Port Talbot); the Neath Blues; all the Bridgend Lads (especially those on Dib's Tours); the 1927 lads; the Ant Hill Mob; the Milford Haven Blues; the Donut Crew; the North Wales Blues; all the lads from the Neville pub; Gethin and Chris (the Original Soul Crew); the Baker brothers; Steven Beards; Pricey; Lez; Jammo; Dowie; Shoulders; Mike Pedric; Premier 1 (Andy); Merlin (Craig); Thomas Fish (Merthyr 6); Sian and Mike (Canton); – plus all the rest of the older lads from Llanrumney, the older Barry lads from the Zoo pub, and all the Merthyr, Pontypool and Risca lads.

To all the lads from Sunderland: Brookie, Daz, Jason, Locky, the Twins, Joe and the many more that I've met who have always made me and my friends welcome and shown us great hospitality.

To Rowland (Pompey), George Calder (Kilmarnock FC), Mark Forester, Fowler and all the lads from Villa. I know the following are your archrivals, but wherever I've bumped into Big Al, Bones and Cuddles from Birmingham City, they've always bought me a drink and made me feel welcome.

To David Williams (author of *Desert England*).

To Mike for all his help (Plymouth), Kadjet (Cardiff), Tony Rees (news reporter), John Newey (WBA), Dave (Boro), Terry Last (Chelsea), Prickett, Ian Woodruff, Adams and Dave Roberts of Newport County, Gilly Shaw (Wolves), Neil, Scoots and Ponch of Wrexham, Alan Swain, Neil, Marc Parcell and Angus (Bristol C), Para Paul (Millwall), Paul (Reading FC), Mike (Wigan), Murco (Stoke City), Tony Reardon (Bolton W), Simon and Ian (AFC Wimbledon), Sam Salim and Mandy McCann (Sheffield Wednesday).

RIP: Derek Ford; Mike Rayer; Budgie and Ginger Jason (Cardiff C); Manny (Bradford C); Lemmy (Newport County).

Special thanks to all the members of
www.cardiffcityforum.co.uk. My own website is
www.annisabraham.co.uk, from which you can
purchase any of my books.

INTRODUCTION

This book is about the lads I've met over the years who all have a tale or two to tell about their times with the Soul Crew, or fighting against the Soul Crew. We will all get slated by the so-called do-gooders, but the fact remains that there was trouble at Cardiff home and away all through the years. Cardiff had a huge mob and were always up there amongst the very best. It's now part of history.

One of the main faces of the 70's was a legend called Frankie Humphries, and during my younger years it was his name I always used to hear. By the 80's, Cardiff's mob took a total turn and changed to a trendy casual look; by '82, a lad called Parsons had come onto the scene big-time, and for the first time ever Cardiff became an organised force. Parsons even came up with the name 'Soul Crew', but, as most Cardiff lads know, he became too big for his boots and was sent on his way.

And so the Soul Crew dispersed into smaller groups such as the young Soul Crew, Ely Trendies, PVM (Port Talbot), Barry Soul Crew Seasiders and mobs from different valleys. These groups were later to be joined by the Dirty 30 (from the docks and Brownhill's), who were one of the gamest firms around. By the 90's, Cardiff had probably 20 different firms and half of them were not even getting on with each other. But as the team declined the numbers got smaller, which eventually started to get everyone together again. By the end of the 90's we even had a mob called the Battle Bus, and on many occasions they themselves would take up to three coaches of good lads.

During the last 30-odd years, some of these lads have fought against each other or against the Soul Crew, but as the years have gone by they've developed a respect for each other and have even become good friends:

Pat from Chelsea is now one of my best mates. He is well respected in the football world and is now a friend to many, but Pat won't bullshit, he will tell you how it is, whether Cardiff lads like it or not. The same goes for my good mates Jonathan and Viking, who I have known since we were kids. I have the utmost respect for them, they will go straight to the point just like they did in their many battles for the Soul Crew.

Over the years of following Cardiff, I have met some good lads and some wankers too. Dave from Palace is another true mate of mine, he won't make out to be a top lad but he's seen a lot and has been involved when it mattered. He will also tell you the truth.

Simmo, who is much older than me and has been around the scene a long time, is a well known character and a very likeable one at that. On many occasions when lads have tried to slag me off, he has been one of the first to stick up for me. He and his wife Pam, who is also well respected by the lads of Cardiff and other clubs, have become true friends of mine.

Three great Valley lads – Big Sam, Gwyn Davies and Paul Corkery – have all written a piece in this book. These lads were there in the days when the crowds were 1,500 at home and 3-400 away. I have a lot of time for them; not only are they good lads, they are Cardiff through and through.

I've known Little Collin since my school days and we have even worked together. He's a boy and a half, one of the smallest lads you will ever meet, but one of the gamest, who would actually put his life on the line for you.

Mikey Dye is one of my oldest mates, a great organiser and a great lad to be with. He's got many tales to tell.

I've had some right laughs with Frankie D through the years and he's always been well up for it. He's another good mate who I could rely on when needed.

I was one of the first to take Jeff Marsh – author of *Soul Crew Seasiders* and *The Trouble with Taffies* – to away games. He's another lad you could always rely on.

Con is a true gent, and we go back to the early 80's. He was a hard lad in his day and, if called upon, would still be there now for you. He's a great laugh to go away with, and so organised. (Almost as good as me! Hee hee!)

It was unusual to have Stefan (Hoffmeister) of Offenbach FC (Germany) with us for a couple of years, but he turned out to be a good laugh and he was able to take the mick out of the opposition on many occasions. Even though he liked Celtic, I still like him and he always took it on the chin about Germany losing the war.

I remember Tonto (Lee Davies) in the 80's. He always was a daredevil, and a good laugh with it, but he was straight in on the action when it mattered. Tonto now follows Wales with a passion.

Gregors and I go back a long way. He loves to wind the opposition up and has probably made more enemies than anyone I know, but I speak as I find and he's always been a good lad to know through the years, and a good laugh with it. He's also probably got the most stories anyone could ever tell.

We all know how good Boro are, and with lads like Diddy with them during the 80's and 90's they knew they had a good firm. I met him at many matches during the years, and Jonathan and Viking have a lot of respect for him too.

Hicky is the greatest legend of all time. I met him when I was 16 years of age, he was one of Chelsea's top lads then and to this day they've never had a better organiser than him.

Simon Neads is the famous 'Neath Punk' who appears in many a book. He can be the funniest person around, but don't get on the wrong side of Simon as he will always have the last laugh. He's a lad who will always be on the frontline, a great lad to know and a good friend too, going right back to the early 80's.

Dave Sugarman got involved in the 80's too, like most lads did. You couldn't help it if you followed Cardiff back then. He admits he was never an out-and-out lad, but he saw the funny side of it. I've got to know Dave well these last few years and he has become a friend.

Mallo was a bit of a tearaway in the 80's, probably because he was the youngest lad at that time down the football and was always trying to prove himself. Well, you did, Mallo, and to this day a lot of lads have plenty of respect for you. We've remained friends for all these years, despite the odd disagreement.

Simon Williams is my mate from the same village that I live in. When I first started getting involved in the casual scene in the early 80's, it was Simon's group that I looked up to, as they were the main dressers at the time and were always there. Even though Simon was one of them, he will quite happily admit he was never on the frontline, even though many he knew were and they were also probably among the original Soul Crew.

Mac is probably the most well known lad Cardiff has, and has earned that reputation without a doubt, being well liked and respected by every firm in the country. We've known each other for well over 25 years and have stayed friends throughout. You will see Mac at every game home and away, as he is one of the most loyal fans we have.

Little Pete (Cardiff City Valleys) is obsessed with the hooligan world and was banned when I was putting this book together. I've known him for years and have always got on well with him, he's game and, though a small lad, he has no fear. Pete probably wishes he was around in the early 80's.

I knew Joe in the 80's and he went on many a trip with us, a good friend during those years and now. He has done well for himself and has totally settled down. Good on him.

Taffy Anton (Port Talbot PVM) is a lad respected even in Jackland, always to be found at the front. I've known Anton for many a year and we have total mutual respect for each other, going back to the 80's. During the writing of this book, Anton was under a six-year ban.

Guff (Port Talbot PVM) is a gentleman and a good person. Way back in the 80's he was as game as they come. He has changed his life, moved on, and now he puts his family and career first. Fair play to him.

The Sam Hammam era created the Valley Rams, when you could have anything from five to 15 coaches going away. Some of them were known as the Valley Commandoes Unorganised, but if any opposition came their way they would have needed to have had their best lads out, as the Valley Commandoes were virtually all the old heads from the 70's and 80's, who feared no one, and with them the Battle Bus mob. Cardiff in the Sam era were probably the biggest firm in the country. The tales they tell are all of their own experiences and, whether people like it or not, it's how they felt about what happened at the time.

I've spoken to all the following lads and met quite a few; even though they follow other teams, I have got on with every one of them and there is total respect for each other. It shows that football lads are not all like animals, as the media makes out. We can sit down and have a drink together and talk about the past; maybe this is what the media can't understand or doesn't want to happen, as it doesn't make a good story for them.

So respect to Danny and Mike from Plymouth (Central Element), Nicky Muff from Leeds Utd (Service Crew), Ginger Bob from Millwall (F Troop), Sooty Jason and J from Birmingham City (the Zulus), Barnsley Five-0, Gregors (QPR) and Mick from Man Utd (the Red Army).

There has been an increase in trouble at football over the last couple of years or so. I'm not sure how that has come about – maybe because a lot of bans are now up, or younger lads are coming through, or maybe it never really went away and has gone underground, with the media just picking up on any incident, from a coin being thrown to a fan being drunk or swearing. The fact remains that any type of trouble nowadays is not on a scale of five per cent of the type there was in the 70's and 80's.

Annis Abraham Jnr.

1
THE RAGING 70'S

(PRE-SOUL CREW DAYS)
Annis Abraham Jnr.

During the 70's, hooliganism was out of control. Hooligans came from every club in the league, from Cardiff to Man Utd. It was different to the 80's: fighting could go on all day, there was hardly any segregation, no CCTV and no police spotters. In those days it was the fans with scarves and football tops that would be fighting.

Cardiff City were going through a bad time on the field, especially after the sale of John Toshack to Liverpool, so all their fans had to look forward to was a punch-up with the opposition. Man Utd, Leeds and Chelsea had thousands of hooligans; even Rochdale, Torquay and Halifax had their own hooligan element. Cardiff was known during this period as a mad and unwelcoming place; you knew that, if you went there, you had to have hundreds of nutters with you just to survive. But Cardiff were never organised, they just had thousands of lunatics who were very passionate about their team. One name who was a legend with Cardiff in the 70's was Frankie Humphries, and the lads that went with him were as game as anyone. The fans we had in those days came from all over Wales, and some even came from Hereford and Somerset to support the Bluebirds. If you had Welsh ancestors, wherever you were living in England, then you gave your allegiance to the Bluebirds.

At home games Cardiff were among the best in the hooligan world, but when it came to away games at places like West Ham, Millwall, Chelsea, Man Utd, Pompey and Leeds, we had the lads but no organisation. It meant that Cardiff came unstuck on many occasions.

I started supporting the City in the middle of the 70's. As a kid, coming out of Ninian Park at the end of every game, hundreds of fans would go steaming past me down Sloper Road, towards the away end, and all hell would break loose. As the years went by, Ninian Park became so intimidating to the away fans that less and less of them came.

In the early part of the 70's, Pompey took a right liberty when, as soon as the turnstiles opened, about 3-400 of their lads were first in and made their way to the back of the Grange End (Cardiff's end in the 70's, now split with home and away fans). As Cardiff fans arrived, bit by bit, Pompey kept steaming down into them and never let Cardiff regroup or get together. To this day, Pompey are the only team ever to take Cardiff's end, as they were kept in there throughout the entire game with about 200 police standing in front of them.

In the 1974/1975 season, Man Utd had run riot and taken over everywhere they went. The Red Army, as they were known, came in their thousands to Cardiff, and boy, did they need them! Every one of them.

Cardiff weren't going to be a soft touch like the rest. They came down from the valleys in their thousands; some had even come down the night before. From early morning on that day, on every street corner there were lads from all over Wales. There were running battles everywhere; every train that arrived was attacked. As soon as they walked out of Cardiff Central, the Valleys were down on them like vultures and never let the Red Army have a minute's peace. They had the shock of their lives. They hadn't been used to such numbers attacking them before, and Cardiff were never going to let them take over their city.

The Valleys had been dreaming of this fixture the minute Man Utd had been relegated from the old Division One. All the way down to Ninian Park they lay in wait, and United had to fight their way through. Both sets of fans battled all the way through the match and gave as good as each other, but, after the game, Cardiff continued to attack them from Ninian Park to Tudor Road to Cardiff Central Station. The Red Army had never left a city in such a hurry before, and those that got away unscathed were the lucky ones.

St David's Day, March 1st 1975, saw the return at Old Trafford. 4,000 Cardiff were allowed to make the trip and everyone was expecting the biggest backlash ever, after what happened at Ninian Park. But somehow it was a total anticlimax. Firstly, Cardiff didn't have the thousands of hooligans that everyone expected to travel; secondly, United weren't as mad at home as they were when they were going away. Cardiff were quite a young firm, and United did have large gangs roaming around, but from the beginning the police had the situation well under control. Those that went said it was still a very intimidating place, but it couldn't be compared to the first game in Cardiff. So, in terms of violence, it ended up practically a non-event, while City got hammered 4-0 on the pitch.

Leeds in the 70's, on the other hand, was one of the most hostile places to go and could be compared to Ninian Park. Five thousand City fans travelled up there for the FA Cup and, before the game, gave Leeds a right shock. As soon as they got off the coaches, Cardiff didn't just wait around to see what would happen – they went berserk and ran Leeds everywhere outside of Elland Road. Leeds were totally stunned when, during the game, a lone Cardiff fan ran on the pitch, kicked the ball in the net, put his scarf down in the goal mouth and kissed it. This sent the Leeds fans mental and they invaded the pitch, with over 40 arrested. During the second half, fighting then erupted on the terraces and continued until the end of the game, which City lost 4-1. As the Cardiff fans came out of the away end, over 2,000 Leeds fans were waiting, baying for revenge for what had happened before the game. They got it too – every City fan who went that day said they received some kind of kick or punch from the Leeds nutters. Cardiff stood and fought back but were taken totally by surprise, exactly as they'd done to Leeds before the game. So, off the pitch, it was 1-1.

And then there was Cardiff v Chelsea. We've always been big rivals off the pitch for the last 40 years, and the subject would fill a book on its own. Throughout this book, with the help of

Chelsea Pat, you'll find many such stories. Both firms have a lot of respect for each other. In 1976, Cardiff did what only Leeds were previously known for, and smashed Chelsea's scoreboard up. But we went further than that after the game, when Cardiff ran around to the Shed end entrance concourse and attacked it. Chelsea never forgave Cardiff for that; in 1977 they came down in massive numbers. Not only did they outnumber Cardiff that day, they were older and well organised. By the end of the day, Cardiff had been run ragged. They stood their ground in the park opposite Ninian Park and went toe to toe with them for a while, but in the end Chelsea's numbers took their toll. On Tudor Road, many from both sides were left covered in blood, but once again Chelsea's numbers won the day.

Spurs brought a mob for the FA Cup in 1977, but it didn't compare to Chelsea and they were smashed by Cardiff.

Millwall have never come to Cardiff in their thousands, but, whether it was ten or 300 Millwall, they were always up for it. They didn't care how many you had, they'd stand no matter what. It happened all through the years, every time they have visited Ninian Park. One evening, during a midweek game in the 70's, about 70 Millwall came down. Not much happened before the game, as Cardiff hadn't been out in force, but afterwards hundreds of Cardiff waited down Sloper Road. The police panicked and tried to get Millwall into the park opposite the ground, as the fighting on Sloper Road was getting well out of control. Cardiff repeatedly attacked the police to get at Millwall, and eventually burst through the lines. The police were made to scatter, but, to Cardiff's surprise, Millwall just stood there. Then about 30 Millwall – who were armed with ammonia – sprayed the baying mob of Cardiff. Cardiff backed off, and with that Millwall ran out of the park, sending them further back onto Sloper Road. But then hundreds more Cardiff surged forward and steamed straight back into Millwall. All hell broke loose and the police went mental too, before they finally got it under control. As the 70 Millwall were being escorted by the side of the Ninian Park pub, Cardiff attacked again and again. To be fair to Millwall, they were fighting the police and some were even getting through, as most of the police were facing the Cardiff. Those that got through got a right hammering due to being outnumbered.

As the streets were now totally in darkness, the fighting got worse; for over half an hour the police had to battle with both mobs, who were intent on getting at each other. By the time Millwall got to Cardiff Central, behind them was over a mile of debris with windows, cars and anything else that got in the way all smashed up. When they left that night, they left Cardiff with a lot of respect for them. Not once did Millwall cower; they had been up for it just as much as Cardiff, the only difference being that Cardiff had the numbers.

I've heard time and time again about how the early 70's in the hooligan world were mental. The following stories run from the middle of the 70's right up to 2010; so see how some of these stories, told by the top lads in football, compare to the old days.

II

NEVER LOOKING FOR TROUBLE, BUT FINDING PLENTY ALONG THE WAY!

Gwyn Davies (CCFC)

I started watching Cardiff City at the age of ten and my first game was sometime in 1965. So I was there at the start, I was there at the peak and I'm still here during the decline of 'football hooliganism'. To those amongst us that say, "It hasn't declined and it is still active," my reply would be that if you had been there in the mid-to-late 70's, you would realise how much it really has.

The Fight or Flight 70's

People who have been involved, or simply caught up, in any incidents of 'hooliganism' will often describe the buzz and the kick they got from such events. In most cases this is the adrenalin rush caused by the 'fight or flight' situations that are part of our makeup. Many people will keep searching for more such buzzes, or even bigger and better buzzes, and these are often the lads who develop into active hooligans rather than 'accidental' hooligans – which I think, if I'm honest, that most of us are.

During the madness around the mid-70's, serious slashings and stabbings weren't even making the headlines because they were such a regular occurrence at games. People nowadays talk of a hooligan code of honour, or rules of engagement so to speak, but in the 70's it was survival of the fittest, there were no rules and very little respect for the law. These were the days when you would go somewhere on a football special train with 7-800 full-on nutters, get off in some city or town centre and not see one copper waiting for you. It sounds unbelievable, but it's true nonetheless.

Usually, when you travelled in such numbers you could look after yourselves in most cases. But going to somewhere like West Ham and arriving in Paddington at 11am, you would soon see that mob of 700 break up into smaller groups all doing their own thing. There was very little organisation, and basically at most times it was every man for himself. Getting to the ground was a challenge on its own; when you got inside the ground, some places would have recognised away ends, but in most cases you just headed for sections which weren't seen as the home fans' end. Often, at the less infamous clubs, groups would mob up, infiltrate and have a go at taking the end, but you didn't go to West Ham, Millwall and the like intending to take ends unless you had a death wish. In lots of grounds there was no segregation, hardly any police presence and, if there weren't enough of you to stand your ground or look after each other, then you just split up and blended in, trying to look inconspicuous.

Mind you, when you went to some of the big city clubs in your Wranglers (jackets and jeans) and wondered why you stood out like a spare prick at a wedding – until you looked around and saw all their fans wearing fashions you had never heard of, let alone seen – you may as well have turned up with a flashing sign on your head saying, "Here I am, please come kick and stab me."

While I may be making light of it now (having come out the other side in one piece), these were seriously scary and dodgy times. Why I or others would put themselves through that week in, week out is beyond me.

It makes me laugh now when people walk the walk, wear the gear and think that they are the new face of 'hooliganism'. My God, nowadays you spend half of your time being covered by CCTV cameras, escorted by hundreds of coppers and hundreds more stewards, helicopters, mobile phone tracing, pre-match combined police force and club meetings, picking through the intelligence and information they have gathered pre-match. You have more chance of getting into a scrap down your local Tesco's than at the football.

I would love the police and authorities to have a couple of months off and to see what happened. I doubt if lots of the brave teenage gesturing and threats would take place if they knew that, outside in the street, they would have to back up such actions. We have all seen a rival fan, safe behind his fence, his row of stewards and line of police, giving it the big 'un with his cut-throat gestures and the big 'you and me outside!' hand signals, knowing he has more chance of meeting the Queen than coming face to face with you. It would be great to see such fans stepping out of the ground and being left alone to back up their actions.

The organising of arranged offs with rival groups did not really get into full swing until the 90's and the advent of mobile phones and the internet. Prior to these times, old scores were still settled and fights were still arranged, there were planned punch-ups but most of the trouble was sporadic, if not inevitable at certain games. The mobile phone and internet era gave birth to a different type of football violence and far more offs and meetings were set up away from the stadiums.

The new technology proved to be a two-edged sword though. Just as the hooligans were getting more up to speed, so were the police, but at a faster and more advanced rate than the rival crews up and down the country.

There is no need for me to go into any detail about what technology is available to the police, but suffice to say that, while it isn't James Bond, it's a bit more advanced than a police whistle and a two-way radio. When you are shown a photograph taken from a helicopter high up above you in the sky, and in that photograph you can read the label on your shirt, then you soon realise you aren't going to get away with much. Does this mean there will be no more trouble at or around football? I very much doubt it, but it will never get back to the scale we witnessed in bygone years.

Now with regard to the title of my chapter, 'Never Looking for Trouble, but Finding Plenty along the Way', I would never consider myself a football hooligan. Mind you, my definition of hooligan might not be the same as everyone else's.

I have witnessed mob rule and anarchy at football. I have

seen people rob, smash and destroy service stations, pubs and shops, and vandalise things just because they knew they wouldn't get caught. I have seen bullying at its worst, away fans robbed of their money, clothes and any other possessions the other group wanted, cars tipped over and windows in houses along the route smashed with bricks and bottles. And at times, Cardiff fans have been some of the worst.

Now that is my image of hooliganism and, while witnessing many such incidents during my younger days and being on the fringe of things, I can honestly say I never vandalised property or bullied others just because I could. In fact, wherever possible I would step in to prevent bullying. When getting caught up in many fights over the years, I would do anything needed to get the upper hand and stay on top, but I have always known when enough is enough and also stopped my mates from causing serious harm when we've had the upper hand. I am not trying to paint a holier-than-thou image of myself, but most people that know me know how I function, and in reality most of my close mates act and think along the same lines, or they wouldn't be my mates.

Some of my best memories in regard to trouble at football involve situations where bullying by larger groups has been turned around and the larger group has come unstuck. I'm not going to write the typical 'ten of us backed off 60, and me and my two mates chased off 20 other lads,' that all gets a bit tired. But to those of you who have won every fight, and come out of every scrap unmarked, having never taken a backward step, I take my hat off.

QPR Skinheads

I swear that, in times past, if I couldn't have run faster than the 20 boys chasing me on occasions, then possibly I would not be here writing this, but sitting in a wheelchair, sucking soup through a straw. One such occasion comes back to me at QPR. It was a typical London game, back in the early 70's. There were possibly 2,000 or so City fans that had made their way up there one way or another. There was no major trouble before the game, but 20 or so of our top boys got into the Loft, had a 20-

second kick-off and then get onto the pitch, only to be booed by every Rangers fan in the stadium, and cheered by all the City fans in the away end, as if they were heroes returning home from a successful conquest overseas.

The match passed without any serious trouble, the final whistle went and we all poured out of the ground, some going this way, some going that way, and within minutes everyone had split up and spread all over. That day I'd gone up there with two mates from Aberdare, Jeff Francis and Needsy, both of them a year or two older than me, who at 17 was the baby of the group.

Now this was the early Doctor Marten era, and many grounds would either not let you in or make you hand over the laces from your boots, or even make you leave your boots at the turnstile in some cases. Needsy, being the great thinker that he wasn't, thought he'd get around this problem by taking a spare pair of trainers (or 'daps', as they were known then) with him in a carrier bag. We made our way back to the tube for our return to Paddington station. Now, while not being known for mass mob hooliganism in those days, QPR were well known for ambushing rival fans on the London underground and had it down to a fine art. I wished someone had told us though, we were like lambs to the slaughter. We went onto the platform and stood amongst hundreds of other fans, some Cardiff, some QPR, most dressed similarly as skinheads, or 'suedeheads' as they were called, and any colours were blue and white, so there were no differences there. The atmosphere was tense but not seriously threatening. However, when the tube arrived and we jumped on, things started getting a bit hairy.

The tube doors opened and every carriage seemed to be packed full with QPR skinheads. We had to get on and just brave it out, but they were the longest couple of stops of my life. Small gangs of QPR were working their way through carriages, intervening and handing out slaps to individuals or small groups of Cardiff they came across. There was no organisation and, unlike today, most of us didn't know which ones were our fellow Cardiff fans. Without having a Frankie-type (undisputed top man at the time) leader on board, none amongst us planned to make ourselves known and were just keeping our heads down.

We arrived unscathed at Paddington and thought we were home and dry. Loads got off and we just hung back. When we walked up the stairs and went to cross the bridge over the platform, we could see possibly 50 or 60 QPR boys standing at the top of the other stairs. Well, they clocked us straight away and we had a choice to either turn and run or just take our chances. We kept walking towards them and suddenly the meanest-looking one stepped forward. "Are you Cardiff?" he said. What could we say? "No, Buttie, we are from Notting Hill, honest!"

We stopped in our tracks, Needsy still with his daps and carrier bag stuck under his armpit. He went to grab the bag, either to hold it while running down the stairs or to keep it safe while we were getting kicked to fuck. But, for whatever reason, the big, bad, nasty skinhead lad jumped back, shouting, "Look out, he's got a gun!" You couldn't make it up, could you? That little jump back was just what we needed, we were down those stairs like Colin Jackson, closely followed by this gang who must now have realised that three dopey boys from Aberdare are unlikely to be walking around London with a shooter in a carrier bag. They really wanted to hurt us big-time now. Those of you that know Paddington will know how long the platforms are, and this one was the mother of all platforms. We had done the Jackson sprint, we were now looking at the Paula Radcliffe marathon. We were running and laughing with fear and you could feel their breath on the back of your neck.

We had no plan other than make sure you can run faster than your mate. But you knew you'd have to stop and take a kicking if they caught any of your mates – not that three against 50 would have done much better than one against 50. Secretly, I was just glad that Needsy was carrying his trainers rather than wearing them; that could have kept him ahead of me in the race for survival, and you don't want to be in last position in those races.

It's hard to work out how you can be running flat out and still have daft thoughts racing around your head. One thing I vividly remember is that all three of us, while running for our lives, were laughing out loud, almost hysterically, but there ahead of us was our get-out-of-jail card. Frankie and 50 of Cardiff's finest were drinking in a bar which was right at the end of the platform; they had seen our little chase and were pouring out of the bar. We were running so fast that we went through the Cardiff fans and got 20 yards out the other side before we slowed down to a stop.

The Rangers fans weren't as lucky. By the time we had turned around, there were a dozen or so sprawled over the platform and some of the lads were chasing the others back up, while others were still taking care of business.

They didn't look like they needed any help off us – thank God, because we were breathing out of our arses. Now, seeing those lads sprawled out across the platform, some with blood pouring from their noses, others with dazed looks and eyes that appeared to be spinning in different directions, all looking sheepish and trying to slope off from further damage, while I was glad it was them having the kicking and not us, deep down I still hoped that it didn't get taken too far. Justice had been done and they'd been sorted, but I did wonder if they would have let us get up and walk away with a few slaps, or would we have been kicked to hell and back, or even stabbed? These were seriously mad times and you never knew how far things could go. At least my conscience was clear and I could sleep easy in my own bed, rather than in St Mary's Hospital, as would have been the case if not for Needsy's trainers.

This was my first taste of fun at Paddington station, and it would not be the last. We have had a few run-ins around there over the years and even now, 30 years later, I still keep looking over my shoulder even if I'm up there on a shopping trip.

III
THE FIRM

THE DIRTY 30 (DOCKS BOYS)

Jonathan Evans (CCFC): Back in the late 80's, Annis had Brownhill's pub and hotel, situated right next to the central station. It was the ideal spot for us to hang out in and a really tough ol' place. (It was no Hilton, I can tell you.) But it was our HQ at the time and we were always there; for a few years it got to see some pretty naughty things happen, plus some pretty funny times too. Especially when Jellyhead got stabbed in the back, he was screaming he'd been cut, so we were all worried about how bad it was until we saw it for ourselves. Let's just say we used a plaster to cover it.

The hardcore of our crew was about 30 strong, hence the name Dirty 30. We were mainly Docks and Grangetown boys, we had a few other lads from all over Cardiff, but mainly preferred our areas. With Brownhill's so close to the city centre, we hit Cardiff's nightclub and football scene with a bang. We were a fucking handful. We had a crew of some of the maddest top boys you could ever meet, some of the toughest lads in the city. Today we are all sadly touching 40 and over, but in the late 80's we were boys – and boy, didn't we grow up fast, fighting blokes twice our age.

Through that period we had to battle out-of-town gangs for the control of the doors of our city centre. At that time you had the rave scene in full swing, where there was big money to be made, and just like all over Britain it exploded in Cardiff. This was all pre-Mac days, before he had control of most of the doors in Cardiff so the togetherness of us, outside of football, was a tight bond and therefore made us stick together at the football. In those days we were a very tight-knit firm.

The Viking was our front man, when any big steroid-head doorman faced us, he was always the one who stepped forward. At one stage when battling the doormen, it nearly got to all-out war; it came to a head one night when over 30 of our lot destroyed their main venue in town, the Ritzy. The whole place was shut down as the doormen got battered and run out, leaving a manager and DJ to run a club that held over 2,000. They were never seen again.

So the Dirty 30 became another part of Cardiff's Soul Crew at football matches. You've got Cardiff's main firm, then you've got the Valley Commandoes who do their own thing, but for big games it's just one firm together.

VALLEY RAMS

Gwyn Davies (CCFC): Chesterfield: not the first place that springs to mind when referring to a spot of bother at the footie, is it? But it certainly nearly caught us out in March 2002. I was responsible at the start of the 2001-2 season for putting together an 'organisation' known initially as the Valley Rams. My plan was to organise some regular transport to Cardiff away games, based loosely around three of the larger valleys leading off of the city of Cardiff: the Rhondda, Aberdare and Merthyr. 'Rams' was a play on the 'sheep-shagger' tag we get labelled with, chanted at us at every ground we visit. Rather than upsetting us, we can usually be seen joining in and dancing along to "Sheep, sheep, sheep-shaggers!" It does confuse the locals somewhat, as they seem to expect us to be destroyed and to hold our heads in shame. Our initial aim as an organisation was to simply provide regular affordable coach travel, which catered more for the 'laddish' type of fan, the type who liked a pint on the way there and also a pint on the way home. I was hoping and expecting to fill at least one bus full on a regular basis for our away trips. Up until now, on a good day, each valley would have scores of lads at these games, all travelling under their own steam in vans, cars, trains and (for some games) coaches. On the big games, each valley could muster several coaches from all the towns and villages in these valleys. On some of the crap midweek games or boring other-end-of-the-country type games, you would have a regular level of die-hard support, but spread out over a large geographical area, making it hard for people to get together as a group. Part of our plan was to give all these people a central booking point and phone number and get them all together, rather than in separate cars, etc.

Our first away game as the Valley Rams was to Peterborough United. The one proposed bus had turned into three, at the next away game it was five, and so on. Within six months we'd drawn Spurs away in the League Cup and finished up filling 32 coaches within a fortnight of the game being announced. It was a logistical nightmare. We had obviously carved a niche for our group, and the more relaxed method of travel was appealing to vast numbers. In no time at all we had to change the title from Valley Rams to the Cardiff and Valley Rams, so many lads from other valleys and the city of Cardiff itself wanted to be a part of what we'd started. The rest is history and ripe for another story at a later date (watch this space).

Anyway, back to the Chesterfield game. We'd been up and running just over six months. We were the most organised/disorganised gang/mob in the country. There were identity struggles, some groups had ideas or visions of how they wanted things to run. We had extremes of opinion, ranging from some wanting it to be a total 'lads up for a bit of organised scrapping' right the way down to others wanting another fully official organised supporters club, with elected officers and a democracy in place. Well, this was my baby, and democracy at these stages was, "This is what's happening, this is where we are heading, join in or fuck off and do your own thing."

We'd hold regular weekly meetings and take them around from town to town, sometimes we'd have 300-plus people turning up – mad, mad, days but great fun. I'd built up a small army of 'reps', as we called them. In most cases these were the well-known and respected lads from many areas, usually lads who had earned the respect by being able to have a scrap, but also by keeping things organised by booking and controlling all the individual coaches. Finding scrappers wasn't the problem, it was finding the ones who could scrap and organise that was the hard part. But we got there.

The rivalry between the Valley Boys and the City Lads was well known, culminating in the mid-70's with almost all-out war. Many times you'd see the look of bewilderment on away fans' faces when they'd be surrounded by police in the stadium for their own safety, only to see massive scraps breaking out all over Ninian Park between rival factions of the home support. It was a scary old place, even for the home fans.

This rivalry didn't just limit itself to Valleys and City, or even valley to valley. I, along with many others, had grown up in a village where all the boys on my side of the street were enemies of the boys on the other side of the street. But our united enemies, which bound both sides of our street together, were the next street in the same village. And the next village down the road were the mortal enemies of our village. To pass through each other's villages, you either had to be mobbed up, tooled up (which at ten was a catapult, at 12 a big stick, at 14 a club or cosh, and at 16-plus a knife – a growing-up game that sometimes had dire consequences) or sneak through under cover of darkness. Occasionally, for the big scraps, two or three villages would mob up and have a go at the townies. The rivalry and tribalism was very much – and still is, to a lesser degree – part of growing up in the Valleys, especially where the reputations and respect earned from previous battles were paramount.

So getting all these boys to mix, meet and travel together wasn't always that straightforward. Often I'd get to a service station or pub, etc, only to be called upon to try and sort some situation out, and I'd have to give out an occasional slap just to keep some order or solve a problem. But thankfully that wasn't every week, and it did get less and less as we progressed.

PURE VIOLENCE MOB (PVM)

Guff (CCFC): The casual scene arrived in Port Talbot due to following Cardiff City and the music. Loyalty to my mates and the travelling away soon took a grip of me, and I was soon wanting to be with the lads more and more. You had many a tale told to you by the older Port Talbot lads from the Sandsfield area of Port Talbot, a right tough old place. The Jacks would never venture there. Many of my mates then had the same concept: "We want more of this!" They remain close friends of mine till this day: Steve, Nigel, Huey, Stavvy, Taffy Anton, Wayne, Vince, PT, Scouse etc, etc.

We soon began to make good friends with the lads from a town called Neath, even closer to Jackland (four miles away). We met Simon (Neath Punk) and Gareth, et al, on regular trips to Neath for nights out and then trouble with the Jacks, when they were returning home from their away games. We soon realised we were becoming a close-knit bunch; the more trips away with Cardiff, the more our numbers grew.

For a laugh one day, we came up with the name 'PVM' (Pure Violence Mob). We never thought it would get around so quickly; all over West and South Wales, lads knew of us. The problem was that every young adult in Port Talbot became linked with these three letters, and every crime was soon blamed on us. We were just football lads, nothing else, and every Saturday we would look for an off. The home games in Cardiff were followed by a good drinking session in a well-known pub called Brownhill's, owned and run by the author of this book. We would then sometimes stop off in Bridgend on the way home from an away game, and always end up in bother. We would go to the away games usually all crammed into a Transit from Port Talbot; on the big ones we would join up with Neath, and maybe have a coach. In the Transit we would have a right laugh, setting off really early, plenty of beer, Huey at the wheel, trying to keep his eye on the road, while there was mayhem in the back. These were the good old days. I bet every lad up and down the country remembers those days.

There were some great days with the Soul Crew from Cardiff, we would sometimes go on their coaches to places like Blackpool, Peterborough, Rotherham and the famous Tranmere trip, then on to Blackpool. We made some really good mates with lads from all over and the friendships are still strong today. The Ely Trendies, Barry lads, Docks boys, Taff's Well lads, Bangor and North Wales lads were all the same as us, up for it.

ELY TRENDIES

Mikey Dye (CCFC): Cardiff City to this day has a massive mob, and can call upon hundreds of lads when needed. Although football violence is a thing of the past (in stadiums anyway), it is not uncommon for violence to occur around the city centres and pubs of every club still. Cardiff's Soul Crew was formed many years ago, in the early 80's, by a lad called Parsons, but by 1984 he had been kicked out by one of the older lads. In the '83/'84 season, me, Jammo and Rayer had travelled to the game at Leeds. We were young, 15-16 years old. We'd boarded the 7.50am from Cardiff, which arrived in Leeds at about 12.30pm. The drink was flowing, and I think it was settling a lot of nerves. This was the Leeds Service Crew we were heading for, who at the time had a huge reputation in the hooligan world. You could feel the tension among our ranks, as if we were in awe of them. In reality, we were.

We passed Elland Road to our left, and we all got up to look at an impressive stadium. We all thought that it would only be a short walk to the ground. How wrong we were. The train just kept on going. Someone shouted, "Fuck me, look how far we have to walk!" in a nervous voice. We were entering unknown territory that day. Last season it was Bournemouth and Bury, this year it was Leeds and Chelsea. We finally came to a halt and piled off. We were dressed in all our clobber and it fucking pissed down all day. My Pringle jumper was soaked and Jammo's wedge haircut was all wet and stringy.

We left the station, all 250 of the Soul Crew. As we looked across the road there were hardly any Old Bill; Leeds had about 50 waiting, so it could have been a great result for the young Soul Crew, although we greatly outnumbered them. The fun that day would have been running them, which is a result in itself. At the time, Leeds, Chelsea, West Ham, Millwall and Man Utd were top of the yobs, and we could have taken a great scalp. Someone amongst our ranks started chanting, "Cay-ardiff!" and most others joined in. Then the Soul Crew chant went up. It was awesome. The football lads in the know travelled by train, sat in the stands and didn't let on how green they were by singing! Leeds fucked off sharp and our chanting alerted the Old Bill, who surrounded us and stopped any possible action. Leeds actually called us the 'Welsh Male Voice Choir' for our efforts. We lost 2-0 and learnt a valuable lesson. From that day on, I have never sung since!

I lived in Ely, an estate in Cardiff which was mostly council houses. Our area was Lower Ely. We could pull together a real tight firm from around our patch, and when they got to know us, lads from Canton, Llanedeyrn, Splott and Whitchurch – as well as most other areas of Cardiff – would come and join us. In Ely we used to knock about by the local shops, especially one called Maggie's Chip Shop (I believe it's now called Chippy on the Bridge). It was situated right by a set of traffic lights opposite the Old White Lion pub. The front of this shop had three sections, each one would step up about four inches to the entrance. We spent many an hour there and it would be the place to meet. It's also the place where we met the author of this book. We eventually got tagged as 'Millbank'. To other Elyites, this was a local junior school. For every person who remembers passing us at this point, I hope we never offended!

We travelled everywhere from the 1981/82 season. Me, Jammo, Rayer, Zub, CC, Zeddie, Mosh and many more. Too many to name them all, but thanks to you all for many great awaydays. I'm 41 now, with numerous court convictions behind me for football-related offences, and in '87 I got a nine-month banning order – yes, just nine months, not prison, and a £400 fine. Most of my mates had convictions for disorder at football, but before jail sentences became the normal thing our lot got out of it all. Only my mate Baggars had done bird for his efforts.

I met Annis around about the '84 season. Two of his best mates, Peter M and Little Collin, had by now started knocking around with us and they introduced us to him. I had heard stories giving him the blame for Bradford in the 1982/83 season, but after hearing his side I don't doubt him. He did his best to get a pub full of Cardiff down to the station, but it wasn't to be. We started travelling together, all young lads but with big hearts. We were known as the Ely Trendies, but we also had a punk amongst us who went by the name of G.

We were at the heart of the travelling. Some lads would wait at the station, ready for the train, but would not travel until we'd turned up. We would always swell numbers by 20-30 which, due to the fact that not many travelled anyway, was considered a large group. By '84, us, Canton, Splott and the Docks would be in harmony. Travelling together, we looked good and we had our fair share of encounters. The laughs, the running of opposition fans and getting run ourselves were always par for the course!

BARRY SOUL CREW SEASIDERS

Jeff Marsh (CCFC, author of *Soul Crew Seasiders*): I grew up on Barry Island, which at the time was home to the Butlins camp, a busy fairground and docks. At age 15, I was a skinhead. Me and all the other boys from school used to hang around the promenade on weekends and on bank holidays, fighting with mods, teds, Asians, greasers or anyone else who wanted to know. We used to have mass stone fights over the fence with English kids from the Thomas A` Becket Homes, who used to stay in the camp on what were known as the 'kids' weeks'. These went on for a good few years, and we used to go down on the railway bank to collect buckets of stones, hiding them in the bushes in preparation for these battles. Many a kid suffered head injuries in these mass rock fights, and the sight of some English twat being stretchered away covered in blood was always guaranteed to cheer us up.

We had some massive brawls with mods, who used to come from Cardiff, Bridgend, Ponty and the Valleys. Most bank holidays it was like a scene from *Quadrophenia*, as running battles took place on the beach or promenade. One time, when I was around 16 or 17, I was sitting on the beach wall with about five other skinheads and some blond kid on the beach below us walked up, offering us out. He had about four or five others with him, so I jumped down and said, "Come on then, let's have you!" He started shouting, "Come on, Cardiff!" and all of a sudden there were about 30 of these bowl-haircutted kids running at us from all different directions. A lot of them had umbrellas and were running at us using them like spears. Someone was shouting, "Annis, here they are!" as we legged it up the steps and away.

That was the first time I came across Annis. Not long after I took my first trip to football, the terrifying outing to Millwall I spoke about in my first book, and, although I hated football, I was hooked on this new gang warfare I'd discovered. Now in the early 80's, mods and skins often used to clash on the terraces of Ninian Park, but that was all about to change. They realised that they were being singled out by the police for attention at matches, while these bowl-haircutted, ski jacket and trainer-wearing Herberts – who at the time were known as 'trendies' – could get away with murder with their boy-next-door appearance.

Before long, all the mods and skins were dressing as trendies and the Soul Crew name started to be bandied about. Instead of fighting, we were forming into one unit with a common enemy, other firms from around the country. It was easy to sort out disputes between different groups by saying things like, "Don't fight each other, save it for the Jacks/Millwall/Chelsea/Pompey," or whoever we were playing next.

I next met Annis when I climbed aboard one of his coaches. I can't remember where it was going, I think maybe Wrexham, but we spoke about the incident on the beach and laughed about it. It didn't matter now, we were all top mates and that was how it was going to stay. After this, I became a fully fledged member of the 'Annis Travel Club' and we travelled all over the place together. In my opinion, if it wasn't for Annis and his organisational skills, Cardiff would never have gained the reputation they did back in those days. The team's performance was terrible, you always knew Cardiff were going to lose. We were stuck in the shit divisions, it was grim, but we travelled everywhere. Rain or shine, we were on the terraces of shitty northern teams, going on the other side's end, confronting much larger mobs and taking liberties. None of it would have been possible without Annis. He used to drive down to us and all round the Valleys, convincing people that Cardiff's honour was at stake. Okay, he was making a few quid off the coaches but we didn't care, as long as we had a bit of fun and a day out.

With the Annis Travel Club we used to go by coach, fleets of vans or by train, using Family Railcards (one adult pays full fare, then an army of 'kids' can go for £1 each) or Persil vouchers to get there cheaply. We used to go into supermarkets with Stanley knives and cut the vouchers off the Persil boxes, walking away as powder poured out everywhere. We went on many adventures to places like Blackpool, Bolton, Stockport, Burnley and Tranmere, but one that stands out is a shitty night match at Halifax, when around 30 of us made the trip. Five or six of us went on their end, but had to get out quickly as loads of Leeds skinheads came into the ground. In those days you could walk all around the ground, so we headed back to the Cardiff end. We noticed that they were mobbing up and moving over towards us, so we decided the best form of defence is attack. We ran onto the pitch and headed for them. Around the edge of the pitch at the Shay stadium was a speedway track, so I grabbed a rock, jumped into the terracing on my own and launched it at them. Next thing, I'm being chased all around the ground by the Old Bill. They decked me and bundled me out and into the van. I was sat in a cell thinking, *This is shit*, and wondering how I was going to get home in the morning when the police came back in and told me I was being released. Annis (who had split his head open when a car he was in crashed as they looked around the town for Halifax lads) had made the coach driver come to the police station and all the boys refused to leave till they released me. The police had been so desperate to get rid of them that they agreed to bail me straight away. A top result, and I won't ever forget it. This is how proper mates should be: never leave anyone behind. I can remember Annis was concussed and covered in blood all the way home, then he ended up in hospital. Apparently, the kid driving the car had only passed his test a few days before and had driven from Cardiff to Halifax! I remember some drama on the way home, after the boys stole some crates of pop from a chip shop and the Old Bill came on, searching us all. We could have done without that. I went to court and got slapped with a £60 fine – it cost me more than that to get back up there. What a joke!

Another mad trip was Darlington, when we left Cardiff at around five or six in the morning, travelled all the way up there and when we arrived the game was snowed off! All we had to show for our trouble was about 18 hours on a coach, and Saint and Greavesie laughing at us on the telly. Mind you, we stopped off in Ashby de la Zouch, had a mass snowball fight and raided a few shops, so that made it a bit more fun. Everywhere we went, towns would be wrecked, pubs and shops smashed, cars overturned and bodies battered. It was fucking brilliant. I used to carry a blade as a matter of course in those days, mostly for slashing seats on Blackpool trams, London Underground trains, etc, and ended up doing two years in one of Her Majesty's hotels for stabbing two filthy Mancs. I do regret the whole business, as I now feel that only cowards use knives. But at the time a few of our lads had been slashed, so we started carrying as a result and the whole thing got out of control for a while. But I don't regret my life as a hooligan, as those were the best years of my life. We were lucky enough to be there through the glory days of the 80's, I had a top time and met some top lads. People can slate Annis all they want, as far as I'm concerned he is a top guy and he made the Soul Crew one of the best mobs around back in the day.

It makes me laugh when I hear people saying, "The hooligans have wrecked Cardiff," and claiming they've supported the club for the last 30 years. The fact is, in the grim days of the 80's, if it wasn't for the 'hooligans' then Cardiff would have had no following at all, and I don't remember us having many scarfers back in those days. I'd say we had around 250 lads who all knew each other, and knew we would back each other to the hilt. Those days are gone now, and the police have definitely destroyed hooliganism. But then it couldn't have gone on forever, as it got out of control and a lot of people got hurt back in those days. With banning orders, CCTV surveillance and massive sentences for what are, in reality, only minor public order offences, only an idiot would want to be a hooligan these days. The worst hooligans I've seen in recent years are the police, who will batter anyone at the football with no fear of reprisals. If anyone wonders where the thugs have gone these days, in my opinion they've all joined the police force.

YOUNG SOUL CREW

Joe (CCFC): After several seasons of attending many City away games, I became part of the younger Soul Crew. The number of our firm was very small, approaching 150 on a good day, but we were a close-knit outfit ranging from 16 to 25 years.

We would share similar interests and fashion sense. I would make regular trips to London to ensure I had the best looking clobber: anything from Cecil Gee to CP Company was a must, and I always found that prices were quite often 50 per cent cheaper than overpriced Cardiff. When wearing this gear, it gave you a newfound confidence that made you think you were untouchable and it was easy to make new friends and acquaintances.

We became a notorious following by emulating the older guys from what is now well known as the Cardiff City Soul Crew. So much so that we even arranged our own coaches to away games and drank/socialised together outside of football. Our favourite watering hole was Brownhill's, where many a good drunken night was had.

Trouble back then was often sporadic and unplanned, not like today's prearranged 'flappy-armed' bullshit.

C SQUAD

Alex Mannings (CCFC): The C Squad is a name used by the Cardiff Youth firm over the past two or three years. In this time, it has risen to one of the most active young firms in the country. Football violence for myself started in around 2001, and my first experience of battle was away at Bristol City in a game which was fairly heavily publicised and used in a TV documentary a few years later. From that time I have seen a seen a change in names and personnel associated with the youth element here: from a few of us tagging along with older lads in the early days to the formation of the more organised 'Creche Squad', which was made up of young lads from various parts of Cardiff and from places as far as the East Valleys and towns like Usk and Cwmbran, a large number of lads from Pontypridd and even lads from as far afield as Carmarthen. The firm was relatively inactive compared to the previous two years or so that I'd seen, though we did travel frequently to various parts of the country where we were often stopped in our tracks by the all too familiar South Wales Football Intelligence Officers. The few occurrences where violence did happen tended to be on 'suicide missions', including a game between QPR and Nottingham Forest where the away team were relegated. There were clashes between the fans after the game, so three of us decided to have a look before being caught up in the melee. After backing Forest down the road with help from a few oaf-like cockneys, we got turned upon by our newfound 'comrades' who by now had realised that we were certainly not QPR. Our accents gave away that we were Cardiff. A few yardie types flashed steel and we were on the back foot, but after a lucky intervention from a well-known face at QPR (Gregors), we were given a pass on the understanding that we spread the word that this individual was still around and kicking! Further occurrences of this nature happened in Bristol and on other occasions in London, as well as when nine or ten of us fronted around 40 West Brom outside Sam's Bar in Cardiff on a Tuesday night, where we were backed off but certainly not disgraced and received praise from some of West Brom's main lads regarding our efforts.

The C Squad came about over the course of 2005, with small pockets of young lads coming together to form the firm we have today. Personally, I was just going with a few of my friends from the Creche days, as many of the lads from that firm had drifted away for various reasons. There were many lads who I'd known from before but hadn't really bothered with in previous years, as well as young lads who were just coming into the fold, and this formed a good mix of lads between the ages of 16 and 21. We associate strongly with many of the older lads and are generally regarded by outsiders as just a part of the Soul Crew, though we do try and make our own way in the football scene and therefore regularly travel independently away from the older generation. As any lad involved in this way of life knows, when travelling away the key to whether the day is a success or a waste of time is avoiding detection when getting to the town or city where your team are playing. More often than not, days have been ruined by the Old Bill collaring us before we've even got across the English border.

One major event where we escaped detection and everything went to plan was in February 2007, when travelling to a league game at Coventry. After a few days of heavy snow and serious traffic disruptions, getting on a minibus and onto the road was something of an achievement on this cold February day. After an early start, the perfect breakfast of lager and adrenalin soon got everyone's spirits lifted as we made our way to the West Midlands. The journey was pretty straightforward, considering the state of the roads after the bad weather, and we got to Coventry in good time. We decided to settle somewhere on the outskirts of the city for the first part of our day, and to try to coax Coventry's firm into meeting us away from the bright lights and CCTV of the city centre. We ended up in a trendy bar in Earlsdon where we were bribed into behaving ourselves by the landlord, who gave us free food and the odd free drink as payment for keeping his bar intact and his other punters happy. After numerous phone calls, it was clear that Coventry's 'Legion Youth' were unlikely to join us in our out-of-town location, so after a few hours enjoying a few quiet beers and planning our next move, we decided to go somewhere more central. On noticing a public bus stop outside the bar, we decided to take this less detectable mode of transport into the city centre. As many of us had been to the city before, we knew our way around fairly well, so we headed towards the main square of this dreary town. After having a quick look in a couple of bars, we decided to stop in a bar in Jordan's Well which is just on the outskirts of the city centre. On ordering my first pint, I heard a shout for us all to leave from one of the lads outside the pub. He'd been told on his phone that Coventry had seen us pass through the city centre and had now followed us down to Jordan's Well. We immediately began marching back towards the city centre. Sure enough, marching towards us in the middle of a very busy road were 20 or so Coventry who appeared to be the youth element. We numbered only 12 going into them, but there was no way we had travelled down here to let them have a result.

The early exchanges were very violent, punches and kicks came in from both sides, as well as many items from the roadworks which were used as weapons. Members of the public looked on in complete and utter astonishment, and this prompted around 40 emergency 999 calls to be made to the police. The violence continued for what seemed like forever, with a few lads taking a bit of a beating. One lad from Coventry was apparently knocked out at one point after running into a fucking lamppost! As the row dragged on we backed them down the road slightly and, at one point, a few Coventry were on their toes. I believe to this day that if it wasn't for two of their lads at the front holding their own, the Coventry mob would have been chased back into the city centre. One of these lads actually made a case to be selected for the England cricket team, after catching a road sign flung by one of our lads in a manner befitting a world-class wicketkeeper, before making me dance out of the way of the return throw! Throughout the fight a number of weapons were seen, including knuckledusters, batons and what appeared to be CS gas, as well as various pieces of street furniture. Coventry eventually regrouped and came back at us, chanting, but this just encouraged us more and we backed them off again with the words, "SOUL CREW!" echoing around the street. Eventually, the Old Bill arrived on the scene, after finally getting through the mile-long tailbacks we'd created. The sirens warned everyone involved to disperse. About seven or eight of our group were rounded up near the scene, and stopped and searched under the Section 60 rules. This would prove to be key for the police further down the line. Our own Football Intelligence Officers were on the scene to make sure all information given by us was correct and, after one arrest (for possession of a knuckleduster), we were ushered into taxis and sent on our way to Coventry's Ricoh Arena. Many of us at this point did not have tickets for the match and were therefore refused entry. Once police realised we were the same group that had been stopped earlier in the day, we were taken in riot vans and escorted to the train station where our minibus driver picked us up. The trip back to Cardiff was a lively one, with everyone still buzzing about how the row had actually gone to plan. Other than a few complaints about ripped Paul and Shark jackets and stained CP Company tops, the trip was basically a disco with the Stone Roses and the Twang providing much of the entertainment. All in all, by this time the day was considered a success.

Other incidents involving our firm in recent times included an away at Crystal Palace, where, after a trip to London on the train, a chance meeting between members of the C-Squad and their cockney counterparts ended in a violent encounter in Thornton Heath. It was a small incident numbers-wise, with only seven or eight Palace lads against around ten young Cardiff. It was the outnumbered Palace lads who called the battle on, but inevitably numbers proved to be their downfall and they were backed off across the road. The incidents were fairly minor, but still resulted in two arrests for the Cardiff contingent. Both were eventually found not guilty, which was good news all round. In the early months of the 2007/2008 season the C-Squad was somewhat depleted, with key members of the group being banned while on bail for the incident which occurred in Coventry. But one game which did attract a turnout was Plymouth away, partly because it corresponded with our favourite Italian lunatic's birthday! Though the lads on bail could not attend the match or go within a certain distance of Plymouth's Home Park ground, this did not stop a very violent incident occurring on the edge of the city where a few of Plymouth's older (and apparently main) lads were taught the meaning of the phrase 'don't judge a book by its cover'. After being confronted by around ten of Cardiff's young lads, they cockily laughed off suggestions that we could compete with them by saying, "Good effort, but we'll let you off this time, 'cos otherwise you'll just get hurt." With this, Cardiff steamed in and a violent battle ensued, with a few minor injuries on both sides. The main blow was dealt to the ego of these Plymouth lads, who certainly left with their tails between their legs. They were by no means bad but had seriously underestimated what was in front of them. There has been no action taken by the authorities in relation to this incident, which is certainly good news for all involved.

Over the last few years there have been many other minor incidents worth a small mention. One of these was following an international game between Wales and Slovakia in Cardiff, where a violent incident occurred involving members of Cardiff's youth element as well as many older heads. After the game a number of Cardiff lads were gathered in a regular drinking spot in Canton when a group of around 25-30 approached, who turned out to be Slovaks. The Cardiff lads inside the pub numbered about 30. They confronted the Eastern Europeans and immediately had them on the back foot. The lads from Slovakia did make a decent effort, but most who stood ended up taking a bit of a hiding before eventually being seen off by the local contingent. Another incident in which the youth were heavily involved was at the Carling Cup Final held down here in 2007 between Chelsea and Arsenal. After meeting a lad I know from Chelsea for a quiet beer, myself and about 15-20 other youth lads got settled in a quiet bar in the city centre, expecting to see a bit of an effort from one of the London firms. Unfortunately for us, there was none. As the day went on we ended up going into the same bars as many of Chelsea's main lads, and even managed to bump into one of the main lads from Swansea who was meeting a publisher to discuss his recent book deal. As an uneventful day came to a close, a few of us headed back to our local pub. After many had left we found ourselves confronted by approximately 25 Chelsea, who backed us down the road and eventually dished out a bit of a beating to myself, another Cardiff youngster and one of our older lads, resulting in cuts, bruises and a couple of smashed windows! These were by no means Chelsea's top lads, but they were certainly cockney geezer types intent on kicking fuck out of anything in their path.

Although there have been many incidents of banning orders being dished out to young Cardiff lads, serious sentences have been almost nonexistent. However, one major coup by the police was in relation to the Coventry City incident, where five Cardiff lads were jailed for a total of 46 months, with all convicted also receiving six-year banning orders. CCTV and a lack of commonsense and loyalty from two other lads involved (who incidentally managed to escape a prison sentence) conspired to give the prosecution a very easy ride in convicting and sentencing us. After serving three months of a ten-month sentence, I came out (as did the others) to a great reception from our older lads, underlining the mutual respect we have for each other. I would like to take this opportunity on behalf of all who were jailed to thank all who contributed to our release fund, which paid for a very lively first weekend out!

Although banning orders and heavy policing limit the activities of us and many firms around the country, success on the pitch resulting in an FA Cup Final and potentially entering European football has certainly spurred the lads on. It would be naïve to say that football hooliganism in Cardiff will not continue long into the future.

IV
A FEW CHARACTERS

THE VIKING

Viking (CCFC): I was born in Cardiff Docks, which is a close-knit community where everyone knows everyone and you look out for each other. I have known Annis since way back in the early 80's, and we've had a good friendship ever since. I started going down to Ninian Park in the 70's. I was a fan for many years, but the atmosphere would soon draw you in and nearly everyone was a lad, either fighting or talking about it. During the early 80's, when I was going around with all the lads, the Docks were always fighting the Ely Trendies outside football and I was always trying to keep the peace. I felt like piggy in the middle. In time, the football pulled us all together and we started hanging around Brownhill's, which was a pub in Cardiff city centre owned by Annis.

The first time the hooligan side of the football became serious was when us Docks lads formed our own firm called the Dirty 30. We were still part of the Soul Crew at the football matches, but outside football, every weekend night we would be battling with the doormen of the nightclubs and any outside gang that came into the city centre and tried to give it the big 'un. Gangs of Birmingham and Bristol came down over the years and tried to walk over our town; they were dealt with and never came back again. Some of the main lads of the Dirty 30 were Jonathan, Pepper, Rusty, Princey, Jellyhead, Big Foot, Bigger, Weller, Porta, Jaja, Farrah, Derek, Starship, Brummie, Toddy and a few more. In those days we were like brothers. We stuck together. Everyone knew they could never run, otherwise it would have been dealt with back home.

I've a lot of respect for teams like Bradford, Newport, Barnsley, Boro and Hull, as they've come to Cardiff and really wanted it. They've gone as far as to bring the battle to us, where most teams don't even turn up, or if they do they make sure they're in an escort. (Tottenham just came to make a show of it and never once tried to break their escort.)

You'll all probably laugh at what I'm going to say was one of the best tear-ups I've ever had. Remember that I've fought Millwall, Cockney Reds, Boro and many other top firms, so I was surprised as anyone when it happened in May '93 in the town centre of Doncaster. We'd just won the Third Division championship at Scunthorpe, and the Dirty 30 had taken a Transit with 15 of our naughtiest lads. Nothing happened in Scunthorpe, we just took the piss, so on the way home we decided to stop off in a sleepy town called Doncaster. We stopped off in a bar and were soon on the piss, celebrating City's promotion. An hour or so later, we were told there was another pub where Cardiff had turned up down the road. It was the PVM (Pure Violence Mob, good lads from Port Talbot), so we all decided we would take a walk and go join them. I could see a few of them standing outside a pub across the road. As I was walking over, a lad of about 19 years approached me and said, "Donny wants it." I said, "You what? Donny wants it? Go and get Donny, I'll have it with him now." Then the rest of the lads burst out laughing and said, "Donny's their firm!" Then suddenly here they were. I couldn't fucking believe it, it was a mob of easily 150, including townies, doormen, football lads and whoever else wanted a fight.

I said to everyone, "Just shut it and walk towards them. As we get closer, just steam the fuckers." My heart was going. There were no more than 30 of us, including the PVM. We were out of our heads. As we got closer, one of their lads came from nowhere and sparked a PVM lad out. That was it, every fucker was fighting. It was right on top from the beginning, but we remained a unit and managed to split them right down the middle. As we were doing this some of our lads were getting clocked, including myself. But we were up for this, and the more I could see some of our lads being hurt the more I wanted to go for them and the more psyched up we were getting. As we had now split them, we managed to back one section of them off. Fuck me, to this day I will never forget the battle. It didn't seem to matter how many punches you threw, they just kept coming at us, more and more of them.

The Old Bill arrived and they just came wading into us, whacking us with their truncheons. We couldn't believe it, as the rest of the police were just shouting at Doncaster to back off while we were getting slaughtered and they were hitting us like fuck. They then marched us to the vans. The only thing the Old Bill did which was decent was to let me and a couple of others go back and carry one of our lads back to the Transit, as he was out cold. As we were walking back with the escort, some of the locals, including the doormen, were shouting, "Fair play to you lot, you're game as fuck." We shouted back, "We'll be back one day," but that day has never come.

I have had many tear-ups, but with the odds so stacked against us we had to give it our best ever, and not even one of us backed off. It didn't even enter our heads, we were in it together no matter what. Yes, we got hurt, but we enjoyed every minute of it.

Is hooliganism dead at football? The day is not far off, due to CCTV, bans and the heavy sentencing. You just can't get away with it today. We've got some real youngsters coming through, but it will never be like the old days and they know it. They're gutted, but that's just the way it is.

MR MAC

Mac (CCFC): Before I tell you a few tales of my years following Cardiff, I've got a short story first.

One day in about the mid-80's, I was standing on the Bob Bank watching the same old shit as usual, so I got chatting to the person next to me for the next half-hour or so. What else was there to do in those days? City were shit, it was either that or fuck off home. Half the time was either spent chatting to fellow City fans and the other half you were usually fighting the opposing fan, if he bothered to come down to Ninian Park. We might not have had big crowds, but virtually everyone down the

City in those days was a game lad. I was a Cougar, a scooter boy, if I wasn't watching the City I was always going on scooter rallies all around the country. Most of the boys I was hanging around with then were into the Jam and the Clash, I still play all that music now on the way to away games. At the same time as the scooter days, you had the mods as well, who were fighting the Trendies and casuals from Cardiff in the city centre on non-match days. Now for the next year or so, all I kept hearing about was the Trendies did this and Trendies attacked us here, etc. One name that kept coming up was Annis's, and a lot of people were stirring it between us both, but somehow we never met and never even knew what each other looked like.

Going back to that day on the Bob Bank: when the match finished, the person I had been chatting to said goodbye and, as he was leaving, introduced himself. I did the same. We both looked gobsmacked and then burst out laughing as we shook each other's hands. From that day Annis and me have been friends ever since, we've gone on many a trip together and had some right old laughs.

I went to my first match with my dad in 1970, when Cardiff were in the old Second Division. For the first few seasons I regularly attended with my old man, but then, by the 1974/75 season, I started going to games with my younger brother. One of the most frightening times was when I was about ten and Man Utd came down to Cardiff with about 10,000. It was mental and I was shitting myself. To this day, I've never seen anything like it. Both sets of fans fought for the whole 90 minutes of the game.

After I left school I trained as a butcher, which was handy for me because the terrace fashion at that time was white butcher's coats, I think Millwall set it off. We had a lad called Frankie Humphries in those days who was the Cardiff leader, he was a legend and the fans used to sing songs about him. He was the gamest I've ever seen at football, but at the same time a real gentleman with it.

One game that brings back some good memories was the FA Cup game at Ninian Pak in 1977. I was actually in the enclosure, standing on the other side of the pitch with my dad. Everton were the team and they had been given half of our home end on the Bob Bank. The match hadn't even started and it had kicked right off; within minutes Cardiff were chasing Everton totally out of the ground. What a sight to see, and I was still only a kid.

On the football side, in 1977 we had a player called Robin Friday for about half of the season. He was fucking brilliant, but at the same time he was as mad as a hatter. He looked like a gypsy, a real scruffy bastard, but had so much talent, he was a genuinely gifted player. Then he just disappeared and, later on in life, sadly died at a young age. But what a privilege it was just to have seen him play in the flesh.

By the 80's I was going to football suited up, and I remember being on the pitch at Loftus Road against QPR in a cup game, having a row in my Armani suit. I personally like the classic labels Boss, Prada and Lacoste, some of the fake stuff and the shell suits the scousers wear are fucking awful. While we're on the subject of QPR, I remember going there in 1990; there was a massive queue to get into the away fans' end, so two of my mates and myself walked around to the other side of the ground and went in the QPR end. As soon as we got in there we let them know who we were and we backed a load of them off. With that, a big gap opened up around us and somehow we managed to stay in there till half-time. It's unbelievable when you think of it, for just three of us. We then jumped over the wall and walked down to the Cardiff end, where all the Cardiff fans started applauding us.

At Wolves away in 1988, in the old Fourth Division, they were top and we were second, and we won 4-1. I was sitting that day in the front of a minibus with about 15 of us and we were stuck in traffic, waiting to pull out of a car park. Before the game we'd had a bit of a result, as we'd run a mob of Wolves outside the ground, so perhaps we were a little confident or complacent after the game. That was when about 200 of them spotted us and surrounded the van. The next thing, the windows were all smashed and they were using scaffolding polls and planks of wood. Fuck me, it was frightening! Then I really thought I was going to die as a breeze block came crashing through the front window and hit me full on. I virtually collapsed in my seat and felt faint, the pain was beyond anything and my ribs felt totally broken.

The driver managed to mount the kerb and speed off along the path, so we just about managed to escape. As we were nearly halfway home, I shouted to the driver to stop and an ambulance was called out to me on the motorway, but I refused to go and said, "Just get me back to Cardiff, no matter what." They did, and I was then rushed into the emergency ward, where within minutes I was being operated on. I was told later by the doctors that I had been near to death, as I had internal bleeding, a ruptured spleen, several broken ribs and other internal organs were damaged. That turned out to be the most frightening day of my football life.

One of the greatest days was when we took over the town of our rivals, the Jacks, in the FA Cup in 1991. That day will live with me forever. Well over a thousand lads from Cardiff went. We did just what we wanted, but the Old Bill couldn't stop us, they had to just keep up with us. At first there were about 300 of us and, up ahead in the main shopping streets, we saw a mob of about 400. We charged, only to find out they were Cardiff as well; then we bumped into a few more hundred Cardiff. The Jacks were nonexistent that day, though it seemed that every window in every pub and shop was smashed to pieces. Maybe they did turn up, as cleaners the following morning to clean it all up.

Wolves are a top firm, who match anyone on their day.

Stoke can pull the numbers and are game.

Portsmouth I've got respect for, as whenever we've played them they have been well game.

Barnsley have come to our place and gone looking for it and they were as game as fuck, they held their own at our place.

We weren't out the night Hull came, but that's not their fault. A hundred and twenty good lads from Hull came to Cardiff on a Friday night, and not many firms can say they have done that.

Boro came to Cardiff and shocked us at 11am. We tried our best but they ran us, on that day in 1994.

I've got a lot of respect for Chelsea and they used to come to ours big-time in the 80's. We always gave them a run for their money.

A lot of smaller clubs such as Chesterfield, Huddersfield, Burnley and Darlington are all from tough northern towns. They might not travel down to us, but if you go up there never underestimate them.

Just to finish off: if Cardiff lose it fucks up my whole week. Even my wife looks out for the score, then she knows what mood to expect me in.

LITTLE COLLIN

Little Collin (CCFC): I was there during the 70's and in the thick of it during the 80's. I've fought alongside the Soul Crew and I'd like to believe I was one of the original Ely Trendies and Soul Crew lads. I hardly go to football now, and when I have it's a totally different scene. It's well and truly over. Those who know me know that I don't give a fuck about a kicking. I've been stabbed, slashed and hospitalised three or four times, and most of the incidents were actually away from the football. I've been beaten up many times at football, but I've given as good as I got. What brings a smile to my face is when you're well outnumbered. I'm going to tell you about two incidents at football. Annis asked me if I would share a few memories; I was more than happy to help as we go way back and have been good mates, at football and outside of football, for as long as I can remember.

A lot has been said about Bradford and I'm sure Annis will tell you all about his own experiences in his next book, and tell you it in full. But here's what happened to me. I was 18 years old when we played Bradford away and I will never forget that fight in the 1982/83 season, as being outnumbered is a big buzz to me. When the odds are stacked against you, you know who your real mates are. You can always sit back afterwards and have a laugh about it.

We boarded the train at Cardiff Central, eight lads and one girl, but I knew the only one I could rely on was Wurzel. Yes, we knew there would probably be some kind of reception waiting for us, as in those days virtually every team in the country made a show. The journey was seven hours long and boring, but I did expect more than eight lads to go. But I still thought it should be fun. Eventually, we arrived at Bradford interchange. We got off the train; there was no reception for us on the platform, so you could feel that everyone started to feel relaxed. We went down the escalators and, as we reached the ground level, I noticed a few lads, I'd say about six. I thought these were their 'spotters'. Little did we know there were many more than six, and a mob of about 60 Ointment suddenly seemed to come from nowhere. Most of the lads with me were edgy, as if to say, *What the fuck are we going to do?* Wurzel and I just carried on walking to the exit where they crowded around. I knew I was going to get a kicking, but that's life. If you don't want to know, don't go! I think Bradford were disappointed with our turnout, and then they just suddenly came into us, shouting, "Ointment! Ointment!" It seemed like Wurzel and myself were suddenly fighting everyone. I hit as many as I could, but the amount of punches that rained down sent me and a few others flying back. I then noticed Wurzel seemed to be getting a worse hammering than me, so I went back and tried to help him as, no matter what, I'd never leave a mate. They seemed to stop for a couple of seconds and we regrouped by the bottom of the escalators. Then they came at us again. Our lot had brollies and they were whacking them, as Wurzel and I tried to punch them back. Eventually, we were forced back up the escalators to the platform. I don't know why, but Bradford just seemed to disappear. Yes, they had a result in their eyes, but if they were so good why weren't we battered worse? I actually felt more knackered than battered, and I was glad that I could finally recharge myself, ready for whatever happened next. Then the Old Bill finally appeared.

At the ground I met my old mates Annis and Mannings. They said they'd heard there had been trouble, but then everyone knew what I was like. I laughed as I told them the story. I've met some of the Ointment on a few occasions for a drink, not on a football day. We laughed about it all and they didn't stop buying me drinks, saying they always had respect for me. We also met about 15 years ago at Valley Parade, against the City, and I think we showed them how it should be done.

A day at a football match was something you looked forward to. You may have wondered, but you never knew what was going to happen. I will give you an example: it was the mid-80's, a Friday night kick-off at Tranmere, which is on the outskirts of

Liverpool. About 15 of us left Cardiff train station at 10.30am Friday morning and made our way to the game. On the train we drank a few cans and played a couple of games of cards; we arrived at Liverpool Lime Street at about 3pm. That gave us four and a half hours of drinking time. We caught a local train to Tranmere and settled in a pub near the ground. Kick-off was drawing near so a few of us left the pub and went outside the ground to see what was going on. Nothing was happening, so we went in. The first half of the game was a bit boring; when half-time came me and two mates decided to get a coffee and something to eat. While we were queuing up, a few Tranmere lads started mouthing off and trying to wind us up. I did get a bit annoyed and said, "Look, if you want to have a go, we'll play along." In the end we exchanged a few words and went back to watch the second half. When the final whistle went we all left the ground and made our way to the train station. The Old Bill stopped us and told us they would take us to the train station. So they dropped us off at a station called Rock Ferry. It seemed a bit out of the way and it was deserted. Hanging around on the platform, waiting for the train, one of the lads went for a walk. He came back, saying that a mob was coming into the station.

This is how it went. There were about five of them to one of us, so the numbers were against us to start with. Then, when they got closer, I could see that some of them were tooled up with knives. I knew this was a bit dodgy and pulled out my Stanley, thinking, *This is it*. I looked around and some of our lads had started off down the track to get away. Things were going quicker than I thought; the next thing I knew, there were only four of us left. This one lad of ours was trying to break up a bench, so I went over and broke it up with him. So there I was, a length of wood in one hand and Stanley in the other. The next thing, there they were right in front of me and all my mates had run. I was on my own again, thinking, *How am I going to get away?* I put Stanley back in my pocket, started to swing the length of wood around and noticed they were backing off. So I had an escape plan. I swung the wood one last time and threw it towards them, turned and ran. I ran as quickly as possible, but inside it was hurting me. I wasn't prepared to be sliced into mincemeat; I would stand against fists, or one Stanley, but not half a dozen. But as I was running, I tripped over the railway line and twisted my knee. I thought, *Fucking hell, I'm in trouble now!* I managed to get up and made my way to the fence, I don't know how but I climbed over it. On the other side of the fence was a housing estate. I looked behind: *Fuck me, they've gone! Thank fuck for that.* Around the corner was a pub where all the lads were sat inside. I went in and sat there talking about what had just happened. Looking back on it now, I chuckle to myself. How did I survive? I guess it was just meant to be. But I will say Tranmere is a fucking rough place, and you need a better mob than we had that night.

I am 44 years old now and, in my opinion, those were the best days. To this day, Annis and Mannings remain my good friends and we have been side by side on many occasions. I would trust those two with my life.

NEATH PUNK

Simon Neads (CCFC): I am not going to go on about me and Annis together at football matches, because I haven't got the time or that big a memory to recall them all. The 80's would be a book on its own. I could tell you stories of Blackpool, Gloucester, Tenby, Bradford and many others, which is nothing to do with football on a Saturday afternoon. But I've chosen Western Super-Mare, which as usual turned out to be fighting with a good laugh thrown in with it.

Before I tell my stories of the past though, I thought I'd tell you a bit about myself. Most of Cardiff know me as Simon from Neath ('Neath Punk'), but the truth is I am a Valley boy and proud of it. I was born in Tredegar and I lived there until I was 15 (I spent my first nine months living in a place called Cwm, near a good lad called Rotter – a very game lad too). As with most lads, I was first taken down the City by my dad when I was nine years old. These were memorable days which will never leave me, and my first match on my own was against Man Utd in '74. I went on an old Charlie Hills bus from Tredegar town centre. Thanks to a Cardiff lad called Coco, who was a legend in my eyes, and many older lads from Tredegar who went on the bus, I became a hooligan on that day. Talk about having a laugh, I was chased back to our bus, thrown around like a used chip packet in Caroline Street and given a few boots up my arse for good measure. Why oh why I had two scarves tied around my wrists that day totally bewilders me, from that day I've always hated United.

I carried on going on the bus with these Tredegar lads, including Porpoise and the strangely-named Bible Eyes. He used to put the fear of God into me at the best of times. Not many games stuck in my mind until the 1977 FA Cup run, and I nicked my first scarf off an Everton fan on the Bob Bank. Boy, Everton didn't half get a pasting in the ground that day! That, sadly, was my last day of being a Commando, as in '78 I moved to the land of the white shite, Neath. But boy, did Neath Blues and myself soon turn it around.

Now let's get something straight: I was first and foremost a football hooligan. I am not ashamed of my past and I will take those pleasures with me to the grave. I have been arrested 15 times at football matches; three of those times have been abroad; I've been deported once. I've had two life bans from Cardiff City and three bans from the courts. I got sentenced to six months in '88, one year in '91 and three years in 2002. At no time have I thought of giving up the path I chose to follow. I have been involved in literally over 100 football-related fights and, in March 1984 alone, I had over 17 against the Pebble Dash Kids (Swansea Jack filth) alone. I have given more than I've received, but yes, I've had my ribs broken by Plymouth, had a fractured cheekbone and nose broken by other firms. I've also had 12 stitches in my head (from a machete) from the gypo Jacks and have even been run over by them. I've been gassed by the Old Bill and other firms. You might think I'd have been put off by this, but wrong. I will give up when I choose to and I feel I can't take it anymore. Like I say, whoever said it's better to give than receive is spot on. As long as those scruffy gypo twats are living next door to THE PRIDE OF WEST GLAMORGAN, WHO ARE NEATH AND

PORT TALBOT BLUES and 150 STRONG, you muppets will never get past us to even take on Cardiff's other firms.

My introduction to the pride of West Glamorgan started on a Monday night in Neath town centre, where my band, the Auschwitz Ashmen, were playing in a bar called the Full Moon. We were in my eyes a hardcore punk band, hence my nickname. Thank fuck I hadn't been a new romantic, it hasn't got the same ring really. In the crowd watching us that night was a lad called Gareth Jones. After Gareth telling me that tomorrow night he was off to see Cardiff v Swansea in the Welsh Cup (1982), I was back into football. Since I had moved down to Neath, I hadn't been for five years. So off we went on the 5.40pm train; we got there at about 6.30pm and I was nicked at 7.30pm, fined £300 and the rest is history.

Over the next decade we held our own and came out on top time and time again. As Toozey, the author of the Jacks book, personally once told me, a lot of it was tongue-in-cheek stuff. I would like to meet any two Jacks who can say they slapped me or Fulman (probably the best lad we had down this way) in those days, so please step forward. I only live three miles from you and some of you have got my phone number. There were only two Swansea lads who would have been able to have a go at Fulman, and they worked with him anyway. With Fulman, you get no change in a row with the guy. I've been with him in at least 30-40 rows and we've only ever come unstuck due to the severity of the numbers stacked against us at the time. This was on two occasions, once when he stood at Swansea Guild Hall and just faced a mass of them and then when we tried to take Exeter's end. A couple of us were left on there and we just fought till we were fucked. There are photos to prove it. I don't mind admitting I got a right old slap off them, unlike most of the Jacks, who say they've never been run or done. Who are they kidding?

Around about Easter 1984, after taking the piss out of the Jacks all day in Swansea, we then marched down to the East Terrace at the Vetch Field. We were 200 strong, all dressers and all laughing, celebrating that we had just run the scum absolutely everywhere before the game. As we got to the

ground, a copper asked us where we were all from. I showed
him my Neath Punk tattoo and that was it, we were off. There
were 200 now on their end, and the best was to come. We all
ran on the pitch towards their North Bank end (when we had
scored), but we were soon driven back by dogs, etc. The second
goal came, and this time we had other plans. We ran to the
halfway line and then faced the North Bank and called them on
(again, there are photos to prove it). We hadn't even done
anything and they were running away. I got right to the fence
and, without a second thought, climbed over and ran straight
in; the scum had all scattered, to my amusement.

I then saw Ginger climbing back over the fence, and the other
198 gingerly walking back to the away end. Did I look for
mercy? Did I fuck, the whole inbred family steamed me. I then
ran into the corner of the North Bank and the East Terrace,
where I was trapped in the corner, I remember seeing a load of
Jack heroes steaming towards me. I thought to myself, *Fair play,
they've come straight from work to the game*. Well, why else
were they wearing steel toecaps and donkey jackets? I was soon
to find out that they were the notorious Town Hill Crack
Commando Squad and I was cornered by about 30 of the
muppets. Fair play, I'd just run the North Bank in half a minute
on my own, and I pulled out a blade (or was it my William Hill
bookie's pen?) and couldn't believe they backed off from four
inches of blue plastic. I got to the emergency gate, tried to crawl
under the fucker and got a bit of a slap. But, thanks to the copper
who pulled me from under the gate, I was then taken to the rest
of Cardiff's travelling support to be given a hero's welcome.

My second story is about the FA Cup saga of 1991 at the
Vetch. For starters, the Neath lads were running all the top Jacks
out of their seats during the game, and you can see this on
YouTube, along with the bastards doing the Canton mile, being
legged by nine Cardiff lads outside the exchange in Canton.

Back in '91, we had one of our biggest mobs out for years and
we met up with the Cardiff lads in the Bear pub in Neath. We
had 40 good lads just from Neath alone. (Would the Jacks have
40 lads living three miles from Cardiff? In their dreams!) We all

made our way to the railway station, a good few hundred lads. That day, Cardiff had over 5000 supporters at Swansea with no restrictions – hooray for the good old days! In total that day we had over 1000 who were lads, and if those Jack twats don't admit it then they're lying to themselves. Their town was run ragged, and even the police have said that we were out of control that day. We had so many mobs out that day that we kept bumping into each other, each time praying it was the Jacks. They must have gone to the rugby for the day. 2-0 to me, I think.

I'm going to finish with 'THE GREATEST NON-EVENT OF THE 80's', the 'swim away'. I'm referring to the gypo Jacks' only self-proclaimed victory over Port Talbot (not Cardiff, by the way). I'm talking 12 people in total, nine Port Talbot lads age 15-19 and three Dinas Powys lads. Let's also get it straight: there was only one old head present that day, and that was Kersy from Barry (Dinas) who was 19 at the time; the other lads were Tongy and Bazza, two 17-year-olds from Port Talbot, 16-year-old Lee Webber, and Aiden (Taffy Anton's brother) who was 15. The only wrong step that they took that day was going back to their cars, about 300 yards from the Vetch Field. Also remember that these boys parked up only three minutes from all the pubs and had the nerve to march around Swansea and give it to whoever they could find. At this time, Swansea's oldest trick was to stay in their pubs until Cardiff had been safely escorted back to the train station and the coaches, so then they would pick them off in ones and twos and their full mob would attack anything up to three cars full of kids. So fair play, when there's 200 onto 12, like there was that day, I don't think even Swansea will get done. When those numbers occur, 18-1 in their favour, I'll take my hat off to them. So the Jacks steamed them onto the beach and then the kiddy fiddlers swarmed all over them. The 12 lads took their only one option and jumped in the shit-filled Swansea Bay. I would have rather stayed and fought than been unlucky enough to swallow a floating turd from the land of the unwashed which is Townhill, you gypo scum! It was dark by this time, so imagine what it must have been like with syringes floating around and a load of bricks raining down on them. Young Lee Webber was shouting, "Come and join us over here!" So why didn't they go in their shitty water? Or was it that they couldn't swim?

Luckily enough for the boys, a few Old Bill turned up and told Swansea to fuck off. Apparently the boys came out like drowned rats; a couple of carloads had come back for them, but when they saw the state of them they said, "You're not coming in the car like that, boys!" Anyway, this has been Swansea's biggest result to date.

You do have some top lads: of the ones I have respect for, Stacko in particular has saved my arse on more than one occasion, as have Boxer, Alan and Laddy. Personally, I know he has upset a lot of people with his book, but Mr Tooze has never given it the big 'un to me or Fulman, so respect where it's due.

DAVE SUGARMAN

Dave, as you will see, is not a hooligan. But if you supported Cardiff through the years, whether you liked it or not, you would probably have got caught up in it. I wanted Dave's story in this book as I thought it would be different, and it sure is. Dave is one of the best writers down at the City and remembers everything. He's known as TLG on the City message boards.

Dave Sugarman (CCFC): Seventeen. That's how old I was when it became painfully obvious that I wasn't cut out to be a football hooligan. My experiences during a six-month period from March to September 1984 left me in no doubt that I was never going to make the grade as a member of the Soul Crew. If you're hoping this will be another collection of anecdotes from somebody who was one of Cardiff's top boys in the 80's, you'll be disappointed. On the contrary, mine is a cautionary tale about a young lad who was drawn to football violence like a moth to a flame, but who soon learned that getting involved was more hassle than it was worth.

My father took me to my first Cardiff City game in March 1975, on the day before my eighth birthday. A trip to Ninian Park was his idea of a special treat. Sheffield Wednesday were Cardiff's opponents on that glorious occasion. The Owls were rock bottom of the Second Division table, while the Bluebirds were just one place above them. Predictably, the match ended in a goalless draw. The crowd jeered, slow handclapped and chanted, "What a load of rubbish!" at regular intervals throughout the 90 minutes. Midfielder George Smith ripped off his shirt and threw it at manager Jimmy Andrews after being substituted. His replacement, Johnny Vincent, missed a late penalty, and City were booed off the field following the final whistle. Both teams were relegated to the Third Division a month later. Happy days.

Although I'd been given a grim introduction to life as a Cardiff supporter, I was nevertheless bitten by the Bluebirds bug and became a City fanatic from that day forward. After my father had taken me to the remaining four home games of the 1974/75 season, I pleaded with him to buy me a ticket for the following season, which he duly did. Our seats were situated in the back row of Block C of the Grandstand, directly in front of the old press box, and the view from up there was superb. I have lots of terrific memories from my first full season as a City fan, which was a very successful one for the club. The likes of Willie Anderson, Adrian Alston and Tony Evans played some brilliant football as they fired the Bluebirds to promotion to the Second Division, but it wasn't just the action on the pitch that kept me entertained. Back then, visiting supporters were usually housed in the enclosure, which was an area of terracing to the left of the Grange End. It was directly below our section of the Grandstand, so those of us in Block C had a clear view of what went on down there. In the mid-70's, the sight of rival fans smashing lumps out of each other in the enclosure was as common as the sound of fireworks on the Bob Bank during winter and the smell of cigars in the Grandstand at Christmas. Teams such as Crystal Palace, Brighton and Millwall brought decent numbers to Ninian during that season, so there were plenty of scraps to be seen on the terraces.

As a young child I was fascinated by hooliganism, but that's hardly surprising as I began attending matches at a time when violence seemed to go hand in hand with Cardiff City. In those days, crowd trouble was such a regular occurrence in and around Ninian Park that I never considered it to be anything other than normal. As far as I was aware, fighting was simply something that young men were supposed to do at the football. There was nothing unusual about it at all.

Sometimes, after matches had finished, the clashes on Sloper Road would get so bad that the stewards in Block C of the Grandstand would advise anyone with women and children to wait in the players' bar for 20 minutes or so. Our exit onto the streets was the same one used by the away fans in the enclosure, so we were told to stay in the ground until things had calmed down outside. I can remember several occasions during the mid-70's when I was sat in the bar, watching through the upstairs window as scores of lads fought pitched battles on the streets below.

Naturally enough, the majority of the football songs I was hearing and learning as I was growing up were about violence, or 'Cardiff aggro' as the boys preferred to label it. City's lads proudly proclaimed they came from the Valleys where the grass was green, and were the hardest fans you'd ever seen. Visiting supporters were warned they'd have to keep off the Grange End if they wanted to stay alive. They were also told they were going to get their fucking heads kicked in, they'd never make the station and they were either going in the River Taff or going home in an ambulance. Ninian Park was such a warm, welcoming place for visitors back in the 70's.

While I'd seen numerous minor skirmishes on the streets and terraces during my debut season as a City supporter, the first major outbreak of trouble I witnessed came at the end of the 1975/76 campaign. The occasion was a European Championships quarter final second leg between Wales and Yugoslavia at Ninian, and the crowd disturbances on that sunny May afternoon were so serious they ended up making headline news all over Europe.

The Yugoslavs had beaten Wales 2-0 in Zagreb a month earlier, so Mike Smith's team had a mountain to climb in order to reach the semi-finals. Nevertheless, the demand for tickets was high and Grandstand seats were very hard to come by. My father managed to get us tickets, although he couldn't get two together. His seat was halfway up Block E, while mine was a couple of rows from the front of Block F. Not too far apart in reality, but it was a little daunting for a nine-year-old to be separated from his dad in a crowd of over 30,000, especially given the volatile atmosphere.

The man who unforgettably took centre stage that afternoon was an East German referee by the name of Rudi Glöckner. He was considered to be one of the best officials in the world at the time, having previously refereed the 1970 World Cup Final between Brazil and Italy in Mexico, but for whatever reason he didn't seem to like the Welsh. Within 20 minutes of the kick-off he'd upset the crowd when he awarded the visitors a penalty despite a blatant dive by striker Dan Popivoda. Defender Josif Katalinski tucked away the spot kick to leave Wales 3-0 down on aggregate and in need of a miracle, although Crystal Palace centre-half Ian Evans equalised seven minutes before half-time to give the home fans a bit of hope.

An unlikely comeback looked possible shortly after the break, when John Toshack scored from close range. A bicycle kick from John Mahoney had set Toshack up, but Glöckner ruled that Mahoney had been guilty of dangerous play and disallowed the goal. Despite the fact that Toshack's effort would have been deemed legal by any British referee, the East German was having none of it, so Ninian Park went mental. Beer cans rained down on the playing surface from all angles, several lads scaled the fences and invaded the pitch in an effort to attack the ref and the rest of the crowd aimed Nazi salutes in the direction of the officials. Play was halted for five minutes and Glöckner threatened to abandon the match, which was something he did twice more before the afternoon was over.

A second Toshack goal was disallowed for offside ten minutes after the first, which prompted another volley of beer cans from the terraces along with more pitch invasions, more Nazi salutes and another lengthy stoppage in play. The crowd's misery was complete when Terry Yorath missed a penalty 12 minutes from time, so the fans contented themselves by abusing the East

German officials for the remainder of the game. Play had to be stopped again after linesman Siegfried Kirschen was hit in the neck by a stone thrown from the Bob Bank. When Glöckner eventually decided to blow the final whistle, hundreds invaded the pitch from all four sides of the ground. Between 20 and 30 policemen sprinted onto the Ninian turf and surrounded the referee in an attempt to escort him to safety and they just about managed to do so, but not without a serious casualty. One of the pitch invaders grabbed the flag from the corner where I was sitting and threw it like a javelin in Glöckner's direction. It landed in the shoulder of one of the coppers who was trying to shepherd him off the field. Images of the stricken officer were used by many of the national and international papers in the days that followed, as Welsh fans were roundly condemned by the world's press. 'Ninian Park's Day of Shame!' screamed the headline on the front page of the *Western Mail*, while talk of possible European bans for both Cardiff City and Wales filled the back pages.

That day was a hell of an experience for a nine-year-old kid and it made a huge impression on me. The atmosphere inside Ninian Park was so hostile it was frightening, but it was also strangely exhilarating. I can clearly remember my bewilderment as the entire crowd were standing and chanting, "Sieg Heil!" at Glöckner during the second half. I didn't have a clue what that was all about, but everyone else was doing it so I joined in regardless. I can also remember my mother giving the old man an almighty bollocking when we arrived back home. We'd returned well over an hour later than scheduled due to a combination of the large crowd, the various delays during the game and the fighting on the streets after it had finished. Mum had heard about the trouble on the news and she'd been convinced that something terrible had happened to us. She was right too. We'd been knocked out of the European Championships.

Three more major outbreaks of violence I witnessed in my first few years as a City fan occurred during games against Wrexham and Everton, in 1977, and Chelsea, in 1979. The

Wrexham match was a dramatic fourth-round FA Cup tie that the Bluebirds won 3-2 courtesy of a last-gasp strike by Scottish midfielder John Buchanan. The attendance at Ninian Park on that occasion was almost 30,000 and the fighting in the enclosure was incredible. It was almost non-stop during the first half. So many lads were involved that the police seemed powerless to do anything about it.

Cardiff played Everton in the fifth round in front of a bumper 35,000 crowd. Some bright spark came up with the idea of putting 4,000 visiting supporters on the Canton side of the Bob Bank, with only a temporary plastic fence separating them from about 8,000 City fans on the other side. The segregation measures lasted all of two minutes. Everton won the tie 2-1, but the scousers who came down to South Wales won't have happy memories of their trip. Many of them got battered.

The Chelsea match in 1979 is one that has gone down in hooligan folklore. A group of around 50 Londoners invaded the Bob Bank shortly before the game started and they were given an almighty hammering for their troubles. There were bodies flying all over the place while it was kicking off. A couple of Chelsea lads got thrown over the wall at the back of the terrace, and about a dozen had to be carried away on stretchers once things had eventually calmed down. There was also chaos outside the ground after the game had finished. Jubilee Park was like a mini-war zone. The press later reported that two pubs in the city centre had been badly damaged, 24 fans had needed hospital treatment and the police had made almost a hundred arrests.

My father usually took me to three or four away matches each season during my first five years as a City supporter. The games he picked were generally local derbies in places like Bristol, Hereford and Swansea. Unsurprisingly, there was always trouble of one sort or another at such matches. He also took me to games against several of the London clubs including Charlton, Crystal Palace and Fulham, along with a couple of England v Wales home internationals at the old Wembley Stadium. They were lively affairs to say the very least. If memory serves, more

Welshmen were using the rotten wooden seats as weapons than were sitting on them during a 0-0 draw there in May 1979. Wembley was a dump when we arrived, but it looked considerably worse after we'd left.

The first time I ever travelled to an away match without the supervision of my father was in April 1981. I'd just turned 14 at the time. Cardiff were playing Swansea in a Second Division game at the Vetch Field, but the old man refused to take me because of the violence during the previous season's fixtures between the two clubs. It was a vitally important match as the Bluebirds were battling against relegation and the Swans were going for promotion. I was determined not to miss it, so my mate Dan Beynon and I cobbled together as much money as we could in the week leading up to the game. After telling our parents on the Saturday morning that we were spending the day at our local youth club, we caught a bus into town, then jumped on a National Express coach and headed for Jackland. Having left Cardiff at around 9.30am, we were able to walk from the bus station to the Vetch without any problems, but we'd arrived so early that the ground hadn't even opened by the time we got there. We were both as green as grass and didn't have a clue what we were doing. We ended up sitting outside the away end for at least an hour before the turnstiles eventually opened.

The terraces began filling up pretty quickly once the ground did open, and it wasn't long before missiles of various descriptions were flying back and forth between the West Stand and the North Bank. I can remember an enormous skinhead dislodging a large piece of one of the terrace steps shortly after his arrival in the away end. Once he'd smashed it into hundreds of pieces, the air was thick with lumps of concrete for a while. About half an hour before kick-off, the word went around that a gang of Cardiff lads were going to attack the north bank at ten to three. Sure enough, when the time arrived a group of 30 or 40 City fans made themselves known in the top left-hand corner of the terrace. It was bedlam over there for a few minutes, until the Old Bill managed to drag them out.

The game itself proved to be a decent contest. The Jacks were well on top during the first half and Leighton James put them ahead just before the break, but he wasted a chance to increase their lead when he had a second-half penalty brilliantly saved by Ron Healey. Striker Peter Kitchen nodded in an equaliser from a John Lewis cross with ten minutes remaining, and Tarki Micallef almost won it for the Bluebirds in injury time with a header that went inches wide. Following the final whistle, Dan and I somehow managed to get back to the bus station unharmed, which was quite a feat considering there were running battles taking place all over the town centre and we didn't know where we were going. I'm certain we found our way to the station more by luck than judgement. After we'd been sitting there for a while waiting for our coach, we were surrounded by a gang of local kids who pushed us around a bit and nicked my beloved City scarf. I can remember being seriously pissed off at the time, but looking back now I reckon we got off pretty lightly considering we'd been wandering around enemy territory like a pair of lost sheep for much of the day.

About 12 months after that Swansea game, I began drinking in my local pubs in the Rhiwbina area of North Cardiff. The regulars in the Deri back then included a group of City fans who were a few years older than me and who were more than familiar with hooliganism. They included the likes of Carlton Jones, Spragg, Dafydd May, Foxy, Simon Williams and the infamous Dai H. The casual culture had begun to kick in by that stage and the Deri crew were already wearing all the right labels. As a young punk rocker, I was none too impressed by their clothes, but I looked up to those lads all the same. Listening to them tell stories of their numerous escapades on their travels encouraged me to go to more away matches.

The 1982/83 campaign proved to be an excellent one for the club and it was also a big learning curve for me personally, as it was the season in which I began to travel away regularly. My usual mode of transport was a coach run by the Barry branch of the supporters' club, but occasionally I'd travel on the train with a couple of my mates from school and a few of the older lads from the pub. I took in a total of 14 away games during an incident-packed year and there are several that stand out in my memory. One was an early-season match at Oxford that ended in an exciting 2-2 draw. City fans celebrated a late Jimmy Mullen equaliser by running riot in the streets around the Manor Ground. A couple of cars got overturned, if I remember correctly. Another memorable encounter was a fiery affair up at Lincoln, where Dave Bennett was sent off, City were beaten 2-1 and I got sparked out in some dingy sidestreet after being caught in the wrong place at the wrong time as I headed back to the bus. I've still got a small scar on my chin from that incident. Then there was a first-round FA Cup tie at Wokingham, where a wall collapsed during the second half, badly injuring a policewoman. A load of us spilled onto the pitch when that happened, and I ended up being spotted on the evening news by my old man. He went berserk when I eventually got back home, which was much later than planned. A couple of our coach windows were put through by a gang of Chelsea fans while we were making our way out of Wokingham, so we had to hang around at a bus depot in Reading for a few hours while we waited for a replacement vehicle to arrive.

The biggest game of that season by far was a promotion battle with Portsmouth at Fratton Park in March 1983. Pompey were top of the Third Division table at the time and Cardiff were second. The match attracted a crowd of around 25,000, which included almost 4,000 travelling Bluebirds. The contest on the field wasn't the best and ended in a 0-0 draw, with the highlight being an incredible save made by City keeper Eric Steele from a Billy Rafferty header. I think it was later voted *Match of the Day*'s 'Save of the Season', or something similar. However, the most exciting action that day took place on the terraces. Fighting broke out in the home end on several occasions during the first half, while the scenes in the away end were chaotic from start to finish. Numerous fixtures and fittings were destroyed, including a huge old clock which stood at the back of the terrace. At one stage during the second half, a mobile hot dog stand that had been parked in a gap between two large sections of the away terrace was smashed to pieces, resulting in burgers, sausages and bread rolls being used as missiles against the Old Bill. I've seen many bizarre sights during my 30-odd years as a Cardiff fan, but that one must be close to the top of the list.

Some of the clashes with the police after the game had finished were amongst the most violent I've ever witnessed. Everything went crazy when a load of Pompey fans started launching bricks and stones into our section from an alleyway behind us. We were locked inside Fratton Park for ages while a huge City mob vented their fury on the local constabulary and there were plenty of injuries on both sides, some of which looked serious. It was also pretty hairy when we got outside the ground. I remember feeling mightily relieved when I eventually made it back to the coach in one piece.

Cardiff went on to secure promotion in the second week of May with a 2-0 victory over Orient at Ninian Park. John Lewis and Dave Bennett scored the goals that lifted the Bluebirds back to the Second Division. Seven days later, thousands of us travelled to a meaningless end-of-season game at Bristol Rovers' Eastville ground, where City fans celebrated the team's promotion by going on the rampage. There was loads of trouble before, during and after a match that is best remembered for an unfortunate incident involving striker Jeff Hemmerman. He'd been brilliant all season and had netted 26 goals in 52 league and cup appearances but, sadly, he damaged his knee ligaments in a second-half collision with Rovers keeper Phil Kite and had to be stretchered off. The injury proved so severe that it effectively ended Hemmerman's career. He did attempt a comeback towards the end of the following campaign but he was never the same player again, and was forced to retire from the game in 1984.

I left school in the summer of 1983 with few qualifications and even fewer ambitions to get a full-time job. Football, music, drinking and chasing young women were the only things that interested me at the time. I did a few fiddles for a local landscape gardener called Keith Oliver, who had previously been City's groundsman for many years, and I also did a bit of labouring work for my mate Tommy, who was a roofer, but apart from that I was perfectly content with life on the dole. Provided I had enough money for football, weekend drinking and the occasional gig, I was happy. Working was for mugs as far as I was concerned.

It was during that summer that I began frequenting a place called the Lexington, which was on Queen Street in Cardiff city centre. It was situated where the Capitol shopping complex now stands. The ground floor of the Lex was supposed to be an American-style restaurant, but in reality it was little more than a glorified burger joint, while the basement was a small bar where all the punks and goths used to hang out. It had a fantastic jukebox which featured loads of great singles by punk bands such as the Sex Pistols, the Clash, the Buzzcocks and the Stranglers, as well as lots of stuff from early-80's alternative acts like Bauhaus, the Cure, Killing Joke and the Psychedelic Furs. I used to love it down there, particularly on Friday and Saturday nights when it was packed with punkettes and goth girls.

Among the many weird and wonderful characters I met in the Lex was a lad called Carlton Seymour. He was several years older than me but we got on like a house on fire, particularly as we were both keen City fans. I think I'm right in saying that Carlton was originally from Aberdare. He was around six feet two inches tall with a wiry frame and a distinctive tattoo of a sheep wearing Doctor Marten's boots on his right arm. Hard as nails, nutty as a fruitcake and pretty much fearless, he'd spent a bit of time behind bars but was one of life's loveable rogues. Despite his obvious faults, he had a heart of gold and was always great fun to be around. We became firm friends very quickly and began going to matches together as soon as the 1983/84 season started.

At that stage, our Saturday routine when the Bluebirds were playing at home would often begin with a mid-morning haircut at Harry's Salon in Mackintosh Place, where barbers Andy and Nicky were both staunch City supporters. They specialised in flat-top and Mohican-style haircuts, so all the sharpest punks and psychobillies used to go there regularly. After Harry's, we'd head to the Lex for a few lunchtime pints, and then it was off to Ninian Park for the match. When the game had finished we'd return to the Lex for a few hours, and then stagger around the corner to Nero's nightclub on Greyfriars Road, where the upstairs bar was full of punks, goths and psychobillies on

Saturday nights. How on earth we used to manage all this with so little money is a mystery, but we usually did.

Overall, the 1983/84 season was a mediocre one for City. The team spent the majority of the campaign in mid-table and consequently never looked likely to go up or down. Nevertheless, we had some good trips to places like Charlton, Fulham, Brighton, Portsmouth and Cambridge, even if the results were a little erratic. By then, the casual look was well and truly established on the terraces, so Carlton and I must have stood out like sore thumbs. He always had a bleached-blond flat-top, while my hair colour and style used to change regularly. At various stages during that particular season it was jet black, orange, yellow, half black/half white and bright red. We both dressed similarly in denim jackets, checked shirts and drainpipe jeans, but while Carlton usually wore a pair of moccasins, I favoured either Doctor Marten's boots or leopard skin-effect brothel creepers. I think it's fair to say there weren't many other lads travelling around the country with Cardiff during the mid-80's who looked like us, which was probably just as well, as we weren't exactly inconspicuous.

As we approached Christmas 1983, Carlton decided that we should get ourselves Pringle jumpers specifically for the football because so many other City fans were wearing them. Consequently, he turned up in the Lex one Friday evening with a couple of brand new Pringles in a Tesco carrier bag. The one he chose for himself was a light blue effort, while the one he gave to me was bright yellow. God knows where he got them from, and I didn't like to ask. One thing's for sure though, he certainly hadn't paid for them as he never had a penny to scratch his arse with, never mind enough money to buy expensive golf jumpers. We wore them to numerous games before the season had finished and, to be honest, we must have looked a right pair of clowns. After all, punk rock haircuts and Pringle jumpers could hardly be described as a perfect match.

In late March, a small group of us celebrated my 17th birthday by travelling up to Maine Road to watch Cardiff take on Manchester City. The Mancs were on the fringes of the promotion race, while the Bluebirds were 11th in the table. We went up there on one of the supporters' club buses, which in those days were far removed from being the pop and crisps affairs they are now. In fact, a couple of us were so pissed by the time we got to Manchester that we could barely stand up. We arrived pretty early and I can't remember any significant trouble before the game, but things became much livelier inside the ground. City took an early lead when Gordon Owen converted a Trevor Lee cross and they played well for most of the match, but sadly they collapsed late on. David Johnson scored an 85th-minute equaliser for the home side and then Graham Baker bundled in an injury time winner from a Neil McNab corner. That was the signal for chaos on the away terrace, as hundreds of City lads began fighting with the police and stewards. Apparently, there were a number of ferocious battles on the way back to the train station, but we didn't take part in any of those as our coach was parked near the ground and the Old Bill had cleared the area by the time they let us out. While we'd lost the game in unfortunate circumstances, the day hadn't been a total disaster as the Manchester fans to our right had been throwing coins at us all game long. Carlton and I picked up that many ten- and 50-pence pieces during the course of the afternoon that we ended up returning home to South Wales with more money than we'd set out with, which was good news for a couple of dole bums like us. Oddly, the 20,140 crowd at Maine Road was the biggest in all four divisions that weekend, which goes to show how far attendances were dipping at the time.

Three weeks after the Chelsea game, City were scheduled to meet Swansea at the Vetch in an Easter Saturday fixture. I initially planned to travel on the football special, which was due to depart Cardiff at around the 1pm mark. However, Carlton insisted that we should leave on a much earlier train as we'd miss all the best action if we went on the special. I reluctantly agreed, so me, Carlton, Dan and another mate of ours from the Lex called Jim Frampton ended up setting off from Central Station at something silly like 9am. I don't remember Jim as being that much of a City fan and I can't recall him ever going on another away trip with us, but the way things turned out it was very fortunate for Carlton and I that he'd decided to join us on this particular occasion.

There were a couple of hundred loonies on the train as we left Cardiff, and plenty more got on at Bridgend and Port Talbot. When we arrived in Neath, everybody piled off and headed straight for an off licence, which was quickly ransacked. It was a boiling hot day, so we spent the next half-hour or so drinking and sitting around in the sun before everyone made their way back onto the train. Upon our arrival in Swansea, we were greeted by a small handful of police outside High Street station, although there was no sign of any Jacks in the vicinity. The Old Bill made a token effort to hold us there, but a shout went up from the front of the mob and within seconds we were all sprinting off in the direction of the town centre. When we got to the Quadrant shopping complex, most of us went inside and it wasn't long before Gilesports had their windows put through. We weren't in there more than a minute or two, but nevertheless numerous items were grabbed from shop displays and lots of damage was done.

After running amok in the Quadrant, everyone started heading towards Oystermouth Road, but the day's entertainment was about to come to an abrupt halt as far as Carlton and I were concerned. A couple of police riot vans suddenly appeared on the scene, so most of the lads began to scarper in the direction of the seafront, but our small group decided to play it cool and keep on walking. We'd been at the back of the mob ever since we'd left the train station, we hadn't done any damage or stolen anything in the Quadrant and none of us had committed any crimes as far as we were aware, so I was confident the Old Bill wouldn't give us any grief provided we stayed calm. However, that confidence was misplaced. As one of the wagons passed us, its back doors flew open and two burly coppers jumped out. They grabbed hold of Carlton, wrestled him to the floor, handcuffed him and dragged him into the van. I couldn't believe what was happening, so I ran towards the driver's door, banged on the window and demanded to know why my mate was being arrested. The driver's response was to tell me to fuck off or I'd be joining him. I protested that

Carlton hadn't done anything wrong and was given the same reply, so I foolishly kicked the side of the van and shouted something ridiculous about the police being fascist bastards. Unsurprisingly, I was sat alongside Carlton in a pair of handcuffs very shortly afterwards.

While we were being driven to the police station, the officer who'd arrested me began making snide remarks about my hair, which I'd dyed bright red a few days earlier. He was sporting a thick, bushy moustache and looked like an extra from a Village People video, but nevertheless he decided that my appearance was worthy of his derision. "Why do wankers like you have such stupid haircuts?" he asked. "The same reason why tossers like you have stupid-looking furry things stuck in the middle of your faces," I replied. Apparently, that was the wrong answer, as he grabbed me by the throat and banged my head against the side of the van. Carlton went nuts and started screaming at the copper to leave me alone, so he was also given a couple of hefty whacks across the head. When things had settled down a little, he quietly told me to button it and said he'd deal with our moustachioed friend later.

When we arrived at the station, and once we'd gone through the formalities of being signed in by the desk sergeant, Carlton was asked if he'd calmed down yet. He confirmed that he had, so his handcuffs were removed by one of the officers who'd apprehended him. After gently rubbing his wrists for a few moments, he casually turned towards the copper who'd arrested me, grabbed him by the ears and butted him in the face. Naturally enough, all hell broke loose and Carlton received some severe punishment, but not before he'd managed to dish out a few decent punches of his own. While all this was going on, I was cowering in the corner. If I'd had my wits about me, I suppose I could have tried to make a break for it, as the station doors were wide open and the Old Bill were too busy trying to control Carlton to pay any attention to me. Still, on reflection, running away probably wouldn't have been the wisest of moves. After all, how long would it have taken the police to track down a drunken teenager with a bright red Mohican?

Once Carlton had been subdued, we were put into separate cells which stood opposite each other. The match was due to kick off at 3pm, and yet we'd managed to get ourselves locked up well before midday. It was almost an hour until anyone else joined us, but the cells started filling up steadily as the afternoon wore on and the lads who were arriving had plenty of tales to tell. Apparently, something in the region of 4,000 City fans had descended on Swansea and there had been pitched battles with the police and the Jacks at the train station, in the town centre and at the Vetch Field. The first bit of information we were given about the game was that it had been held up for a few minutes shortly after kick-off when around a hundred Cardiff supporters invaded the pitch from the East Terrace and confronted the home fans on the North Bank. Then the coppers told us that the Bluebirds had taken a 2-0 lead. That news was greeted with prolonged cheering and a spontaneous burst of City songs from most of the cells. Next, they informed us that the scores were level at 2-2. Finally, they took great delight in telling us that Swansea had come back to win 3-2. To begin with, nobody believed it and everyone thought they were winding us up, but then a few boys who'd been nicked after the final whistle arrived and they confirmed that the final score was indeed 3-2 to the Jacks. Dean Saunders had scored two of their goals, including the winner. I was gutted, especially as defeat for Swansea would have seen them relegated to the Third Division.

The eventual number of lads arrested on what had been a very busy day for the boys in blue was 68, and more than two thirds of us were Cardiff supporters. Therefore, some of the cells at Swansea Central were packed to overflowing. At one stage, my cell contained no less than nine of us, including a well-known Bluebirds fan named Seddie. He told me he was going to give up football as he was getting himself into too much trouble. Three weeks later, I spotted him on the Ninian Park pitch battling with a group of Sheffield Wednesday fans after the last game of the season had finished, so that's one resolution that didn't last long. Carlton's cell contained four other Cardiff lads and an ugly Jack skinhead. Suffice to say, he was given a hard time for much of the duration of his stay, but nevertheless the filthy bastard still managed to spit across the hallway at us on several occasions.

After our statements, fingerprints and mug shots had been taken, the lads slowly but surely started being released. As Carlton and I had been amongst the first to be arrested, I naturally assumed that we'd also be amongst the first to be let back out again, but that's not the way things panned out. In fact, we were the very last City fans to be released along with five other lads, most of whom were Cardiff-based. It was fast approaching midnight by the time we were finally let out of our cells. While we were being turned loose, the coppers informed us that the last train back to the capital had already gone and there were no more services that night as the following day was Easter Sunday, so we were well and truly knackered. No explanation was given as to why the seven of us had been detained for so long, but in our case I reckon it was a straightforward act of revenge for the incident in which Carlton had nutted the officer who arrested me.

While we were standing around in the foyer planning our next move, a couple of the lads poked their heads out the station door and spotted a group of Jacks across the other side of the road. They were obviously waiting for any stray City fans to emerge, but none of us were in the mood for any more hassle. We just wanted to know how we were going to get home, so initially we refused to budge. The desk sergeant told us he couldn't care less how we got back to Cardiff, but he wanted us out of his station. After a few minutes of angry bickering, he made arrangements for us to leave via the back door and get a lift in a riot van to the outskirts of the city. From there, he expected us to either hitch a ride or walk home.

The van dropped us off at a roundabout on the A483 just outside Swansea. After a brief discussion, we decided our best bet would be to walk the remaining six miles to Neath and see if we could arrange some sort of transport from there. As it had been such a hot day it was still pretty warm, so at least the temperature wasn't a problem. We christened ourselves the Magnificent Seven and set off on what proved to be an eventful late-night hike along the side of the dual carriageway.

We hadn't been walking for more than a quarter of an hour when one of the lads spotted a white Transit van moving slowly past on the other side of the road. The driver wound his window down and shouted a tirade of anti-Cardiff abuse, so we returned his insults with interest and thought little more of it until a few minutes later, when the van reappeared on our side of the carriageway. On that occasion it was travelling considerably faster. As it drew level with us, the passenger door opened and one of the occupants hurled a couple of bricks in our direction. I couldn't believe it. Thankfully, nobody was seriously hurt, although one of the boys did get hit on the leg if I remember correctly. The van went past once more a short while afterwards, but by that time we'd collected up a few bricks and stones of our own. Once we'd lobbed them at the vehicle, we decided to make ourselves scarce for a while in case the driver went back into the centre of Swansea and called up some reinforcements. After leaving the side of the dual carriageway, we walked through a series of fields for the next mile or so, and then returned to the road. There was no sign of the van for the remainder of our journey.

It was around 2am by the time we made it to Neath, and naturally enough everything was shut when we got there, so we decided to head for the station and keep our fingers crossed that some kind of train would eventually turn up. Happily, we didn't have to wait more than half an hour before one did. To be honest, I can't really remember what sort of service it was. It might have been a Royal Mail train or something similar. All I know is that we were very glad to see it, and although we ended up going back home in the middle of the night, we were all in remarkably high spirits by the time we pulled into Cardiff Central.

The Magnificent Seven returned to sunny Swansea a few days later for our initial court hearings. The majority of the 46 City fans who'd been arrested on the Saturday were on the same train as us and plenty had brought mates along with them, so it was like a mini-football special. There were some chaotic scenes in and around the court buildings after we arrived. Fighting broke out on the steps outside on a couple of occasions and the proceedings inside had to be halted numerous times due to a variety of misdemeanours from those in the dock and the public galleries. They included the chanting of football songs, the screaming of insults at the magistrates and police, the smoking of cigarettes and the drinking of alcohol. After hearing the ludicrous charges that were being levelled against us, Carlton and I pleaded not guilty, so we were granted legal aid and our case was adjourned.

The police had concocted a ridiculous story that involved us being seen leading a large mob on a destructive rampage through the Quadrant and then being arrested after a violent confrontation with a group of Jacks near the seafront. They made out that we were the imaginary gang's ringleaders. It was a complete fabrication, but it was worrying nonetheless as the charges were serious and the alleged offences were at the top end of the public order scale, so the punishments were likely to be harsh. The Swansea-based solicitor we were appointed was very sympathetic to our plight and he seemed to genuinely believe the Old Bill's allegations against us were false, but he warned that there was every chance we'd be found guilty as it was our word against theirs. He predicted that Carlton would be looking at several months inside due to his previous convictions, while I would probably be liable for a heavy fine because it was my first offence. However, he added there was a possibility we could both get custodial sentences if the worst came to the worst, as the police were clearly trying to make examples of us.

It was around six weeks before our case was eventually heard. In the meantime, Carlton dreamed up a hare-brained scheme that involved our girlfriends, Judith and Carol, turning up at the courts with cushions stuffed up their dresses in a bid to convince the magistrates that they were pregnant. He told us he believed this would result in more lenient punishments if we were found guilty. Thankfully, he was outvoted three to one. When the day arrived, the girls opted to simply try and look sad instead. I can remember feeling extremely anxious as we re-entered the court building, and Carlton was as quiet as I'd ever known him to be. Jude and Carol were alongside us to offer their moral support, while Dan and Jim were present as our witnesses.

The two arresting officers were first to give their statements, and fortunately they weren't particularly convincing. They offered up no evidence other than what they had allegedly written down in their notebooks on the day and they had no witnesses, so our solicitor got stuck into them and managed to pick several holes in their story during his cross-examination. Carlton was up next, and his testimony was a nervous one. He looked worried throughout and didn't speak very well at all. I followed him, and although I was shaking like a leaf as I made my way up to the stand, I grew in confidence when I got there and ended up putting in a fairly decent performance. During one heated exchange with the prosecution solicitor, I even managed to make the magistrates laugh with a sarcastic remark about the quality of his questioning technique. Dan was called up next and he did reasonably well for us, although he wasn't in front of the court for long before our solicitor played his trump card. That was Jim, who neither looked nor sounded like a potential football hooligan despite having a flat-top haircut. He proved to be a brilliant witness. Jim was a well-spoken lad and he delivered his testimony calmly and confidently. Having eloquently expressed his outrage at the inaccuracy of the police evidence, he then gave his own version of events and stuck to it rigidly under questioning by both solicitors. By the time he'd stepped down from the stand, the prosecution's case was in tatters. In the end, the magistrates retired for little more than a couple of minutes before returning to declare a verdict of not guilty on all charges. I don't think I've ever felt so relieved in my life. When we got back to Cardiff we celebrated our acquittal with a few beers in the Lex, but we didn't stay there long. To be honest, I think Carlton and I were too drained to genuinely enjoy ourselves.

While my arrest in Swansea and the subsequent court case had been an experience, it wasn't one that I was keen to repeat in any great hurry. Therefore, I promised myself that I'd be much more careful at future matches, but it wasn't long before I was in trouble again.

Three weeks into the 1984/85 season, Cardiff played old enemies Leeds Utd in a midweek fixture at Ninian Park. Leeds were top of the Second Division table going into the game, having won all four of their previous matches, while the Bluebirds were rock bottom, having lost all three of theirs. City's attendances were getting so bad at the time that only 6,800 supporters turned up on the night and a large percentage of those were from Yorkshire. Despite the team's pathetic start to the campaign, they began this particular match brightly and took the lead in the 25th minute when Paul Bodin struck from close range. Scott Sellars equalised for the visitors on the hour when he crashed in a 30-yard thunderbolt, but Phil Dwyer secured a well-deserved victory for the Bluebirds ten minutes from time when he powered home a header from a David Tong free kick.

The atmosphere on the Bob Bank had been superb all night despite the small crowd, although the Leeds fans in the Grange End didn't look very happy. As we exited the ground from the alleyway behind the Grange, loads of Yorshiremen were hanging over the back wall throwing coins and various other missiles down at us, and they were getting plenty back in return. The gates to the away end were locked as usual, so the bulk of the visiting supporters were contained, but Leeds also had around 50 lads in the Grandstand who were able to leave Ninian at the same time as the City fans. Fighting broke out from the moment they ventured out of the ground and the police were taking no prisoners, so things got ugly very quickly. Although I was supposed to be careful and I should have been heading straight home, I just couldn't resist joining the mob on Sloper Road. The whole situation was much too exciting to ignore and my adrenalin was pumping, so I chose to stick around. A minute or two later, a line of angry coppers charged into the City boys with their truncheons flailing, so I jumped into one of the gardens opposite Jubilee Park and ducked down behind a hedge. I imagined that would be the best way to avoid a battering, but it didn't prove to be the wisest move I've ever made. Having waited for a few moments until I thought the coast was clear, I stuck my head up above the hedge to see what was going on. Out of the corner of my eye I spotted a copper lunging towards me, but I didn't see him until it was too late. Before I was able to take any evasive action, he'd swung his truncheon and smashed it into the side of my skull. I hit the deck like a nine-stone sack of shit, and for a while I didn't know who I was, where I was or what I was doing there. It felt like my head had caved in.

As I slowly clambered back to my feet, the officer who'd clobbered me grabbed me by the scruff of the neck and dragged me out of the garden. I'm absolutely certain he was going to arrest me, but then he was attacked by several other Cardiff lads, so he let go of me and turned his attention to them. I made my escape while I had the chance and staggered off in the direction of the city centre, where I caught the next bus to Rhiwbina. The pain inside my head was already severe, but it got a whole lot worse during the journey home, as I was treated to a loud and lengthy analysis of the match by legendary City fan Dai Hunt. Although he's as mad as a box of frogs, Dai is about as genuine a Bluebird as you could ever wish to meet. However, he is positively the last thing you need when you've got a screaming headache.

While I lay in bed that night, unable to get comfortable because of the pain I was in, I asked myself if getting involved in football hooliganism was worth the kind of hassle I'd endured during the Chelsea, Swansea and Leeds incidents. After a couple of sleepless hours, I decided it wasn't. Ever since that day, I have always endeavoured to stay out of trouble at the football, but as I'm a Cardiff City supporter and a regular away traveller, it hasn't always been easy. Although I've consciously avoided confrontations with rival fans and officers of the law, I've nevertheless ended up in a whole host of tricky situations over the years. For instance, I was arrested before a Friday night game against Chester in 1989, having allegedly been seen fighting with Bristol City fans a month earlier. Thankfully, my explanation for what had happened with the Wurzels was accepted and I was let off with a warning. Then I was subjected to a dawn raid following the infamous home match against Swansea in 1994. That was a straightforward case of mistaken identity. I was released without charge after a few hours of questioning once the Old Bill had established I wasn't the man they were looking for. There was even an occasion in 1987 when I got head-butted by a police horse during a disturbance outside a train station in Stoke, but the less said about that incident the better. Life as a Cardiff City fan often has its ups and downs, but one thing's for sure, it's rarely dull!

* * *

Unfortunately, my story has a sad postscript. I lost touch with Carlton Seymour during the late 80's when he moved to London. While he was living there, he apparently fell in with some heavy characters from the West End who were involved in all manner of dodgy activities. After marrying a Swedish stripper, he moved over to Holland for a brief period and then worked in Bath on his return to Britain. It was while he was living there that he disappeared one weekend in 1998, and he's never been seen since. Although the police are still in contact with his friends and relatives from time to time, they haven't got a clue what happened to him, as his possessions remain untouched and his passport has never been used. He is listed as missing presumed dead. If Carlton is still out there somewhere, I'd like to think he may get to read this and he may even be tempted to get in touch. Like many, many others, I would dearly love to hear from him again. If he's no longer with us, then I'd simply like to say thanks for the memories, mate, and rest in peace.

V

THE LONDONERS

A DAUNTING TRIP TO COLD BLOW LANE
Millwall v Cardiff City, 6th December 1975
Paul Corkery (CCFC): We had travelled to London on a coach from the valleys; there were three coaches in a small convoy as we arrived near the ground. It was always a daunting trip going to Cold Blow Lane in those days; this Third Division match was to be one of the most terrifying. I was 16; most fans on the coach were of the same age apart from the organisers and a couple of old people down the front. We pulled up near the ground, outside a shell of a burned-out terraced house where a racist-motivated arson attack had killed some of the occupants a few days earlier. The atmosphere amongst us changed from banging the windows and 'flashing v-signs' to passers-by to a sudden realisation that this was not a normal away trip.

A few minutes later the three coaches turned into a sort of wasteland-cum-car-park, and two Millwall nutters ran at our coach, banging on the side, frothing at the mouth like rabid dogs. A copper with a dog chased them off. We got off our coaches and were glad to get inside the ground. We were in a corner with a floodlight pylon blocking part of the view; there were about 6,000 inside the ground, with under 300 from Cardiff. We had a small seated area to our left that ran the length of the ground, the rest of the stadium was terracing and there was very little sign of fencing or police. There was a thin line of coppers to our left, providing some sort of barrier from the home fans. The vast majority of Millwall lads seemed to be behind the opposite goals or on the terrace near the halfway line.

Millwall's chant in those days was a haunting dirge: "We are *Milllwallll*. We are *Milllwallll* . . ." I can't remember the other chant they kept blasting out, maybe it was "Cum on you lions!" Whatever it was, I can remember thinking to myself, *What am I doing here?*

The match was underway and we soon took the lead, much to the annoyance of the home fans. We then went two up and our captain, Phil Dwyer, accidentally poleaxed a Millwall player. Suddenly, from the seated area, a Millwall fan ran on the pitch and tried to punch Dwyer. Fortunately, Dwyer was a big bloke and no harm was done before stewards dragged the fan off the pitch. The atmosphere was getting alarmingly scarier by the minute, and it appeared to me like the Millwall fans were congregating closer to us. The thin line of coppers looked a poor defence to me, and I started looking around at our fans. I counted about 40 who were maybe able to hold their own; there were another 100 or so around my age and the rest were families or old people.

Fifteen minutes into the game and, unbelievably, we scored again. It was now 3-0. The excitement of the goal was short-lived; the Millwall fans behind the opposite goal had now moved to the side of the ground and were heading towards our end. I can't remember if there were fences at the Den, but if there were they weren't very good. Slowly but surely, the growing mass of angry fans were making their way towards the thin line of coppers; like a knife through butter, they steamrollered their way to our small section. A mass brawl broke out and, luckily for us, there was a lot of confusion: Cardiff punching Cardiff, Millwall attacking Millwall. It was chaos. The police were powerless and outnumbered, but did manage to get some fans into the relative safety of the seated areas.

We were forced outside the stadium, where the fighting continued. The police had more numbers, but we were trapped by the turnstiles and forced to climb over a spiked fence. I was helped over, looking back on a scene of flying boots and fists, people bleeding and getting knocked out. The police were vainly waving their truncheons, trying to break it up. There were about 50 of us outside now, with five lads on the other side of a fence calling to us. Me and my mate climbed over and joined them, thinking it was the best option . . . *wrong*.

There were now only seven of us, and we were isolated from the rest who had been forced to go in the other direction by the police reinforcements. On the other side of the fence were the Millwall fans. They spotted us and we ran towards a small wall – where, behind it, a large hedge would provide perfect cover – with a mass of Millwall lads now in pursuit

Without a thought, I cleared the wall with the other lads and fell almost headfirst into the bushes. Unfortunately for us, they weren't actually bushes but the tops of trees, and we plummeted through the branches to the floor, 20-odd feet below, into a blackberry bush and brambles. There were five of us on the floor, stunned, bruised and covered in blood, leaves and thorns. We looked at each other and laughed. *Fuck me, that was close!* Above us we could hear the laughter of the Millwall lads, peering over the top.

We were in the grounds of a big house. We headed towards an open window and climbed in, unsure if the Millwall lads were still behind us. It was a hospital, and a porter asked us what we were doing; we explained and he took us to his office. We had no idea of the score, or how we were going to get back to the coach. Time was moving on and we decided to draw lots to send one of us back, to let people know where we were. Hopefully, the coach would pick us up. A tall, skinny kid lost and was charged with getting back to the Den alone, to sort out our rescue.

Twenty minutes later, a Cardiff fan came into the porter's lodge. I knew him from Merthyr, and he said we had to go with him back to the coach. He had a Millwall scarf on, acquired from a victory some of the lads had won earlier, probably the only victory off the field that day.

There were seven of us again as we walked towards the stadium. It was quiet outside, walking down the terraced street, but you could hear the crowd inside the Den. There was still ten minutes left of the game, so we needed to hurry back before it finished.

We could see where the coaches were parked now, there were six or seven police horses nearby with riot vans and lots of police. We were less than 400 yards from them when a large gang came around the corner and the police forced them in our direction. We kept walking, heads down, until they spotted us and a roar went up, "It's fucking Cardiff!"

They were sandwiched between us and the police. Luckily, not all of them realised who we were and we ran straight through them. We got another few clips, but some of us managed to punch a few of them and suddenly we were in front of the cops, with their truncheons in their hands. They pushed us behind them and formed a shield to get us to our coach. It was like a scene from *M.A.S.H.*, with bloodied bodies and people in bandages all telling their tales. We found out then that we had won 3-1.

NEVER TAKE CARDIFF LIGHTLY
Ginger Bob of Millwall is old school and was there right through the 70's. He's still going, just like they do at Millwall, I don't think they ever give it up. Bob's one of the main faces at Millwall and is well respected by all who know him. I've had the pleasure to meet him on a number of occasions and he's just like Chelsea Pat, with plenty of stories to tell of the old days, so when he agreed to give me some stories for the book I knew I was getting them from the horse's mouth and not any secondhand tales.

Cardiff City v Millwall, 27th March 1976
Ginger Bob (Millwall): Older Millwall over the years have come to respect Cardiff's firm, as they have always come to Millwall – be it the 70's, 80's or 90's, they have always turned up, no matter even if their team was bottom of the league.

One of the games that I will always remember was Cardiff v Millwall at Ninian Park. I remember it was a top of the table Division Three clash and, at the end of the season, Cardiff went up and we went up instead of Palace. We had all got the early morning special. About 500 Millwall were on the train with about 300 boys all together, and all of the 300 were quality top Millwall.

If I remember correctly, we got to Cardiff about 12pm and the place was swarming with Old Bill, all waiting for us. We were put straight into an escort and marched to Ninian Park and, other than the odd Welsh nutcase sticking his head out of some pub window, it seemed pretty quiet. Along the way, a few Millwall had given the Old Bill the slip, as the streets had been quieter than even the Old Bill had expected, so they weren't on top of us anymore and eventually about 40 Millwall had got away. We were feeling pretty confident, as the year before about 60 Millwall had run Cardiff out of a section of the Grandstand at Ninian Park, which was the away end at the time. Fair play to Cardiff for trying, not many teams outside London have tried to infiltrate the Millwall section before. I know it was at Ninian Park and it was their manor, but at first they gave us a bit of a shock. Though we soon sent a hundred taffies packing, it seems we were lulled into a false sense of security because of what had happened that season.

My best mate, Dave Rand, was like a brother to me and at the time was Millwall's main lad (from the mid-60's to the mid-70's). He was also known by Millwall as the Captain; because of his black beard he looked the spitting image of Blackbeard the pirate. He and another guy called Winkle ('cos he had a massive cock) had also given the escort the slip and decided to go into the Bluebirds Supporters club bar for a drink. They had managed to sneak in as I think you had to be a member in those days, going by what they later told me.

After ordering one drink, they were immediately sussed, but their luck was in as at the same time about 40 of the rest of the Millwall, who had also slipped the escort, came steaming straight through the doors – game on. Then, fucking hell, over 200 Cardiff attacked them, led at the time by a bloke I later found out was called Frankie Humphries. Millwall were smashed and ran right out, leaving Dave Rand and Winkle behind. Dave was hit over the head with a wooden chair but managed to stay on his feet, and even though he was staggering around and the blood was pouring out, he knew that no matter what he had to stay on his feet, as if he went down it was curtains for him. By now they were both at the front door and fighting for their lives. Finally, some luck really did come their way, as two of the doormen stepped in and stood between them and the mob of Cardiff. One shouted, "This is enough!" and shielded them till the police came, who then took them to hospital for stitches and a lot of bandaging up.

Dave got back to the ground just before half-time, looking like the Red Indian Geronimo with a whole bandage covered in blood wrapped around his head. I've since met one of the doormen from that day when I was down for the Millwall and Man Utd FA Cup Final, I listened to his side of the story and it was the same word for word.

Anyway, back to the match: it was the usual abuse and banter bandied about between the two mobs. "You're going to get your fucking heads kicked in!" and "We'll see you all outside!" came from the taffies. At the end of the game, when we came outside, fuck me, there must have been over 2,000 taffies waiting for us and on this occasion the Old Bill seemed to be very thin on the ground. The taffies had filled the main road and were refusing to move; the thin blue line of Old Bill tried to escort us, a mere 300 lads. As we walked along at a slow pace, the taffies attacked both sides of the escort; our ranks stayed together and, with the Old Bill having a right baton charge at them, between the two of us it meant that the taffies weren't having much success. So we were able to hold them off.

However, on the way back to the train station, maybe another 200 yards or so further down the road, myself and about 20 top Millwall were all at the back of the escort, where there were a lot less Old Bill. Cardiff were able to do their best – and I mean *vicious* – attacks. We decided to make a sort of stand and went for it, a proper toe-to-toe. Fuck me, it was tiring, as when we threw a punch they must have thrown a dozen back. In the meantime, unnoticed, one of our guys had drifted back into the middle of the Cardiff hordes who, upon sussing him, battered him to the floor and were mercilessly kicking him. I recognised him as my pal Winkle, who had previously been fighting in the Bluebirds club with Dave Rand (it just wasn't his day).

That day in Cardiff I had a brand new cashmere jumper on, nice strides and, to my eternal regret, a pair of Hush Puppies, instead of my usual steel capped boots like the rest of Millwall.

When I had seen Winkle being attacked by Cardiff, I took it upon myself, and without any communication to the others, to do a charge into the mob. The adrenalin was pissing out of my ears, and at first I stunned the taffies who were kicking Winkle. I was able to drag him back into the escort, he was semiconscious by now. I then had a bit of a battle with two taffies, I hit one with my right hand flush (they had attacked me from the side) and he was out cold. I then managed to hit the other one with an uppercut and had him on his arse. Winkle was still lying on the floor, and the escort was all over the place. I was then clocked by another two taffies. This time I kicked them in the bollocks – it was a painful lesson for me as well, as I was wearing Hush Puppies. (I never wore them again.)

I managed to drag Winkle once again back into the escort. At the same time I was punched, nutted, even bitten, everything you can imagine from all sides. It must have been the adrenalin that kept me going and kept me upright, if I had gone down it would have been RIP Bob and Winkle. As I reached the escort, Millwall at the back saw my predicament and finally came to my aid. Between the lot of us we managed to shore up the escort and some vicious toe-to-toes took place. Police reinforcements eventually came to the back, while at the same time taking Winkle to hospital. Now, with protection at the back of the escort, we were moving forward instead of continually walking backwards or running back to help others. The taffies were still coming at the escort and the Old Bill were fighting them back from all angles.

As we looked to our left, to our amazement and shock, we saw the police fighting with four girls – two black and two mixed race (obviously Tiger Bay). They were about 17 or 18 years old, wearing multicoloured tops. The Old Bill had decided to turn these girls virtually upside down to reveal they were carrying blades for their Welsh male counterparts. We had never seen anything like this before, and people think Millwall are crackers. Anyway, murder continued all the way to the station, but somehow with no one dying (fuck knows how).

In those days Cardiff station had a big wooden gate outside it, and once they had pushed all our lot inside they locked it with huge padlocks. A train was now waiting for us and the police were concentrating once again on the taffies outside the station. They temporarily forgot about us – bad move, as only 50 Millwall got on the Penny Lane train, leaving 250 of us on the platform. The police had gone, thinking we'd gone too, but as the train had left we'd gone through to another platform and waited there for ten minutes quietly.

The police were still battling with the taffies, but had managed to clear them from outside the station. Myself and a few other Millwall rallied the troops and said we'd been humiliated by the Taffies and what they'd managed to do. "We are Millwall, the best fucking firm in the country, and we are not leaving it at that!"

"Come on, let's fucking do 'em!" the cry went up. It was dead outside the station as the Old Bill and Cardiff were well away from the front. Another big roar went up and we smashed the gate down and steamed forward like Vikings. "WAR! WAR! WAR! WAR!" we shouted as we went looking for the taffies. We then smashed anything in our way, pubs, cars, and anyone who looked like they could fight. "Come on, we're Millwall!" we shouted as we headed straight into the Old Bill. They charged us with horses, dogs and batons, eventually getting us on the next train home whether we liked it or not.

That was a typical away day in the 70's, if you had the arse to go to a naughty gaff.

I'll NEVER FORGET THE BOB BANK AT NINIAN PARK IN '79

In the 70's and 80's, Hicky of Chelsea was one of the top names in the hooligan world. His nickname was 'the General'. He now lives in the Philippines and gave me his story on his way to see Chelsea v Man Utd in the Champion's League final in Moscow. Here, he tells about a visit to Ninian Park which he will never forget.

Cardiff City v Chelsea, 20th October 1979
Steve 'Hicky' Hickmott (Chelsea): I was born in 1955 in Kent.

First game: Chelsea 1965/66, Chelsea 5 v West Ham 5.

Biggest thrill: Chelsea winning FA Cup against Leeds 1970, 2-1; also, taking Arsenal's North Bank more than once.

Biggest disappointment: losing to the Yids (Spurs), FA Cup Final 1967 and League Cup Final 2008.

Nicked: Ipswich away '72 (fined); Sheffield United away '74 (three months detention centre); Liverpool away (suspended sentence); Birmingham away (six months prison); Villa away (fined); Spurs home (fined).

Not guilty: Spurs away '72; Arsenal away '72; Millwall home '76; Cambridge away '78; Birmingham away '81; Villa away '81; Scotland '82.

In 1986, I was nicked for affray and charged with six years of conspiracies at Birmingham, Everton, WBA and Chelsea home games. I was sentenced to ten years plus five years to run concurrently; I served three years ten months and was released on appeal, due to police fabricating evidence, in November 1989.

In 1991 I moved to Thailand, and have lived there and in the Philippines ever since. I was part owner of the Dogs Bollocks Bar, Pattaya, Thailand 1996-2002, where I have enjoyed the company of loads of Cardiff City lads over the years – including some who were on the Bob Bank that day.

It was the beginning of the 70's, the Watney Cup. Cardiff were at Stamford Bridge and Chelsea hadn't played them for years. The cheeky bastards had arrived early, around 11am, and they took over the Britannia pub opposite the Britannia entrance. They had blue/white/yellow scarves, same colours as us; I thought they were Chelsea until we heard the accents. There were about 150-200 of them, not a big firm in those days, but big enough to surprise us three weeks before the season got going.

We had enough lads for our first attack, around about 1pm. There were no Old Bill, as nothing was expected to happen, and as there was no police intelligence in the good old days we were able to attack the pub. We steamed into them from two directions along Fulham Road and up Britannia Road; plenty of bottles and glasses were thrown, as well as the odd punch, but the fuckers stood firm outside the pub. We needed more of us. Luckily, more and more kept coming and so the next attack had them on their toes, trying to get back into the pub; some sprinted away to safety while others got caught and battered. Then the

Old Bill arrived and pushed us back while they escorted the Cardiff mob into the North Stand end of the ground, as in those good old days there was no segregation either. (Hee hee!) So we followed them in and took liberties; we battered them throughout the game. Finally, towards the end, the Old Bill finally took control of the situation, put them on their coaches and sent them packing.

Go forward to 20th October 1979, Cardiff away in the old Division Two. We left Tunbridge Wells (Kent) early, picking up lads at Bromley, Lewisham and outside Stamford Bridge. Sixty lads on a 45-seater coach – those were the days. Cider drinkers, glue sniffers, dopeheads and nutters heading toward the M4, but not before we stopped and robbed an off licence of a large amount of alcohol. *Cardiff, here we come!!!*

The plan was to meet up with two other coachloads from other parts of London, get into Cardiff and kick the shit out of them. We arrived around 2pm with no police escort; we could see the ground in the distance, so we disembarked and headed towards the ground and the Cardiff end, the Bob Bank.

We met a few more on our march to the ground, there were around 80-100 of us all lined up at the turnstiles. We'd agreed not to talk, we didn't want them to know we'd arrived; we would have soon been sussed out via our accents and that could have fucked up our surprise. We entered in an orderly fashion and gathered at the top corner of the Bob Bank, towards the Grange End which is a huge side terrace. We looked around for the other Chelsea lads that had agreed to meet us at 2.30pm. Where were they? *Fuck it,* I thought, *let's just do it now.* We headed across the terraces, about halfway down the chant went up: "Chelsea aggro! Chelsea aggro!" We got stuck into the Cardiff lads on the edge of the main mob, there must have had between 2-3000 on this end. At first, as we were laying into them, they tried to back away, but the sheer weight of their numbers stopped them backing off. They stood and fought us and then – *fucking hell!* – they came down on us from everywhere and a huge row broke out. Chelsea fans on the far end and the other side of the ground were chanting "Chelsea aggro!" and "North Stand, North Stand, do your job!" It was coming well on top now; we were getting battered down the terraces, fighting for our lives, and their whole mob descended upon us. We got smashed to fucking pieces and were now backing off, or in some cases running for our lives. Why can you never find a copper when you need one? We tried to regroup at the top left corner but it was all too late, we needed reinforcements and there weren't any. We were fucked.

Cardiff now had 30 of us surrounded; we were already battered and bruised in that top corner, and they just came at us once again. We'd lost all the other lads and now we had hundreds of Cardiff coming at us. Some of our lads went over the wall – at the back of a huge, sloping drop – back to the place where we'd entered. There were more taffies kicking the shit out of us as we fought our way back to the turnstiles. It was a fucking disaster!

At the front of the Bob Bank, my mate Melvin, who had been beaten to the ground, was now being stretchered out along the side of the pitch, covered in blood. The stretcher bearers stopped at an open gate to the terraces, whereupon Melvin got off and went through the open gate, into the baying mob of taffs on the terraces. It was a fantastic sight, all of the taffs running from one nutter. Then the Old Bill took over, put him back on the stretcher and got him back to the safety of the Chelsea end, where around 2000 were still chanting, "Chelsea aggro!" Chelsea won the game 2-1.

With no police to hold us in the ground, we just piled onto the surrounding streets looking for the Cardiff firm. As we rounded a corner we could see hundreds of them, chanting and running towards us. They were on the grass in a park, with a three-foot-high metal spike-topped fence between us and them. We took the fence out of the ground and charged towards their mob, using it as a huge battering ram. Fights broke out on all sides, but we had the spikes and used them to back the taffies off. The rout had started. Cardiff were now in full flight across the grassy park in all directions; some of them tried to fight back, but the full force of their original attack had been broken. All the way to the train station you could hear, "Chelsea aggro!" Cardiff made the odd stand a few times, but it didn't last long. We got back to our coaches while the rest went for their trains. As we got on, we realised we had lost badly in the Bob Bank that day, but we were the more organised and better fighting force on the streets of Cardiff.

Thanks for making it a great day to remember.

NON-STOP RUNNING BATTLES

Chelsea Pat: Firstly, I'd like to say thanks to Annis for asking me to give my views and horror stories about the CCFC. I've got lots of good mates at Cardiff and they have always made me welcome. They are genuine people and straight as an arrow. If they don't like you, you'll fucking know it!!!

Over the years, I've fought against the Soul Crew – or the Bob Bank Boys, as they were known to Chelsea and QPR. I've gone to Millwall v Cardiff with some Millwall mates, and watched two huge mobs fighting the Old Bill to try to get to each other, and I've been the guest of the Soul Crew in later years. The friends I've made are mates for life, and friends come before football. I'll tell the stories about when we've been run by Cardiff and when we've chased after Cardiff, and I'll tell it as I saw it. So if you don't agree with me, then in Mickey Francis's words, "write your own fucking book."

When I first started going to football in the mid-70's with my father, he took me to see QPR, our local team. He wouldn't take me to see Chelsea, my own team, because in those days Chelsea and Man Utd were always in the papers, causing trouble, wrecking cities, etc.

After a year or so, I started going to football with my mates from the street. At QPR, I used to stand behind the goal with my dad, but now I moved to the back of the Loft End; when I used to sneak off to Chelsea matches, I'd stand at the back of the Shed.

The first time I came across Cardiff was in the League Cup night game at Loftus Road in the late 70's. We were all standing at the Loft End when we heard a chant from the South Africa Road, which runs parallel to the stadium – "*CAYARDIFF!*" – as maybe 1,500 fans came running down the road. All the QPR ran across the Loft into the part that overlooks the South Africa Road. "WE'RE THE LOFT BOYS, WE'RE THE LOFT BOYS, WE'RE THE LOFT BOYS, SHEPHERD'S BUSH!" "WE'RE THE BOB BANK, WE'RE THE BOB BANK, WE'RE THE BOB BANK, NINIAN PARK!" came back the taffs. The taffs maybe had 2000 fans in the away end, and maybe 50 came onto the Loft that night, but they got chased off. "RANGERS AGGRO!" and "YOU'LL NEVER TAKE THE LOFT!" were the QPR war cries. After the game there was murder. All the QPR left the Loft and gathered outside the Springbok pub on South Africa Road, maybe 600 strong. Out came Cardiff, and from the ground up to the old White City station road to White City underground station, there were non-stop running battles. You couldn't say if there was a winner. "WE'RE THE BOB BANK!" "WE'RE THE LOFT BOYS!" continued the rallying cries, plus a few, "You're going to get your fucking heads kicked in!"

The next time I came across Cardiff was with my brother Johnny, who wasn't feeling too lucky. Johnny had been to seven matches and every one was a fucking riot. To this day he will never step inside a football ground because of what happened. His first game was QPR v Bradford City, a Tuesday night League Cup game in the mid-70's. Bradford brought about 3000 fans and maybe 1000 hooligans. Outside the ground there was massive fighting, all the way past the greyhound station, past White City underground station, down to Shepherd's Bush Green. There were charges and countercharges as hundreds and hundreds on both sides attacked each other. From where we were it looked like QPR had the better of it, but if Bradford lads disagree I won't argue. (We were only kids.)

The next one was Arsenal v Chelsea at Highbury. As my brother liked Arsenal, my old man insisted I take him on the North Bank. Bad fucking move. As soon as the teams came out, we realised Chelsea had half of the end. There was fucking murder, it seemed like the whole end was fighting. We got beaten that day 5-2 and I got beaten when I got home, as my old man thought I took Johnny in the North Bank because I knew there would be trouble. (You can't fucking win, can you?)

The next time was Chelsea v Cardiff in a night game. I was told to stay in the ground after the game to wait for everyone to leave, to make sure that if there was any trouble we would miss it.

Anyway, in the ground rumours were going around that Cardiff had done Chelsea outside the Britannia pub opposite the North Stand (away end). A Chelsea fan had been stabbed too. As you can imagine, we didn't need any encouragement to stay inside the ground. After the stadium emptied we walked towards Fulham Broadway tube station; as we entered the station, we saw a mob in green fight jackets, skins, punks etc. All of a sudden it was, "I'll give you a CEEE, AYY, ARR, DEE, EYY, EFF, EFF, *CAAAAYAARDIFFF!*" I shit my pants there and then. My poor brother was on the verge of tears, especially as he was wearing a Chelsea scarf for safety after what had happened at Arsenal. We managed to get onto the bridge that splits the platform from the city trains to the Wimbledon-bound trains on the other side. Cardiff came piling through. "We hate the Cockneys!" boomed down the stairs. All of a sudden, I saw a few black faces pushing up quietly behind them, then I heard the roar: "WE'RE THE NORTH STAND, WE'RE THE NORTH STAND, WE'RE THE NORTH STAND, STAMFORD BRIDGE!" Cardiff ran down the stairs with Chelsea behind them; fair play to them, they made a stand halfway up the platform. As about 30 Cardiff stood, the rest came running back down and a classic toe-to-toe took place on the platform, which spilled onto the train. Fuck knows how the train pulled off, it must have been rocking all the way to Paddington.

My brother, who was now in bits, swore never to go to football again. I said, "Johnny, you're fucking lucky, you should go every week, you're a walking lucky charm for a punch-up!" Ha ha!

CHELSEA ARE MAD!
Cardiff City v Chelsea, 5th September 1981

J. Kagad (CCFC): I remember informing all my friends at our local hangout (the bomb patch in the Roath area of Cardiff) that I was attending the Chelsea game and their comments on the lines of, "Bloody hell, Chelsea are mad!" and, "I'd watch yourself down there!" To which I would defiantly reply that I was not at all worried

The game that day was played in beautiful sunshine. We stood in the family enclosure, due to the fact that if you found an adult to escort you in, your entrance fee was 30p. When I arrived in the ground I was amazed and impressed to see all the Chelsea fans with their yellow away tops in the Grange End, singing away. Early on, Peter Kitchen scored for Cardiff but Chelsea rallied and won 2-1.

Throughout the game there were outbreaks of ferocious fighting in the two sides' enclosures. Suddenly I wasn't safe and this scared me. Maybe I should have listened to my friends in Roath, after all. When the game ended, everyone left the ground as normal, but the faces of the older lads were different that day. They seemed to be pre-empting the ensuing mass skirmishing that by now seemed inevitable. They were tense, aggressive and antagonistic.

Vincent and I were outside very briefly. We were walking away from the ground when we bumped into Vincent's older brother, who told us in no uncertain terms that we would be best off out of it, as there was "going to be murder" at any moment.

Roar!!! Chelsea are out and there is mass panic amongst the group of early teens that I am with. Chelsea then make four or five charges, the panic spreads and worsens and I am petrified. Chelsea are now in the sidestreets also, and there seems to be no escape. I just want to vanish into thin air when we see Vincent's grandfather coming out of a betting shop, he lives a couple of doors away and takes us to the safety of his flat. This is a first-floor flat and is on the main road where chaos is ensuing. For the next five minutes I watch from the safety of that flat, transfixed by the bedlam of the street outside. Vincent and I then make our way to Cardiff Central bus station. On arriving at the station, there are still pockets of trouble while we wait for our bus.

That night, I made my way to the bomb patch and informed my mates, who earlier had the foresight to know that if you were too young to defend yourself, Ninian Park was not the place to be. I informed them all of the day's happenings, and that's when it happened. I realised I was in a real-life adventure that day and I wished we could play Chelsea every week. I felt like a rock star.

DON'T EVER UNDERESTIMATE THE TAFFIES

Chelsea v Cardiff City, 15th October 1983

Chelsea Pat: I remember the talk during the week: there was to be a meet at the bar in Paddington station in the morning, so bright and early that I was at the pub by about 11.30am. By 12.30 we had about 25 boys. It turned out there was a documentary about football violence being made the same day for LWT and they were filming in the Swan at Fulham Broadway, which was one of our main pubs. Apparently, most of our lot wanted to get their boat races on TV. It wouldn't happen nowadays and that's why it was such a shit turnout.

About 1pm we noticed ten dressers had come off the Cardiff train and they were stood on the concourse, staring at us lot. Three of us walked over and, before we reached them, these Cardiff, who were younger than us (about 16 years of age), nervously edged over towards a group of transport Old Bill who were at the end of the platform. "No trouble, boys," one of our lot said, "we just want to know how many you are bringing today." The Cardiff boy in a light/dark blue waterproof Patrick jacket said, "We've got 300 lads, but they all got off in Slough and went on the piss so we're not going to get to your place until late."

"Fair enough, mate," we said. To be honest I wouldn't have fancied our chances with our 25 against 300 of Cardiff's finest. We all then went back to the bar, had one more and then headed up the taxi rank onto Praed Street to get the underground.

As we got to the top of the ramp, we noticed about 40 lads drinking outside the Dickens Tavern. "How the fuck did they get past us?" I said.

"Never mind," said one of ours, "it's game on. Come on, you taffy bastards!" We charged towards the Cardiff, who had just woken up to the fact that they were being attacked. As one they turned and ran back into the pub, closing the door behind them. We were all stood in the street, feeling pleased with ourselves, when the door went flying open and glasses, ashtrays, barstools and even a plate of spaghetti came flying towards us. I picked up the board outside and launched it into the mob of taffies who were now slowly edging out of the pub. This backed them off at first, but more and more glasses came at us and we were now backed off into the street.

Cardiff then poured into the street with at least 100 boys. There must have been about 60 in the pub when we ran the first lot in. After standing for a while under a constant bombardment of glasses, the old cry of, "Fucking stand, Chelsea!" went up. A sure sign that we were about to be put on our toes. Anyway, we got chased round the corner back into the station, but Cardiff stopped at the entrance, luckily for us. I think they thought we were leading them into an ambush, so they didn't follow us.

Back at the ground, apparently the Cardiff who had come on coaches had got run by Chelsea down at the Princess Royal, all the way up to the North Stand entrance. Later this incident appeared in the documentary they were filming that day. It shows about 150 Chelsea chanting, "Ooo, ooo, ooo," as they chase Cardiff up the street, and then the Old Bill nick a wedge-headed taffy in a ski jumper, tight Lois jeans and Nike Wimbledon trainers for trying to do a suicide stand after all his mates have fucked off.

After the game, (the other Cardiff boys did turn up late, by the way, and got drenched on the North Stand), there was talk of revenge for our little reversal before the game, so it was all set for round two at Paddington.

We had about 200 waiting at Paddington, when all of a sudden the shout went up, "Here they are!" Up came the Cardiff boys in an escort and they were pushed through the middle of the station by the Old Bill, with us lot trying to get at them from both sides. As they got to the platform entrance, me and Brains fronted a few of them and they backed off. This Old Bill saw what was happening and jumped between us, drawing his truncheon and shouting at me to get back. I'll never forget what happened next. A Cardiff lad lent across the copper and spat a big greeny, which hit me full in the face. I was fucking speechless. Brains was crying with laughter next to me, but I swear to God I was incandescent with rage. If I had caught that cunt, I would have beaten that prick to death, given him the kiss of life, then beaten him again. To coin a phrase, I would have done *28 Days*

Later on his fucking head! Anyway, I could keep my rage in check until the return a few months later.

Mikey Dye (CCFC): We had about 160 and it was chucking it down. While holed up in the Dickens pub, it was decided that we would get to Stamford Bridge for about quarter-past three. *How stupid,* I thought, we would miss part of the game. But I soon discovered why. Being a young whippersnapper back then, I didn't realise it was unwise to arrive early. But we would turn up and make an entrance, whether it be on the high street or in the ground. As it was, the Chelsea lads were all in the West and South Stands and, as we all walked in together, they all rose and applauded us. Were they applauding our arrival or taking the piss out of our lateness?

TEN MEN WENT TO MOW
Cardiff City v Chelsea, 31st March 1984

Dave Sugarman (CCFC): A game we had been looking forward to for months – the visit of arch enemies Chelsea to Ninian Park. The Londoners were joint-top of the table and their fans were the undisputed heavyweight champions of the hooligan world at that point in time, so the fixture promised to be a stern test of Cardiff's credentials both on and off the field. To say the afternoon proved to be an eventful one would be something of an understatement. By the time it was over, I was left with cuts, bruises, aching limbs and a nagging feeling that perhaps this hooliganism lark wasn't all it was cracked up to be.

During our pre-match drinking session in the Lex, Carlton demanded that we sit in the Grandstand as opposed to stand on the Bob Bank for this one. He'd heard on the grapevine that Chelsea were planning to take over the Grandstand, and he'd also heard that a lot of our top lads were going in there in an attempt to stop them. He told us he felt it was our duty to join up with them and do our bit, so that's what a small gang of four or five of us decided to do. Apart from Carlton, who was in his early 20's, the rest of us were teenagers. The group included an old mate of mine named Vaughan Roberts, who I've been friends with ever since we were toddlers. I was skinny enough back in the 80's, but by comparison to Vaughan I was like some kind of muscleman. He was so thin it was unbelievable. There was more meat on a whippet's lip. Nevertheless, I remember we were full of ourselves on the long walk to Sloper Road and we were proudly singing Cardiff songs all the way to the ground. Luckily, we didn't bump into any of the 4,000 Chelsea fans who were making their way to Ninian Park, which is quite surprising in retrospect.

When we arrived at the turnstiles, we paid to get into Block A of the Grandstand and took our seats in the middle rows. There appeared to be plenty of City boys around us, including a couple of faces I recognised. One of them was Marksy, a lad from Aberdare who I didn't know well at the time but who I became friendly with a few years later. With his long hair and droopy moustache, Marksy was an unmistakable figure in those days. He looked like a cross between a Mexican bandit and Dylan, the hippy rabbit off *The Magic Roundabout*, although he definitely had more in common with the bandit than the rabbit. While he wasn't the biggest lad in the world, Marksy always seemed to be there or thereabouts whenever it was kicking off and he was never afraid to get stuck in.

We confidently began chanting Bluebirds songs shortly after the teams took to the field, and I was immediately struck by the fact that so few people in Block A were joining in. Chelsea looked to have occupied every part of the ground other than the Bob Bank. There were visiting fans in the Grange End, the Canton Stand and both enclosures, and it was soon evident that there were also plenty of them in the Grandstand. City started the game brightly and were well on top for the first quarter of an hour. By that stage, a suspicious gap had begun to open up all around us and it was becoming apparent that there were no more than 30 or 40 of us in total. To make matters worse, it was clear that most of us were kids. Then the visiting fans struck up a chorus of 'One Man Went to Mow', which was Chelsea's anthem at the time. Cardiff supporters also often sang that song back then, so we decided to join in. The problem came when the London lads stopped at "three men went to mow", while we stood on our seats and carried on until we reached "ten men went to mow", which we followed with a chant of, "*Keyaaardiff!*" That was like a red rag to a bull as far as the visiting mob was concerned.

All of a sudden the Chelsea fans in Blocks A and B turned to face us and started punching the air while bellowing, "War! War! War!" They then began clambering over the seats towards us. There must have been a couple of hundred of them, and many were considerably bigger and older than our lot. The majority of us instinctively backed away into the top right-hand corner of the stand, as that was the only place we could go, but two or three lads decided to throw caution to the wind and steam into the visitors. Those brave souls included the indomitable Carlton, who was in his element. He managed to take several Chelsea boys out of the fray before they were able to drag him down.

I was on the outside of our group towards the left. The first Chelsea lad to reach me was an enormous acne-scarred monster with a face like a bucket of smashed crabs. He towered over me and shouted something along the lines of, "Come on, Taffy, let's 'ave it!" in his broad cockney accent. He effectively stuck his chin out and gave me a free shot. My legs had turned to jelly by this point, but I summoned up all the courage I had left and attempted to hit him as hard as I could. He barely flinched. If the truth be told, I'm not sure if I even connected properly. I thought my life was going to end there and then, so I just curled up into a ball, hedgehog-style. In fairness to him and the other Chelsea lads alongside him, they didn't go over the top. I was given a few cuffs around the head, a couple of blows to the back and a boot or two in the ribs, but I came out of the encounter unscathed apart from some minor cuts and bruises.

Meanwhile, Vaughan hadn't fared quite so well. He'd been at the front of the group when Chelsea attacked and was thrown around like a rag doll. He was also booted down the stairs just as the police began pouring into the stand. It obviously wasn't his lucky day, as he was grabbed by a copper and mistakenly thrown back into the Chelsea mob, where he was subjected to another kicking. While all this was going on, midfielder Roger Gibbins had apparently put City into the lead with a spectacular volley, but we hadn't seen it. At that point, Carlton was busy fighting, I was busy being hit, and the only thing Vaughan was seeing were stars.

Once the Old Bill had managed to restore some sort of order, they quickly decided to get us out of the Grandstand and put us on the Bob Bank. As we began moving out of Block A, a very strange thing happened. The Chelsea fans in the stand began applauding us. To this day I'm not sure why they did that. With the exception of a couple of individuals, it wasn't as if we'd managed to offer much resistance, but it appeared we'd amused them all the same. Perhaps they were acknowledging that we were mainly a bunch of kids and that we'd at least attempted to take them on, even if it had proved to be a really bad idea from our perspective.

After getting us out of Block A, the police took us down the stairs and under the stand. While they were doing so a roar went up outside, which turned out to be City fans celebrating a Gordon Owen penalty. Incredibly, our team was 2-0 up against the league leaders with a little over 20 minutes played, and yet we hadn't seen a goal. We were then led out into the players' tunnel and kept there for a minute or two while the Old Bill prepared to escort us around the pitch. As we were standing in the tunnel, Nigel Vaughan stroked home a Karl Elsey cross to give the Bluebirds a 3-0 lead. I didn't see that happen but several others did, so they started jumping up and down and the rest of us followed suit. Seconds later, a Chelsea fist came flying over the enclosure wall and caught Vaughan right on the side of the head. I think it's fair to say he wasn't having the best of afternoons, and neither was I. City had banged in three goals in a sizzling seven-minute spell, but I hadn't had the pleasure of seeing any of them.

As the police began escorting us around the pitch, we were spat at from the enclosure and had coins thrown at us from the Canton Stand. There were Chelsea fans everywhere and they weren't happy, which was hardly surprising given the score. We got another round of applause from the City fans on the Bob Bank as we were being led onto the terrace, and they sang 'We're Proud of You'. While that was undoubtedly well-intentioned, it wasn't much of a consolation for the hammering we'd been given, especially in Vaughan's case. He'd taken such a pounding that his legs had gone, so he was effectively being held up by the copper who was escorting him. Carlton was a different matter altogether, though. As a natural-born hooligan he'd been having a whale of a time, and was as happy as a pig in shit.

Cardiff continued to play well for most of the game and looked destined to run out comfortable winners until Kerry Dixon pulled a goal back for Chelsea in the 84th minute. The Bluebirds started to panic at that stage and conceded another goal a couple of minutes later, when Colin Lee scrambled the ball home from close range. Nevertheless, they still seemed certain winners, so hundreds of Chelsea lads began pouring out of the ground as the game went into injury time. A large mob of them made their way around to the back of the Canton Stand and, for a brief moment, it looked like there was going to be murder, as the Bob Bank gates had been left wide open by the stewards. Only a couple of coppers and a solitary police dog stood between the rival factions, but one of them quickly managed to swing the gates shut while the other sent his dog flying into the Londoners. They probably averted a mass brawl by doing so.

Within seconds, another loud roar went up inside the ground, so those of us who had congregated at the top of the slope on the right-hand corner of the Bob Bank headed back towards the terrace, while most of the Chelsea mob ran back into the stands. It transpired that the visitors had been awarded a penalty after John Bumstead had blasted the ball at David Tong during a goalmouth scramble. The referee adjudged that Tong had handled the ball, although television footage later showed it had struck the midfielder on the right side of his chest. He even had a mark on his shirt to prove it, but the ref ignored City's protests and Nigel Spackman converted the spot kick to rescue an unlikely draw for Chelsea.

After the final whistle, the supporters on the Bob Bank suffered the indignity of being kept inside the ground while the visiting fans were let out. When the Old Bill finally did open the gates for us, they formed a human barrier which they maintained right up until we got to the railway bridge next to the Ninian Park pub. From that point onwards it was mayhem. Loads of Chelsea boys were still rampaging through the area, so there were running battles all the way back to the city centre. The scenes on the streets leading to Central Station were unbelievable. There were hundreds of lads from both sides heading in the same direction and fights were breaking out all over the place, but nobody seemed sure of who was who. As we ran past one of the Chinese supermarkets on Ninian Park Road, I had a big Chelsea lad breathing down the back of my neck and screaming, "Come on, you taffy bastards!" I spotted a milk crate full of empty bottles on the pavement, so I swooped down, grabbed it, swung around and launched it at him all in one movement. He crumpled in a heap, although I didn't hang about to see if I'd done him any damage for fear of him getting back up and killing me. Instead, I ran all the way back to my bus stop on Kingsway.

Having had more than enough excitement for one day, I decided to go straight home once we eventually got into town, but Carlton and the revitalised Vaughan opted to stay and have a few pints in the Lex. Later that evening, they ended up drinking and swapping stories with a group of Chelsea lads who Carlton had become friendly with on the gig circuit. Something that surprised me when I read the local newspaper reports over the next couple of days was the fact that the police had made a total of just 38 arrests. That was amazing considering what had gone on in and around Ninian Park. My guess is they'd been so busy trying to keep the rival mobs apart that they didn't have the manpower to detain many people.

The *South Wales Echo*'s report included a large photo of the fracas in Block A. In the accompanying text, journalist Joe Lovejoy wrote: "This is the picture that sums up one of the main reasons why attendances at Football League games have halved since the Second World War. As we watched the skirmishes between rival sets of so-called supporters on Saturday, one season ticket holder told me he no longer takes his son to watch Cardiff as he fears for his safety. It seems the Grandstand no longer guarantees immunity from these hooligans who travel to matches intent on causing trouble." I must admit I felt a bit guilty as I was reading that, especially as the photo featured a father and his young child who had got caught up in the middle of the disturbance.

WHAT A FUCKING DAY!
Cardiff City v Chelsea, 31st March 1984

Chelsea Pat: Ah, the famous 3-3 draw, which I would put in my top ten in matches for trouble before, during and after the game.

Dave Jones did a very good summary of what happened from a Cardiff point of view in the *Soul Crew* book, and Annis has asked me to write it from the Chelsea side. Luckily, would you believe there is actually a tape knocking about of the actual match? A 90-minute videotape with no commentary. Fuck me, I was laughing my head off; it is non-stop action in the Grandstand and Canton stand with fans being led around the pitch and coppers dragging lads out, etc. I'm glad I watched the tape, as the memories of back then are not the sharpest, so it was a good help.

The morning of the game, we arrived about 1.30pm. The first train had already dropped a big firm off and they had already clashed with Cardiff. The Old Bill tried to hold us at the station entrance, but if I remember correctly there was a John Menzies shop in the station and we all cut through it and escaped into the city. Soon, the Old Bill saw that everyone was now out of the station and jogging down the road towards the ground. They just said 'fuck it' and let everyone go, so we were about 600-handed walking towards Ninian Park with the Old Bill behind us. It was God's grace that we didn't bump into Cardiff, because there would have been murder. In fact, we didn't see one boy all the way to the stadium.

In the early 80's all of our firm used to go into the seats, because at the end of the match you never got held back and you could leave five minutes before the end and walk outside, or attempt to invade the home section as the home fans were leaving. Anyway, as usual we all piled into the seats in the Grandstand and the Canton stand (we had a fucking massive firm that day).

We were surprised to see a small firm of Cardiff in the seats next to us in the Grandstand. There were only about 70 of them and they were soon getting terrorised, so the Old Bill and stewards took them down into the enclosure and round the pitch to put them back in the Bob Bank. Not to miss a chance of mischief, a load of our lot jumped on the back of the Cardiff escort going back to the Bob Bank. As they passed the Canton stand, the Chelsea mob in there steamed down and a few punches were exchanged through the fence.

The Old Bill then opened a gate on the Bob Bank to let the Cardiff lot back in; when it all kicked off the 20 or so Chelsea invaders got sussed as they entered the gate. Apparently, this is where some Cardiff got squirted with ammonia as the Chelsea boys were being driven back out.

Throughout the game there were so many incidents that I can't possibly remember them all. But with ten minutes to go we were 3-0 down; we were now sat in the Canton stand and could go wherever we wanted, as the Old Bill didn't have a clue. The shout went up: "Come on, we're leaving!" With that, about 250 of us walked round behind the Canton stand with the intention of getting on the Bob Bank.

I can remember us walking through all the early leavers, looking up and seeing two lads at the top of the stairs, staring down at us. They both sussed us and ran back into the Bob Bank; within seconds, hundreds of Cardiff came flying down the stairs towards us. Game on. It went toe to toe for about 20 seconds, until we started to get the upper hand and chased Cardiff back up the stairs into the home end. Apparently, the Chelsea in the Grandstand saw all the Cardiff run back onto the Bob Bank, and then they all tried to leave and join in the fun. For whatever reason, we all stalled at the bottom of the stairs, enabling one fucking copper and a dog to pull the gate shut on us. Cardiff then came back down the stairs and we all started to trade punches through the gate, until the Old Bill forced us back onto the road.

There were now thousands of Chelsea boys outside, while the Old Bill locked Cardiff in the Bob Bank. It's the first time I've ever seen the home fans kept in while the away fans were let out. About 500 of us walked up to the Ninian pub and plotted up, there were no Old Bill with us. About five minutes later, some Chelsea came under the railway bridge and were calling us up the road. Obviously it was going off outside the ground, as everyone charged down the street. I don't know exactly what happened, as the Old Bill now chased everyone back to the Ninian. It apparently went mental outside the stadium, with Chelsea getting the better of it but Cardiff giving a good account of themselves.

Back at the Ninian we started to walk back towards Canton, and we noticed a load of Coronation-type backstreets leading back to the road towards the train station. As we reached one sidestreet we couldn't believe our luck, as at the top of the road was a huge mob of Cardiff, 5-600 handed, about the same as us. The Old Bill were behind both mobs, so this was it! "Fucking walk at 'em, don't run at 'em!" went the shout. However, being young and keen and daft, some people walked quicker than others. At the other end of the road, Cardiff came charging towards us, launching everything at us. We noticed that Cardiff were getting closer but at the same time slowing down. The charge had now slowed to a jog, then to a walk, then, at about 100 metres, to a stop. Then we could hear, "Cardiff stand!" as they started to backpeddle up the road. On the junction of the main road they managed to regain some composure and made a stand right across it.

Us lot (the younger ones) reached the junction first and bounced up and down in front of the Welsh hordes. "We're fucking Chelsea, come on, you mugs!" Just then, the biggest skinhead I've ever seen came out of the Cardiff crowd and fronted the lot of us. I nudged my mate C, who is one of the gamest, most fearless football lads I've ever met. "Go on then, C!" I shouted as the skinhead called us on.

"You fucking go on then!" said C, not keen on being killed first.

It was then I noticed a draft behind me. In our haste to get to the fight we'd left the rest of our mob still casually strolling down the road, about 100 metres behind us. Luckily for us, it was as Cardiff started to sense the chance of a turning point in the row that a police van pulled up in front of them, while another drove straight at us, sending our whole mob scampering back down the road. Further on, we cut down another sidestreet and were now behind the Cardiff mob, with a few token Old Bill in the middle. It went mental all the way back to the bus station, with Cardiff going toe to toe with us, then backpedalling, then standing again, all the way back to the train station. I couldn't believe how many Chelsea had been busted up with bricks and bottles, etc.

When we got to the train station, it was only then that we realised how many lads had been hurt. There were loads of cut heads, busted hands, etc. It looked like we had been in the wars, literally. All the talk on the train was of what would have happened if we'd got on the Bob Bank. In my opinion, I think we would have got killed. From my experience of going on the other team's end, you need three things: the element of surprise, to get behind the home mob and to hold the high ground. We didn't have any of this with Cardiff. Also, when you go on a home end you can end up fighting everyone from hooligans to fans, even women and children want to kill you.

As we got off in London, a ticket inspector said, "Fucking hell, boys, who have you been fighting with, the Welsh rugby teams?"

"Near enough, mate, near enough," said one of our lads, sporting a nice black eye and chipped front tooth ensemble.

The inspector then said, "Good result on the pitch."

"Are you taking the fucking piss?" I said angrily.

"You drew 3-3, mate, you scored three in the last five minutes."

We just stood there openmouthed. There had been so much trouble, we didn't even think of the score. What a fucking day!

PS. To the fucking huge Cardiff skinhead – I still see you in my nightmares!

FULL TURNOUT

Millwall v Cardiff City, FA Cup 26th January1987

Mikey Dye (CCFC): This was the third round of the FA Cup and the draw was made on Monday at noon. We all eagerly anticipated this moment and wondered who we would be drawn against. We were young lads of 16-20 years of age, travelling regularly, and we were really up for anybody.

I remember being on dinner at work and Radio Wales was on; the draw began, teams were coming out thick and fast. Suddenly, the number representing Millwall got drawn, my stomach was churning and my brain was full of excitement. I was thinking, *We must be drawn soon, there's not many left!* Then another number, the commentator says, "Cardiff City," well I leapt and bounced around, what a fucking draw! The adrenalin was running through my body. *Fuck, how many will go? How will we get there? Will they be out for us?* So many questions were running through my head. That day in work seemed to last forever. Finally, home, shower and out. We all met up as usual outside Maggie's chippy, Ely Bridge. There was a full turnout of Ely Trendies for this one. The game was in three weeks or so. That evening, all our lot were about. Annis pulled up in his car with Chrissy B, Darryl and Richard E. We decided on the 07.45 train to Paddington, straight across to Soho to drink there. We knew the younger element of Cardiff would be going, and a lot of older ones went on the special.

The day of the match finally arrived – January 10th 1987 – and my chosen attire consisted of a Fila BJ top, Lois jeans and a pair of red Adidas Munchen trainers. I knocked for CC, then Jammo, and met the rest at the bus stop by Ely Legion. Caught the bus to Cardiff Station, and about 60 of our lot (I mean our age group, 16-18). By the time of departure we had at least 100-120, all champing at the bit, virtually all the younger lads of Cardiff, probably not more than three over 21 years old.

The Smoke was beckoning as we alighted from the train. Some of our lot filled the air with, "*Caarrdiff! Caarrdiff!*" but we quickly told them to shut up. We got to Soho just in time for opening, we filled two pubs opposite each other and settled down for a few hours. Our young firm were ready for anything and anyone, but this was somehow different. It was the capital of football hooligans and we were going to the most notorious of them all. At about 13.30, Rawlings got up on the table and said, "This is the big one, we're here for Millwall, let's fucking show 'em!" With that, the air filled with evil chanting and threatening songs which made the ball on my Fila BJ bounce! We left the pub and headed for the tube which would take us to Kings Cross, where fighting broke out with the Old Bill all over our youngest lad (15 years) not having a valid ticket. Then it was off to London Bridge to change for Bermondsey.

On arrival at London Bridge the Met Old Bill were everywhere; they gathered most of us up, but Annis, Jerky, myself and a few others managed to slip through, so we headed to Bermondsey on our own without the police escort. When we finally got to Bermondsey, our throats were dry and stomachs churned at the thought of what awaited us. How I wished I was in that escort right then! As we left the tube station we climbed the steps towards daylight and the air was full of familiar chanting. Lo and behold, it was only our boys in the escort being taken to the ground. So we hastily walked on the opposite side of the road to them with not a bushwhacker in sight. I vaguely remember something going on at Millwall with regards to the way the club was being run, and Millwall boycotting the game. Which could explain why there was no welcoming committee!

During the game, Annis and Little Collin had done a mad one and gone out of their seats on the side by the away end. Millwall had soon sussed them and our spotter (Jeff Richards in those days) came to their rescue. I heard later that Little Collin hadn't given a fuck and had called it on.

The match passed off without any real incident until they tried to keep us in. In those days Cardiff would do the usual thing and try to wreck the ground to get out, and a few pipes etc were thrown at the Old Bill holding the gates shut. Millwall that day were a letdown, that's the only time they have never really turned out for us.

We arrived back at Paddington where the Old Bill were putting Cardiff on special trains home. Not us though, we didn't want safety on a special train and we broke out in song: "We're the Service, we're the Service, we're the Service, Ninian Park!" and our 90 or so went home in more comfort in one of those shit special trains. (A few lads never returned that day and were arrested and put on trial, just like Chelsea, West Ham, etc, were in those days.)

Personally for me, season '83/'84 was the best, as we had just gained promotion and were in a division that housed some of the greats of that time, in Chelsea, Leeds and Birmingham, followed by back-to-back trips to Man City, Pompey, Middlesbrough and Newcastle all later on in the season. This was also the year that Cardiff were dressing rather smartly. To most, this was the beginning of something that would take over our lives. Some of these trips mentioned above always had a good turnout for the train, with anything from 100 on the train to Oldham and as many as 800 for Pompey.

KNIVES AT THE FOOTBALL
Orient v Cardiff City, 20th February 1988

Lee 'Tonto' Davies (CCFC): I hadn't had much experience with knives at the football and certainly never carried one myself. But one incident that has stayed with me right up until today happened at Leyton Orient. It was the hundredth anniversary of the FA or something, and there was going to be a mini-tournament at Wembley with every team's last five league results taken into account to decide who qualified. Cardiff only needed a draw at Orient; needless to say, we got stuffed 4-1 or something and that was the end of that. But at the final whistle Orient managed to get onto the pitch, so obviously we tried to do the same. I managed to get on but the police and stewards stopped most of the others. I was hardly likely to have a go at Orient on my own, so I tried to blend in and find my way out of the ground. While I was still on the pitch, three lads came over to me. I thought, *Bollocks, now I'm fucked*, but luckily they were Cardiff and had recognised me, so we decided to stick together and get out of there as soon as possible. When we were out of the ground and on the street, these three lads (who, inside the ground, had seemed like they wanted to be on the first train back to the valleys) went mental. Anyone who looked like a lad was getting it, these three didn't give a shit. Almost the second we got out of the ground, they ran straight into a mob of about 30; by the time I knew what was happening, they'd had a kicking, the police had turned up and they were already fighting with the next lot. By the time we got near the station we must have had over a dozen offs; the truth is that I couldn't wait to get on the train, these blokes were dangerous. The usual lads I went to football with knew what they were doing; this lot just had a death wish. We'd managed, by some kind of miracle, to get to the station in one piece and I thought it was all over. But no chance, not with these three around. There was a hill to the right of the station with a pub at the top of it; outside this pub was a tidy little firm of maybe 20 or 30 lads. They could have stayed there and enjoyed their Saturday afternoon pint, but these three lunatics decided to have a go at them and began charging up the hill with me in tow. At first, I thought we had them worried; they didn't run but they didn't come at us either, they just stood there. It didn't take long to work out why. By the time we reached the top, we were out of breath and knackered; that's what they were waiting for, and that's when they came at us. Straight away we were on the back foot, as they kicked the fuck out of us all the way back down the hill. I tried to fight back, but for every punch I threw they must have landed ten, they were just hitting me for fun. The next thing I knew, I was grabbed around the neck and pulled through a small gate onto some steps. These steps were a shortcut to the station about halfway down the hill, and it was one of the Cardiff lads that had pulled me through and then closed the gate. I don't know why he'd pulled me through and not one of his mates. I think I'd probably been knocked out because I don't remember fighting, just being pulled to safety. Once we were stuck on the wrong side of the gate, the other two lads were brought over to us, held there and slashed in front of us. We'd already taken a kicking and that should have been that. The way I see it, if you put yourself in a position where you're likely to get a kicking, that's your own fault; the bruises go and your eye normally reopens within a week. You should be ready for your next off by the time the next match comes around, and that should be as bad as it gets. There was no need to cut them up as well.

When travelling away, we always made a point of trying to get ourselves onto other people's home ends; probably because we were always guaranteed an off, even if it never lasted too long. The easiest way to do this was just to hand over your money at the turnstile, keep your mouth shut and hope for the best. This method worked more often than not, and once, at Southend, came with a bonus. When I paid to get in I was also given a raffle ticket for a free draw that was going to take place at half-time. I couldn't believe my luck when they announced the number – I'd won a Flymo. I never did collect my prize though; we'd kicked off in their end before the game had, and by half-time we'd been thrown out and had to pay a second time to get into the Cardiff end. (No free raffle this time.) So I figured it might be pushing my luck a bit by trying to claim it.

HAMMERS, BARS, KNIVES AND BOTTLES
QPR v Cardiff City, Late 80's
Chelsea Pat: QPR drew Cardiff two years on the spin, and there had been trouble at both games but the second one stood out. Before the game it was unusually quiet, with no Old Bill on the Uxbridge Road. As I walked down with two of QPR's main boys, B and Gregors, we passed the police station and drew opposite with the House of Pies chip shop. As I glanced over, a bus pulled up at the stop next to the chip shop. In front there were four football chaps, two eating chips and staring across the road at us. We clocked them looking at us and all seemed to stop at the same time to stare at them.

"What are you looking at, you English cunts?" said one of them as he dropped his chips and bowled into the road. As we all looked at each other, the rest of them came over as well.

"Fuck this," said B. "What did you say, you fucking Cardiff cunt?"

We flew off the pavement towards them. "Come on then!" As we shaped up to our Welsh counterparts, the bus pulled off to reveal about 40 of their mates all stood there eating chips. *Oops!!!*

"Come on, you cockney cunts!" Cardiff charged into the road.

"Baked potat'er!" (see you later) I called. Fuck me, I have never run so fast. As people that know me will tell you, I'm not built for speed. I turned into Lime Grove and could still hear the roar behind us. "Don't fucking leave me!" I screamed at B and Gregors, as they started pulling away. I could hear B laughing, "Keep up, you fat cunt, they're right behind ya!" I somehow found a second wind.

I later found out they'd given up chasing us virtually straight away, but the other two kept me running as they thought I could do with the exercise. Fucking comedians!

After the game, QPR mobbed up at the Cunningham pub – maybe 200 of them with hammers, bars and knives and bottles People were sick of the taffies, who'd taken liberties once too often over the years. A couple of scouts plotted Bloemfontein Road and, as Cardiff turned towards Shepherd's Bush, tried to bait them to walk the opposite way, towards where QPR were waiting no more than 200 yards away. But Cardiff never bit. I'm glad in a way, because if they had come down that road there would have been a bloodbath. It was pitch-black, there were no Old Bill and with that amount of weapons someone would have been killed, without a doubt. Fair play to QPR: they later took over 100 to Paddington, but the Old Bill stopped them on Praed Street. They were well up for it and respect should be given to them.

GREGORS

QPR v Cardiff City, 28th September 1988
Mark Gregory (QPR): I have supported QPR from the early 70's. I'm in my late 40's now, and I've seen it all through the years. It was really nice of Annis to ask me to go down Memory Lane with Cardiff and QPR. I've got big respect for him as a mate, we go back to the 80's, and I have also got a lot of respect for Cardiff as a mob. When I was very young, in the early 70's, Cardiff always had a good rep for coming to QPR and getting away with murder. My first encounter was when we were playing them in a night game, and all the older firm told me, "Gregs, don't worry, you'll see them in the Loft tonight." Fuck me, it was a buzz to be with the older firm, as I was a youngster waiting for the row to happen.

The Loft used to have a big middle entrance that everyone used to stand on; on the righthand side of this entrance, all the older guys stood at the top of the stairs, looking down at the turnstiles to see if any mob tried to sneak in. As we were looking down the stairs, from our left we heard a massive roar from the T bar entrance: "CAAYARRDDIFF!" With that, everyone ran up to the back of the Loft so they couldn't get behind us and take our end. I was rooted to the spot, watching all the gorillas, as I was only 11. They were going toe to toe in the middle of the Loft. I did think of getting involved, until this fucking monster with a beard ran past me screaming, "Come on, you English bastards!" and headbutted a Rangers fan. It was the first time I saw a full-on fight at QPR of that type, and I was hooked. The Old Bill must have had a time-out, because you couldn't even dream of it happening nowadays.

QPR had the higher ground and forced Cardiff down the front, and then the Old Bill took them out and then marched them onto the pitch at the away end. You could hear from the away end, "Cardiff aggro! Cardiff aggro!" and from the QPR end, "You'll never take the Loft!" At the end of the match, hundreds and hundreds fought with bottles and bricks and anything you could pick up from the ground. It went from the away coach park in the dog track via White City station up to Shepherd's Bush Green. It made Roma v Lazio look like a slight disagreement. Being so young, I skipped all the way home and couldn't wait to tell my school mates and recruit a teenybopper mob to ambush the Welsh cunts next year.

Over the years, I came into my own and became a well respected face at QPR. With some rival mobs, I also became a hate figure and a target. I don't regret that, as I've always put myself at the front. Being so small, I made up for it with bottle, a little bit of front – and sometimes a big mouth! Sometimes being small makes you a bigger target than if you were seven foot tall, and my big mouth made things worse. With my cockney wit, I used to love mugging the other mob off. Given that most of these firms were cavemen, I became Public Enemy Number One. Every firm that came to QPR would say, "Where's Gregors?" or, "I'm going to kill that cunt Gregors!" and they're still saying it to the present day. Don't get me wrong: it's a pain in the arse when both the firms and the Old Bill make a beeline for me, but it goes with the territory. QPR have got a naughty firm that can match anyone on their day, especially in equal numbers. Some of our top boys are quality, as lots of the mobs that took us lightly found out the hard way – especially if they bumped into the C Mob, or the Northolt Mob, or 'my little firm' from the Notting Hill and Ladbroke Grove area. We used to do our own thing, and you wouldn't want to meet us in a dark sidestreet.

My Chelsea mate, Pat, reminded me of a night game in the late 80's against Cardiff, in the old Littlewoods Cup. At the time, we used to meet in the Bushrangers opposite Goldhawk Road station. I talked Pat into going to Paddington to meet Cardiff off the train, to tell them not to get off at the Bush but to stay on for one stop and get off at Goldhawk Road, where we could play with them. Pat didn't fancy it, because Cardiff fans were a bit barmy at the time, and if you tried to organise something with them they'd be quite happy to put you in hospital just because of your accent. But somehow I talked him into it. When we got there, I was beginning to think Pat was right. There were about 500 monsters on the train and, as they came onto the concourse, it was like an invading army screaming abuse at anything that wasn't Welsh. Pat said, "I fucking told you, Gregors, you can't talk to them, they'll kill you as soon as look at you!"

"Fuck that, watch me!" I said as I bounced into a group of about 20 of them. I told them I was QPR and told them to bring it on. As I walked back, Pat's mouth was so wide open you could have put a football in it. "It's called bollocks, Pat," I said as I smiled and walked past him. "Well, if you're a black cat, you little cunt, some of your lives have fucked off," said Pat.

Anyway, back to the Bushrangers. QPR were about 100-handed, waiting with no Old Bill around. The game was a 7.45 kick-off, it was now 7.30 and everyone said they weren't coming, so this whole mob left and walked to the ground without seeing any Cardiff fans. However, I was banned at the time, so I was stood with Fat Pat and his postman mate, Steve, outside the White Hart pub opposite the police station and 100 yards from Shepherd's Bush station. Steve the postman had just bought a massive pizza from Domino's across the road and was offering it to me and Pat. Pat was on a diet at the time (again), so he refused it, but you could see he was gagging for it. Anyway, as I shared the pizza, a huge mob walked out of Shepherd's Bush station. When I say 'walked', that's putting it mildly; they charged down the road and battered anyone who looked like they could throw a right-hander. They got opposite us and turned down the sidestreet next to the police station. I thought, *I'm not having that*. Pat second-guessed me and said, "Don't you fucking dare, Gregors!" Too late. I'd followed up behind them and said, "Oi!" With that, they all stopped and turned around, I said, "What time do you call this? Where were you at Goldhawk Road?" There was a spilt-second silence, and then they turned as one and charged. Steve had a big slice of pizza in his mouth at the time; that went west. Fat Pat broke the 100-metre record for 18 stone, and me . . . well, I'm Gregors. They lost me in the confusion, sometimes it pays to be lucky and small. After the game there were more scuffles, but nothing major. It's a shame the meet didn't happen before the game. It would have been special.

Back in the early season of '99, we hadn't played Cardiff for a while and we heard they were coming in masses to QPR. It was a League Cup night game again and it brought our biggest turnout for a few years. That night we heard that Cardiff were massive in Hammersmith (early doors) and they were also firm-handed in the Walkabout pub. But later on, as the day wore on, QPR had an early meet at the British Queen on Uxbridge Road; some nosey youth had scouted Hammersmith and said Cardiff were huge, and that it should be good later. Late afternoon, me and my mate Sean went for a stroll, but at the same time I had to be careful, as some Cardiff would beat me as if I was a Swansea fan if they recognised me.

As bad luck would have it, I got a call from my girlfriend. She'd been called to work, so I had to go and take care of my boy, who was only six. I was gutted, as I knew tonight would be special. My boy, myself and Sean were headed down the Uxbridge Road, towards the Prince. Sean was dressed like an advert for Burberry and, as we drew opposite the White Hart, five lumps appeared out of nowhere and fronted us. "Come on, boys, we're Cardiff!" I thought, *Shit, what about my boy?* I'll never forget the cunt: he had a white Timberland cap and jacket, and was raging drunk. He turned to Sean and said, "You look like a boy, come on, Sambo!" As my mate is half-caste, this didn't go down well. "Come on, we're Valleys!" My mate lost it, so I tried to get between them and said, "Leave it out, mate, there's only two of us and a kid." Luckily, that prick's mate pulled him away.

We'd gone about 50 yards when the same cunt came running up behind us and started again. I turned to Sean and said, "All yours, mate." Fair play to Sean: he said, "No, Gregors, what about your kid? We've got all night for these mugs." I was fucking fuming. I couldn't believe that anyone could front us with a little kid. What a fucking liberty! "Forget about it," said Sean as we continued walking down Uxbrige Road. Something made me look around, and I saw that little knob who'd given us shit joined by about 30 or more, now marching quickly to catch us up. I then heard those immortal words, "I'm sure that's fucking Gregors!" To make it worse, I'd looked around as the geezer said it, so they must have thought, *Bingo!* Just as I was thinking, *We're fucked,* the mobile went. Apparently, QPR's mob were rioting with the Old Bill, about 300 were up ahead of us. The caller said it was really bad, with flares, gas and all sorts of lovely stuff. I thought the best thing to do would be to walk towards the riot and draw these Cardiff into QPR's spider web, and then serve the cunts up.

As we got closer, you could see something was going on up ahead but, unbelievably, the mob behind us still hadn't sussed it. We could now see the British Queen and the Old Bill were in Roman army battle squares, trying to contain the riot. The Cardiff behind had now sussed it and said, "Fuck that," starting to walk back. One of them walked over to me and said, "I know your big mouth, don't I?" I replied, "I'm Gregors," and with that he jumped back like I had rabies. I clocked some QPR lads who were nearby and said, "Come on, they're here!" But they didn't fancy it. Luckily for me, about ten of our main lot had slipped through the Old Bill and come over to me after I'd told them about the liberty that had been taken. They were raging. "Come on, let's get the cunts!"

About ten – and it was a naughty ten, trust me – followed up behind that Cardiff group as they turned into Bloemfontein Road. A mate took my son to one side and said, "Payback time, Gregors," so we roared up. Cardiff turned and faced us, bouncing up and down, then one of then shouted, "They've got fucking blades!" and with that they started to backpeddle. As we pursued them, they made a stand at a skip. *Here we go*, I thought, then, just as it looked like it was going to go mental, they all turned to run. I soon realised why, as hundreds of QPR came running up the road behind us. The Cardiff boys had run to the corner of Bloemfontein Road, where it turns towards the stadium to South Africa Road. However, they stopped on the corner and turned as a huge Cardiff mob joined them. *Armageddon, here we come*, I thought, as hundreds of lads flew into each other all across the street. The Old Bill lost control and nobody budged. In the end, however, we started to back Cardiff up because of our huge numbers, so we claimed that row on points.

Everyone was being dispersed and, as I was banned, I couldn't go in. So I stood opposite the ground. Behind me, towards White City station, a huge roar came as about 400 Cardiff shirts came running down South Africa Road; they steamed across the road and attacked the Springbok pub, which was full of QPR shirts. A huge shirt v shirt battle took place before my eyes. I was laughing my head off, as I hadn't seen this for years. As the Old Bill got between them, they pushed the Cardiff shirts towards the ground. In amongst them, I noticed a few dressers. As I was looking at them, one knocked out a QPR div who was minding his own business. My big mouth opened as usual: "Oi, ya doughnut, why ya hitting clowns?" As a war of words took place, I was suddenly surrounded. I thought, *Oops, oh shit*. "You look familiar," said the Cardiff lad who threw the punch. Luckily for me, a QPR spotter stepped between us and said, "What are you doing, Gregors?"

"Fuck-all, I know them," I replied. *Phew!*

The Cardiff barmies were now passing us by, singing, "Wales! Wales!", only to be joined by a mob of QPR barmies singing, "England! England!" It took about two seconds for the third riot of the day to kick off. There must have been a thousand barmies and boys and normal fans going at it hammer and tongs. The Old Bill completely lost it again and chaos reigned. A big gap opened next to us and a big taffy (who was a ringer for Annis) wearing a Burberry shirt bounced into no-man's land, offering everyone out. "Oi, mate," I said, "bounce 20 yards down the road where there's no Old Bill." With that he said, "What do you mean, boyo? I've bounced 200 miles from Cardiff to get here." I had to laugh. It's not like me to be lost for words. Nice one, mate. 1-0 to Cardiff.

While the game was on, I went back to my mate who was looking after my son, He said he would keep him at his house for a few hours after the game, so I could go back for round two. As I reached the ground, the Old Bill, who had had a bad night all round, decided to let everyone out together. *Hello*, I thought. We'd just started to get together when a wicked 40 v 40 row broke out. Everyone was taking lumps out of each other and one Cardiff geezer, wearing a woolly hat, was double game, flying into everyone. He looked like he'd snorted a kilo of Charlie in one line.

Just my luck then that he came at me. I ducked down and threw an uppercut. Fuck me, he was out before he hit the floor. One of my mates laughed and said, "You win, Gregors, what do you want, a coconut or goldfish?" It all soon died down and I went back home. As I got home, I got a phone call that a van load of taffies had chased three QPR boys who, unluckily for the taffies, had made it to a naughty pub where some of our top boys were drinking. Fair play to Cardiff: they jumped out of the van 15-handed and squared up. However, they couldn't have been in a worse place or caught by nastier people. It kicked off and a few stood for a short while, then they ran and left the van. One Cardiff guy, probably the driver, stood and, along with another four who got caught, took a terrible beating. It's every chap's nightmare to be caught like that, but when you put yourself on offer these things happen. It's just a shame that, when it goes Pete Tong, it's always the game lads that get caught. Afterwards, on the internet, some Cardiff cyber warriors had said QPR had taken liberties with the mob in the van and were out of order.

Just remember, boys, who started it: Cardiff had chased QPR but came unstuck. Sometimes, shit happens. If you play our game, you've got to learn to live with it.

In the 2007 season, we played Cardiff again. As usual, we were looking forward to it, and as it was at the start of the season it was even better.

We've had a tasty youth mob for the last few years, and they'd been on the phone to Cardiff youth to sort something out. But for one reason or another, nothing came of it. I've got nothing but respect for QPR youth. They've proved themselves again and again over the last few years, and have some right game cunts among them. It's good to know that when me and the older main firm knock it on the head, QPR will still be a mob to respect.

Before the game we had a solid turnout at the British Queen, about 100-handed, but the Old Bill have wised up and now block the corner of Uxbridge Road and Bloemfentain Road before the game. It only took 30 years for the cunts to suss that one out. The first bit of action came about 1pm, when they marched Cardiff barmies down from the walkabout, maybe 1500 of them. As usual, you would have trouble telling the difference between divs and mob, as the shits were growling at bystanders and offering everyone out who looked like a QPR fan.

I'd already plotted up on the Uxbridge Road with some of my mates. I knew this couldn't be it, their firm hadn't arrived yet. About five minutes later, another escort came down but this one was surrounded by the riot police. *Here we go*, I said to a mate. As they got closer, all you could see was 200 bald 40-50 year old Honey Monsters marching down the road, the nearest thing to it would be the baldies gang out of the 70's film *The Wanderers*. Fuck me, they didn't half look the part! As they got level with us, the Old Bill clocked me, ran over and surrounded me. Obviously, all the Cardiff looked over and one said, "That's Gregors." I thought, *Oh bollocks*, as the whole mob pushed towards me shouting insults and threats. I said to the Old Bill, "You caused this, you better make sure they don't break through." As this was going on, Cardiff all of a sudden stopped worrying about me and charged up the road, only to be beaten back by riot Old Bill.

Apparently, QPR had come running down from the British Queen and, on seeing the Cardiff escort, started throwing bottles, bricks, etc. The Old Bill got between the two mobs and started to push Cardiff up Bloemfentein Road, towards the ground. My new ban was in force, so I couldn't walk in Bloemfentein Road. I stood on the corner, watching the Soul Crew getting marched to the stadium. As they walked past, this massive cunt who I can only describe as Bluto – the bearded villain who was Popeye's enemy in the cartoons – slipped the Old Bill and bounced over. "We've got a massive mob here today, boyo, you've got no chance." As usual, my mouth went into flight mode: "Yeah, mate, you've got a good mob, but we've got a brilliant mob. If you get to this point after the game, don't turn towards the station, turn right towards our pub. Then we'll see who the governors are."

With that he looked at me kind of funny. "Don't I know you from somewhere?" Then you could see it dawn on him. "You're fucking Gregors!" I kept quiet as I took a few steps back. *"Fuck me, this cunt has no neck,* I thought. "Yeah, I'm Gregors," I said. "I've been waiting six years to get my hands on you, I really fancy my chances with you," said Bluto. With that I just started laughing. It was lucky the Old Bill started to take an interest. *Well, Bluto, I'm sorry I ain't got no spinach, so that's out the window.* Then, to top it all, he said in a right valley accent, "Jog on, Gregors." I thought I'd split my sides laughing as I walked away. To be honest, I was just happy the big ape didn't get his hands on me.

After I left the area, a sniper firm of Cardiff came later and attacked the QPR pub called the Adelaide, opposite the British Queen. There were a few chaps in there at the time, including one of our main boys and his 15-year-old son, who they happened to front first. Bad move. The fights spilled out of the Adelaide and drew the attention of some of our boys who were banned and were drinking in the British Queen. So the Cardiff mob got hit from both sides and got a good slap. Apparently, there was a German with them who was quite game. Some of our lot thought it was Ronald from Cologne, but that was shit. I knew he was with Chelsea Pat in the stadium and some of Pat's

Kiwi mates from Belushi's pub, who were just there to watch the game. Obviously, the German was guesting with a mob of Cardiff that day. I'm sure he'll think about coming back to West London, after his stay in Hammersmith hospital.

After the game QPR were 200-handed, a fucking wicked mob. We came down the backstreets onto Goldhawk Road. Someone in front shouted, "Cardiff are up ahead!" With that we charged. Imagine the buzz: no Old Bill, your mob's full strength and about to clash with a respected foe. As we approached Goldhawk Road station, we saw no Cardiff. Just fucking Old Bill, trying to block the road off to Shepherd's Bush. We cut down Shepherd's Bush market, towards Shepherd's Bush station. Bad fucking move. As we reached the top of the market, 200 riot Old Bill in full gear just charged us. They went berserk. Heads were busted left and right. God knows how many went to hospital. As usual, you couldn't see any police numbers. I suppose the best firm in the country won the day again. Unfortunately for us football hooligans, the best firm always wears riot gear.

Later on that season, QPR were at Palace and Cardiff were at Charlton. As we were very active this particular season, it didn't take a scientist to figure out that we might cross paths. We'd gone to Palace and, to be honest, it was shit. So a small mob of our youth thought, *Let's have a look at Paddington to see if Cardiff are still about*. Bad move. As they left the station, they were surrounded by about 20 Cardiff grizzlies who, for whatever reason, didn't go to the game. All they kept saying to them was, "Where's Gregors? If you see him, tell the little cunt he's dead etc, etc." One of our youth, God bless him, said, "Fuck you, if you got something to say to Gregors, tell him yourself!" Luckily, these Cardiff were alright and gave our little young mob a bit of a squeeze!

The next time I saw the Rangers youngster, I told him it was really nice of him to stand up for me but he shouldn't have put himself on offer. A few hours later, three of our boys who are known to like a beer had decided to follow the QPR youth to Paddington to be nosey. As they were on Paddington station concourse, a black homeless nutcase approached them on the ponce for beer money. As the QPR boys were pissed, they gave him some money and started having a laugh with him. Out of nowhere – *boom!* – they were surrounded by about 20 Cardiff dressers who fronted them, asking, "Who are you lot?"

"We're QPR and we're here for you Welsh cunts!" said one of the QPR fellas. Before anyone could react, the mad black homeless guy bounced into the middle and started to do kung fu moves, saying to the taffs, "You fuck with my mates, you fuck with me! Come on, I'll fight all of you!" Cardiff backed off, to think about how to deal with this headcase. As they were getting their heads around it – thank fuck, as otherwise our lot would have taken a pasting – the Old Bill stepped in. My QPR mates said they never found out that mad geezer's name, but if he reads this book he has free beer in the British Queen next season.

FAIR PLAY?
Enfield v Cardiff, FA Cup, 11th December 1988 (Spurs)
Guff (PVM – CCFC): Recalling the FA Cup game away to Enfield on a rainy Sunday, boy, I miss those trips still. On the Saturday I hired the Transit; how I ever got it, after the state we used to return them in, is a puzzle – always full of used cans, fag ends and the old mattress in the back. For this trip to London, the same old faces were up for it: Huey, Vince, Taffy Anton, Stavvy, Webber (only just turned 16 at the time, but always game, sadly no longer with us – RIP), Steve, Nigel, Kenny, Aidan, the Charles brothers, and a few others, about 15 of us in total. Small in numbers but we were all up for it, with no fear whatsoever.

We all thought that one of the London firms would show; it might be little Enfield, but that's how the surprises usually happen. We did think it would probably be Spurs, and with them in mind we got tooled up. One of the lads worked where they made windows and so he got small iron bars, about 18 inches thick, just in case it came totally on top.

We got into London and then headed out to Enfield and saw Cardiff had a fair old following there already. After parking up in some terraced street, all of us did the usual thing and met all the lads who had travelled up. Once in the ground there was the usual heavy police presence, so not much really happened. We all decided at the end of the game we would go off on our own, and probably bump into Spurs if they had bothered to show up. As soon as the final whistle went, with a 4-1 win behind us, we were off and got back in our van and sat there for a while. We watched the train mob being escorted and, finally, the Old Bill were gone as well.

We then drove off, but within a minute or so we spotted about 20 lads in a sidestreet. This was our chance, we all thought. We parked up in the next street, but no sooner had we parked than the mob had noticed us. The only problem now was the mob had grown to about 50-odd lads. We were already out of the van and outnumbered, but there was no way back now. So we just stood in the middle of the street, waiting for the now charging mob that was heading straight at us. It went into the usual toe-to-toe, but soon they were waiving Stanleys at us, shouting, "Yids! Yids!" and they were really going to fuck us. One of our lads managed to open the van door and got our bars out, but oh no, could you believe it? The Old Bill turned up en masse at our end and Spurs fucked off, leaving us by the van. We couldn't believe it, we had just held out against big numbers and were just about to defend ourselves, and we were nicked.

We were all handcuffed there and then, I think about 12 got nabbed, and given the usual few head slaps like they used to in those days. Then we were off to the local police station. Webber was taken on his own (juvenile), the rest of us were kept in a room together over the next hour. We must have had at least a dozen police look in at us. Then each one of us was led out, myself and seven others were released onto the streets of London while the others were kept and charged, including the driver. We had to dash across London to make the last train home. The others were eventually let go and were back up in court on the Tuesday. It looked like they charged whoever's face didn't fit, or who they disliked.

In court, Stavvy said that the bars were all in there because he was making rabbit hutches for his sister; that statement made the *Evening Standard*. The following home game, we were all slated in the match programme for the trouble; they said it marred the day and that the club had nothing to do with this 'extra-match entertainment'. The fact remains that, in my estimation, 90 per cent of the fans in that ground that day were lads.

A few weeks later, a well-known Spurs lad from Port Talbot invited two of the lads on a Spurs coach to Bradford away in the cup. They were all Spurs lads and guess what? On the coach were the lads we had it with in Enfield. On this trip, they said to our lads, "Fair play, your lads stood against us when you were totally outnumbered." Our two lads were well looked after by them, that's why being a lad at football is a funny old game. One minute you want to batter each other, next week you're drinking together.

MOST OF WEST LONDON WERE OUT THAT DAY
Hayes v Cardiff City, 21st November 1990
Chelsea Pat: Ha ha! Let me tell you about Hayes Town FC from West London. If all the local football lads followed that team, it would be like going to Millwall in the 70's at Cold Blow Lane. It seemed that most of West London were out that day, some of the best quality boys from a dozen different mobs. You had lads from Chelsea, QPR, Arsenal, West Ham, Man Utd, Millwall, Brentford, etc – all coming together when Hayes got a decent FA Cup draw.

Over the years Hayes have slapped Swansea and Peterborough, taken over Fulham and done Northampton away – and, as everyone knows, back in their day Northampton at home were no mugs. They also turned up at Ninian Park, but, as Lakey [Anthony Rivers] says in his *The Soul Crew* book, there was no Cardiff mob out that day. Lakey also mentions Hayes had a massive mob out because of the liberties Cardiff had taken at QPR the previous season. No, mate! As soon as Hayes drew Cardiff, about ten mobs around London woke up to the chance of a good punch-up. It's a shame they moved it from Hayes to Brentford, because it would have been carnage.

Come the night of the game, I was with about 25 QPR. There were Chelsea faces everywhere when we arrived in Brentford. When we went into the first pub, a sea of ugly faces all turned our way and then slowly went back to their beer when they realised we were cockneys. Every pub was packed solid with chaps and my hand was getting sore from the amount of handshaking I was doing, as I was seeing people I hadn't seen for years.

"Why is it that you get on with every cunt?" said an annoyed Gregors (QPR), who was glaring at a load of Cockney Reds (Man Utd) who were returning the stare with interest.

"Now, now, Gregors, we're all Hayes tonight," I said with a grin.

On to the game. In the stadium Cardiff had a shit turnout of a couple of hundred fans, if that. It looked like we'd come down from Shepherd's Bush for nothing. As me and my mate Smithy didn't go in, we walked past the away end to see a young Cardiff lad being thrown out by the police. I called him over and at first he was understandably wary.

"Nah, mate, we're sweet," said Smithy, "we just want to know if you have any boys down."

"Only about 20," he said.

"Is Annis there?" I asked.

"Yeah, he's inside."

"Fucking hell, I haven't seen him for about three years," I said. "If you see him, tell him I'll be looking for him." We walked away as a nosey policeman came over.

After the game, about 3-400 lads gathered across the road from the away end. Apparently, Cardiff had been cheeky in the ground, so there were going to be no squeezes for them. The police did their best to break up everyone, but because it was dark and I don't think the Brentford police were too clued up for that sort of thing, we were all still there when Cardiff came out.

The next I saw was a group of about 25 lads walking up the road, with a few Old Bill protecting them. They might as well have painted them bright yellow, as everyone moved towards them. Within minutes there were 60 in front of them, 50 behind them and 200-odd walking beside them. They were dead men walking. In the middle of it all, I could hear a familiar voice screaming, "Keep together, don't let them mingle in!" Fuck me, it was my old mate Annis! I couldn't believe it. He was as white as a ghost, but he was still barking orders to hold it together.

I was so pleased to see him that I bowled straight through the Old Bill, right up to him. "Annis, my old mate, remember me?"

"Pat, you Chelsea bastard!" He hugged me. "What you doing here, mate? This has turned into a nightmare for us."

"Just keep your head down, you've got no chance tonight," I told him. "There's about 300 top boys from all over London, looking to pay you back for 30 years of Welsh hospitality."

The next thing, I was grabbed out of the Cardiff escort from behind by an angry Chelsea copper. "What are you fucking doing, Pat?" he growled.

"I'm collecting my money," I said.

"What money?" said the copper.

"We had a bet that Cardiff would need an escort after the game. He lost," I said, pointing at Annis.

"Get your fat arse over the road before I fill it with my boot, you cheeky cunt!" roared the Old Bill. I didn't need to be told twice. Anyway, I was glad to see that Annis and the boys – Jonathan, Mallo, etc – managed to survive what was a dodgy night for them. Believe me, if it had been at Hayes FC they wouldn't have been so lucky.

AT THE NEW DEN

Millwall v Cardiff City, December 9th 1998 (Auto Windscreen Shield Cup)

Chelsea Pat: I remember when this draw came out of the hat, the first phone call I made was to Annis to confirm that Cardiff were going and the second was to Ginger Bob, for him to invite me over.

I didn't need a second invite, being a nosey cunt, and the night game in a Mickey Mouse cup game at Millwall had all the ingredients of a messy and ugly night out. Anyway, over at Millwall there was a bit of a slow turnout at the meet, probably 50 or 60 grizzlies in the bar. The mobile phones were soon going and the story was that Cardiff were at the Elephant and Castle.

Gregors (QPR), who was guesting, jumped in a car to go and have a look with some bushwhackers. He rang back and said, "You won't believe it, but they've started to walk down the Old Kent Road about 100-150 handed with no escort." The atmosphere completely changed, and the talk was of how we were going to get to the Old Kent Road to meet our Welsh counterparts. Vans and cars were mentioned, and as the wheels were put in motion another call had come through saying that Cardiff had cut off the Old Kent Road and were heading back to London Bridge. Apparently, they had been arguing that no one knew where they were going and they would probably miss the match if they got lost. Fair enough, I suppose, and that is Cardiff's problem: they should unite more and would then be probably the number one firm in the country, with their numbers.

Anyway, about half an hour later someone runs in the pub and shouts, "They're coming off the station!" With that the mob – which was now about 80 – steams out and runs down towards the Cliftonville pub by the railway bridge leading up to the stadium.

We all stood on the corner as the Cardiff escort turned and headed towards us. "BLUEBIRDS! BLUEBIRDS!" chanted the Welsh hooligans as they moved towards us.

"Come on, you Welsh cunts!" The Millwall charged across the road at the front of Cardiff's escort. Some Cardiff had got through the escort, but the numbers were so small that they eased off when they saw the amount of Millwall that had filled the road. It was getting dark now and the street ahead looked a nasty sight, with two mobs baying for each other.

Fucking hell! Millwall were rabid to get at Cardiff and the Old Bill were really struggling to hold them back. One guy had got rugby tackled by two coppers and was still crawling on his fucking hands and elbows towards the taffs, shouting threats. What a fucking headcase!

As they marched under the railway bridge, Millwall charged the escort from behind with a deafening roar. Fair play to Cardiff, they turned and fought back; some Cardiff picked up the police railings and threw them into Millwall. Then they went through the Old Bill and brought the fight to Millwall. Respect.

The Old Bill were smashing both firms' kneecaps with their steel batons and a police van drove between them. They charged Cardiff down under the bridge, while a second lot of Old Bill lined the road to stop any Millwall following.

A bit later on I was stood with Terry, Ginger Bob's brother, when what I can only describe as a two-legged wooly mammoth came over for a chat. Fuck me, he looked like Giant Haystacks' big brother. "Well Terry, you've got to give it to Cardiff, not many would come here for a nothing game in the night and come looking for it, that's a lot more than Chelsea or West Ham would ever do," said the mammoth.

I glanced at Terry out of the corner of my eye to see a nasty smile playing on his face. "Have you met Pat from Chelsea, he's one of their boys?" (Cheers, Terry, you cunt!)

"Oh, sorry mate," said Haystacks, "I didn't know you were Chelsea."

"That's alright, bruv, don't worry about it," I said. *Phew*. To be honest, that big cunt could have said Chelsea got battered by Orient and I wouldn't have said anything.

Later, Bob was laughing when Terry told him what happened. "What do you lot eat to get so big?" I asked Bob.

"Grilled West Ham fans with Chelsea sauce," shouted Terry across the pub.

"That makes sense," I laughed.

During the second half of the game, a couple of Cardiff Valleys had the bright idea to leave early, obviously to get home. Bad fucking move. They were captured by a nasty mob of Millwall who came out of some houses as they walked past. Apparently, the taffies were given a savage beating and one of the Millwall filmed it on his phone and texted it to a Cardiff lad in the ground, to wind Cardiff up. Fucking sick or what?

I tell you what – and this is honest, knowing Millwall the way I do: those taffies got off lightly. When it comes to things like that, Millwall are fucking ruthless. They were really lucky they didn't get cut or, fucking worse, end up brown bread.

I was in the area with Gypsy Ben when Millwall rioted after the Brum game. Trust me, when you've seen as many riots as I have, you know what you're talking about. Seeing a police horse getting chased down the road with no one riding it really showed me something. Millwall are absolutely radio rental.

ONE BY ONE THEY WERE RELEASED

Brentford v Cardiff City, 28th December 1998

Taffy Anton (CCFC): Another game that sticks in my mind is Brentford away, when well over 5,000 City fans turned up. We were really doing well then, on that rare occasion. And what a turnout from the PVM and the Neath lads: we had a good 50, all dressers in Armani and Lacoste. Amongst the lads were Neath Punk (Simon), Huw, Guff, Vince, Aiden (Bro), Fulman and many more.

We arrived at Brentford about 11am and went straight into the Bricklayer's Arms. It was already packed with Brentford lads (probably half of them being Chelsea). I was playing pool with one of the lads, while the rest of the boys were outside drinking in the sun. With that, a load of cockneys started being abusive to my mate and I, calling us 'taffy wankers'. All hell broke loose. I just lost it and went steaming straight in, and all the boys outside piled in as well. You had pool balls, glasses, everything flying around, and as the battle went on we were backed up by the Docks Boys, continuing into the street where quite a few Brentford got cut badly. Eventually, the Old Bill arrived and over 30 Cardiff got nicked, including my brother. I managed to make a quick escape and got myself to the ground.

It was unbelievable. Outside the ground, thousands of Cardiff were locked out and so hundreds were making their way into the home end. Cardiff were on all sides. While the match was going on, apparently hundreds of Cardiff were steaming the turnstiles and gates to get in. Eventually one of the gates was smashed through, so in some areas of the ground it was well and truly rammed. Scuffles were breaking out in the home end all the way through the game, our support that day had well and truly surprised the Old Bill.

But my joy was shortlived, as I was pulled out by the police on suspicion of a serious assault. I pleaded my innocence and said that I didn't know anything about it at all, and eventually I was let go when the game had finished. After the game, we headed back to the police station to get the boys out. One by one they were released, but with no sign of my bro. So I waited there and, some three hours later, he came out and a big cheer went up. I gave him a big hug as he was now a fully fledged hooligan. What was unbelievable was that every one of the 30 lads was let off.

THIS WAS PROPER!
Cardiff City v Millwall, 7th August 1999

Dave Chappell (Crystal Palace): Ah, Millwall, the boys from Bermondsey. What a prospect! The first game of the season was Millwall at home and I had to have a ticket for this one. How the game wasn't rescheduled I'll never know. Still, I didn't want to miss it. A ticket was purchased in the Bob Bank and off I set. I stayed at Annis's on the Friday night in order to get to the city centre early Saturday morning, as we'd been told Millwall were due to arrive early. Around 9am, the first train pulled in with 30-40 Millwall on. They got run within minutes of entering the town centre, but it wasn't Millwall's main lads, it was kids. When the second train arrived it was a different story. This was the true Millwall – all men, no kids. Fuck me, they looked the business! Millwall were put into Sam's bar and a few other bars in Mill Lane, and surrounded by police. While Millwall were being escorted to the bars, around 4-500 Cardiff were battling the police on Penarth Road to get to their London rivals. This was fighting with the police like I hadn't seen before. This was proper Cardiff, using planks of wood, missiles, anything they could lay their hands on, while Millwall took the piss outside the bars.

Me and Annis managed to stay inside the city centre and were watching Millwall, but you could see Cardiff charging towards the adjoining bridge. Millwall were eventually escorted off to the ground once the roads ahead had been cleared of Cardiff. We were told to get to the Severn Oaks Park as Cardiff were going to ambush the escort. This possibly might have worked if the police hadn't tried to land a helicopter in the middle of two mobs. The police escort managed to get Millwall into the ground without any more trouble. Inside there was an evil atmosphere, with both sets of fans hurling coins, lighters, etc, at each other, as well as numerous insults. The game finished in a 1-1 draw, with both goals coming from the penalty spot. I couldn't wait for the game to finish so I could see what would happen afterwards. When the final whistle went, for some reason the police allowed us to exit via the back of the Grange End. This meant more missile-throwing from hundreds of young casuals as we were walking behind the Millwall end. The police were trying to contain Millwall while Cardiff were gathering serious numbers outside the ground. The numbers must have been up to a good 1,000 lads, all waiting ready for Millwall to come out. When they did it was mental. Millwall came out from underneath the Grandstand, and those that were first were some of the gamest I've ever seen. Cardiff were like locusts, all over them, attacking them and driving them back into the ground. The Millwall who came out first got hammered, well and truly fucked. As always, the police eventually separated both sides and had the unenviable job of getting the City fans to disperse. They kept making baton charges into us on Sloper Road and Penarth Road, the result of which was bruised legs for yours truly. We made our way back to the city centre and had a few beers, as another good day with Cardiff came to an end.

Mac (CCFC): the first game of the season at our place in August 1999 was another day to remember. We were massive that day, probably one of the biggest turn outs since the 70's, anything between 1,000-1,500 lads. We had been trying to get at them all day, as the Old Bill had stopped and even banned us from drinking in our own town. There had been a small mob of about 30 Millwall in a pub at 11am, but there was no real toe-to-toe as a mob of Cardiff got to them and wiped them out.

Then, when about 300 Millwall arrived and plotted up at Sam's Bar in Mill Lane, the shout went up a mile away in Grangetown and over 600 lads ran up Penarth Road. Two police motorcycles rode through the crowd of Cardiff and one was dragged from his bike; the police on horses were attacked by the Cardiff fans too, and at one stage a police helicopter landed in a park about a quarter of a mile from the ground, it actually hovered between us and Millwall to keep us apart. So you could say that before the game was a bit of a non-event between us and Millwall.

After the final whistle, well over a thousand lads were waiting outside the ground and the Old Bill tried and tried to move us. During that time some Millwall managed to break out, but the moment we saw them we steamed straight into them and totally hammered them back into the ground. It was so bad that they were fighting one another to get back inside, but I've got total respect for them. They had brought the fight to us, and not many firms do that.

Later on that season, when we played Millwall at their place, we had a mob of well over 700 and some of the faces I hadn't seen for years. We were awesome that day, and I heard Millwall were good too. But the Old Bill won, as they had wall-to-wall police wherever we went. Coming out of the tubes we couldn't go left or right, and it ended up as a non-event. In my opinion though, Millwall are one of the top firms of all time, although the old Den was a nasty place to visit.

Jonathan Evans (CCFC): Now I'm not going to say too much about Millwall, as you know their rep, but when they came to us in August '99 they came properly unstuck. They came with a firm. They didn't fuck about. They came looking for it. The Viking and I told our lot to meet in our local, the Neville in Grangetown. Millwall arrived in Cardiff early; we had a few scraps early on but nothing too major, as there were too many Old Bill. By 2pm we had a huge mob of lads at the pub, at least 600 strong; we decided to try to get at Millwall, who were in the city centre, so we had to make our way from Grangetown by going through the sidestreets. But trying to take a large mob like that through is impossible, especially in Cardiff. We tried our best, but got baton-charged back by the Old Bill; planks, bricks, you name it and it was thrown at them for at least half an hour, while a dozen Old Bill on horses charged at us time and time again.

Millwall were being escorted tightly by the Old Bill all the way to the ground, but we still attacked the police bubble they were in, with a police helicopter landing between us in a park at one stage. What a mad sight! So no proper punches were thrown before the game, which was a proper disappointment. The game itself was a bit lively: objects were being thrown back and forth, as were all the usual chants, but after it was game on. This was what we'd been waiting for. As we came out of our end, Millwall burst out of theirs and we had hundreds ready for it; there's a CCTV video of our numbers and it doesn't lie. But I'll give respect to those Millwall lads, because they are the only side I've ever seen doing what they did: after we were both forced away from each other by the police, Millwall went back into the ground, ran along the side of the pitch and burst out the side of the family enclosure gate. Just as I was calling our lot to go through the same gate, we met head on; the Viking, myself and Rusty went straight in, no bouncing about and all that bollocks. Their front line got smashed bad, and it was great because they were forced back into the enclosure and back up the stairs. As we went forward, their lads were left behind on the floor; those that weren't KO'd were hammered and laid out on the ground as hundreds of Cardiff poured through. Fourteen were taken to hospital. It was proper naughty. They were all dodging to get away from us, but they got properly done. It was a good result, but I've got to give those lads respect because they were the gamest London firm to come to us.

Millwall v Cardiff City, 4th December 1999

Jonathan Evans (CCFC): In the return game we took over 800 boys to Millwall. Me and the Viking drove up, and as soon as we got there the Old Bill were on us. I'm sure they had our mobile numbers tapped, as it was proper strange. Anyway, we had no chance of avoiding the police with the size of the mob Cardiff had that day. We got to South Bermondsey and there was a massive police presence, which prevented any trouble, but somehow I still got nicked before the game. Some bollocks charge again, another night in the cells, but never mind; shit happens.

Cardiff v Tottenham, FA Cup 7th January 2002

Tottenham weren't much better. In fact, all they did was sing. I'll give them credit though, they've got good voices. Some of them came the night before and got to a pub in Grangetown, but the Old Bill just kept baton-charging us away. On the day of the game they did fuck-all. They were put in a bubble and marched through Grangetown, happy to stay in their escort. Again we tried our best to attack, five attempts were made. Before we burst out of the side entrance of the Grange pub, I said to the boys, "If I go out first, make sure you all follow behind me." Everyone did. Spurs saw us and just started singing, they made no attempt to break the bubble. They were a proper disappointment. As I've been saying, I'll always show respect to lads who've earned it, and Spurs were a different animal at home. By then though, I was in prison for the game.

It was a midweek game. Our lot did travel to London, so I can say what they thought of Spurs. They told me they were fucking good; both sides had over 700 boys out and Spurs were game. I don't think either side could have claimed a victory that night, but our lot have told me they were very impressed with Spurs. I hope they feel the same as we do, because it's all about respect and they have ours. So do Millwall, for the part they played that day in August '99. Even though they came unstuck, I thought they were as game as fuck.

FRIGHT HEART LANE
Spurs v Cardiff City, Carling Cup, 1st October 2002
Chelsea Pat: When the draw came out of the hat my phone blew up. You've got Cardiff, who must have been the only firm in Britain to get better and BIGGER as time went on. They had a bigger firm now than in the 70's and 80's, though I suppose it also could be that over time everyone else got smaller and they stayed the same. As the team was shit they seldom played the big boys, so stories of their continued huge numbers were all second- and third-hand. Some are based on fact though, as I'd discovered a year earlier.

Tottenham were arguably one of the best firms in the country, so it was a proper clash of the heavyweights. The weekend before the game, the Yids were playing Boro in the cup while Chelsea, my team, had West Ham. After the game we were about

200-handed outside our pub, listening to our mates from Boro as they taught Spurs a lesson on the Seven Sisters Road (the noise in the background was unbelievable) by live action from a mobile phone. Judging by this, I didn't fancy Spurs' chances on the Wednesday, considering Cardiff would have at least 1,000 boys. However, fate is not without a sense of humour!

A train strike on the Wednesday fucked up the trains, so Cardiff had to make their way down in coaches and minibuses. They provisionally arranged to meet in Enfield, and me and Bully from Chelsea, Ronald the German and another pal arranged to meet them. However, when we got there was a pub on our left and outside was a six foot two black geezer with dreadlocks and a black Stone Island hooded jacket. He smiled at us, revealing more fucking gold teeth than even I've got. Sometimes you get a feeling that this is not going to be your day. Then this fucker went back into the pub. "We've been sussed," said Bully. "Just keep walking," I said as we quickened the pace, glancing back every few seconds. We stopped in the next pub to catch our breath. "Fuck me, that was close," Bully said. "What's the matter with you? You look like you've seen a ghost."

"I hope you've written a will, Bully, 'cos we're fucking dead," I said. "Look over your shoulder but don't make it obvious." As Bully glanced back, 30 Yid youth waded into the bar and ordered drinks. "Drink up," I said to Bully.

"Nah, take your time, they ain't sussed us," said Bully.

"Bully, I'll fucking kill ya if that Rasta walks in here and clocks us! They will dissect us."

"Alright mate, you're right," said Bully, "let's fuck off."

Anyway, fast forward two hours and we met Annis at a petrol station. When we got there, we jumped in a minibus with some of Annis's mates. As we approached the ground, I noticed we were coming towards the home end. Normally, when Chelsea play (unless we've done a sneaky one), we come from the other side. But as we crawled through the traffic we got caught in a jam. The next thing, hundreds and hundreds of lads came running down the road towards us, both on the pavement and through the traffic.

"Oh my God," came a Welsh accent from the back of the van.

"I take it that this lot ain't yours then?" I said.

"Nope," said the voice.

"Right," I said, "nobody say nothing, I'll do the talking."

Around the van, the charge had now slowed to a jog then to a walk. As they walked past the van, all heads faced our way. All of a sudden, the driver door got pulled open from the outside and loads of hate-filled faces crowded around the open door.

"Come on, you Welsh cunts!" said a big skinhead in a CP Company jacket.

"What you fucking on about?" I said. "We're fucking Yids! The row's back down there! Call yourself Tottenham? What you going this way for?"

"Oh shit, sorry mate, we thought you were taffies."

"Yeah, do I sound fucking Welsh, you mug?" And with that I pulled the door shut.

Nobody said a word until we'd driven through hundreds of them and reached the away end. I will never forget how, as we stopped, I looked back and everyone was as white as a ghost.

"Anyone got a dustpan and brush?" said the driver.

"Why?" I said.

"'Cos I think I've shit all over the seat."

With that we all cracked up laughing. What a fucking escape! I had visions of those squaddies caught at the IRA funeral in Northern Ireland in the 80's, and it definitely would have gone that way if one of them had recognised me. Luckily, the van had nothing that was Welsh on it either.

During the game, the stories were coming back of Cardiff being picked off in small mobs as they made their way to the ground. To be honest, I wasn't surprised. As much as I hate the Yid cunts, the mob they had out that night was top draw. They would have done anyone that night and, after what had happened the previous Saturday against Boro, it was even more credit to them to pull a mob like that.

In the stadium, Cardiff had at least 1,000 lads but, because of the train strike, they were all over the place. If the train strike hadn't have been on, I reckon there would have been total carnage and it would have been very hard to say who'd have come out on top. After the game, they tried to hold us back but Cardiff burst through the gates. You could see groups of Tottenham hanging around everywhere; we crossed the road, Cardiff steamed towards one group of Tottenham and battle commenced. After about five minutes of running battles it calmed down, but, to my horror, when we reached the corner all of Cardiff turned right towards White Hart Lane station, where all their coaches were parked. I had to go left towards Seven Sisters and I'd lost Bully and Ronald. I was on my Jack Jones. *Fuck me,* I thought, *I'll never reach home.* I must have been pulled at least three times by groups of Yids on the main road.

"Got the time, mate?" "I'm Spurs." "Oh. Sorry, mate."

"Where you from, mate?" "Tottenham." "Sorry, mate."

"Where you from, you Cardiff cunt?" "I'm a Yid, mate." "Sorry, mate."

I called this a St Peter moment – whereas he denied knowing Jesus, I denied being Cardiff three times. Over all the years, that was one of the dodgiest nights for me personally. When I next met Annis, we were laughing our hearts out about it. I was later told by some Cardiff that, as they were marched down the road, there was a tennis court and about 30 Cardiff burst the escort to run through the court into a park. Unfortunately, they were met by 400 Yids coming towards them. Bad move. The rest of the Cardiff escort battled with the Old Bill to try to reach their mates, but were batoned back. However, a large mob of Cardiff had managed to sneak out and ran some mobs of Yids right by the park. The trouble was that they were running into the middle of nowhere, they split up into smaller and smaller groups and eventually got picked off again.

Not a good night for the Soul Crew, but sometimes circumstances (the train strike) dictate the outcome rather than the strength of the actual mobs.

Dave Chappell (Crystal Palace): Brilliant, another must-go game. I got down to London and met Lakey and a few of his mates in the daytime, and had a mooch around some shops before making our way around the dreaded M25 to Tottenham. We met up with Annis's car load and a minibus full of lads on the A10. After a couple of beers it was time to go to White Hart Lane. I went in the car with Annis, his partner Jo, Michael and a lad called Brian, we parked up in one of the many housing estates near the ground and started to walk. Phone calls were coming in thick and fast, saying Spurs had a top mob out and were attacking Cardiff at every opportunity. Darkness had now set in and you sensed trouble. Everything around us felt dodgy. We were walking parallel to a park and could see a pub called the Artichoke in the distance, with a lot of figures milling around outside. It was decided that I'd walk ahead and, if they were Spurs, then with my accent I'd talk and Annis and co could walk on. We were well outnumbered and we would have been fucked. Fortunately, it turned out to be Cardiff; pleasantries were exchanged and we carried on to the ground.

The phone calls were right, Spurs had a top mob out: all colours, shapes and sizes filled the streets around the ground. The police were holding them back, allowing Cardiff fans to get in. Unfortunately for us, the Met decided they were going to make our group of five walk through the Spurs mob and all the way around the ground to the away end, to 'teach us a lesson'. One copper saw sense eventually, after much arguing, and allowed us through – *phew!* As we approached the turnstiles, about 150 ticketless Cardiff fans kicked a gate open and all got in. In the ground, all the talk was on Cardiff being picked off in dribs and drabs. The game was terrible and Spurs won 1-0. The final whistle went and we were told we were going to be escorted out of the ground. Fortunately, it was in the direction of the car. If we had parked anywhere else it could have been a dodgy walk. Out in the street, Spurs were being held back on both sides of the road by the police. All of a sudden, the roar that we all knew went up and, fucking hell, Spurs were attacking the police, Cardiff were attacking the police and it was going off everywhere. There were loads of running battles, and fights kicking off in the car park. Outside the ground it went mad. Cardiff were now together and there must have been at least 600 lads who were all trying to get at Spurs.

There was too much going on all around to focus on one thing. The Old Bill were desperately trying to get Cardiff moving back onto the coaches but it just wasn't happening. There was too much going on; there was a large mob of Spurs trying to get through the park on our left. They were being monitored by a helicopter and Cardiff were trying to get into the park to stop an ambush. Every side road and alley had police at the end of it. Spurs were trying everything, it was manic. Full marks to Spurs: they were awesome that night and certainly gave us as good as they got. They deserve honours, even in my book!

We got back to the car and we were all buzzing – what a top night.

I'll also say thanks to Annis and Michael for stopping me from getting mugged at St Albans train station, where they dropped me off. Cheers for noticing the lads following me.

WEST HAM HOME AND AWAY, 2003-04 SEASON

Jonathan Evans (CCFC): We played West Ham after Tottenham. West Ham did fuck-all, nothing. They brought about 200, drank in town with the Old Bill outside, and were happy to be escorted to the ground in a bubble. They made no attempt whatsoever to look for it, whereas we got bird for trying to attack them. I got nicked before the game, a rocket was fired at the police lines to try and break them and I got charged with an attempted GBH Section 18 (wounding with intent) on a copper. I got a Not Guilty, but had six months bird on another charge. Viking had four fucking years for his part after the game, as Cardiff tried to ambush West Ham in Grangetown. The judge, on sentencing, said it looked like a scene from Beirut, but not one punch was thrown after the game. What a fucking liberty! In the return game at Upton Park, West Ham got done and Cardiff took the piss: we ran them ragged after the game, down every sidestreet all you could see were the backs of West Ham. Out of about a dozen battles that day, they stood only once and then got savaged by our numbers. We must have had 5-600 lads who had travelled that day, and some had never forgotten the times we'd been battered there in the late 70's. So I reckon we finally settled the score.

Although West Ham weren't up to much at their ground or away, the old ICF were undoubtedly the governors back in the old days. But times change. I guess the new West Ham aren't a patch on the old ICF, who had their reunion back in 2001 – when 400 of them went to Manchester – and would never have been turned over.

VI
THE MIDLANDS

FAKE MEMBERSHIP CARDS
Northampton v Cardiff City, 28th December 1986
Lee 'Tonto' Davies (CCFC): About this time clubs were introducing membership schemes to make sure home fans only got into the home end, but if you were smart enough there were always ways around that. One Sunday we had an away game at Northampton; we'd been to another match the day before, which was something we used to do if Cardiff didn't have a game. I remember once watching the first half of a game at Elland Road and then the second half of one at the Odsal Stadium, but I don't know where I'd been before the Northampton game. All I can remember is driving overnight and arriving in the early hours of the morning. When we arrived, we broke into their supporters' shop and borrowed a pile of blank membership cards (we left everything else, so I doubt anyone even noticed we'd been there). We got a local phone book and filled out the membership cards with names and addresses; all that remained now was to wait for the train to arrive and hand them out. When the train arrived we gave them to anyone who'd take them. The plan was to get as many of us as possible into Northampton's end, while it was my job to go into the Cardiff end and get a mob together there. It was arranged for half-time; we were going to cross that stupid bowling green they used to have at the county ground (we'd already been in earlier that morning and opened a gate at the back of the away end) and onto Northampton's end, but things didn't go as planned. Firstly, only about half a dozen managed to use the fake membership cards, and from what they told me later they were

given a hard time by Northampton police. They had their feet stood on so they couldn't move and their hands held behind their backs. Unfortunately, there was nothing they could do except wait for half-time and for us to arrive. On the stroke of half-time about 150 of us squeezed through the small gate and onto the bowling green, only to find the police were one step ahead of us and lined up on the far side. The presence of the Old Bill was never a problem, so we ran towards them. As I got closer, they didn't look too concerned that 150 lads were about to attack them. When I looked behind, I realised why; I was just in time to see the last Cardiff fan disappearing through the gate, leaving just two of us to have a go at the Old Bill. I certainly didn't fancy our chances. I don't remember, or didn't see, what happened to the other lad who stood, but I was knocked to the ground and literally trampled on as they ran over me to try and make a few arrests. I was dragged across the grass to the edge of the pitch, by an old fat sergeant who was sweating and wheezing by the time he'd got me off the bowling green. All he could manage to say, when he handed me over to a young copper, was, "Here!" When the sergeant went back to make a few more arrests, the young copper asked me what he was supposed to do with me. I told him the fat bloke had said I had to be put back in the Cardiff end, and I couldn't believe my luck when he did exactly that. What a result!

After the game, outside the ground it was mayhem. We had running battles with the police, all the while trying to get at Northampton. I also had another run-in with my fat friend from the bowling green; luckily, he didn't recognise me, but as usual the Old Bill managed to get on top and eventually got Cardiff onto buses and drove us back to the station. A few of us managed to avoid the transport they laid on by using the usual blag that we'd driven up and the car was in the car park, and for once it was true. When the buses were on their way with a police escort, we spotted a small group of Northampton calling us up a sidestreet away from the Old Bill. We didn't need to be asked twice, and went running straight into them. Our numbers were pretty even and they gave it a good go, but eventually we started to get on top and they backed off. One of their boys was keen as mustard and wanted a one-on-one with me, so we made our way into another sidestreet while our boys ran the rest of Northampton's mob. Once we were alone, he put his hand in his back pocket and told me he was going to cut me. Obviously, I wasn't too keen for this to happen, but I was no mood to run either so I told him to go for it. Sometimes it gets you like that: you know that if you thought about it you'd have it on your toes, but you don't think and there's no fear – just the buzz. He went to pull out his blade and I just looked at it with a smile on my face; to this day, I don't know what an illiterate moron like him would be doing with a biro at a football match, but that's what he was waving at me. By the look on his face, I knew he'd pulled out the wrong tool. So I took my chance and went for him; he took a couple of good blows before he went down, but what with firmly keeping hold of his pen in one hand while trying to find his knife with the other, he didn't put up much of a fight. It was at this point that the police made an appearance, the sound of sirens getting louder as their van headed towards us. Now it was time to run. As I was having it on my toes, I looked behind to see if the Old Bill were giving chase. Luckily, they were too busy picking my new friend up off the road and putting him in the back of their van. A concealed weapon at a football match – now there was a naughty boy who wouldn't be sleeping in his own bed that night.

PAPER COSH TRICK
Peterborough v Cardiff City, 1st October 1986

Lee 'Tonto' Davies (CCFC): Away at Peterborough, we'd managed to get into their seats early and were waiting to see where it went from there. There was a while to go until kick-off, it was pretty empty (although it never really filled up at London Road) and it wasn't long before the dozen or so of us were spotted; neither did it take long for Peterborough to get a mob together and have a pop. Fighting in the seats was always tricky, so when they came at us we just stood our ground; they were unbalanced and falling over in their haste to have a go, so even before they reached us we had the upper hand. Then we attacked. As we went into them, I was more concerned with tripping over seats and going down than I was about the punches being thrown at me. That's when I got gassed. All I saw was a plume of white mist coming for my face; I instinctively scrunched up my eyes and covered them with my hands. Then I felt some punches and went down. I don't know if I'd been punched to the floor or had tripped over something, but I know that fighting with your eyes shut and your hands cupped over your face is not a tactic I'd recommend. While on the floor I took a right shoeing, but it didn't last long because the boys had seen me go down and had come to my rescue. I took my hands away from my face to pull myself up and began to open my eyes; as I did, there was no burning sensation. As they focused, the first thing I saw was torn newspaper over the floor – they'd done me with the old ripped-up-paper-in-the-face trick. Apart from a few bruises on my back, the only thing that was really hurt was my pride. Still, you live and learn, and on the bright side it did give the boys a reason to take the piss out of me for the rest of the season.

"HEARD OF THE SOUL CREW, PETERBOROUGH?"

Peterborough v Cardiff, 17th October 1987.

Chelsea Pat: Back in the mid-80's I used to knock about with a mob of Northern Chelsea from Middlesboro and Birmingham, who were double game and, over the years, got a big rep at Chelsea. However, fighting wasn't their only talent. These boys were expert in the art of breaking into fruit machines. This, however, was never my cup of tea. I never had the arsehole for thieving, and I'd rather fight ten geezers than steal a packet of Polos.

Anyway, a couple of mates of mine said they were going to Peterborough on a fruit machine tour and would I like to come? "Sure," I said, on the understanding that I was going to stay out of the mischief. "No problem," they said, so off we went. We arrived in Peterborough and settled down in a pub/hotel opposite the station. My two mates started to play the machine and, looking around, we were the only people in the bar besides a half-sleeping barman.

I settled down with my pint and gazed out of the window. I

remember looking up at the clock which said 11am above the station exit, and then I was distracted by a huge mob walking out through it. "Oi, who the fuck are these cunts?" I shouted as I ran to my two mates by the fruit machine. Before we could react, the unknown mob swarmed into the pub and, from being empty, it was now packed with over 300 lads. Anyway, due to our casual dress (if I remember correctly, duffle coats were a fashion, the type with the wide wooden buttons), we were soon surrounded by about ten lads. One of them was a big lump with red hair. "Heard of the Soul Crew, Peterborough?" he said.

"Nah, mate, wrong mob, we're Chelsea," I said.

"What are you lot doing down here?" said another taffy.

"We've come to see Annis, he's a mate of mine," I said.

"Okay, I don't think he's here yet, but you're more than welcome to come with us," said another lump.

"Cheers, mate." Thank fuck it was Cardiff who walked in the pub, as I knew a few of them and if it had been anyone else we could have been in trouble.

Anyway, as we were giving out the introductions, Brummie Andy said, "As you're all here, you couldn't stand around this fruit machine while we break into it? We'll give you a drink."

The taffs didn't need asking twice. *Crack! Bang!* And the next thing the drinks were on us. Our newfound Welsh friends invited us to go to the game with them and meet up with Annis. As we were leaving the pub, I got a tap on the shoulder. It was my old mate from Cardiff, Fisher, who was a mate of Nicky Parsons who I knew at Chelsea. Fisher told me that he and Parsons had recently fallen out, resulting in a fight. That was their business, but it was good to see Fisher as he was a proper boy and as game as anyone.

When we got to the ground, all the Cardiff mob had seat tickets and, as we didn't, we told them we'd meet afterwards for a drink. As we were stood there another mob of about 60 Cardiff turned up, led by my old mates Zeddie and Dyo. Zeddie used to come to Chelsea with me now and again and I'd regard him as a good mate. He's now on the straight and narrow and you'd never believe, looking at him now, how much he loved a footie tear-up. He was a right chap in his day. Anyway, we got talked into going into the ground with them, and the first thing I noticed was that this little mob weren't as friendly as the Cardiff mob from the pub. "Argentina! Argentina!" they chanted, and a few glanced over at us. This didn't go down well with my mates. "Come on, Pat," they said, "let's fuck off. I don't want to listen to this shit, we've just been in a war with Argentina." As we were discussing it, my mate Zeddie came over, ashen-faced.

"Pat, I'm so sorry," he said, "but you lot better leave, because they are talking about serving you lot up."

"It's okay, Zeddie, we won't put it on you, mate. We were leaving anyway."

As we were leaving, the main mouthpiece of this group came out of the toilet and fucking withered as we all stared at him. I'm sure he pissed his jeans, as he couldn't get back up into the terrace without walking through us. But we're not liberty takers, so we just laughed at him as he ran past us. And you know what? I've never seen him since.

Outside, we walked around to the Peterborough end behind the opposite goal. As you looked from the home end, Cardiff's main mob was up in the seats to our right, about 300-handed. The away end directly opposite had an open terrace on our right, which contained about 50 Peterborough casuals plotted up next to the away end. We hung around to see what might happen. At the end of the game, Cardiff steamed out of the seats and charged straight across the pitch to the small mob of Peterborough facing them. Peterborough ran down to the wall and stood until the last few seconds, as Cardiff climbed the wall. With that, Peterborough turned and ran out the back of the stand. Then the Cardiff mob turned their attention to us but, luckily, the Old Bill made a line in front of us. Cardiff then went on their usual rampage. On our way back to the station, we bumped into Fisher and the big redheaded lad from the pub. They said they'd seen Annis in a car and he'd been looking for me. When I told them what had happened in the away end, they went mental.

"Who were they, Pat? Fucking point them out!"

"It doesn't matter, no one got hurt, so forget it," I said.

"It does matter," said the redheaded lad. "Those bully cunts tried to take liberties with four blokes. Promise me, Pat, if you see them, point them out."

"Okay," I said, but there was no way I was going to do that.

We reached the station without further incident and said goodbye to our newfound friends. On the way back to London we all laughed, as we promised ourselves to make sure we checked the fixture list before any more unplanned weekends away.

THEY WERE AS GAME AS FUCK
Peterborough v Cardiff City, FA Cup, 14th November 1987

Taffy Anton (CCFC): One of my best experiences of the 80's was Peterborough away in the FA Cup third round. We left Port Talbot in a van about 8am, with some of the rest of the PVM following us. There were a solid 20 of us: Vince, Guff, Nigel H, etc. We got to Posh about 12 noon and, as we walked over the bridge by the ground towards the town, we bumped into about 20 of their lads and had a bit of a standoff with them, nothing really to write home about as the Old Bill did the usual thing. Through the town Cardiff were everywhere; pubs were packed full of lads from all over South Wales; near kick-off we all made our way to the ground, bumping into quite a few of the lads who had now moved to London. The match started with a cup atmosphere and, as usual, Cardiff let their massive support down. When we were losing 2-1, with about five minutes to go, I decided to leave the terrace. As I got to the turnstile to go out, I pushed it and found that the doors opened. I rushed back in and shouted to the boys, "Come on, the gates are open!" With that, a good 50 of us left and bowled around to the home supporters' side terrace. We were soon on the side of the terrace by the pitch, but – can you believe it? – we weren't attacked by their lads. We actually got attacked by old men with their umbrellas and shirties shouting at us to get out. Before we knew it, a few of us were actually injured by fists, boots and umbrellas, I can even remember Darryl being knocked to the floor. Fair play, in their younger days they must have been good lads.

Eventually we stormed onto the pitch and ran towards the

main home end, goading the Posh lads behind the goal. I'll give them their due, they climbed over the fence and confronted us head on. On the pitch we fought a running battle for a good five minutes. What a buzz! They were as game as fuck.

Little was I to know that, two weeks later, I'd get a dawn raid from the Posh police. Me, Nigel H, Jammo, Mikey Dye, Billy and some of the original Soul Crew, Gethin etc, all ended up nicked for it. I ended up with a one-year ban, which in those days was a lot, and 60 hours community service. Hee hee! I miss the good old days.

THE ZULUS
Birmingham v Cardiff City, 14th October 1989
Joe (CCFC): I am from the northern city suburbs of Cardiff and started following Cardiff City in 1983, when I was a young teenager. Back then we were in the old Division Two. I would look forward to games against the likes of Man City, Newcastle and Chelsea, as they always brought large away support and contributed to an amazing atmosphere at Ninian Park. We would often see our attendances double in size at these prestigious games.

I initially attended every home league game with my uncle, wearing my beloved City scarf. I would stand on the cold Bob Bank terraces and can often remember watching a section of supporters in the Canton stand, which would usually be between 150 and 200 young casuals. (I later found out that they were the young Soul Crew.) I was intrigued by their behaviour, fashion and witty songs.

The first incident that affected me was against Leeds United, in September 1984, when my uncle's car had its windows smashed. Ironically, it was not the away fans but the home fans who did it, and the sole reason was because his car had a Leeds number plate. From that moment on, the other side of football intrigued me more.

As I grew older, I started to go to Ninian with my friends – Julian, Popeye, Paddy, Dog and Jacko – leaving the City scarf at home. I had become more aware of the terrace culture and fashions, and wanted to get more involved.

Over the next few seasons I gradually became more involved with the trouble associated with Cardiff City, while following my beloved Bluebirds.

Birmingham City (the Zulus)

Annis and Mojo arranged two coaches for the Birmingham City away game, one was filled with guys from the docks and the other with Cardiff, Valley and Barry boys. Although I arrived early for that evening's game, the coaches didn't leave till 6pm because of internal strife – mainly Cardiff fans refusing to pay on Mojo's coach. Annis's coach was all up and running, lads paid up and driver happy, whereas everyone on Mojo's coach seemed to want to take the piss out of him. Mojo has come a long way since then, as he now represents the lads in court as a criminal solicitor and has even become a FIFA agent with a lot of Cardiff players, amongst others, on his books. But back then, Annis had to come on Mojo's coach and in the end everyone paid. Happy days, we were off and running.

We travelled up in eager, yet nervous anticipation, as we all knew Birmingham had a fearsome reputation both on and off the field and would be more than a match for our relatively young firm. One of my mates, Brummie (Steven), knew the area very well, as he was originally from Birmingham and directed our two coaches to Digbeth. For anyone who hasn't seen this part of Birmingham, it's rundown and just behind the Bull Ring. It'd been through a period of neglect and many of the buildings were derelict. However, some of the city's oldest pubs can be found in this part of the city. The whole area was extremely dark, dreary and industrialised, which only added to the tension and anticipation of the possible events that evening.

As kick-off was fast approaching, 100 of us decided to park in Digbeth and walk the 1.5 miles through the cold, dreary backstreets of old Birmingham to St Andrew's Stadium, home to Birmingham City. On the way we encountered small groups of Birmingham fans, but they were easily chased off and did not put up much resistance.

As we approached the ground, the game had already kicked

off and a few of the main lads suggested we should attempt to enter the Spion Kop stand, a large terraced area for the home fans. We thought this suicide mission was a good idea and would only enhance our growing reputation if we managed to get a result against such a fearsome firm.

We made our way across the gravelled façade, arming ourselves with bricks and debris, ready for the inevitable confrontation. Viking, Annis, Jonathan, Little Collin and a couple of other lads were going through the turnstiles. If I'm honest, a lot of other Cardiff didn't seem up for it and stood well back, singing, "We're the famous football hooligans!" and Cardiff City songs, which not only brought the attention of the Zulus but also let the Old Bill know we were there. The few who were already in the turnstiles were then attacked by dozens of Birmingham and had no other choice but to retreat.

We charged across the façade, throwing various items at the Birmingham mob, to help the lads by the turnstiles who'd managed to catch the Brums offguard. They quickly retreated back into the home section and only a few blows were thrown between the rival fans. We were rapidly gaining confidence but, not to be outdone, it didn't take the Zulus long to realise we were low on numbers in comparison. They quickly began to fight back and again several blows were exchanged. Then, almost as quickly as the event unfolded, it died down as the police baton-charged; a few of our guys sustained injuries, but in the scheme of things we were lucky. Given our numbers we had obtained a result and, again, our reputation was on the up. But, in all honesty, the mass numbers the Brums had down at the turnstiles would have eventually done us. We were starting to feel that we were not a firm to be messed with, as we'd gained the upperhand on other occasions, seeing off firms such as Wolves, Bolton Wanderers and Exeter.

We thought the night's events were over, especially as the police were aware of our presence, but both us and the police were very wrong. During the match, which was attended by 600 City fans, 12 of our group had decided to leave the ground about five minutes from the end of the game and look for the notorious Birmingham Zulu firm They were not to be disappointed. Some of the 12 consisted of Little Collin, Jammo, Annis, Jellyhead, Brummie, C Beer and Darryl. We all tried to follow them but were soon stopped by the Old Bill.

When the game finished and they let us out, we all turned left and said to the Old Bill that our transport was down there. We could hear shouting in the distance and, with that, Brummie Steve came running back saying our lot needed help and were taking a bit of a pasting. We all tried to force our way through the Old Bill, to no avail, but we were soon able to get down to our boys when half our Old Bill left us to rush down and stop the fighting. As we got down to the other side of the stadium our small group were surrounded by Old Bill; they weren't being arrested but helped back. The area was now completely under control by the police and our lot looked like they had just been at General Custer's last stand.

Our small group sustained many injuries, but one guy who sticks out in my mind was Little Collin, both of whose eyes were pumping blood out. Apparently, when about 60 Zulus had charged at our 12, he ran on his own straight into the middle of them. Annis and Jellyhead had gone in to help him, but Collin by this time had fought about six of them on his own and had taken some real punishment for his madness. Jammo and Jellyhead had been knocked to the floor and stamped on, all of them had sustained injuries. They had been done, but they were all laughing about it when we finally managed to regroup. The lads wanted revenge and, on our walk back to Digbeth, at any point that the lads saw any Brums, they flew through the police escort and had a couple on their toes.

When we got down to Digbeth, the Zulus were standing around all over the place. Our lot got smacked back a number of times by the Old Bill, with the Zulus smiling and laughing at us, which got us more wound up. A few charges and roars went up and the Viking went mental, fuming that he hadn't been there earlier. He, in particular, wanted revenge for his mates. Eventually, the police managed to gain complete control of the situation; we were ordered back to our coaches and escorted back the 100 miles to South Wales.

The feelings on the coaches were of relief and exhilaration. We knew deep down that the Zulus had won the night, but they can never say we didn't take it to them and we felt our reputation was enhanced once more.

A HILL TOO FAR

Northampton v Cardiff, 14th May 1998

Frankie D (CCFC): I've been frequenting Ninian Park since the age of 11, in the days of the old Grange End. I am now 43 and reflecting on a hooligan past where I have been banned from watching games, cautioned, thrown out of grounds and made six court appearances. I have seen some nasty and extremely ugly incidents over the years. Although not the worst, Northampton in the 1997/98 season sticks in my mind.

I think it was primarily because it was Northampton, who do not have a history of football-related violence. It was a hot day in Northampton. We had travelled there for the League Two play-off semi-finals' second leg. We needed to win to get to Wembley. The ground held 8000; our allocation was 1500, which would include 500 lads. We left Cardiff around 9am for a 7.45 kick-off, leaving us plenty of time to look around the place and find a suitable pub. Our minibus was full: 16 lads, all game, all dressers, and all veterans of football-related disorder. It was a while ago, but the names I remember are Rawlings, Alan, Emlyn, Little Collin, Patrick, Annis, Frankie D and Huw Boy. Apologies for leaving anyone out due to different faces being on different trips. A sell-out crowd at Northampton was easily expected, as it was a crucial game set to bring out Northampton's best mob ever. The excitement was unbearable. We got into Northampton around 2pm; we quickly looked for a pub close enough to the ground but not close enough to attract the attention of the OB. We found a suitable pub sometime later. A couple of Cardiff scarfers came in and said they had been chased by a mob of Northampton from a pub perhaps half a mile away. It was not 30 seconds before we were in the van, vexed and ready to confront Northampton for the first time today. We left the van in the middle of the road and headed for the pub doors; it was not long before we were spotted and an estimated 100 Northampton came out. We were not deterred by this, continuing our charge towards them only to be pelted by bottles and glasses. Little Collin got the closest, only to retreat under the hail of missiles.

I was surprised by their action as this was a perfect chance to give some of Cardiff's top boys a good kicking, bearing in mind the numbers: seven to one. We stayed our ground until the police arrived on horseback and with dog handlers. In a way they saved us from being cut to pieces. We made our way to the van as quickly as possible to avoid any confrontation with the police. A funny moment came as Huw Boy chased the van wearing a white shirt covered in blood, tearing it off so as not to attract the OB's attention.

We knew the OB would come after us, so we needed to get the booze off the van. We travelled perhaps a quarter of a mile and got out with the cans and started walking. We knew if the cans stayed on and the van was searched, this would be a perfect opportunity to send us back to Cardiff. The driver stayed with the van and was pulled by the police, who did a stop and search looking for anything incriminating. They found nothing and let him go too. We walked to a large grass area where 20 known Cardiff casuals from Ebbw Vale were sitting. We told them about our incident at the pub; they too had had a confrontation with the same group. We sat together discussing our course of action, as revenge was necessary. As time passed more Cardiff joined us, our numbers were swelling but time was pressing on. I was getting very restless and walked off alone to do a bit of spotting. I arrived at a kind of retail park with different branded burger outlets, etc. Then I found a pub that had a few doormen. I was convinced this had to be where they were. I approached confidently so as not to attract attention. The doormen asked me what team I supported. In my best Northamptonshire accent I said, "Northampton." The pub didn't look big from the outside, but as I got inside I'd estimate it to hold a thousand. It was packed.

I took a good look around, as if I were looking for someone. There were really loud chants of "England!", and lads standing on tables waving flags. They were obviously excited and no doubt saw this as England v Wales as much as Northampton v

Cardiff. This raised my suspicion very quickly that we may not be dealing with Northampton. This was a mob of around 500 good lads, probably cockney lads that came along for a pop at Cardiff. It was not long before I left this highly-charged and intimidating atmosphere. This was their mob, all grouped up, so this was where we had to come for the off. I made my way back to the grass area to tell the lads what I'd found. They quickly got up onto their feet, by this time we had about 60. "Come on, Cardiff, let's do it!" We left like a pack of wolves. It was a real buzz. We didn't have to walk far: 300 of them were heading towards us. It was our first toe-to-toe of the day. Outnumbered again, we charged towards them; punches and kicks were exchanged, then it was like the Grand National, with police horses everywhere. The police pushed us back down the hill. This turned in our favour, as Simmo's coach had just arrived. It swelled our numbers and made things a little fairer. It was kicking off everywhere. We chased Northampton away; the OB had now regrouped and baton-charged us to the turnstiles. They were not messing, so into the ground we went.

In the ground there was a lot of chanting. It was a real cup-tie atmosphere, with a real buzz of expectancy from both sides. We were 1-0 down from the first leg and 1-0 on the night. The game was not in our favour, so a result off the pitch was on our minds. As the game went on, the OB started to put on their riot gear. No doubt they'd sensed the mood. They began to remove all the advertising boards – something I can honestly say I've never seen before.

Lakey got about 30 of his lads. They were making their way to their end; we followed. The OB didn't catch on straight away, but when they did they locked the gates and stopped more Cardiff leaving. About 40 of us managed to get out. It wasn't enough, but we had no option. We walked around to their end. The OB had other ideas, and headed us towards a grass bank where some 800 ticketless Northampton were watching the game. It was inevitable we would get a good row. This was a situation where most teams would run. We didn't. We are Cardiff and we are fearless. This was one of the best positions a hooligan could find himself in: a mob right in front of you; the adrenalin pumping. A standoff ensued, our 40 to their 150. Then Annis steamed in. Around five Northampton attacked him. I backed him up, it kicked off. There were bodies everywhere. It seemed to go on forever, it was one of my most memorable toe-to-toes ever.

It was inevitable that the numbers would get the better of us, and we were forced down the hill. It was a scrap that was to leave us battered and bruised, but it wasn't over. We then regrouped and charged back up the hill towards them. Anyone that's been to Northampton will know how steep this hill is, we were knackered just climbing it. We then had our second toe-to-toe in our small numbers. We gave it our best shot, but we did get done. Once again we were forced back down the hill. We were exhausted. I remember Emlyn shouting, "Come on, lads, one more time!" Up the hill we went, we were like a depleted army but we were not going to lose face.

I remember making my third trip up the hill when, from a distance, we heard chants of "Soul Crew!" The game had finished and the gates were open. We gained instant strength; it was now kicking off everywhere and Northampton were running. But there always seemed to be smaller Northampton mobs appearing. The battles went on for around half an hour before the police finally took control.

I got back to the minibus, where I was greeted by ripped shirts, cuts and bruises. It was a good day out. We left Northampton and headed home. We stopped on the way at a pub in Silverstone, where we sat down and discussed the day's events. We virtually all admitted that, if it were a boxing match, then Northampton would have beaten our 40 on the hill on points. But we were convinced that it was not Northampton. We know that London mobs turn up anywhere they can to take on Cardiff, and Northampton wouldn't have that good a mob. But I feel our 40 can hold their heads up.

HOOLIGANS IN UNIFORM
Stoke v Cardiff, 30th April 2000
Big Sam (CCFC): I will give you my version of the events when my club, Cardiff City, played Stoke City in a promotion/

relegation clash in April 2000. I was one of the thousands of Cardiff fans who travelled that day – including very many from the valleys of South Wales, where Cardiff have a huge following, Merthyr, Rhondda, Aberdare, Pontypridd, Tredegar, Rhymney, Ebbw Vale, Mountain Ash, Maesteg, all big valley towns with big Cardiff followings. This is our version of the events that took place that day – no lies, no bullshit, just the truth of how we were treated by a police force who were a disgrace to their uniform, and the South Wales press and TV companies who, in their own way, were just as bad as the police. Wankers, the lot of them!

The people who were at the Stoke game that day have all got similar stories to tell. I just happened to have been asked to tell mine, with a little help from a few of my mates. So here we go then, make of it what you will.

"Right lads, we've all got to go! Another fucking relegation battle on behalf of our beloved Cardiff City!" This time we were playing Stoke City, who were going for promotion big-time. If we got relegated it was back to the dungeon: Division Four for us old bastards for, what, the third, fourth or fifth time? God knows, I've lost count of how many relegations we've had over the years. Apart from being a top Division One team, Stoke have got a well-respected firm, 'the Naughty 40', respected not just by Cardiff but by everyone who knows anything about football lads. So for this one everyone had to get off their arses: off we jolly well go!

The game itself was put back to a Sunday afternoon, with a 2pm kick-off on police advice in case of trouble. The funny thing was that most of the trouble would be caused inadvertently by the police themselves – the wankers! As the game was on a Sunday, most of the Valley lads couldn't get to Cardiff early for the trains. You've got more chance of winning the lottery than getting a train early to Cardiff on a Sunday morning, never mind getting one back home. So it was coaches for us lot, and loads of them. I spoke to my great mate Desy from Barry, and they were taking coaches as well. It had all the makings of a very interesting day.

Years ago, the Valleys and Cardiff lads never used to get on. I personally used to hate that, but it's different now. Thank fuck, as we all support the City, but the Barry lads and us have always been great mates and always will. Many of the Valley boys are ex-miners, ex-steelworkers, ex-everything because everything's been fucking shut down. South Wales in general is a working-class area and not very affluent at that. There is a huge support for the City in the Valleys and most of the lads don't give a fuck about anything else except the City, beer, women and a tear-up. There is fuck-all else to do. Watching the City, good or bad (mostly bad), is still a release from everyday things, and I should imagine it's the same at working-class clubs like Stoke, Millwall, Pompey, Boro, Wolves, WHU, Sheff Wed and United, Sunderland, Hull, etc. Myself, personally, I've always felt cheated by my club, the police, the Welsh FA, the media – especially the fucking one-eyed, rugby-orientated, bullshitting Welsh media – my club, for selling any decent players we ever had, and various chairmen for shafting us big-time. Then there's the police for treating us like fucking terrorists – I've lost count of the 'bubble' games we've had, it's no wonder we've played up over the years. The Welsh FA are a sack of shit – the sooner we come under the English FA umbrella the better – and as for the Welsh media, they're obsessed with the egg (rugby) and slate my club and our fans for any little incident. The reason for this little rant will become clearer as the day at Stoke unfolds.

We had two coaches from Merthyr, all the usual suspects were there: Meathead, the Neck, Bonker, Ritchy, Mad Jack Lewis, Taylor, Ted, Sapic, Carlton, the Foley Clan, Stud, Hooker (who has sadly passed away since), Skull and his crew, and many of the Valley Soul Crew lads. On the way, we met many other coaches from all over South Wales. The weather was fine and everyone was confident of what we were about to face, but some of the actions of this particular police force surprised even the more experienced campaigners amongst the lads.

Off we go then: we leave Merthyr on the Heads of the Valleys Road, M50, M5, M6. Everyone on the coach is bouncing. Bonker gets up and says, "Anyone who runs gets a fucking kicking and can fucking walk home." Everyone laughs. "Let's have it!" We can't wait to get to Stoke. We get calls on our phones to say the Old Bill are waiting for us, so we take out coaches off the motorway to a place called Stone. We find a boozer called the Poste and we have a few beers in there. There's no trouble, it's nice and quiet, as it was shut when we got there early. After an hour or so we mount up and head for Stoke. As we get off the motorway there are a number of roundabouts. As we approach one of these we see fucking hundreds of police. There are Cardiff coaches and vans in the lay-bys, and on the inside lane, as far as you can see, the police are everywhere – and I mean everywhere.

The police were holding us in a lay-by, hard shoulder and inside lane of a dual carriageway. I don't really know how many coaches or vans were there, but there were loads. We must have been held there for 20-30 minutes, and everyone was getting really angry with the police when they started to move us out. But at least we were on our way. As we approached another roundabout, the Britannia Stadium was straight over but all the coaches and vans and the law turned right. Where the fuck were we going now? By now it's around 1.30pm, the game kicks off in 30 minutes. The law then directed all coaches and vans into a huge compound/waste ground at a place called Trentham Gardens. The number of police there was unbelievable and the vast majority of them were in full riot gear. You could only see the tossers' eyes. This place was like an internment camp for terrorists or illegal immigrants, the nearest thing to ethnic cleansing without being fucking shot! There must have been 7-800 of us, probably more. They had this metal detector like they use at the airport where you walk through and an alarm goes off. This detector was placed in the middle of the waste ground. The police were obviously hoping that we'd all walk through – all 800 of us, mind – and that they'd find knives, axes, machetes, guns, rocket launchers and maybe a fucking tank, the stupid twats!

Our bus was way back in the queue and there was no way we were going to make the kick-off, as it was 2pm already. A copper got on the bus and told us that the kick-off had been delayed for

30 minutes. On some of the coaches upfront, the lads started piling off, stripping off and running bollock naked through the metal detector. It was fucking hilarious, and mad at the same time. As this was happening, Des from Barry jumped on our bus to say we were 1-0 down in the game – which the Old Bill had said was put back 30 minutes, the lying bastards! *Fuck this!* Everyone piled off the coaches and vans. It went potty. For all their armour, no one gave a fuck about the police. It was chaos for a while. After what seemed like an age, but was probably only minutes, a no-man's land appeared. (How the hell that happened, I haven't got a clue.) An inspector told us to get on the transporters and they would take us to the ground. He got called every name under the sun and claimed there had been 'a misunderstanding', 'wrong information', etc. Now we may not be the most intelligent set of fans, but for fuck's sake, how thick do they think we really are? The lying twats!

On one of the vans they found some tools. It was the guy's work van and I know him well. He's from Aberdare and he'd forgotten to empty it – a bit dopey, but it happens. They found Stanley blades, hammers, shovels and a fucking huge disk cutter. The law and press later had a field day with the disk cutter incident, but the cutter was as big as the bloke that owned it. How the hell could he get it through the turnstile and, if by some act of God he did, what was he going to do with it in the ground? Chop a fucking stand down? I ask you . . .

Anyway, we eventually got to the Britannia Stadium. It was half-time, fucking great, 1-0 down, could it get any worse? Well, it sure could, and it would. We got off the coaches and vans and we got searched again. "Fuck me, are they all queer up here or something?" At the same time the lads on the trains were arriving. They had had similar problems to us. There were around 400 of them, so with our lot there must have been 1200-1300 Cardiff outside the ground at half-time, and people wonder why we got angry. Finally in the ground, the second half had already started and we were still 1-0, staring relegation in the face again, but I don't think most of our lads gave a toss after the way we were treated by the law. There was a lot of posturing and gesturing, and a few surges by both sets of lads during the second half, but nothing really happened. One incident summed up the day so far, and the police attitude in particular. We went 2-0 down but managed to pull a goal back, 2-1, and we were on top when we had a corner with five-ten minutes to go. A wall of riot police were facing us all along the byline and Andy Legg, City's fullback, could not take the corner because a fucking great big police horse stood on the corner flag, and the twat would not move. We were all waiting for the horse to cross the ball. We lost 2-1.

Everyone was in a foul mood and out we went. Anyone who has been to the Britannia Stadium will know that the coaches, vans, etc, are parked in a compound which is fenced up all the way around as you come out of the ground. To the left there is a high bank, maybe 40 feet above the compound. A lot of the Stoke fans were up there, chucking objects into the packed solid compound. A few of us got to the perimeter fencing, trying to pull it down. A few of the Stoke lads were trying to get it down as well, but the riot police waded in. Me and Bonker got battered by their truncheons. I had my kneecap split open and I was gassed. Bonker got truncheoned on his back and head, and got gassed. Then it really kicked off. The lads had had enough of the riot police and attacked them, scattering them everywhere. The police regrouped and attacked Cardiff, driving the lads back. It was total chaos. This time, Cardiff got organised and attacked the riot police again, driving them up the banking and along the top of the fence. The riot police were on their toes, the horrible bastards got what they fucking deserved! Hours later, everyone was rounded up and put on buses, vans or trains out of Stoke. One amazing thing about the day: I don't think there was one punch thrown between any Cardiff or Stoke lads.

Finally, to round off a really mad day, our coach was on the Heads of the Valleys Road, approaching Merthyr on the way home, when it caught fire. The back wheels were ablaze and the driver only pulled into a petrol station. Jesus Christ, how dumb is that? I've never seen 50 lads get off a coach so quickly in all my life, we were like rats leaving a sinking ship. Out through the emergency door, the shithouse door, the sunroof – it was abandon ship time. Looking back, we laugh about it now but at the time we were shitting ourselves.

The next few days and weeks, our fans got slaughtered in the press and on local TV. I also believe Stoke fans had the same bad press, but the truth of the matter is that the policing that day was of the lowest calibre. In our opinion they were to blame for 90% of the problem: their attitude, their ignorance, their lies and their complete mismanagement, along with their bully-boy tactics, caused the chaotic scenes at Trentham Gardens and the Britannia Stadium. They were nothing but a disgrace to their uniform.

Ten months later the arrests started. I personally had a dawn raid. Seven charming officers, two of whom were from Stoke, came through my front door, took me to Llanishen nick, charged and bailed me. I'm not 100 per cent sure, but around 60-70 got raided. But the real sickener was our glamorous South Wales press printing mugshots of Cardiff supporters on the front pages of their papers for days. I always thought you were innocent in this country until proven guilty. Again, I'm led to believe the Stoke lads had the same treatment as our lot. Isn't it strange: two working-class sets of fans treated like shit?

The South Wales press were a disgrace. Good people lost their jobs due to wankers, and when it came to court some of the banning orders were unreal: anything from three-ten years, and for what? For complete mismanagement by a pig of a police force that treated us (and probably the Stoke lads) like shit and with a complete disregard for our human rights. No wonder the lads reacted like they did.

Cardiff also lost and got relegated three days later – again! Stoke went up, and both sets of fans got hammered in the courts and press. They called it one of the worst cases of football violence ever, when in truth the biggest hooligans that day were the fucking police.

THE ZULUS IN CARDIFF FOR THE 2001 WORTHINGTON CUP FINAL

Sooty Jason (Zulu, Birmingham City): Firstly, I would like to thank Annis for the chance to give my views on the disorder between the Zulus and the Soul Crew. Although I have not had the chance to meet Annis, I have spoken to him a number of times over the phone thanks to a good friend of mine, Chelsea Pat, who I've known for a number of years.

2001 saw Birmingham City play Liverpool in the Worthington Cup at the Millennium Stadium. We set off for South Wales in the car around midday; calls were made to say that there was already a good firm of Zulus in Cardiff. After arriving in Cardiff around 2.30pm, it wasn't long before we were spotted by some of the Soul Crew. "Birmingham, are we?" said one.

"Yeah, I'm Birmingham."

"Well, your lot are in the RSVP Bar up the road. We'll see you lot later." Knowing the Zulus were going to be in Cardiff in big numbers, the Soul Crew were ready for us.

The afternoon passed off without any major trouble and by early evening we were easily 300-handed. Ten of us walked through the shopping centre and bumped into a few Cardiff lads. The chant went up: "*Zuulluu.*" A handful of punches were exchanged and a couple of bins thrown; the police came in with their batons. Due to a heavy police presence, it was hard for the Soul Crew to get into the centre of Cardiff where the Zulus were drinking. So they had to wait till late evening.

During the evening, a few pubs got smashed and a policewoman got hurt as the Zulus fought with the police at the Philharmonic pub. Shortly after, a number of Zulus who were in a pub drinking with a few Liverpool fans were attacked by a group of Cardiff hooligans. The fighting spilled out into the street, till riot police came into force to split both groups apart, which led to many arrests. Throughout the night, incidents took place with the Zulus attacking both police and locals. I remember walking through Cardiff with a small group of the younger Zulus when we heard, "ZULU!" and the sound of smashing glass. We ran to a pub on the corner where it had kicked off with the Soul Crew. Bottles were thrown till the police arrived in number and separated both groups, using dogs and batons. Battles like this were constant throughout the night.

After I got split up from my group, I walked up a road next

to a group of lads who just happened to be Cardiff. I was on my own and expected a kicking. But the one Cardiff lad who to this day has become a good friend of mine, named Peter, said I was okay and that they were "not bullies". I was then taken to a pub where there was a large group of Soul Crew; due to the incidents that had gone on throughout the night, I was very nervous at first, but I became relaxed in their company. I now have a lot of respect for the Soul Crew. You could see Cardiff were well up for it. But I would like to finish off by saying how well I was looked after that night. Although I wasn't involved in any of the disorder, many a time I've heard stories retold by other well-known Zulus from that fateful night. The Soul Crew are without a doubt one of the best firms in the country, and many Zulus have a lot of respect for them due to three decades of similar incidents. The aforementioned is what I witnessed of the day in question.

MAID MARION WAY
Nottingham Forest v Cardiff City, 23rd August 2003
Jonathan Evans (CCFC): We've got some naughty villains in our crew, so it would be a good battle if we ever met head on with other firms like Man Utd, Chelsea and Birmingham. I've met a lot of good boys over the years, especially in jail, I was once down the block in Dartmoor for a few months on G.O.A.D. [good order and discipline infraction], and got quite friendly with a lad from Derby. He used to tell me about the rivalry with Forest and admitted they had a good firm, so when we went to Forest I half expected a good row. We went by car and met in the Robin Hood, about two miles outside the city. One of the boys was talking the usual bollocks to a lad from Forest: "How many you got? Where are you?" I grabbed the phone off one of ours and asked the Forest lad, "Where the fuck do you want us to go?" "Maid Marion Way," he told me. "Okay, right, we'll be there." We got a good mob of 70 together that day, all good faces. There were a few chats about what to do and where to go; I was in a people carrier with seven of our lot, Viking was with me. So I got us all ready and

said, "We're here now, it's what we've come for, they've called it on and we're going!" So a convoy of cars set off, we were the lead car, and as we were driving into their city centre I could see their mob in the distance crossing the road, about 250 strong. We got clocked, so I made the driver park up bang on Maid Marion Way. *Perfect*, I thought.

I look around and the rest of the convoy misses our turn, so only three cars pull into the car park. I don't give a fuck, so out we get. I walk straight out of the car park and over to Forest, the Viking is right behind me, the police quickly come between us and them, and with that another mob of Forest come up behind us. *Bang!* We're over the metal barriers, straight into them; there are about 15 of us, all good boys, so we're not worried about numbers. As we steam towards them they back off straight away, they have about 50 of them but no bottle, and as we're going into them there's our police spotter (Potatohead) fronting them. Suddenly, their lumpers feel a bit brave and start bouncing around; we give it to them and it soon sends the rest packing. (Their papers will show them covered in blood, looking well done.) The 15 of us are rounded up, put in a bubble and marched to the ground. We meet up with the rest of the convoy, they're gutted that they missed it but I think a few were glad they took the wrong turn. They know who they are and I've told them what I thought of them.

After the game, Forest came out on the bridge and surrounded Annis, his missus and two mates: 50 onto three lads and a girl, fuck me, that's brave! They even had his missus by the throat but, thanks to Taffy Anton and his little crew – who hadn't been to the game and were just coincidentally walking across the road – steaming straight into Forest and backing them off, those three lads and a girl were prevented from getting a hammering. They knew where we were parked too, and the brave bastards did our windows and tyres while we were at the ground. It was perfect for us really, because we had to stay a bit longer. As we were standing by our three cars, we got chatting to a few Forest boys; they said how good they thought we were and that they would try and bring it to us at Cardiff. As we were speaking, there was a roar from a sidestreet and about 60 lads came steaming at us. The cunts had kept us talking while they got their lads together.

At this time there was one copper between us. Once again we went straight at them; they stopped dead in their tracks, like they'd hit an invisible wall, and then started to bounce around. (I hate that crap.) Then, the strangest thing that I've ever heard of at a football match occurred. As they backed away from us, one or two of them were saying, "They're too big, they're too big." These weren't kids, mind, but part of their main firm. I know we had some big lads there that day – the Viking is six foot three and I'm nearly 17 stone – but fuck me, what's all that about? It rattled my head. They didn't want to know, no bottle whatsoever, those Forest lads, and as for them coming to Cardiff – not a chance, total bullshit. I read that Boatsy said they had over 400 – well, they must be the invisible men, because no one had seen a mob that size all day. They had 25 in a pub on the way into the city centre, and when a carload of our lads found them and said, "Wait here, we'll be back," they were gone like a flash. That big firm they talk about was no more than 80 on the train, and happy to be in a bubble.

WE DON'T MAKE THESE DECISIONS
West Brom v Cardiff, 14th February 2004
Big Gwyn (CCFC): Then there was West Brom away. Now the game I'm referring to took place at the Hawthorns in the 2003-2004 season – I think. I have never been one for stats such as dates and scores, etc, from games played previously, and unless something totally dramatic happened on the pitch in that particular game, then I have serious problems remembering anything about it. I can't even put it down to my age because I've always been the same.

However, if something happened with regard to the fans, then usually it's stored in the memory banks for the long term. That doesn't just mean remembering the trouble that might have broken out, but also the craic that occurs amongst the fans, such as where I was when I first heard a particular chant, or saw someone in a mad outfit, or things like Ronnie Rock at Tranmere (a well known lad who is harmless but drunk more often than sober). I had gone down to the concourse under the stand at half-time, to see Ronnie up against a wall with a copper facing him. The copper had both his hands on Ronnie's shoulders, holding him against the wall, and I thought, *Oh fuck, what's he done now?*

I approached the copper in a nice, conciliatory manner, trying not to make things worse than they were, and said, "Everything okay, officer? If Ronnie is playing up, I'll sort him out and get him away from here, even put him on the bus if he's causing problems," trying my best to stop him getting arrested and possibly banned. The copper smiled at me and replied, "I ain't arresting him, mate, I'm just holding him up," and as he started removing his hands off Ronnie's shoulders you could see Ronnie sliding down the wall with both his eyes spinning and his legs collapsing, like Bambi on ice. Fucking priceless!

Anyway, back to West Brom: this game, due to the West Midlands police's wisdom, had been changed to an 11am kick-off. Again, there was no consultation with supporters groups, etc, just a case of, "This is what we are doing. Take it or leave it." Well, lots of people left it – but I don't mean that they left it by giving the game a miss, what they left was the organised travel on the coaches, which had been proving so successful at so many other clubs we'd visited.

Part of the reason the police had arrived at this early kick-off time was to stop our fans getting up there early hours and drinking in all the pubs in West Bromwich. Now if they'd have spoken to us in advance, we'd have explained that we could arrange, as we had done at lots of other clubs, to stop well outside the city, along the route at such places as Tewkesbury, Worcester, Bromsgrove, etc, in pubs that were glad to welcome us and would often ring me in advance to bring the till-swelling revenue that we provided with such gusto. We would then happily turn up at their allotted rendezvous point for an escort en masse to the stadium, job done and quite straightforward.

What the forward thinking brains of Britain's finest police force hadn't worked out was that this early kick-off would lead to loads of our fans saying, *Fuck them, we'll make our own way up* (mostly by train), and either stay up there for a good drink afterwards, or wander into the centre of Birmingham and hang about New Street station, having a scout about for any likely lads passing through, as so many do on most Saturdays of the football season.

So they created a nice little powder keg, which did lead to trouble breaking out in several areas in and around the station. What it also did was spread the match-day police resources all over the place; instead of having possibly 80 per cent of the travelling fans coming on organised coaches, they were now looking at possibly 60 per cent of ours coming from all directions and at various times. They had to have coppers spread out here, there and everywhere, New Street station being just one location; they had to have a presence on stations all around the West Midlands, including the Metro-type stations they have up there. Also added to this, lots of lads had taken up vans and cars, parking these all around the area and planning to go back there to have a few pints after the game.

So, all in all, it was a policing nightmare. The City supporters club still had their normal allocation travelling on their coaches, and these are the fans you can count on week in week out to turn up everywhere; the numbers were pretty consistent and Vince, who runs this club, had got it off to a 't'. Vince will be the first to tell you that, while the Rams were taking so many coaches to away games, there were more positives than negatives for him and the official supporters club.

One such was that we at the Rams tended to attract and look after all the nutters (and I say that in the nicest possible way!). This left the family element that predominantly used Vince's coaches to travel unhindered and unmolested. My God, I've been around the block a few times and there were times when, if I fell asleep on one of our coaches, then I would do it with one eye open. Another benefit to Vince's group was the fact that, until we had started using coaches, the supporters club tended to get the brunt of the silly, over-the-top policing, with long delays at R/V points and top-to-bottom bus searches. Now, in most cases, when our group and their group turned up together, it gave the police the chance to see which tended to have the risk element on board, so all their energy was expended on us.

Up until these times, we used to believe, with some justification, that the police and authorities tended to view all Cardiff fans as Genghis Khan-like invaders out for rape and plunder. This now gave them the chance to see that this wasn't the case, and often Vince's group would be allowed to have a separate escort, with no searches, and to be taken quickly away from the R/V point, possibly to protect our own family groups (from the accompanying Rams coaches), who in truth weren't out for trouble, just a good day out watching the football, or a day on the lash, letting your hair down and not necessarily breaking any laws. Regulations, yes, but that's a totally different argument and one that more or less led to us finishing off the Rams travel group.

Whereas at the onset they were happy to see that, if they handled things well, then in most cases no laws would get broken, it soon got to the stage that regulations were now the main focus. Yes, we have to have rules and regulations, but we also need to have people that can apply these properly and use them to their advantage at times.

One of the daftest rules relates to alcohol. At rugby you can turn up pissed, drink in the stadium, even drink in your seat while watching the match, and this is all good 'rugger' fun, the occasional mass brawl or damage in a pub is seen as a bit of hijinks. Yet at football, you could turn up at a stadium and if an awkward copper was having a bad day, you could be arrested if he smelled drink on you, no matter if it was one pint or ten. For those that say it doesn't happen like that, let me tell you I've lost count of the occasions I've seen it happen and tried to stop someone getting arrested.

Yes, if someone turns up pissed and staggering all over the shop, then fuck them off and if they don't listen, then yes, you may have to arrest them. But there are so many variables to this equation, and at the end of the day it's down to attitude and different approaches from different forces and even different officers within that force. It's a bit like a risky lottery.

And then to compound this problem, they will enforce this law/regulation to the letter; yet when they do let you in, you are then allowed to drink to your heart's content as long as the game isn't being played and you're in view of the stadium. Mad as fuck!

But the main law/regulation that caused most confusion, depending on where and who you were dealing with, was the drinking-on-coaches law – as applied to football, mind, because rugby or horseracing doesn't matter and you could fall off those coaches as drunk as a skunk.

Travelling on organised compliant coaches that turned up at R/V points at allotted time slots was the one mode of transport where you weren't allowed to drink. Trains, cars, vans, etc, no problem, and even if you had a minibus that this non-drinking law applied to, in most cases you could get by unnoticed and be parked up in some sidestreet with no searches or delays.

So it was almost like an incentive to travel any which way you wanted to, rather than via an organised method, if you wanted to have a pre-match drink. Surely it would have made sense to do the exact opposite and say to fans, "If you travel on recognised compliant coaches to the game, you can have a drink on board or we can arrange to find suitable premises near the ground where you can all drink together, while making things easier for us [the police] to look after things."

But there you are. Who are we to have an opinion? Even if it's one that, when seconded by police forces, helped things work like clockwork in most cases.

Now back to West Brom, which is a classic example: the coaches were told they'd be searched on arrival and escorted well out of the force area, preventing anyone having a drink before or after the game. So instead of the possibly 20-plus coaches the Rams would have had that day, we took around ten. This meant at least 500 of our regulars were now off the leash, so to speak, and boy, did those 500 (along with the few hundred regular independent travellers who would also be there) make them work for their money that day.

Our ten coaches had made their way up as normal, heading for the R/V point at the service station on the M5, just three miles or so down from the Junction One turnoff to West Brom. The supporters club coaches got there in advance of us but were nowhere in sight; what had happened was that they'd got there, hung around looking for the escort, which hadn't turned up, and so after waiting a good while they decided to push on the last three or four miles on their own.

Our coaches were now doing similar things, and as they turned up in ones and twos, they had a quick look, saw no coppers there and pushed on, thinking, *Fuck you, we came on time, you weren't there, so we're off.*

What had happened, as we found out later, was that the plans to meet and escort our coaches had been shelved last-minute because Cardiff fans were arriving and showing up all over the place. Police resources were reallocated to all these 'hot spots', but someone had forgotten to tell all the coaches and they were just left to work it out and do their own thing.

This meant that you had the eight or so supporters' coaches ahead of us and mixed in with the thousands of cars, vans and lorries all heading off at Junction One, which is one of the busiest junctions in the country on a normal day, let alone on a match day at the Hawthorns.

By the time our coach had got within sight of the junction, I could see the chaos ahead of me. It was gridlocked and the traffic was queuing down the slip road, hundreds of yards back down the slow lane of the motorway. After what seemed like ages, lots of had started getting well pissed-off; we could see the floodlights but we weren't getting any closer to them, so people started getting off in dribs and drabs and walking up the slip road.

This all started off with good intentions, but that soon changed when some of us noticed something happening up on the roundabout about 200 yards in front of us. We could make out that one of our coaches was surrounded by a good mob of 60 or so older lads who, in fairness, looked the part, rather than your spotty-faced wannabes that we see so often.

We didn't know what had taken place, but it was quite apparent that something had happened. We found out minutes later that it involved one of our Rams coaches that was being looked after by one of our reps, Keith Harman, ably assisted by his missus, Jo. Now Keith knew the score and had been in plenty of scrapes over the years; he wasn't a bully but he

Left: Some of the original Soul Crew.

Right: Gethin, Glen, Wurzel and the Barry Lads.

Left: Conrad, Daryl, Simon ('Neath Punk'), Jammo.

Right: The 80's, when young Cardiff would invade Newport.

Left: The Valley Commandos who loyally follow Cardiff everywhere.

Right: Some good lads from Simmo's 'Battle Bus', on an away trip stop at a service station.

Below: The Soul Crew messing around inside Ninian Park.

OUR BITTER ENEMY

Left: Cardiff fans invade the North Bank, Swansea, in the 80's.

Right: One lone Cardiff fan in the Jack End of the Liberty Stadium. He later became known as 'the Ginger Ninja' as they couldn't put him down.

Left: The Soul Crew at the Liberty Stadium, Swansea.

Right: Cardiff v Swansea, Ninian Park, 2009. The police struggle to hold back Cardiff fans.

Left: Standard Liege fans looking for Cardiff fans in Belgium, 1993.

Right: The Soul Crew attacks a Burnley minibus, 1992.

Left: Newport at Ninian Park, 2008.

Right: Our main police spotter knows the Soul Crew well.

Above: Cardiff fans waiting for Millwall, 1999.

Right: Ely Trendies at Barnsley away: Zeddie, Peter M, the author and Mikey Dye.

Left: Cardiff lads from Section A, the Grandstand, Ninian Park.

Below: Cardiff v Millwall, 1999: Cardiff fans try to get to the town centre.

Left: The Zulus at Ninian Park, 2006 – 150 of them. They didn't arrive until 3.15.

Right: Cardiff battling with the Old Bill at West Ham, just after they had scattered the ICF, 2004.

Below: Cardiff hooligans invade the pitch to get at Leeds, 2002.

Above: Cardiff fans at Stoke, 2000.

Right: The Old Bill draw their batons against Cardiff fans outside Bramall Lane, Sheffield, 2005.

Left: Cardiff fans outside Molineux after a riot with Wolves fans, 2004.

Left: Sam Hammam (centre) throws a surprise champagne reception at the Swallow Hotel, for Mansfield away. Seen with him are the boys: Simmo, Mojo, Mallo, Joe and many other lads.

Right: The Barry Lads who went everywhere with Cardiff in the 80's.

Left: The Bridgend lads (with the author at the centre) occupied one of 30 coaches going to 'Jackland' (Swansea), 2008.

Right: The Docks Boys at Viking's wedding, Cardiff.

wasn't one to shy away from trouble. What had happened was the bus he was in charge of had got stuck in traffic on the roundabout just as this group of West Brom had got there; we'll never know if they planned this, but if they had then it worked out well for them in the short term, because Keith's bus had been isolated from the others, which were stuck and spread out from a few hundred yards back to over the next half-mile or so in the queue.

This mob had managed to open the front door and were giving it the big 'un. Now on a normal trip, Keith's bus would have been rammed to the roof with some of our more dodgy characters, but these were the very ones who had now gone up on the train because of the WMP plans. So Keith's bus had mostly families and a lot of youngsters on board, and when Keith piled off the bus (with Jo backing him up), most groups of serious lads would have given them a pass. But not today. So you had one lad and his missus trying to calm things down, and he took a real belting right-hander off one of them. Jo managed to drag him back on the bus before he took a kicking as well; luckily, the queue started moving and they got away from the trouble. Keith was bouncing and, when word spread (like wild fire, as it does), everyone was livid and out for some revenge.

It didn't take us long to get it, because as we came up onto the roundabout we could see this mob had grouped up on the other side of the main road, possibly waiting for their next victims, but this time we were on foot and not stuck on a bus. I was in the front group, which contained mostly lads off my bus from Aberdare and Mountain Ash, not all blokes, and we even had some kids along with their dads. But nevertheless, we had 30 lads who I could count on if and when it kicked off. The good news just coming up the slip road behind us was that there were another 30 or so lads, and 100 yards behind them were another 30 lads, and this was being repeated back down through this nightmare traffic jam. Amidst all this chaos were two or three coppers with a worried look, you could see them thinking, *Oh fuck, if this kicks off we ain't going to be able to stop it,* and kick off it did.

When West Brom saw our motley crew walking towards

them, they came straight at us. We put the kids and their dads at the back and spread across the road as best we could. It started with a few small scuffles rather than an all-in scrap, Puggsy from Mountain Ash was toe to toe with one and Mad Andy was having it off with a big black monster of a lad. Some were dancing around, but there must have been around ten or so small one-on-one scraps spread all over the road, with these three coppers trying their best to calm things down. One of their lads was bending over one of our boys who was on the floor; I ran in and booted him off and, five minutes later, found his tooth stuck in my shin bone. Great shot – not!

But they weren't backing off, and must have felt quite safe having a big, wide road behind them leading up to the Hawthorns, with possibly hundreds more of their lads ready to back them up. But luckily for us, some of our other groups had seen what was going on and came running in from the side of these lads, getting amongst them from side on and behind them. This spooked them and blocked their escape route off.

It's funny how these things happen, and anyone who's been in such situations will know what I mean. A group of 60 lads can within seconds turn into 20; somehow people just slope off, blend in or simply disappear, but I've seen it happen on more than one occasion and, if I'm honest, I've done it myself in certain scrapes, or when two vanloads of riot cops suddenly pulled up with all guns blazing, so to speak.

The 20 or so lads still having a go backed their way off through the now greater numbers, some of these sprinting up towards the Hawthorns shouting their heads off. The other 30 or 40 lads they'd had must have either blended in with us and were keeping their heads down or had just sloped off. I now knew that we would soon be facing a load more West Brom lads when they'd heard what had gone on, and sure enough, you could see hundreds of them making their way down towards us.

Our numbers by now had swollen to more than enough to look out for ourselves, and there were more joining all the time – not all blokes, as I've said, there were quite a few kids and parents amongst us, but nonetheless enough of us for a full-scale 'off' if they wanted one. The police were now starting to get their act together and turning up here and there, and you could hear the dogs giving it the big 'un. A couple of ours had been nipped or had their trousers ripped and were now having a go at the coppers; there was the oft-witnessed pushing and shoving, and lads shouting out, "What's your number?" while West Brom were still coming down the road towards us.

I have recently seen the police footage of the next few minutes' action, and it was strange to actually look at events from all that time ago. One thing I didn't notice at the time was how happy everyone was. It was mad, you had dogs biting people, some people arguing the toss with any copper who'd listen and a couple of hundred West Brom who were now no more than 50 yards away from us. But most of our lads present had big smiles across their faces.

The police had been caught with their trousers down; for some older heads amongst us, who'd grown up with such events happening every other week, it was like a throwback to their youth, reliving what they thought were long lost days. As I keep saying, these blokes don't come intentionally looking for trouble, but if it happens they're not shy in coming forward.

It was on us now, and the police were doing their best to keep a separating line across the road. I was up at the front with the Aberdare and Mount boys, and could see West Brom posturing and dancing around in front of us, with none of them really prepared to get into us, when suddenly one lad lunged forward; he got knocked to the floor by a couple of stiff ones and, next thing, he'd got this big fuck-off Alsatian biting into him, almost lifting him off the ground and shaking him. He was yelping like a good 'un, it was funny as fuck.

A couple more tried to get into us and Mad Andy, still buzzing from earlier, gave one of them a good clout just before a copper got hold of him and pushed him back on the pavement. It was all over bar the shouting now, and you can see on the video all of their lads getting pushed up the road, moaning like fuck, with all of ours laughing and smiling as if they'd just been to the seaside.

We now had police coming in from everywhere, and while

they'd missed out on the serious stuff and had been as much use as an encyclopaedia in Swansea, they were determined to regain some authority now and decided to bubble us up, walk us past the away end and take us on a 20-minute hike before arriving en masse at the away turnstile 15 minutes after kick-off.

But there we are. We don't make these decisions, we are just the people who have to live with the results of them.

The West Brom matter didn't end there on that day. A good few weeks later we were playing Blackpool away and we had five coachloads of Rams stay up there for the weekend. It came about that one busload of the biggest, ugliest, maddest lads you wouldn't want to meet in a church, let alone a dark alley, decided to break up the return journey by stopping off for a pint on the way home. They decided that a pub in the Midlands area would be a good spot for a nice break.

So one of the large pubs used by West Brom fans was chosen and, at 1pm, 50 of our cultural attachés made their way through these pub doors. Big Sam reckoned later that he'd never seen so many people intently staring at the telly and afraid to look anywhere else. It's a bit like playing hide and seek when you're a kid; if you close your eyes and can't see who's looking for you, then that means they can't see you either.

It wasn't the best plan, and Ketty grabbed the biggest one in there. "Do you know who we are?" he asked.

"Y-yes," came the reply.

"And do you know what happened last month?" Ketty asked.

"I heard something about it," the lad replied, but instantly added that neither he nor anyone else in that pub had been involved, and the lads involved tended to drink in another pub in town.

"No problem," said Ketty, "phone them and tell them we are here and we'll wait for them." You can imagine the landlord thinking, *You dare, mate, and you're banned for life.*

Nothing came of it, mind, as the lad reckoned there was no one about. Our lads didn't create any problems there and didn't bully anyone, but the message had got out: sleep with one eye open if you hurt one of ours. I bet West Brom fans still check if we're playing Blackpool away every Sunday before popping down their pub for a pint. LOL.

I PREDICT A RIOT
Wolves v Cardiff, 25th September 2004

Stefan (Offenbach FC, Germany): I moved to South Wales the following season. Being a website and graphic designer, I accepted a position in the Welsh capital and was from now on able to follow my team week in week out for the next few years. Through my new contacts with the Rams (a supporters group who organised away travels), I got in touch with Annis Abraham and met him on several away trips. We've had good chats about football, especially about the City. He is CCFC mad, like myself, only he's been there a long time before me and, of course, always was and still is much closer and better informed about what happens inside our beloved club. It was actually Annis who nicknamed me 'Hofmeister' (well, it's still better than 'Schweinsteiger'), and whenever I come to Cardiff, we meet up for lunch and watch the games at Ninian from Block A of the Grandstand.

A funny annecdote happened when I spent Christmas with my family: we were at my parents' house when my mother called me to tell me there was a documentary about Cardiff City on the telly. You guess who they had on, and when they showed some of those Cardiff nutters my mum was in disbelief when I told her that quite a few of them were my mates . . .

One of the most talked about incidents in the last few years happened at Molineux, when City defeated Wolves 3-2 in 2004. Our club had just sold Earnie to West Brom and we were in the relegation zone, when my favourite player Graham Kavanagh scored our winner. A strong away support with almost 3000 Cardiff fans made their way to Wolverhampton. Still inside the stadium, we were overjoyed with the three points. News quickly made the rounds that Wolves were outside, trying to get a piece of Cardiff's reputation.

When I came out, a battle was already on. Wolves were running down to meet Cardiff and our lot were running straight in their direction. It was a short but heavy encounter, with Cardiff battering their Wolves opponents. Actually, it looked more like fathers smacking their teenage sons to teach them a lesson, due to the age difference of the two mobs. The police soon became involved, trying to separate the two, but it backfired as the now enraged Cardiff fans had switched their combat mode from stand-by to battle. A police car was wrecked; luckily no policemen were inside, but Cardiff were in running battles with the West Midlands Police. The situation calmed down and everybody made their way back to their coaches. The whole escalation of violence could have been prevented, if the police would have kept the Cardiff following inside the ground until the Wolves boys left or, should I say, had their own go with the WMP. This failure caused another incident at Wolves the following season . . .

Arriving at Wolves, our CD player played, 'I Predict a Riot', which caused laughs as we were looking at an army of coppers outside. It was brilliant timing, as we were stunned by the large amount of officers dressed in combat gear, waiting for us. The atmosphere was aggressive, the whole walk from the coach park down to Molineux a line of coppers with helmets, batons, shields and dogs on both sides. A dog almost bit me as I walked past him, I heard that others actually were bitten but I didn't see it. I watched the game from the main stand that day, meeting an old friend from Germany who wrote an acticle about Wolves. That's why I cannot comment on what happened inside the away stand at half-time, but I saw riot police steaming from pitchside into the away section and quickly hitting out after anyone standing near the aisles. I heard it kicked off properly inside, but again I didn't see it.

I left the ground with two minutes to play, I expected the WMP to lock the away fans in and guide them to the coaches afterwards. My plan was to be out before anyone else, so I'd be able to walk to the coach quickly and not have loads of coppers pushing me all the way up to the coach park. How little did I know? By the time I walked around the stadium, Cardiff were allowed to leave at the same time as anybody else, but as soon as the last City fan left the stadium riot police started to push and provoke the away followers. There were people (Wolves and

Cardiff fans) queing at a burger van, who all of a sudden felt the baton and were under attack. Although our fans were not in a fighting mood at first, it led to Cardiff fans turning on the police and, after several fans (including myself) got hit and a guy with crutches was hit on the ground, Cardiff fought back and hit out at every copper they could get.

All the way back to the coaches, Cardiff battled with the WMP, leaving quite a few Cardiff fans with open headwounds and two officers were taken to hospital. I remembered a documentary I saw, *The Battle of the Beanfield*, when armed coppers hit out at a peace convoy full with hippies. I soon felt like one of those travellers, I didn't do anything but was left unable to defend myself against a brutal attack carried out by those who claim to represent the law.

Cardiff's reputation went sky-high afterwards amongst football lads, shirts and scarfers of other clubs. But to the police it was a treatment us Cardiff fans deserved, because we're animals . . . and Welsh anyhow.

THE TRUTH BEHIND THE WOLVES RIOTS

I've known Big Sam since right back in the dark old days, when lads like him were the only support we had. We've been together through the good and bad days, stormed boardrooms, met every chairman and rallied the fans when the club was sinking. You won't get a better fan than Sam, but he's also been one of our main lads from the Valleys.

Big Sam (CCFC): Kevin Murphy is my name, but most people know me as Big Sam. I am from the Merthyr area of South Wales and live in Aberfan, a mining village that has had more than its fair share of tragedy. Merthyr is a big Valleys town and, along with many other areas such as Aberdare, Rhondda Valleys, Pontypridd, Caerphilly, Mountain Ash, Tredegar, Ebbw Vale, Pontypool, Rhymney and loads of others, there is a huge Cardiff City support. Even in my village there are around 30 season ticket holders, plus others who go on a regular basis.

I have been following City for over 40 years and my first away game was Leicester City, August '69. We won 1-0 and Tosh scored the winner. I was a 15-year-old skinhead and, along with thousands of others, we loved this club they call Cardiff City. Over the years of following City I have been involved in incidents up and down the country; it happens, and I'm not apologising for it. In the bad old Division Four days, Cardiff's lads were the only ones who used to travel – well, not the *only* ones, but we were always there. I don't think there are many City fans who haven't been involved, somewhere or sometime, with rival fans. That's fair enough, but the shit we had to put up with from various police 'firms', especially West Midlands and West Yorkshire, beggars belief. The Met ain't so bad really – they would rather give you a good kicking than do the paperwork, bless them!!!

I have been asked by Annis to give a version of events that happened when we played Wolves away in October 2004 and March 2006. I have known Annis for years; a few people slag him behind his back, but if you cut his arm he bleeds blue, 100 per cent City. That's good enough for me.

Wolves away was a special one to me when I went there in the late 80's. We won 4-1 by a Gilligan hat trick and it was as rough as fuck. It was a big game back then and it's a big game now. Wolves have always had a good crew and can pull big numbers as well.

Wolves v Cardiff City, 25th September 2004

As we were travelling up with the Valley Rams coaches, Big Gwyn had to meet the West Midlands police 'firm', ha ha! Police told him no alcohol on coaches. Gwyn said, "Okay, then we will take three coaches and the lads will make their own way to the game. Police said, "Okay, have a few beers," so then we took 23 coaches and most of them were full of our Legions of the Neanderthal. Jesus Christ, we have some right beauties following our club! I honestly believe we have got more nutters who follow our club than any other in the country, must be something to do with the water down here – or the 'bow.

During that meeting with the West Midlands Police, Gwyn was told that any Cardiff coaches turning up would be held, searched and put in the ground early. Charming, that! So basically we were not welcome in that shithole called Wolverhampton. We decided two days before to split up; as it turned out, our coach and five others went to Bromsgrove, others went elsewhere.

Bromsgrove: nice town, stopped there many times over the years for a few beers on the way home from away games *oop north*. Our six coaches were rammed with lads, so when we got there we split up. There are plenty of pubs in Bromsgrove, so there was no problem getting a beer; we were all over the place and there was no trouble anywhere. We don't go smashing up towns – contrary to what people think. No plod, a few beers . . . lovely. It was around 11am, and the police found us at 11.05am . . . amazing.

We had been in a pub about an hour when Tony Rivers (Lakey) came in with Gilly, Wolves' main lad, so we were told. I'd met Gilly before and he seemed a decent bloke. He told us Wolves had 200 lads in Bilston – where the fuck is Bilston?????? I would have thought they would be in Wolverhampton, where Wolves play, but there you go. We knew we had a nice crew on the train. But many of our lads don't like fraternising with the opposition and told him to fuck off, so he went and took Lakey with him . . . probably to another pub.

We left Bromsgrove around 1.15pm-1.30pm, I can't remember the exact time, the Old Bill watching everything we did. Bromsgrove to Wolverhampton isn't too far. On the way, one of the lads had a call to say there had been trouble in Wolverhampton already . . . interesting!!!

Police escort as usual all the way in. When we pull up, we get the usual warm welcome from the West Midland Police (firm) – you know, the shoving, searching, bullying, verbal abuse and general intimidation. I wonder what these chaps are like when they get angry, ha ha! Anyway, fuck them, we had come across these twats before, and it is my opinion they are nothing but bullies in uniform – and what a uniform, wow! They look like a cross between Darth Vader and a Muslim woman. We could only see their fucking eyes and they were armed to the teeth; there is no talking to these twats, I hate them and I'm not just saying this. But our lads don't give a fuck for them, we are used to being treated like shit; give Cardiff fans RESPECT and we are fine. Treat us like shit and you will have major problems. It was a half-mile walk to the ground across a car park and dual carriageway, down a hill and into the ground. All nice and quiet before the game. The calm before the storm.

It was either half-time or during the second half that one of their stewards said to Keith Cooper (Cardiff fan and a retired ref), who was standing close to us, that a few weeks earlier Wolves were home to Wigan and after the game, as the Wigan fans left the ground, the Wolves lot came down the hill, battering the Wigan fans and families as well. Believe what you want, but he also said that they quite often attacked visiting fans in that area after games and that the Old Bill knew about it but did very little. *Should be very interesting later,* we all thought.

Final whistle went and City won a belter, 3-2. Most stayed behind to clap our team, who thoroughly deserved the cheers and applause. Right, out we go, happy as Larry. When we get out, all hell breaks loose. Wolves came steaming down the hill and were throwing everything they could: bricks, bottles, crash barriers, the lot. Only this time they were playing Cardiff City. Love us or hate us, Cardiff lads will always have a real go, and if ever a club picked a wrong day to attack us, Wolves did. We had a huge crew out and as always we were up for it.

City's lads went steaming into them, no bouncing about or poncing about, this was football violence at its best/worst, call it what you like. Our lads went straight in and backed Wolves right up the hill, battering every one of them that got caught or tried to stand. I don't care what anyone says about that day, our lads were awesome. There was so much fighting going on between Cardiff and Wolves, and Cardiff and the West Midlands Police firm, you wouldn't believe it. I'm not naming names or anything, but all the known lads and young guns were having a real go and doing themselves proud. After all, the Cardiff support were violently attacked by the Wolves firm, who apparently did this quite often and got away with it. But not today. I won't describe in detail who was doing what or what was happening to this person or that person or that person, because these incidents only happened a few years ago and people tend to say, "Aye, aye, he's bullshitting," but this was very tasty and Cardiff lads were quality.

Don't forget that when the Wolves lot first attacked the Cardiff support there were families, women and kids amongst them and when they were throwing everything, they didn't give a fuck who they hit. A lot of people could have got hurt and if it wasn't for our lads, a lot of people *would* have got hurt. A lot of our so called 'proper' fans – and they are good people, by the way – often put down the antics of our lads, but I can assure you that over the years, at various grounds around the country, the so-called antics of Cardiff lads have saved many of our 'proper' supporters from having a real shoeing and this Wolves game was one occasion.

After Cardiff backed Wolves up the hill, there was a bit of a lull, then Wolves came back again. This time they were vary wary. Again Cardiff went at them and yet again we backed them off. This time though, the tossers from the West Midlands Police Force had entered the fray. Ha! This police force seems to hate most football fans and us in particular.

The pushing and shoving started, so the lads started shoving back. They then started to hit out willy-nilly with their truncheons, so the lads fought back. Self-defence, yeah? So now not only were we fighting the Wolves crew, the fucking police were having a go as well. Fuck me, it was like being in the German army during World War Two, we were fighting on two fronts. Cardiff support that day numbered around 2,300, of which at least 800 were lads, and the West Midlands Police were cracking everyone, they didn't give a toss who they hit. It was chaotic, mad, there was so much happening all over the place and some of the situations going on were outrageous, hilarious. The police firm had formed a line three quarters of the way up the hill, the hill that City had sent Wolves packing up. These were the finest Robocops – armed to the teeth, you could only see their eyes – trying to get Cardiff back down the hill. If you have ever been to Wolves, when you come out of the away end there is a hill to your right. That's the one the Wolves lot came down and went back up. There is another hill/incline right opposite the away end; the police were trying to get us down one hill and up the other to get us back to our coaches, cars, trains, whatever. We had Wolves and the police in front of us and Robocop behind us. A recipe for disaster, methinks . . .

At the bottom of the two hills/inclines, it started to go off with the police. About 20 yards up the second hill, a patrol car pulled up and two Old Bill got out. They were surrounded by some Cardiff lads and I think they shit themselves, because they forgot to put the handbrake on and the fucking car rolled down the hill into a crash barrier. It was soon dismantled by some of the lads. All of a sudden a shout went up, a lad from Pontypridd (who now lives in Cardiff) said, "I've dropped my phone!" and, unbelievably, the Old Bill and Cardiff lads involved in this particular fracas bent down and picked up not his phone, but the police radio out of their wrecked car. It had a curled aerial on it. We burst out laughing, the Old Bill went potty and so we started fighting again. Fucking amazing!

Not only had we seen off the Wolves lot, we were now having a go at the Old Bill, big-time. Our lads were going mad, now a police van had its windscreen put in. One of the our cheeky lads then took a packet of biscuits off the dashboard of the van, and anyone who was walking up the other hill must have seen the little dance routine of this line of Robocops who came jogging down the hill behind each other, towards us. The last one tripped and a few of them went down like skittles. Wicked, that!

The trouble finally died down and we made our way back to the coaches, trains, cars, whatever means of transport we got here by. There were some comments made by police, which personally I did not hear, but very good friends of mine did and I totally trust and respect their word. These are a few of them:

"It was like watching boys fighting their fathers and Cardiff are the daddies."

"Fuck me, Cardiff's got 800 no-necks."

And on the way back to the coaches, a great mate of mine was approached by a copper who said, "Well done, those wankers deserved a kicking, they've been bullying other fans for years." My mate said, "Yeah, and a police officer's saying that." The copper said, "I'm a BAGGIES fan!"

I've not mentioned anyone's names, or who did this or who did that, because this is recent history and you never know what the West Midlands Police fucking Force might come out with. All I know is that Cardiff City's lads, firm, supporters, call 'em what you like, were violently attacked and responded with a venom that few, if any other clubs in these isles, could manage. It's just in us and always will be.

Wolves v Cardiff City, 11th March 2006

At the game two years later nothing happened between either set of fans, but at half-time, there was a major incident under the stand where Cardiff's fans were. I was at the game, but because I don't like spending at away grounds I stayed on the terrace. (Ha ha!)

Here is the eyewitness account of a 16-year-old girl who was there with my youngest daughter who was also 16 – hardly battle-hardened hooligans. The young girl's name is Jamie Lee Francis and my daughter's name is Kate Murphy. Please read it and make your own mind up.

The day of the Wolverhampton Wanderers away game was a complete and utter palaver. To start off, we were told of two different rendezvous points, then when we eventually arrived at the correct point we were kept in a yard for at least an hour. We were then taken straight to the ground, along a retail park road on a Saturday afternoon; it was utter chaos, as you might expect. There was no forethought, as per usual, from the West Midlands Police Force. What's the point in bussing us in and bussing us out in a so-called 'bubble' game with no freedom, if they are going to allow us to walk side by side with the Wolves fans to the ground without blocking the road off and diverting the other fans?

When we eventually got to the ground, there were maybe four turnstiles and easily 1,000 fans trying to get in all at the same time. Instead of staggering the bus arrivals, they forced us all to arrive at once and we descended upon the ground together. I myself missed the kick-off due to this lack of organisation.

Despite what other people and the police say, to me there wasn't a bad atmosphere that day in the ground. At half-time, me and my friend went under the stand to the bar to get a hot drink. As usual the underneath was busy, full of fans singing and queuing to get served. I can honestly say that I witnessed the bar staff serve not one but multiple fans with alcohol; then, for some reason, they refused to serve one bloke with beer. They said, "We cannot serve alcohol at half-time," to which he replied, "I've just seen you serve people for beer!" And with this the fans started singing, "We want beer!" There were no threats or violence in this, just general banter. But the bar staff stopped serving altogether and started to pull the shutters down. The next thing I knew, a swarm of riot police came wading into the packed bar area.

I moved out of the way and was shielded by a few men. Some of the police officers were like something possessed, swinging their collapsible batons with intent. They hit anything in their path, without concern for age or whether there were women or children caught up in the commotion. It got so bad at one point we were forced back up into the stands for our safety. The next thing we knew, the police had come up into the stands and were battering fans who had not even been in the bar area. Many fans and myself were forced onto the pitch for pure fear of being hit by the police. The violence in the stands continued for well over ten minutes and forced the second half of the game to be delayed. The West Midlands Police were totally out of order that day and have still not been reprimanded for their actions.

A few weeks later there was a meeting chaired by Sam Hammam, which I attended to state that I witnessed beer being served that day. Not only was I called a liar by one of the more 'mature' (shall we say) stewards at the club, but it was also suggested by Sam himself that I mistook coffee for beer, to which I replied, "I may be only 16 years old but I know the difference between a cup of coffee and a pint of beer." It was also suggested that people had purchased beer before the game. One response that sticks in my mind is, "By half-time that pint would have been as flat as a witch's tit, and there was no way it was bought before the game." That still makes me laugh to this day. It infuriates me that the club once again refused to support the fans and that still, to this day, the events have been swept under the carpet.

That's the totally honest account of a 16-year-old girl. After this game, Jez Moxey, Wolves chief executive, banned Cardiff fans from Molineux and for fucking what?????? For being hammered by those pigs . . . Mad, ain't it?!?!

Most Cardiff fans believe the West Midlands Police wanted revenge for what happened two years earlier, and I repeat that we were attacked by Wolves fans. That's not a problem, we defended ourselves and done the biz; the police didn't have a clue what to do and started having a go at us, so we took it to them and they didn't like it. What do they expect us to do? Lie down and let them batter us?????? Fuck that.

If people leave us alone, we are fine. Fuck with us and you've got major problems.

THE ZULUS IN CARDIFF

I was contacted by some lads from Birmingham who wanted to give accounts of their visits to Cardiff. I was away on my honeymoon in 2006, so I can't comment. What I've been told is that the Zulus didn't arrive till really late, but when they did they were really up for it. The numbers they had in the ground that day were massive, and in this day and age that doesn't happen very often. The Zulus in the 80's and 90's were always one of the biggest firms around and one of the gamest, and judging by what they brought to Cardiff in 2006, they are still very active. I would like to thank Sooty Jason (Zulu) for helping to get these stories to me and being a sound lad.

Cardiff City v Birmingham City, 26th August 2006
J (Zulu, Birmingham City): Birmingham City were due to play Cardiff City at Ninian Park for the first time in a number of years. Due to previous incidents involving the two teams' supporters, both in fixtures of years gone by and in recent years when the Blues have played final matches at Cardiff's Millennium Stadium, and also because both sets of hooligan groups belonging to the two clubs would like to think of themselves as, on their day, one of the top hooligan firms in the country, the fixture promised to be a somewhat explosive affair in terms of off-the-field activities.

Because of the interest that this fixture would also undoubtedly generate from our friends at the West Midlands Police and South Wales Constabulary, the Blues lads making the trip down to Wales that day knew that something a little different was in order, if we were to have any chance at all of avoiding police detection or getting any sort of hooligan firm anywhere near our Cardiff counterparts. So at 6am on the day of the game, a good firm of Zulus both young and old met up at one of the Zulu pubs at the time, Billy's Bar. By 7am the pub was full and, shortly after, many of the lads set off for South Wales in cars with the intention of rendezvousing in Newport, Gwent. Before moving on to Cardiff, however, a good firm of 50 Zulus, a large percentage of them young, who were travelling to South Wales on a coach decided that driving down the motorway towards Cardiff would bring unwanted police attention to the rest of the Zulus, who were meeting up in Newport. So therefore they would go a different route to Cardiff, taking them a good hour out of their way but avoiding any South Wales motorways, as well as the all-important police checkpoints.

After a long journey through South Wales, across to Merthyr Tydfil then down the A470 and some other winding Valleys A-roads, the coach of 50 Blues lads finally landed at a pub in the Welsh town of Barry, only nine miles away from Cardiff. But as it was the other side of the city, we expected no police attention. The Blues lads had a quick drink in Barry, while three 15-seater minibuses and a seven-seater taxi were called to take them into the Canton area of Cardiff. The plan was that the taxis would meet up, again to avoid police detection, at a location inside one of the large parks right next to Canton, where the firm of Zulus could then walk together unopposed out into the Canton streets, towards where they believed the main Cardiff pubs at the time were located. However, due to part of this park being closed off on that specific weekend, added to the fact that two of the useless minibus drivers hadn't got a fucking clue where they were going, the firm of 50 Zulus from the Barry coach were forced to reunite at a pub just outside the Sophia Gardens park on the edge of Canton. Which was the only factor that I believe alerted the

South Wales police to the arrival of the 50 Zulus right in Cardiff's backyard.

As soon as the last minibus taxi arrived at the pub, so did one police van which could only follow, radioing frantically for back-up. They could not contain the firm of 50 Zulus as they started to walk through the Canton backstreets. The Blues, after only a couple of minutes of walking through the streets, were alerted by the shouts of some Cardiff fans at the end of one of the side roads; the police following then started shouting for the firm to keep walking straight ahead. So the Zulus, of course, started to pick up the pace and turned down the sidestreet. They saw that on the left-hand side of the opposite end of the street was one of the Cardiff City hooligan firms' pubs, the King's Castle. The 50 Zulus started to jog up the road towards the pub, as did the police. As the firm of Blues reached the pub, a firm of Cardiff hooligans burst out of a side entrance into the road, chucking beer bottles and pint glasses at the Zulus. The Zulus, not tooled up in any way, made a brief charge towards the pub and, with only a handful of punches exchanged, sent the Cardiff lads tripping over themselves and backing off into the doorway they had just burst out from. From the look of shock on the faces of the Cardiff lads who appeared in the road first, I believe that they did not anticipate the number of Zulus that had suddenly appeared to face them in the road right outside one of their main pubs, or the Zulus' willingness to engage. A second van of South Wales police had arrived from round the front of the pub; together with the vanload of police who had been shadowing the Zulus, they now formed a line in the road with their backs to the pub and batons drawn. Facing the firm of Zulus, they now started to force the firm away from the pub and down a main road in the direction of Ninian Park.

Although it was later brought to light that Cardiff's main firm on this date were in fact at a different location, in the Grangetown area of Cardiff, before kick-off, as this incident took place the firm of Zulus were not to know this at the time. I personally believe they deserve full credit for making the effort to get a firm of 50 lads into the heart of Cardiff's territory with very little police presence. At no time did Cardiff ever know we were coming, and that's how we work. A South Wales police officer also said to one of the Zulus, "Fucking hell, I've never seen the Cardiff back off like that before, they normally don't even back off from us!" – a quote which generated much amusement amongst the firm of Zulus throughout the day.

The Cardiff City Soul Crew are, without doubt, on their day one of the best firms in the country and this very minor incident outside one of their pubs is not in any way seen as a firm-on-firm result. It was just a brief incident that took a lot of effort and planning on the Zulus' part to be executed, in an age when it's hard for a firm to even move without the law breathing down their necks, let alone to come face to face with their rivals. It will be interesting to read or hear the Cardiff City Soul Crew's take of the day's events, but hopefully the respect that I know a lot of Zulus have for them will be reciprocated.

Throughout the rest of the day, incidents took place of both firms attacking the police while trying to reach one another, although the incident that took place outside the King's Castle was by far the only real chance the two firms had that day to properly exchange pleasantries. After that, the police slowly started to descend on the firm of Zulus as they continued to walk through the streets of Canton and, within about five-ten minutes, South Wales' finest had 50 of Birmingham's finest cornered in a Cardiff backstreet. Fair play to Cardiff: as the police now escorted the Birmingham Zulus through the streets, taking them the long way around the ground to the away turnstiles, the streets all around were filled with what looked like hundreds of Cardiff lads trying the best they could to break through the police lines, and get to the road where the Zulus were being escorted. But, sadly, the time had already passed and the police were now well on top of the situation. The 50 Zulus were then escorted to the ground without further incident.

Inside the ground, midway through the first half, trouble between the Birmingham City away following and the police occurred as a result of the Cardiff stewards trying to forcefully eject a Blues fan. The South Wales police entered the away end at the front of the stand, which sparked off a crowd surge that forced the police back down the stairs, over the advertising boards and onto pitch side. The police were then pelted with bits of ripped-up seating from the front of the stand and lumps of concrete terracing from the back. This trouble inside the ground later resulted in prison sentences for some of our lads.

Although no major disorder really took place on this day, it was for those involved one of the most eventful awaydays that you will get to experience in modern times. What I have a written about the day's events is an eyewitness account of what took place, although because of the recentness of the day in question – added to the fact that I am still an active member of the Birmingham City Zulu Warriors – I hope you can appreciate why I have failed to specify any personal involvement in the day's events.

THE THOUGHT POLICE
Coventry v Cardiff City, 10th February 2007
Big Gwyn (CCFC): Well, this century started with a bang, it was the Sam Hammam era and the Valley Rams era. I won't bore you with how the Rams were formed or why we walked away from organising travel in 2007, but while those involved with running this group have stepped back officially, a lot of what the Rams created still exists, and the people running coaches from all four corners of South Wales are more or less the same people who were key to the Rams organisation. Suffice to say, the police, the club and the authorities now spend far longer chasing up people to find who's going where and tracing their movements en route now that the Rams hierarchy has stepped down.

We had set ourselves up to be used as scapegoats in the latter stages. It was beginning to seem as if any fan that was seen as drunk or being a nuisance was automatically assumed to be part of the Rams group, and what were we going to do about it? It was almost as if they were no longer Cardiff fans, nothing to do with the club and only our responsibility. Fuck me, we were the only ones doing this for fuck-all amongst all those involved! We had the police, the club, the stewards, even the football licensing authorities, all paid employees, yet it was down to our little band of volunteers to ensure that these thousands of lads behaved like choirboys when, six years earlier, the authorities were amazed and grateful that we'd finally helped to stop the major disorder that plagued our club.

The pubs had stopped being trashed and the services were no longer robbed, which was great, but the biggest problems now were, "Johnny is standing up to watch the game, and not even standing behind his allocated seat number!" 'Scuse me? I thought we were helping to stop mass disorder? Now they were trying to turn us into Big Brother and the Thought Police.

Coventry

One such instance springs to mind during the last year or so of the Rams. We were in Coventry's Ricoh stadium, placed in our segregated end with large sterile areas each side of us, keeping us safe from the massed Coventry firm. NOT!

However, what this sterile area did was allow the same chavvy teenage element I mentioned earlier (you know, the ones who are hard as fuck behind a fence) the opportunity of being within shouting distance of our fans. Most of our fans were standing, as usual, to watch the game, no problem. Other Cardiff fans that want to sit down will usually go in front of these lads or sit around the fringes. Job done. We sort it out amongst ourselves and we all get to watch the game as we prefer, while standing or sitting next to the mates we choose.

For this match, showing my age, I'd sat on the right hand side of this group; about four rows lower than us was a group of four lads all around 15 years of age. They were no problem, they looked like decent enough kids with their feet on the first rung of the 'watching football away with my mates, rather than my dad' ladder.

The match was well underway, with the normal chanting going on, Cov's chavs singing at us and pointing, etc, and our fans responding. Then along came a big, hard, bullyboy steward and his two sidekicks, he grabbed the lad nearest to him and shouted, "Oi, sit down in your seat or you're out!" It was a bit heavy handed and it looked like he was picking the easy option, considering we had a thousand gorillas ten seats or so across, doing the same. The young lads looked quite frightened, they didn't argue and just sat down.

A few minutes later the old chant goes up – "Ten lads, you've only got ten lads!" – and our young lads are singing along and pointing over at the Cov fans. Well, Billy the bullyboy steward comes across and threatens the lads again, saying that, even though they were now sitting down, if they pointed at the Cov fans again that would be seen as threatening gestures.

In all fairness to these now shook-up young lads, they stopped gesturing and kept watching the game. Well, fuck me, five minutes later the bullyboy was back again, but I couldn't work out what they had done wrong now. So I listened in and heard him saying he'd seen one of the youngsters looking at the Cov fans, and if he looked at them again instead of looking at the game, he'd be out on his ear.

That was the last straw that broke the camel's back for me. I had to intervene, and said to the steward that if they'd paid to come in, and wanted to spend all the match looking at Cov fans, then they would and he could do fuck-all about it, and if he didn't fuck off he'd have a thousand nutters climbing over the seats to make sure he did.

He chose the wise option now that a 'grownup' had got involved, and went and hid somewhere else. Mind you, I spent the rest of the match waiting for a tug for daring to stand up to the Thought Police. There are people out there who really want us to watch football in a different environment to the one that most football fans want. It is a major concern and, while we can't allow trouble or racist abusive chanting, the day we have to sit down all match, not sing, not point, and are even told where to look, is the day when I and many others will choose to spend their money elsewhere.

VII

THE NORTHERNERS

MAN UTD – THE RED ARMY

From this day, Manchester United's Red Army had total respect for Cardiff and they knew that, if they ever came back to the capital of Wales, they wouldn't be able to terrorise it like they had done to virtually every major city in Britain and Europe. I have met a lot of United's lads over the years, including Mick, and they have always been honest about this day.

Cardiff City v Manchester Utd, 31st August 1974

Mick (Salford MUFC): It was the year that my club was relegated and, in my time of watching them, one of my only few bad memories. But, as to the hooligan side of it, it was a great season and I will never forget going to Cardiff.

I was just a schoolboy and, although I'd been to plenty of games at Old Trafford with my mates, I'd only been to a few away games where there had been much trouble at that time.

The Cardiff game was unlike anything I think I have ever seen before or since. We expected an 'interesting' day, to say the least, but nothing prepared four kids for an afternoon of absolute mayhem, the likes of which, I'm sure anyone who was there will heartily agree, has never been seen since – with perhaps the exception of Man Utd/Man City, Millwall/West Ham or Leeds/Man Utd.

United fans were largely untouchable in those days, with their sheer weight of numbers plus a ferocious bravado that wouldn't allow them to back down from any resistance. Even the southern counterparts – Chelsea, West Ham and to some extent Millwall – were still lagging behind in both exploits and organisation.

So it was with that air of self-confidence that we arrived at Cardiff train station. "Manchester, la la la! Manchester, la la la!" rang out all around as we walked and swaggered our way towards Ninian Park. We were with the big boys now, the Red Army, it was the exhilaration of being surrounded by 200 or so 'grown men' of 20-plus.

There we saw a group of about 200 lads. A cheer went up, these were more of our own, we assumed. To this day I'll never forget the scene. A handful of our lads from across the road ambled over, a reuniting embrace was no doubt to follow as these old friends joined the throng. Suddenly, I noticed the crazed grin on the face of the approaching stranger and, even with my limited knowledge of football away trips, I had a feeling all was not well.

Our 'mate' simply smashed his fist into the face of one of our lads. "Bloody hell, they're taffy twats!" came the cry. This one lad began wading into at least ten of the United group, bodies were going down all around. His 199 or so mates did very little to assist this one maniac – either they were terrified of the situation or maybe knew his capabilities. Maybe this was Frankie Humphries, the legend from the newspaper stories.

At last the two mobs woke up from just standing there watching and charged into each other. Now when people say 400 fans were fighting 'toe-to-toe' they usually mean half a dozen at most, with the rest milling about looking stupid, but this was as it sounded, and I've never seen anything like it since. It was a full-scale riot.

My mates and I stood there dumbstruck. It was well over 30 years ago and I would love to be able to recall how I joined in the scene of carnage, downing all-comers, but as a young boy I was horror-stricken and frozen with terror. I remember one policeman ambling by and peering round the corner to see what all the noise was. He took one look at the scene and carried on walking. Classic!

By this time most of us had been split into small groups, and the walk to the ground was quite simply a journey you only have nightmares about. On every street corner the sight was the same, people scurrying around in all directions. I saw one outlandish figure – a United fan – in a white boiler-suit and black bowler hat, giving out instructions. All around were cries of, "Here they are!", "Don't run!", "I've got one!" "Over here!" It was total confusion, a tidal wave of thundering red Doctor Marten boots and tartan scarves. This was fucking mayhem!

We arrived outside the ground and met up again with some faces from the train. Some looked dazed and confused, others bloodied but still up for it. "See this," said one half-caste Londoner with a bloody nose. "The next taff I see, I'm going to give him three of these." We all laughed loudly at the ridiculous statement, though some of the characters I had seen at the station, with scars down their faces and smashed noses, really did seem to want more.

We started queuing at the rather oddly named 'Bob Bank', whatever that was. Suddenly a group of Reds walked past us, full of contempt that we were planning to go into our own end. "Not in here, you idiots, it's all down by the so-called 'Grange End'." We followed our lads and paid in at 'the Grange'.

As we prepared to pay our money, I noticed some of the lads around us were tying their scarves around their waists out of sight. I now realised that occupying the home end was more of a military operation than a consumer choice.

We gathered 'inconspicuously' at a point close to the fence which had a huge no-man's land separating the rival fans. Insults were traded for half an hour, a few blood-curdling screams of bravado followed by a couple of half-hearted charges by either side at the fence. A fat Cardiff fan with a scarf round his wrist, and tomato sauce stains around his chin, shouted something indistinguishable and launched a wooden stake, like a mini-telegraph pole, into the baying United mob.

A few cheers rang out as it hit an unseen target. Instantly, a piece of concrete was hurled into the Cardiff boys to my right and I could see a small group of people huddled round a fallen comrade. The reality that someone really could die here today (possibly even me) hit home.

As if it wasn't bad enough, things were about to take a turn for the worse. A small group of taffies began to take an unhealthy interest in the dozen or so lads to their left (us). One lunatic with a severely scarred face wandered over. "Not singing, boys? We all sing in here, you're all a bit quiet today. You are all *Car-diff*, I hope?" I froze, virtually shitting myself, and we knew they weren't going to go away now their suspicions were aroused.

The scout ambled back to the main group to report his findings. After a brief chin-wag amongst themselves, three or four more came over to ask more questions. Guess what? It was those lunatic taffies who attacked us earlier by the train station.

Then some of the top lads from the Red Army came flying over and said, "We'll give you a song: UNITED! UNITED!"

That was the signal for all-out attack from both sides. The dozen or so United lads charged upwards at the massed ranks of blue-scarved taffies in a suicidal attack. Fists flew and a massive gap developed between the fans as the visitors gained some amazing ground. I hid behind one of United's lads.

Suddenly the 'Red Sea' in front of me became just a pond, as the Cardiff boys realised the small numbers involved in the suicidal mission. It finally stopped as United's lads ran straight out the entrance they had come in.

The four of us were now totally left on our own. We should have followed. It was now clear that we were in serious trouble and we seized the chance to make for a gap in the faltering fencing, weakened by numerous charges. We raced towards the safety of our fellow fans, who, to our horror, on seeing the oncoming mob charged into us, and a number of fists flew before our identity was established.

We were suddenly being applauded like heroes, as though we ourselves were on the suicide mission – which I guess we were. I don't really know what I was thinking, I was still in a daze. One minute I thought we were dead, the next we were heroes. As huge lumps of brick, concrete and wood were flying over from both sides, the police were desperately trying to contain the two lunatic mobs who charged continually at the terrified looking thin blue line, and at several points it looked as though the fence would give way.

As a veteran of away trips at home and abroad throughout the 70's, 80's and 90's, I can honestly say I couldn't imagine the carnage that would have taken place had that terrified police line given way on that day.

Thankfully it held, and despite sickening chants of "Munich!" and occasionally even "Aberfan!", the severe injuries were low. Sometimes I think about that day and I'm shocked nobody died. People were being carried out from both sides on stretchers, many with horrifying head wounds. Struggling yobs were being plucked from both ranks by those policemen plucky enough to try. Others were met with a volley of missiles and feet.

Every so often, a small group of United fans would emerge in the home section and the same scenario would be played out – a suicidal charge followed by submersion beneath a frenzy of kicks, stamps and punches.

We decided it was time to get away from this area. We got as far away as possible and just stood there, watching the war continue.

The match continued but I don't know how, as today it would have been called off within seconds of what I saw that day. On the final whistle, both sides burst from the terraces into the street.

Just as before, during the game, it had seemed that I had an awful knack of arriving just as major disorder was breaking out, so it was to be the pattern on the journey back to the station.

Sporadic bottles and missiles flew, but no major incidents occurred until the station was in sight. Suddenly, this was to be the major convergence of both main mobs, and hundreds of Cardiff and Manchester boys tore into each other. There was none of this bouncing about of the modern 'offs', as they became known. No pushing the bloke in front of you into action in order to hide behind him. Just straight in, no mouthing, fight till you dropped.

I will tell you this: not only was I relieved to be on that train home, but so were many of United's top lads.

United's Red Army that season went to all the other towns and cities and pulverised them. Years on, we've had many a battle on foreign ground but nothing will compare to the hatred and violence I saw that day from the taffies.

Cardiff fans continue to wreak havoc around the country and somehow have got bigger in numbers, while other firms have either dwindled or even vanished. Believe it or not, that day got me hooked on being a hooligan and years on I was part of the Red Army.

IT WAS THEIR DAY
Cardiff City v Sunderland, 3rd May 1980

Mallo (CCFC): SUNDERLAND brought thousands and thousands and they were in all the sidestreets, looking for Cardiff. They even attacked Cardiff in the Wells pub and forced them back into Canton; they actually outnumbered us that day, over 10,000 of them. They had fans in all parts of the ground, but those that did try to venture on the Bob Bank didn't stay long as that was the one place that they couldn't take a liberty. A lot of our lads didn't even turn out, but that's not Sunderland's fault – it was their day.

THE EARLY 80's: THE THIRD DIVISION WAS TOUGHER THAN WE THOUGHT

Simon Williams (ex-director, Cardiff City): I remember Annis when he was a kid, as he was about seven years younger than me and, by the time he was 15, he was hanging around with all the older lads and eventually going to all the away games with some of the top lads at the time.

I've never ever pretended to be one of the top lads, but just one of the lads who enjoyed the scene. All who know me will agree with this. I've supported Cardiff City Football Club for 40-odd years now, and all the boys I used to go to games with were a great laugh, top boys, many of whom used to travel with me week in and week out to every game, for more years than I care to remember. They were Paul ('the Rumney Baboon'), Tony (Nanna), Little Collin, Dave ('the Postie'), Dai ('Hooligan'), Mark (from Portmanmore Road, Splott), Carlton, Dav, Jonna, and probably some great lads that I have missed out . . . sorry.

I have seen both sides of this great and famous football club, from the terrace all the way to the boardroom where I was a director for three years, under the Rick Wright regime in the early 90's, and then back to my season ticket in Section A of the Grandstand. The club is in my blood, it's a massive part of my life, and now my son, who I take to most home games is also addicted to this great tradition. This is Cardiff, and we are Cardiff's 'Blue Army'.

I've seen it all with the City, from small scuffles to near riots.

I've been there when the crowds have been as low as 1,500 and I've been there when Ninian Park has been packed to the rafters. I also got to know the lads on the terraces who eventually became the original Soul Crew, in the early 80's. It was the 1982/83 season which stands out in my mind, as that was the year that you could say Cardiff terrorised the Third Division and it was the year that the Soul Crew was formed.

Lincoln City v Cardiff, 13th November 1982

Everybody was looking forward to Lincoln City away, as most of us had never been to Sinsil Bank and also Lincoln were one of our main rivals for promotion from the old Division Three, back to the Second Division.

We all met up early at Cardiff Central station and travelled by Intercity train via Birmingham New Street to arrive in Lincoln at about 12.30pm on the Saturday. We made camp in a local pub near the ground and, up to this point, there had not been any major disturbances that I can recall, just the odd scuffle and mini -battle around the streets of the town centre.

I had travelled with the same mates that I went with for most games, Paul, Little Collin, Dave and Tony, all great guys and very, very game lads. There was also a lad called Parsons from Cardiff, who at the time lived in London. Many, including myself, felt Parsons was the one who started the Soul Crew and also came up with the name. He was a leader and a game lad, but at the same time he upset many a Cardiff fan with his obnoxious attitude.

We stayed in the pub for a while, until everyone who was supposed to be coming had arrived. After leaving the pub, Parsons wanted us to all go in the seats in the main Grandstand, which was something that most firms had now started to do around the country. There had been a lot of rumours coming back to us that a few skirmishes had already taken place between some of the Valley lads and Lincoln. So off we went, about 40 of our lot to their home section seats in the ground.

The game passed by pretty uneventfully, as at half-time we were all allowed to wander around from the stand and near to the pitch side unchallenged. This gave Parsons the idea that he wanted everybody onto the pitch at the final whistle. The main bulk of approximately 1,500 Cardiff fans were fenced off to our left on an open terrace. At the final whistle, when I think we'd lost 2-1, we rushed onto the pitch and basically just meandered around the penalty spot. Some of the lads were urging Lincoln, who were not fenced in, to join Cardiff on the pitch. This they did in their hundreds, there must have been about 40 Cardiff on the pitch and 300 Lincoln. I remember thinking, *This is not too clever,* it was well on top, with no chance of the main Cardiff firm helping as they were battling with the Old Bill themselves, trying to join us. Cardiff stood their ground in the centre circle before eventually being legged out of the ground by biting, snapping Alsatians and the Old Bill whacking their batons into us, along with hundreds of Lincoln fans baying for blood.

As soon as Cardiff got outside the ground it went mental. Lincoln were well up for it and very game, and at one point it looked like we were going to get overrun again. However, as soon as the massed ranks of the main throng of Cardiff lads arrived from the opposite side of the ground it was pretty much all over, with Lincoln having to retreat as fast as they had attacked us, as wave after wave of Cardiff's firm attacked them.

There were outbreaks of trouble all the way back to the station, mainly damage caused by marauding Cardiff supporters attacking or damaging pretty much whatever got in their way. I was later told that Lincoln had battles with the Valley lads who had come by vans and buses.

On the trip home, someone had a radio and we all listened to the sports report at 5-ish about the trouble that had just unfolded via the national radio station.

When the train pulled into Birmingham New Street, Cardiff all disembarked. There were probably 50 or 60 lads on this train, the next one due in had the bulk of Cardiff. People were milling about the concourse, waiting for the connecting train to Cardiff, when somebody shouted that West Ham's ICF had just arrived on one of the platforms. Cardiff went steaming down the escalators and straight into what must have been only about 20 to 30 ICF. Cardiff, through their sheer numbers, were having the better of this until another train pulled into the station within minutes of the first, packed with West Ham. They poured off and went straight into Cardiff, who had to make a quick retreat up the stairs as overwhelming numbers were piling into the Soul Crew.

Up on the main concourse, after being backed right off, the Old Bill and their dogs restored order and normality. We all kept thinking, *If only the next train of Cardiff would arrive,* but that was half an hour behind us so West Ham won the day.

This was one of the best away trips in the promotion season and all credit has to go to Lincoln City's lads.

Wigan v Cardiff, 16th April 1983

The old Springfield Park ground was the scene of probably the longest battle I have ever witnessed on another team's end in all my life. I had travelled up by car with my usual mates and, after parking up a few streets away from the ground, we saw a few well-known faces outside a pub near the ground, so we headed for a drink there. We had a few drinks and then waited to see what the order of the day was going to be.

After a few outbreaks of trouble before the game between small mobs of Wigan and Cardiff, Parsons had the idea that everyone was going to get organised and get on Wigan's end. And so all the lads who had been drinking together at the same pub close to the ground left en masse, about ten minutes or so before the kick-off, unbelievably unimpeded by the police and left to their own devices, but making no noise and trying to look very inconspicuous.

After queuing up and getting into the ground, about 30 or so Soul Crew made their way over to the fence on Wigan's end, closest to the main bulk of the Cardiff support. I think the local constabulary had forgotten about this fixture, as they just did not turn up for a very, very long time. As soon as the game started, so did the trouble. The two sets of fans on Wigan's end just went at each other toe-to-toe for what must have been the best part of five to ten minutes, uninterrupted by the police. Eventually, the police arrived to try to restore order, which after several arrests they did. Cardiff were all led out of the end and allowed entry into the away terracing. (How things have changed.)

During the game there was a lot of chanting from both sides. You could sense that as soon as these two sets of fans could get at each other then they would, and they did. Outside, both sets of supporters charged into each other and were both as up for it as the other. As we had to get back to our car, friends told me that this went on throughout the whole walk back to the railway station, as both mobs fought running battles with each other and the Old Bill lost control of the situation many times. Wigan wanted it as much as Cardiff that day and took the fight to the Soul Crew who were happy to oblige, honours even. It was a day that would betalked about for the rest of the season by the lads. This was a top away game between these two clubs, which has never really been rivalled in all the fixtures between the two since.

At certain places we travelled we expected it, but Wigan and Lincoln had showed the Soul Crew that they couldn't take the mick on their manors.

NOT MUCH HOPE FOR JUST 14 OF US
Middlesborough v Cardiff City, 5th November 1983
Mikey Dye (CCFC): We caught the 04.30am train on Saturday morning, and this was the day I first met Rawlings. Fourteen of us travelled, including Zeddie, Rayer, Little Collin and myself. As we changed trains at Bristol Parkway, I heard a voice from behind shout, "Cardiff Trendies!" I was dressed in a Patrick windcheater, which we were wearing way back then. Rawlings linked up with us and on we went. We arrived at Darlington about 11am for yet another change, and this was where we came across a spotter. *What the fuck is that all about?* I thought. He was a Boro spotter, checking how many we had. We boarded the train and the Old Bill were with us. He said to us, "Be careful up here, boys, Leeds came out of the station last week, all 300 of them and were run back inside." *Fuck,* we thought, *not much hope for our 14 then!* The Old Bill saved us that day, with Boro trailing our every step.

HILARIOUS
Oldham v Cardiff City, 19th November 1983
Mikey Dye (CCFC): We had 100 on the train and as we headed

for the ground, which we could see just across a large recreation field. The only thing in our way was a four-foot wall. As we gathered momentum and started to trot to this wall, the first few reached it and just went for gold, leaping over without giving it a second thought. The next thing we heard was a lot of shouting and swearing, so we looked over and saw the lads rolling around in pain. There was only a fucking eight-foot fucking drop on the other side! How no bones were broken that day, I don't know, but the sight of those lads rolling around was fucking hilarious!

WHAT A FUCKING LETDOWN

I first met Muffy when I lived in Bradford in the early 80's. It was in unusual circumstances, to say the least, which I have written about in my autobiography. He knows my thoughts on Leeds, so we've always agreed not to discuss them, and that way we've stayed good friends. He was a good mate during the 80's and still is today. Fair play to him, he's Leeds through and through, but Muffy is a lad who will stand by your side no matter what. He's probably one of their gamest lads. Leeds don't rate many other firms – in fact I don't know anyone, from Millwall to Man Utd, that they've got an ounce of respect for. Perhaps this was one of the main reasons I disliked them so much when I lived up that way for over a year. Anyway, here is Muffy's story about Cardiff.

Cardiff v Leeds, 11th February 1984
Muffy (Service Crew, Leeds United): I've been a Leeds fan since I was knee high. My dad, though, was Bradford and the rest of the family were too, but Leeds was the team for me and will be till I die.

If ever there was an appropriate way to meet a football hooligan, then it was going to be a kick-off, not anything major but a bit of a set-to. I was 15 years old at the time and was on my way to see Leeds v Chelsea. It was the 1982/83 season and you couldn't get any better than that fixture in those days. I was at Bradford train station at 9am with a couple of my mates, Woody being one of them. We were school kids at the time but were already into the casual scene, and had been watching the

Leeds Service crew rise to the top, so playing Chelsea was far better than going on a geography field trip to Hebden Bridge.

Ten minutes to go for the train, 20 minutes to Leeds Central, then we would be in up-and-coming hooligan heaven. We didn't have to wait too long, as I felt a whack straight to the side of the head. I stumbled back and, as I did, looked up to see a glimpse of a fleeing sheepskin, faded jeans and a pair of Adidas trainers. We were at it already. Not sure of what had really just happened or who it was, we decided to get the next train to Leeds and we would then be amongst our own.

Twenty four years later, I and my family would be sat at a table alongside Sam Hammam and his wife and many Cardiff lads, celebrating the wedding of the very person who had given me that first taste of the enemy's fist: Annis.

Over the years, I have witnessed and been involved in many incidents with Annis, but for now it's the ones involving his beloved Cardiff City and the Soul Crew which I write of. It took a couple of years to come across a Leeds/Cardiff game, after many stories from Annis and members of the Bradford City Ointment, so it was with great anticipation that I found myself again in Leeds at ten in the morning.

Having been to many a game up to then, it was well known that many firms didn't come to Leeds. Whether through fear or lack of organisation, I do not know. So Cardiff's arrival was a great shock to Leeds. The Black Lion pub was just about to open for the day's gathering and around 50 Leeds were already waiting for the doors to open, not even thinking of Cardiff.

From the entrance of the Black Lion, you can see the arrival of anyone coming into Leeds city centre via the train station. You could wait all day long in the hope of some firm being daring enough to have a go, which was what we longed for. Ten minutes is all we had to wait that day. They were here en masse, around 250 of them had made the trip from South Wales to have a go at Leeds. Numbering 50-60 in total, we thought, *Yes, here we go, this is it!* What a fucking letdown! Because up to then it seemed they would be coming straight at us and with no escort whatsoever, but no – I had two years of tales of this and that, and what Leeds got was a hard-looking Welsh male choir. They started singing behind the barriers, "*Ca'rdiff! Ca'rdiff!*" and with that the Old Bill came from everywhere and that's where it ended.

I did hear from other Leeds lads that a rogue coach of Cardiff attacked the Peacock pub at 3pm and chased a few Leeds. A pity they didn't get there earlier.

We would meet some months later down in Cardiff. In those days, Leeds took various divisions of firms to matches, one being the lads from Bradford. On a good day we could number over 100 easy, and some good lads came from Bradford who followed Leeds. We had many a Saturday night battle with Bradford's Ointment in Bradford town centre. So for the trip to Cardiff we had a very good coach full.

We made our way to Cardiff via some country villages. Our coach driver, being originally from South Wales, took us to Penarth Road and dropped us off. The 50 of us then made our way for a mile at least to Ninian Park. We never saw a single lad – another letdown. It was now approaching kick-off, so we went in. Nothing happened during the game, but after it the 50 of us came steaming out straight for the Soul Crew. We were met by hundreds of lads and yes, we were backed off, but for Cardiff to claim that as a result with their numbers, well, that's up to them. I will admit that, when I was on the floor, lads who I've got to know from Cardiff over the years and who came to visit Annis when he lived up this way – Mannings and Little Collin, Moorie, et al, etc – saved me from a hiding. I owe you one.

Annis later laughed at me and said, "You idiots, you walked down a road no one ever uses!" Once again, we decided not to talk about Cardiff/Leeds, as we would not agree on anything.

I never came to the FA Cup match in Cardiff in 2002, as I was abroad. I had enough texts from Annis though, after the game, laughing at us. I know for a fact that over 200 of Leed's top lads went to Hereford before the game and tried their best to get into Cardiff, and near the end they also fought like mad to get out on the streets, knowing Cardiff were massive that day. Also, when Cardiff played their first league game up here for years, when we were first relegated, we had thousands of lads out for Cardiff, fighting the Old Bill outside the ground for over two hours, and many went to prison for it.

Annis still says Cardiff are way ahead of mighty Leeds in terms of lads. Well, we beg to differ once again.

MUSTARD ATTACK
Newcastle United, 25th February 1984

Mikey Dye (CCFC): Yet again we were on the 04.30 train: Peter M, Rawlings, Rayer (RIP), myself and not too many more. On arrival there was yet another welcoming committee, but also the Old Bill and a welcome lift to St James' Park for the match. While inside we got chatting to the NME (Newcastle crew), and all was going well until a top Newcastle lad took exception to this and proceeded to squirt mustard at us through the fences keeping us apart, but only directly hitting Rawlings who was wearing a white Tacchini tracksuit top. The man Rawlings went loopy and would have killed him if he'd had his way. We lost the game, with that curly permed git Kevin Keegan scoring twice.

ALL ABOARD THE DOUBLE-DECKER
Man City v Cardiff City, 24th March 1984

Mikey Dye (CCFC): We took the train for this one, a big turnout of about 200 all dressed to the nines. Man City were called the Maine Line then, but we didn't give a fuck, we were going to Manc land. We downed some ale on the way up – I was a four-pack man back then, no more, or I'd be unstable on my feet!

Our train pulled in and we surged off. There were hardly any Old Bill at the station platform. We went outside in search of the waiting Manc mob. We were not disappointed. Outside were maybe 50 Man City, but also two double-deckers to herd us to Maine Road. There were also police vans, dog handlers and horseback riders. The Mancs didn't reckon on so many coming, but the police had it sorted. Or had they? As the dibble forced most of our lot onto the buses, me, Jammo, CC, Peter M and a few others waited till the end, baiting the Mancs. After about five minutes or so, we could see that about 30 of us couldn't get on the buses due to their being full. The buses were rocking back and forth by now. Anyone who has ever been upstairs on a double-decker when it rocks with 80 idiots on board knows what I mean – Pepsi Max has got nothing on that!

By now, all the Old Bill were busy trying to control the bus situation. This was our chance. We headed for the Mancs and fair play to 'em, they duly obliged. They were into us, with punches and kicks thrown from both sections and the famous standoffs every now and then. It all lasted only 60 seconds before the Old Bill were on top, manhandling everybody. The fuckers had ripped buttons off of my brand new G2 shirt, which I'd bought in London only the week before. That's life, I suppose, but I thought, *Fuck, another £50 down the drain!* The police had ordered another bus for us stragglers and within ten minutes it arrived. We boarded with no problem, but only after our day had been made. Man City brought a coach to us with their mob later on that season. It was the first organised coach that I'd witnessed, but the day went off without any trouble.

A CASUAL'S LEARNING CURVE
Huddersfield Town v Cardiff City, 28th April 1984
Mallo (CCFC): Then I went on my first away trip to Huddersfield, with one of the smartest casuals around, Mikey Dye. We set off from Cardiff Central station, mostly casuals on the train, but there were some ugly-looking blokes that day with Cardiff. Being a bit weary of how loudly they were drinking, smoking and playing cards, I decided to stand in the corridor near the toilets. We arrived at Newport and more Cardiff lads boarded the train. Then we were off up north; when we finally arrived, we walked out of the station, into the main street and up about 100 yards. This black guy in a green beanie hat started bouncing around and throwing punches, he was like a maniac. Then, suddenly, a large mob of Huddersfield appeared and they were armed with bottles and bricks. They were soon throwing bottles, etc, at us, Cardiff had to retreat at first but were soon into them. When all they had left was their fists, it soon became a proper toe-to-toe. My heart was racing: *yes*, this was it, I was actually having my first fight and I was hooked.

After the game I was on the train on the way home; I was taking a lot of stick, mostly from an older guy. As I was still on a high I was having none of it, he may have been ten years older than me but I thought, *So what?* We ended up having a row on the train, where I got the better of him; he soon took me on board, but I was no mug. I was not your normal youngster that would keel over easily. Later, after years of following the City, we then became good friends.

I wanted more and more of this new culture. I was growing up quickly and loving it. I started to collect glasses in a well-known nightclub – yes, a night club at 13 – so I could get money to travel and watch the City.

Then it was the family rail cards, with me being the adult and taking four blokes all with moustaches as kids for a pound. This lasted for a while, but I got rumbled with Annis, Darryl, Collin, Beer and co, when we went to a night match in Bury.

THREE NORTH-EAST FIRMS IN ONE DAY
Hartlepool v Cardiff, 23rd August 1986
Annis Abraham Jnr. (CCFC): At the end of the 1985/86 season, Cardiff City were relegated to the old Fourth Division for the first time in the club's history. As if that wasn't bad enough, it was almost like the Football League deliberately rubbed salt into the fans' wounds when the fixture list for the 1986/87 campaign was announced. They gave us a 600-mile round trip to Hartlepool on the opening day of the season. What a way to welcome us to the dungeon that was.

The club was in a terrible state on and off the pitch at the time, and crowds at Ninian Park were down as low as 1,800 on occasions. Many so-called City supporters had turned their backs on the Bluebirds, although the young Soul Crew hadn't. Cardiff's away following was often tiny during the mid-80's, but we were among the small number of fans who stuck by the team regardless of what division they were in and what sort of results they were getting. Although the opening day of the 1986/87 campaign was sure to be a very long one, we were all up for a journey to the North East.

Believe it or not, we had as much fun in those days travelling to places like Hartlepool, Scarborough and Darlington as we did when City were playing away to some of the bigger clubs. You never knew what to expect when you were turning up at a northern lower division club for the first time and there were hardly any Old Bill on duty at some of the smaller grounds, so we usually had a laugh.

In the weeks before the Hartlepool game we sorted out a batch of cheap family rail cards. When we eventually caught the train there was about 80 of us, and most us were travelling on dodgy family tickets. The lads I was with included Viking, Beer, Rhys, Rusty, Rawlings, Jonathan, Derek, Dowie and Steve from Llanrumney. Some of the Ely Trendies such as Dyo (Mikey Dye), Jammo, Sissy and Jerky were along for the ride, as were a number of the Barry Casuals including Darryl, Kersey, Melvin, Bowcher and Staples. You could say we were one big happy family!

The night before the trip, 40 of us had been over in Barry Island for the evening and we ended up staying out until the early hours of the morning. Our train was due to depart at around 5am, so it was pointless going home. Most of the lads were so drunk by the time we left South Wales they just wanted to sleep the beer off, but amazingly a few managed to stay awake for the whole journey.

As we were leaving Cardiff Central station we were apparently spotted by the police. They phoned ahead to Bristol Parkway, where we had to change trains, and told the local Old Bill to expect us. When we got to Parkway, two of Bristol's finest came over and told us they thought the Cardiff coppers were winding them up when they'd said 80 of us were heading their way so early in the morning. We assured them we wouldn't cause any problems and said all we wanted to do was sleep. Surprisingly, they let us board our train with no objections. I think they just wanted to go back to sleep themselves.

We arrived at Darlington station at about 10am. As we were waiting for our connection to Hartlepool, we noticed a load of local lads further down the platform. They were setting off to watch their team play a Third Division game in York, so Rawlings wandered over and began chatting to a group of them.

They numbered around 50 in all, and they looked a decent little firm. Most of them were a good few years older than us and they were dressed in all the right gear. Jonathan, Viking, Darryl and I strolled over to where Rawlings was standing and listened to what was being said. Rawlings told us they were asking who we were and he said they were talking about how much they hated Hartlepool, but I sensed they were just weighing us up. Then this fat Darlo lad looked down his nose at us and sneered, "You Welsh wankers won't be able to do anything in Hartlepool anyway. You're just a bunch of kids."

Having some chubby northerner taking the piss out of us was all the encouragement our boys needed. A roar went up and everyone was straight into them. Without going into too much detail, it's fair to say that the Darlington lads came badly unstuck. There were bodies flying everywhere for a couple of minutes until the Old Bill flooded onto the platform and split us up. After things had calmed down we couldn't help laughing at the local boys. They had tried to belittle us but it backfired on them big-time.

The transport police ushered us onto the next train, and about nine or ten officers followed us onboard. It was their intention to escort us straight to Hartlepool, but we had other ideas. This particular train was one of the local services that stopped at every station between Darlington and Hartlepool, so when it pulled into Stockton-on-Tees we jumped off and legged it out onto the streets. The coppers tried their best to stop us, but as soon as we made it off the platforms they were powerless to do anything as we were out of their jurisdiction.

We managed to find ourselves a nice little pub within a few minutes' walk of the station. I promised the landlord we'd fill up his tills and said we'd be the best behaved football fans he'd ever encountered, provided he didn't telephone the Old Bill and let them know where we were. He had no problem agreeing to such a deal and was as good as gold with us all lunchtime. We kept the doors firmly closed and made sure everyone stayed inside the pub in an effort to avoid detection. Either the police couldn't find us or they couldn't be bothered to look, as we managed to stay there for almost two hours without any interference from the local constabulary. When we were ready to move on, I asked the landlord to show us the best way to Hartlepool. He said a bus pulled up outside the pub every half-hour and it went straight to the town centre, so that was that. Pretty soon, 80 pissed-up Soul Crew youngsters were on a double-decker bus heading for Hartlepool, and it was rocking. Literally rocking at times!

As the bus arrived in the middle of the town, one of the lads at the front of the top deck shouted that he could see a load of mods a bit further up the road. That was like a red rag to a bull for us. Back then, mods had become an unhealthy obsession for our firm of young casuals. If we weren't fighting with other football fans we were fighting with mods, so the bus started emptying and half of our drunken loonies were staggering down the street, chasing after them. To be honest, we must have looked a right bunch of clowns. We made so much racket that the mods were on their toes long before we got anywhere near them. Although we didn't manage to give them any grief, what we did do was alert the Old Bill to our arrival. The next thing I knew, there were coppers everywhere and we were all running off in different directions. It didn't seem too bad at the time, as we'd agreed beforehand that if we got split up we'd meet up later in Hartlepool's seats. Things didn't work out quite that way though.

Plenty went wrong before we got to the ground. Jammo's small group walked into the middle of a shopping square and stumbled upon 50 Hartlepool lads. By that stage he was pissed out of his brain, so with only a handful of boys behind him he just went for it and steamed straight into them. When we caught up with him later it was obvious he'd had a right kicking, and apparently he didn't get much in the way of back-up from those who were with him. The local lads had even nicked his shoes, which was out of order, although, to be fair, Jammo wasn't using them anyway as he could hardly stand up!

I was in a group of about 20 and we were involved in a few scuffles with the Hartlepool fans on the way to the Victoria Ground. I remember they were pretty game and never once took a backward step. The Old Bill had to get between us on several occasions before we got to the ground. When we eventually did arrive we went straight into the main grandstand as arranged, but we were disappointed to find the others hadn't managed to join us.

Nothing much happened for the first half an hour or so. Then we noticed the enclosure below the stand was suddenly starting to fill up, but the lads who were arriving weren't Hartlepool or Cardiff supporters, they were in fact Middlesbrough fans. The situation was that Middlesbrough Football Club had gone into liquidation over debts of £2 million a few weeks earlier. As a result, the bailiffs had locked Ayresome Park and Boro were left with nowhere to play. A group of local businessmen were supposed to be putting a rescue package together, so the Football League allowed Boro to play their opening Third Division game against Port Vale at Hartlepool's Victoria Ground. Bizarrely, instead of their match being played the following day, it was scheduled to kick off in the evening just a couple of hours after our match had finished.

As we approached half-time there must have been 150 Middlesbrough lads in the enclosure below the stand, and they were making sure we knew they'd seen us. I felt like we were sitting ducks. During the interval some of them began making their way up the steps towards us, so a few of our lot ripped out a load of plastic seats and began hurling them at the advancing Boro contingent. From that moment onwards it was chaos. At first the Boro lads backed off and a few of them even spilled onto the pitch, but then they got themselves together and began charging up the stand towards us. More seats were thrown at them but they were returned with interest. For a couple of minutes the air was thick with missiles going in both directions. Meanwhile, a large percentage of the 600 Cardiff fans in the away end were attempting to invade the pitch and come to our rescue. The Old Bill really had their hands full trying to keep the City mob under control. A few lads did make it onto the pitch and Dowie was one of them, but he was immediately bitten by a police dog, so he got himself back into the away end a bit sharpish.

It didn't take the Boro boys long to get decent numbers up into the stand, and we had no chance against them. When they reached us we attempted to stand our ground for about 30 seconds, but it was a pointless exercise so we began to retreat. That gave Boro further encouragement, and they not only kicked us down the stairs but battered us through the turnstiles as we were trying to get out. I took a fair few slaps, as did Beer and Dyo. Viking and Derek did their best to fight back, I could hear Viking shouting at Derek by the turnstiles to hit them as hard as he could and to smash them, but they didn't last long before they had to clamber over and join the rest of us outside the ground. Luckily, nobody sustained anything more than minor cuts and bruises, which was amazing considering the punishment we took while we were trying to escape.

Beer was seriously pissed off with what had happened and demanded that we try to do something to get our own back, so we ran around to the stand's main entrance and tried to make our way down the players' tunnel. However, the Old Bill saw us and managed to stop us before we got very far. We told them we were only trying to find the away end and, surprisingly, they believed us, so they led us to the Cardiff section and let us join up with the rest of the lads. As soon as we got into the away end we began swapping tops with the boys who were already in there, just in case the coppers decided to come looking for those of us who had been involved in the battle with Boro in the grandstand.

The match ended in a 1-1 draw, with striker Rob Turner scoring City's goal. Afterwards, the Old Bill had a nightmare job as they tried to escort hundreds of us back to the train. There were lots of Hartlepool lads about and there were plenty more Middlesbrough fans arriving for their game, so by the time we reached the station it had kicked off numerous times. No side could claim any sort of victory though, as the police were generally on top of things. Nevertheless, I should mention how impressive Boro's firm looked. Despite the fact that their club was at death's door and they weren't playing in their home town, they still had a large number of lads out. The transport police arranged a special train to take us back to Cardiff and at least a dozen officers joined us for the journey. Nobody was really bothered, as most of us were knackered and just wanted to sleep after such a hectic day out, which is hardly surprising under the circumstances.

When we got back home our phones were red hot. Bear in mind these were the days before mobiles and the internet, so information didn't travel anywhere near as fast. Those who hadn't been with us up in Hartlepool wanted to know what had happened, as the trouble had made the national news on TV and radio. There was also plenty of press coverage over the following few days. The media seemed amazed that the first outbreak of violence of the new season had occurred at a Fourth Division match. The fact that the start of the second half had been delayed for 15 minutes while the police tried to calm things down was the major talking point.

Cardiff City were destined to spend ten of the next 15 years in the league's bottom division, but although the football was often rubbish, most of us stuck together and kept supporting the team all the same. The 80's and 90's are now considered by many fans to be the worst period in the City's history, and that's fair enough really. The club was often in turmoil back then, but the Soul Crew lads still managed to have plenty of good times. Having said that, the day we spent up in Hartlepool in August 1986 was definitely a one-off. After all, I can't remember any other occasion when we had to take on three rival mobs in one day!

A MARKED MAN

Stockport County v Cardiff City, 22nd November 1986

Tonto Davies (CCFC): Coppers can spoil a good day out, and I'm not talking about the ones who steam in with their batons waving. Because let's face it, when that happens then we're all up to something we shouldn't be and probably deserve it anyway. Besides, most of these coppers are shit-scared youngsters who'd rather not be in the middle of two warring firms. The ones I'm on about are the arseholes who got bullied at school, probably wet their beds until they were well into their teens and have now been given a little bit of power they can use to spoil your day.

I met one of these on a trip to Stockport. We'd just arrived and I was getting off the train; before my Adidas-clad feet had even touched the platform, he was on me. He had me around the throat, held me up against a wall, treated me to a sly dig in the gut and said, "I know who you are, I'm watching you." What the fuck was all that about? I was a nobody who'd never even stepped foot in Stockport before this day. The guy clearly had issues. So it was out of the station and onto the first pub. A few of the boys went straight to the ground and managed to get us tickets for Stockport's seats, so all that was left for me to do was get pissed. But that proved easier said than done. I bought my first pint and settled down while we waited for the next train to arrive with the rest of the boys. I must have only been there five minutes when my policeman friend came in, pulled me off the chair, held me up against another wall (I was getting sick of this), and treated me to my second dig in the ribs of the day. Then, not content with just the physical abuse, he told me I wasn't allowed to drink and that I was banned from every pub in Stockport; if he caught me in another boozer, he was going to nick me. So what do you do? Easy, find another boozer. At least I managed to drink a pint in my next port of call, but while I was at the bar, ordering my next one, the Old Bill came in again. This time it was a different copper; he ran straight towards me and I thought, *Bollocks, nicked again!* As it turned out, this one was cool; he told me the other copper picked on someone like this every time a team with a reputation came to town. He also said the other copper was on his way and I should hide in the toilets until he was gone. This game of cat and mouse went on all day. Eventually, we got to the ground and into the seats, and guess who turned up after about 30 seconds? He stood in front of me with his back to the game, and his big size twelves on top of mine so that I couldn't move; he didn't even let me up at half-time for a piss. His reasoning was that I'd paid for a seat and I was going to sit in it. I didn't see any of the game, but he ended up doing me a favour. At the end, Cardiff managed to get on the pitch and have a go at Stockport's end; once it had all died down, the only way off the pitch for Cardiff was through a corridor the police had formed with their dogs. So I might not have seen a ball kicked that afternoon, but neither did I have teeth marks in my leg to nurse on the way home, like most of the boys. I think that was the one and only time I've been to Stockport.

Nowadays it's all too much for me. I actually got called a "geriatric hooligan" a few weeks back, and I'm only 40. In the past they would have just locked you in the back of the van until the game was over, then put you on the train home. Now, with CCTV everywhere, you can expect a knock on your door weeks after the event and a banning order for the same offence; things have definitely changed. I think I'd rather sit at home with my shirt on and wait for the results on Sky.

But then again, I've never been to the Liberty Stadium.

TALES OF THE UNEXPECTED
Boro and Cardiff are very similar when it comes to the lads, and there is a lot of respect for each other's firms. Here are a couple of stories from a Middlesbrough lad called Diddy.

Cardiff City v Middlesborough, 8th January 1994
Diddy (Frontline, Boro): I met the author of this book many years ago, at Darlington v Cardiff, and have kept in touch with him since. Annis has asked me if I would like to write my account of my visits to Wales.

It was the FA Cup 1994. When the draw was made, I was buzzing. We'd never played Cardiff for as long as I could remember, and they were a big name on the hooligan scene. To visit a different ground where we'd never been, a different firm and a new challenge – a lot of our lads were looking forward to this one!

My day started about half past five in the morning. A dozen of us decided to go by train, as Cardiff was a long haul by road and so we'd travel in a bit of comfort. We had to get the train from Leeds, which was about five-ten miles outside Leeds city centre. What a great fucking start! So our only option was to start hitchhiking in twos and hope we got there in time. Dark and cold, at around six in the morning the odds of us all getting there didn't look great. But somehow, lucky as fuck, all of us got there with time to grab a bacon bun outside the station. When I went to the counter to pay my £42 for the train ticket, my luck was in again. I put my money on the counter and the bloke pushed my tickets through the glass window, he never took my money and turned away. So I just grabbed my tickets and my money and was off like fuck, laughing my head off. Unbeknownst to me at the time, the day was going to get even better!

The main crew of Boro lads were travelling down by coach and parking up at Newport, then getting the train in. But the coach was a fucking wreck so they still hadn't arrived, and were going to get into Cardiff half an hour or so behind the rest of us, which wasn't what we'd been hoping. Pulling into Cardiff station around 11am, the nerves started to kick in. The whole 15 of us, not knowing what awaited us, were on edge. We got off the train and were surprised to see only one or two police in the station, who didn't bat an eyelid at the 15 of us walking through. Out of the station, we walked into sunny daylight, not knowing which way to go. We walked straight ahead, then right, looking for a boozer so we could get out of sight. As we turned right there was a big pub over the road, and I'm not going to lie: my first thoughts were, *If this is full of taffs, we're fucking dead!* But there was nobody outside and, luckily enough, nobody inside waiting to steam out at us, as we'd imagined. After all, this was Cardiff, and with their reputation that's what we thought would happen. There was another boozer over the road, the Albert, so we decided to get in there, get a pint, and see where the rest of the lads were.

We phoned one of the lads on the bus and they were at Newport, just about to get on the train. They were 20 minutes away, so I said to my mate on the bus I'd walk back to the station to meet them coming off and take them to the pub. Now 50-odd lads walked out of the station and the copper there never batted an eyelid. *Result!* We were now 60-70 strong and no law knew we were there. More surprisingly, up until now we hadn't seen any Cardiff lads. More and more calls were being made between the Boro lads who were coming by car or minibus, telling them the name of the boozer we were in, and so all the time there was more Boro arriving into the pub, boosting our numbers and our confidence. Upstairs, there was a big window looking out to the city centre; this was where quite a few of the Boro lads had gone, and I was up there when we spotted the first few Cardiff lads – only three of them, but right opposite our pub.

One of them walked over and went straight into our pub downstairs, so I decided to go down and listen to what he was saying. He was by himself and talking to my mate Doozer, so I went over, introduced myself and started having a crack with him, "Where's your lads?", etc. He was saying nobody was about at the moment, as they weren't expecting us to come that early. But it was something Boro had done for years, getting in at 11 bells. The Cardiff lad was sound as fuck, and on his own. He was called Jonathan and it was not our way to take liberties, so he was given the respect he deserved for walking into a pub full of opposition lads. We swapped phone numbers and said we'd keep in touch, especially if we got a draw. Then they'd have to come to Boro!

Jonathan left with a shake of hands and admiration from me and Doozer. For all he knew, we could have been a bunch of wankers with no morals and slapped him about. On the other hand, we knew he was having a good look at what we had in the boozer, but unbeknownst to Jonathan most of our lads were upstairs – which we'd both laugh about in a year's time at Swansea! Anyway, roughly an hour or so later, by which time more and more Boro had arrived at our boozer, I was upstairs near the big front window when the shout went up: "They're here."

Stretching my neck so I could see down the high street to our right, I could just glimpse a mob of Cardiff heading our way. "Come on!" we shouted to each other, as we all pushed and shoved to get down the narrow staircase. (At this point I want to state that all I can say is what I witnessed, as everyone knows what happens when two mobs with big numbers clash. Everybody has their own little stories.)

Concerning the numbers on each side, opinions vary, so all I can do is guess. I'd say roughly anything between 80-130, with Cardiff having anything between 70-100. But it happened quickly and it was 14-15 years ago. We were at some double doors on the lefthand side of the pub, we opened them up to get out and were showered with bottles, glasses, etc. The doors shut until the shout went up: "Fucking get out now!" Then the doors opened and out we piled, steaming straight into anybody in front of us.

We never took a backwards step and, when we piled out, the mob of Cardiff got split into two. There was a corner opposite and half of the Cardiff backed off down one street, while the others backed off to where they'd come from. We stayed tight and went at one mob that backed off – the ones that stood got done – and then went at the other mob, who ran back towards the station. This went on for a couple of minutes and, as anyone who's been involved would know, that's quite a long time. Eventually, the mob nearest the station just melted, so our attention went to those to the right of us. With us all together, mob-handed, the Cardiff didn't stand a chance; they got backed off a couple of hundred yards, we slipped down a sidestreet and ended up right outside the Millennium Stadium. Until then, I was completely unaware how close the stadium had been to us. The police arrived en masse and wrapped us all up together, but by this point we weren't too bothered as the damage had been done. We were escorted up to the ground, with just a bit of verbals as we passed the Ninian Park pub.

After the game we were expecting a very hostile reception, but the police had it all boxed off and there was very little trouble, if any. We got escorted back to the station, and the main crew got escorted back to Newport, where rumour had it that Cardiff were waiting, but the rumours were false. Boro drew 2-2 and the replay at Boro gave Cardiff the chance of revenge. But, with it being a midweek night game, the lads that did come got collared on the coach on the motorway into Boro, Nothing of note occurred and Cardiff won the replay, which was typical of Boro on the pitch.

A year later and Boro got Swansea away. So I rang Jonathan, whose number I'd kept. Again, I got on the train with about ten others, got off in Cardiff and met Jonathan, leaving the rest to carry on to Swansea where we'd meet back up with the Boro who'd travelled by coach, van and car. I met Jonathan and it was like we'd been mates for years. He was as sound as fuck, and so were his three mates who accompanied us in the car to Swansea. When I mentioned what had happened last year with us, one of his mates turned round and said Jonathan had left our pub and gone round the Cardiff pubs, trying to get a mob together saying, "C'mon, there's 50 Boro in the Albert." At that, Jonathan butted in, "Yeah, I didn't fucking know there was another 50-60 of you upstairs!" At that, all of us just laughed like fuck.

On arriving at Swansea, a call was made to see where our mob was. We met them in the boozer our lads had occupied, roughly between 50-80 strong. The Cardiff lads were quite impressed with our turnout, considering the distance. Everyone got chatting and Jonathan asked if we wanted him to take us to their boozer. We all nodded and off we set. We ended up right outside the ground. As soon as we were within yards of the pub, Jonathan and a few Boro were straight into them. But this time the police had cottoned onto us, so it was very brief. Once in the ground, standing behind the goal, I could see Swansea lads pointing at us as if to say, "What the fuck are Cardiff doing with Boro?" Jonathan then explained that he was well known by a lot of the Swansea from past experiences. It was funny looking at their puzzled faces.

After the game there were bits and pieces of trouble, before I went back to the station and Jonathan and the other three Cardiff went back to their car. After this day, me and Jonathan became really good friends, meeting up the following year at the England v Scotland game at Euro 96, where we had a good firm. In the years since I've met him several times: when I've gone down to Cardiff for their play-off game at the Millennium stadium against QPR; when they got promoted; then away at Millwall, when I've got to say that the mob they took there with them that day was the biggest I've ever seen, 600-700 strong! I also went down last season when they played Brum with three other Boro lads, but remained in the pub due to a ban. Every time I've been down, we've been treated with respect.

During the last 14 years or so, I've come to know via others that Jonathan, Viking and a few others are some of the main faces at Cardiff. I think I can safely say that I can count them as good friends, and not once has anybody said a bad word about Boro. In fact, they've praised us since day one. My own view is – and not everyone will agree with me, even some of my Boro mates – that I've seen the numbers Cardiff can muster, from a capital city with all the surrounding valleys etc, and on their day they must be up there with the best of them. But the day we went to Cardiff, we had the better of it; nobody can take that away from us, and I know for a certainty that Cardiff put us up there with the best they've come across.

All in all, it was a day I'll always remember. We had a good off with one of the main firms in the country and came out on top, but I also made proper friends because of it.

To all of the Cardiff lads I've met over the years – respect!

BATTLING WITH MANCS AT NEW STREET STATION 2002

Mikey Dye (CCFC): One of my favourite battles was the scrapping and running of the Cockney Reds at Birmingham New Street station. We travelled by train to Northampton and found the game was called off, deciding to stop off in a pub. Anthony, Robbie, Morg, Justin, GV, Pernny, Lucky, Bags and a few more names were on this outing. At about 4pm we decided to make our way back to New Street, as the Mancs would be coming through. We left the station to make our way to the Wetherspoon's in town for a quick few, and guessed on the reds coming through about seven-ish. We had a bit of banter with a gang of Asians at Brum, who barged into us on purpose. One barged me, so I turned and fronted him. We squared up and he went to headbutt me, but I moved out of the way and Goughy was into him, throwing numerous punches. Before we could do anything it was all over, with our lot actually saying, "Pack it in, they ain't worth it!" Fair play, there were only about six of 'em. When we left this pub we returned to New Street, where our main group drank up and left. Justin and GV were lagging behind, as they left the pub about five minutes after we did. Then guess what? The Asians had mobbed up and waited for the main group to leave, attacking our two stragglers and causing them cuts and bruises. But that's what it's all about.

On arriving at New Street, we went in the pub on the station and, after about ten minutes, a policeman came in and closed the pub. He wanted us out of the way because the Cockney Reds were due in. We were not happy, but there was no beer so there was no point in stopping. We headed for the platform and made our way down the stairs for the train. Lucky Evans was just being thrown off the chugger for smoking! The copper who was dealing with us pleaded to the guard to let us on, but the guard wasn't having any of it. Me and young Anthony, who is a quality lad, decided that if he couldn't get on the train then none of us would, and made our way back up the steps. On reaching the top, fuck me, the blue of Brum had turned to the red of Manchester! These were the shirters – where was the mob? With that, we saw their dressers; we were all pissed but ready – although a bit unstable. The Old Bill didn't know what to do. There were 20 of us, two cops and Man U's mob coming up the stairs. We surged forward to where the platform was and, as we got near, the local plod surrounded us, pulling us all against a wall. Normal people were getting out of the way, but we surged again to break out of the police hold and tried to get into Man U, who by now were coming into view. As we got into a few of them, I went to lash out at one Manc and he raised his leg (it was warm, so he had shorts on). He showed me his Cardiff City tattoo as if in his defence, so I had to ask the question, "Who the fuck do you support?" To which he gave no reply. We let up a roar of "SOUL CREW! SOUL CREW!" and barged through again, but this time the truncheons were used to strike us. I remember crawling on the floor, with two of ours doing the same, while the truncheons rained down on us. Fuck me, we had some bruises! While all this was going on, apparently the rest of Man U had heard the roar and ran back down their stairs. All the riot cops were there to contain us. The dibble were very heavy handed, and we did have three arrests for public disorder – two of them receiving heavy fines for their troubles. By then I'd got back on the train to head home, and my phone was red hot with people ringing me to ask what had happened. News spreads fast in the soccer world.

MINNOWS SWIMMING AMONGST SHARKS

Chesterfield v Cardiff City, 30th March 2002

Big Gwyn (CCFC): Chesterfield away was meant to be a chill trip. There was no history of real problems and, while they could always muster a tidy little mob, it was very much a case of minnows swimming amongst sharks. So no one was expecting problems, no battle plans were in place, and in fact we were so complacent that we'd booked a hotel in the town where 40-odd of us were staying for the night. We were taking around 12 or so Rams coaches up that day, and the 40-odd that were staying were made up of small groups from several buses who'd get off the coach they'd travelled up on and all come home together on the one coach that was staying up there. It sounds easy, but believe me, it was another logistical nightmare.

It was my suggestion to make a night of it in Chesterfield; I'd lived up there for a 12-month or so many years ago, for my work. The place was well known for nightlife and shedloads of tottie, a good mix for our travelling Rams. I was more than convinced we could have a good fun night without any running battles, but I couldn't have been further from the truth.

One of the attractions of travelling on a Rams coach was the drinking culture we fostered, or rather harnessed. Because the Rams didn't invent drinking at football, but we did identify early on that we could use the drink culture as a carrot to get people on board in an organised group. Our plan from the early stage was to identify fan-friendly pubs along the route there or going home, and if possible near the grounds we would be visiting. I'd contact these in turn, trying my best to charm the landlords and assure them that I wouldn't be turning up with Genghis Khan's Mongol hordes. We would offer a bond of £200 and tell them that they could hold on to this money to cover any damages (luckily there never were any).

The older, more respected heads amongst us made sure that the younger hotheads behaved and didn't mess up our drinking privileges. Anyone who stepped out of line wasn't banned, but a couple of them were smacked or put in their place and simpled in front of their mates. This usually did the trick and often they would apologise (when sober) and get back on track, or fuck off and do their own thing. Our reputation for keeping order and control amongst ourselves soon earned us notice, especially amongst pubs the length and breadth of the country, but also amongst some more forward thinking police forces, like the West Midlands. NOT!!!

This progressed as far as publicans phoning me if they knew we were in the area, and asking us to call in with the guaranteed till-bursting revenue we would bring along. Thinking back now, I should have been a bit more switched-on and asked for a few bungs. The police realised the potential of keeping us together, rather than having us spread out all over the county, travelling via all modes of transport and drinking in any pub that let us in or was to timid to stop us swarming over them. Many times we'd be approached by the police, asking us to set up either some pre-match meetings or emails, with them asking what they could do for us and us telling them what we could do for them. Sometimes they would promise us things then stitch us up, forgetting we'd be back next year, so they'd soon get the chance to see which option was the easier to manage. But negotiating and even talking to this mob of hooligans (as we were and still are seen by many) went against the grain amongst some of the higher ranked, public school-educated match commanders.

One such incident was the first game at Wigan away. We'd arranged with the police to take all our coaches to the JJB Stadium. They had arranged a nearby pub for us all to go to: job done, 12 coaches of Rams, straight to the ground, straight off the bus and into the pub, a good swig and into the game; game ends and you come out onto the coaches and head home.

Sounds simple, and it can be. But what they decided to do at Wigan was to let us all get into the ground and then turn up in ten vanloads and search the coaches, top to bottom. Now, one of the unwritten perks we allowed the lads was that – for these long away trips, i.e. five hours on a coach, rather than stopping on the way home for a drink, etc – we'd allow them to keep a few cans in their bags as long as they were locked under the coach for the return journey.

The drivers would then get ten or so miles en route, find

somewhere safe to pull over and allow the lads to get their drink and have a safe trip home, without the worry of stopping off in towns for drink and food and all the problems that would often cause. But the police, on finding this stash of the dreaded alcohol, thought they'd solved the crime of the century. Bags were thrown onto the floor and stamped on, smashing MP3 players and, in one case, a lad's insulin and needles needed for his return journey.

Picture the scene at Wigan: I get to hear of this smart piece of police work; I then speak to our police FIO who, in all fairness, is switched on and can see the broader picture; but at the end of the day, he is only a constable and there is only so much he can do. We both speak to the match commander, who is proud of his great police work in finding some cans of alcohol stashed away for the homeward bound journey. I then point out to him that he will now need to block every exit on the way out of Wigan and on the route home, because as soon as these lads see a gap they will be down there looking for refills or simply finding a pub to stay and drink in. It was funny to see the realisation dawn on him. He'd been quite clear in stating the law to me, in as much as the only place you could not drink on the way to football games was on the coaches, to which I replied, "No problem." So the 2,000 or so Cardiff fans you had safely wrapped up in stadiums would still come next year. Not in a recognisable, compliant convoy of coaches, but in scores of vans, minibuses, cars, etc. These would be parked all over Wigan, and his officers would be running around like headless chickens, trying to stop disorder. You could see the panic set in; suddenly, you had a load of police vans bringing back these dozens and dozens of bags and dumping them outside the coaches. Many of them had been stamped on; many were just strewn around the coach park. (How were they to know which bus they'd come off?) But it got sorted to some degree; not everyone had their correct bag or correct amount of drink, but at least the damage was limited. The next year came along and they took an almost grovelling approach, offering the world to keep us on the coaches and sticking to the plans we'd set up the year before.

Meanwhile, the forces that worked with us usually spoke highly of the cooperation and better behaviour they'd come across. However (and this is a story for another day), these authorities would soon start moving the goal posts and, while initially they were happy to allow a few perks and were pleased with the results, they would soon be limiting the perks and demanding even bigger and better results. Six years ago, they were happy if they got us out of town with no riots or major public disorder occurring. Soon, they would be complaining about the amount of litter that 15 coaches would discharge, and that some of the lads had even been drinking. Shame on them! Drinking on a day out at the football! Who did these hooligans think they were?

Anyway, while every day didn't work out as we planned, most did and we were having a good time of it. The arrest figures that had kept us at the top of the disorder league of shame started to decline. So not only were we delivering a plan that worked, we were also giving them documented proof that a little joint enterprise would suit all parties.

Chesterfield was a bread and butter game to us. There was no expectation or real history of serious trouble, and we were not expecting any. The police had promised to put us all in a pub near the ground and keep us together. When we were around a couple of miles out of Chesterfield, I had the sense that things were a bit tense. Out-rider motorbikes started picking up the coaches as they appeared. Nothing new there. Then we were taken to a large pub with a large car park and there were police everywhere, but again it nothing new to us. Everyone was Section 60'd while getting off the bus and, while not a new phenomenon, it did seem a bit over the top for a Chesterfield game. As happened at lots of other away games, the lads on the coaches would get calls from their mates; some had made their way in cars and vans, but would still want to meet up with us. The atmosphere was guaranteed, and there was also the safety in numbers approach at some of the more high-profile games we encountered.

Again, this was another bonus and spin-off effect of what we were doing. By allowing a huge mob of us to stay together, this usually attracted a lot more Cardiff fans to the same pubs as us and would make policing us easier, as long as they didn't wind us up too much. Because suddenly you may have up to a thousand people drinking in one or two pubs close to each other, a powerful mob if the need arose, but also a massive deterrent to any hostile away fans who wanted a pop at us. My God, they couldn't have got within a half-mile of us, and if they did, with the numbers we had, they'd have been slaughtered.

We started getting calls off small groups of Cardiff that had gone into the city centre; they had also said there was a huge police presence in town that day. I spoke to our FIO, who couldn't say too much, but it became clear later why they were all so tense. Chesterfield had got a huge mob together for this one, and we found out later from police sources and other lads that some major faces from several clubs in the area had got together for a united Yorkshire v Cardiff confrontation. This was kept quiet from us and thank God because, while not looking for trouble, the majority of our lads would be straight in at the first chance of a ruck. That's just the way it is and I make no apologies for that. Leave them alone and treat them with respect and in most cases you'll get no problem, but throw down a gauntlet and they'll be right up for it. If the word had got out, while we had scores of coppers around the pub they'd have needed a small army to keep these lads away from the town centre. They'd have run the two miles into town if they thought there was trouble brewing.

Anyway, we had our pre-match swig and were taken into the game. There were stories of minor offs taking place before the game; sadly, many scarfers and family groups were getting picked on and some had got slapped. This had wound the lads right up and, after the game, loads tried to break through the police cordons around the coaches. There were a few minor arrests but no real disorder. Our group of 45 (the overnighters) stayed together and got lumped in with the couple of hundred lads who'd come up by train for an escort back to the station, or in our case the hotel at the bottom of town. It was like a military operation, helicopters hovered above and every junction we passed had a cordon of vans and coppers sealing it tight. They took us a really long way around and did all they could to avoid the town centre, where most of the 'Yorkshire United' mob had gathered.

When we approached the station, we said goodbye to the train lot and were then taken down to our hotel. Our bus had gone there directly after dropping us at the game and all our bags, etc, were collected from the bus and we booked in with no problem. One of the more senior coppers asked me what our plans were, and I said we'd just go for a pint or two later in small groups, rather than fully mobbed up. He asked me to try and keep it to as late as possible before heading out of the hotel, not to draw attention to ourselves and to hopefully let the Chesterfield mob disperse. We were happy to do this; most of us wanted a bath or shower and 40 winks before the forthcoming night on the town. We all planned to meet in the hotel bar around 7pm, and shortly after most of us were in place.

We got to hear when we were at the bar from four of the lads who had come back around the 6.30pm mark. These lads had not been with us at the game, they were all serving bans for previous trouble in years past. One had a five-year ban and three of them had three-year bans and were not allowed near the game. These four lads had an afternoon pub crawling around Chesterfield and had met no problems until after the game, when the pub they happened to be in turned out to be the main Chesterfield pub. This had filled to the brim around 5.30pm, with masses of Yorkshire's finest who had spent the previous half an hour making token attempts at getting to our escorted mob, while also attacking a few families who'd parked their cars in the town centre.

This is one of the problems of being a Cardiff fan, we are all seen as fair game and any code of conduct goes out of the window when we are in town. Kicking some bloke up the arse when he's getting in the car with his wife and kids is seen as a major result for a wannabe lad. It's a bit of a two-edged sword. Some of the non-scene Cardiff fans hate the Soul Crew image or tag our club carries, but many times they've been glad to see 20 or 30 of our best come around a corner or into a pub just as they're about to be attacked by the local yobs from whichever town we're in. As was the case at Molineux, when their Subway Army came down the hill, wading into all the normals. Men, women and children were fair game, until the lads came out and battered them senseless back up the hill. Even the more 'anti-hooligan' Cardiff fans were cheering the lads who scattered the Wolves lads all over the road and the banking outside Molineux.

Back to the four lads in the pub post-Chesterfield match. They had managed to keep their heads down and blend in. Luckily, there were so many strange faces amongst the Chesterfield mob that no one really picked them out. That is, until one of them had to get a refill at the bar and didn't have enough sense to realise that, "Oi, Butty, three 'bows and a lager when you're free," in a strong Welsh accent would attract just the slightest attention. It spread like wildfire. One of the lads was in the bog and, just as he opened the door to return to the boys, he could see all the Chesterfield bouncing around the bar, calling it on with the three remaining lads. He was weaving his way through when it went mental: glasses, chairs, ashtrays, the full armoury was flying at the lads through the air. The police were outside and heard the commotion, but because of the chaos in the packed pub, some people were trying to get out and the coppers were trying to get in. The three lads were holding them off with chairs, and then one lad was stuck in the middle of the Chesterfield lads thinking, *Oh fuck, how do I get out of here alive?*

Luckily, as is the case when there are that many people trying to attack so few, they tended to get in each other's way and the lads, while in danger, did not take too many direct hits. Finally, the coppers got in and got the lads out. By now the floor was inches deep in smashed glass and there were tables and chairs all up-ended. It was absolute chaos. The four lads now safely outside were buzzing on adrenalin and giving it the big 'un now, taking the piss out of how, even with those numbers, they hadn't got battered. But it was more the relief of getting out alive that had them buzzing.

They were taken in a van and dropped off at the hotel, where they had great pleasure in each telling us their own version of events, while slagging off the dopey twat who had ordered the drinks in the strongest Rhondda accent heard *oop north* for a while. All this excitement was adding to the buzz going around the hotel bar; while most of us thought the main event had taken place, a few of us still half expected a bit of 'afters' possibly a little later on. And afters there would be aplenty.

Around the 7.45 mark, I told the others to stay put while me, Dean and Bombers went up the hill to the first pub for a skulk around and to see how the land lay. It was a typical man's pub, 30 or 40 people in the bar, a couple of possible lads, but nothing too naughty. No one seemed to be staring or sussing us out, a few lads were on their mobiles but, possibly being a bit naïve or not too paranoid, I didn't pay too much heed to this. We had one pint and then went back to the hotel. We said it looked okay and we would head up there in dribs and drabs, have a pint and then see how it went from there. By now our motley crew had a few more numbers. Flahty, whose wife was a local, was staying up with his in-laws, thank God, because he's a great lad to have with you in a scrape, and two or three others who lived around the Nottingham area were staying with us for a pint. So all in all, besides the four Ferndale girls who had come with us (tottie on tour – anywhere for a night out, but a great little gang), there were also two old blokes: Corky, with his one leg, and the bus driver. But we did have a good 35 or so lads who could be called upon if need be, and soon enough they would be.

There were still a few small groups of lads in the pub, but no staring or eye contact. But one or two did leave within a few minutes of us getting there, and a couple of our more switched-on lads started getting twitchy. Carlton locked one of the two doors from inside, saying, "If they're coming in, they're only coming in through one door." I was popping in and out, looking up and down the hill, but not seeing anything out of the ordinary. I was starting to relax.

Back in the pub, I'd just got a full pint when Ian shouted out, "Here they come!" Everyone went to the window, but it was just eight or nine lads walking down the hill and heading for the pub. I just thought they were out on the piss. They came in through the one open door; the lads let the first three in and then knocked the next two sparko with stools. I thought, "Fuck me, that's a bit heavy, lads!" The ones who hadn't got in ran for their lives down the hill, and the three that had got in took a few slaps and were allowed to run back out.

Then the shout went up, "Here they are!" I looked up the hill and could see a good sized mob, but they were being joined by more and more still coming around the corner at the top of the hill. Everything was rushing through my head. I'd brought everyone into this and I felt a massive responsibility. One of the lads chucked a stool through the pub window out onto the street, perhaps it was a message to say, "Bring it on," perhaps it was a plan to have one less window they could smash through onto us, but either way the sound gave me a start. "Come on, outside, all of us!" I shouted We had limited options: stay in the pub, possibly getting trapped – fuck knows how many were coming down at us, but at least outside we'd have a chance to weigh it up; also, if it got too heavy we could back our way down to the hotel. But then I started getting paranoid, thinking, *Perhaps they have planned this well and, if we back off down the hill, what if they have another mob waiting in a sidestreet at the bottom of the hill and we get stuck in the middle?*

I'm also thinking, *Look, an hour or so ago there were 300 coppers crawling around here, surely they will soon get back when the shout goes up?* Was I wrong with that one or what? I'm shouting at the top of my voice, rallying the troops and trying to make them think I'm hard as fuck, even though my arse is twitching slightly. I'm shouting, "Everyone stick with me, anyone runs or takes a backward step and they're dead!" It sounds mad now and as corny as fuck, but this was quite scary and also as exciting as hell. Anyone who's had a taste will know what I mean. I was trying to size things up, but it didn't look good. We were halfway down a hill. They were on top, coming down at us, there were 35 or so of us and what looked like 150 plus of them, and that's just the ones we could see. To make matters worse, also at the top was a big fuck-off skip, with enough ammo to start a war. They were chucking everything at us, bottles were smashing around us, bricks bouncing off cars, bits of timber, even tins of paint. But any initiative they had wasn't used fully. Instead of rushing down the hill and swamping us, they were only taking tentative steps forward and still chucking everything they could, while we were getting right pissed off and sensing their indifference to a full-scale scrap. We started going up the hill at them, spreading across the road, giving them an easier target for missiles, but it did make us look like more of a threat. A couple of our lads had picked up some of the shit they'd thrown at us and were lobbing it back at them, but it's a bit harder throwing uphill.

As we got to the top of the hill it now looked like a bombsite. We'd been outside now for what seemed like ages, but in reality it could only have been a few minutes and there was still no sign of the police. Let the battle commence. We were now face to face with their mob and, while they were giving it the big 'un and dancing around, no one was stepping forward to have a pop. There would be no problems there because we had plenty who were right up for it now, especially the Rhondda boys who were annoyed at having their drinking session interrupted. Stick, the Rhondda rep, got straight into them, followed by his brother who was one of the banned lads from the pub incident earlier. Two of theirs went down and none of their lads helped them, yet they were still dancing around, making all the noises and shouting out threats, mostly to wind each other up and get a bit of bravery going amongst them. Our lads, on the other hand, weren't doing much shouting but were now picking out targets. I couldn't believe it, we were squaring up one on one all over the place, and other than those we were scrapping with the rest of them were just looking at each other, hoping someone else would fill the breach.

All this just added fuel to our lads' tanks and they were now in full flow. There were quite a few lads sparked out or rolling around the floor; out of the corner of my eye I could see the four girls, the driver and the two old guys standing against a shopfront as if watching a prize fight. There was no panic, they were chatting and smoking away as if this was an everyday occurrence. (Mind you, in Ferndale it's not far off the truth.) I was making myself as visible as possible; at six foot six and 20 stone that's not hard to do, but it's always good to keep the big ones at the front and the little ones behind, it does make them think twice. Now, as I was going up the hill, someone had thrown a mop or some sort of brush at me; it had a lime-green luminous handle and I'd caught it in mid-air and was now waving it over my head like a light sabre. Dean reckoned I looked like Darth Maul from *Star Wars* going up that hill, waving this light sabre around. These Yorkshire lads must have thought they were extras in a film, and if you'd seen some of ours you'd understand where I'm coming from. George Lucas would save a fortune on makeup if he made a film up here in the Valleys.

Fuck me, where are the coppers? I thought. We must have been at it now for over ten minutes, and that's one hell of a long time in a full-scale scrap. At one time I was going to ask for a time out, but didn't think it apt. One thing I'll never forget is seeing this one lad amongst us who I'd never seen before, but he stood out at well over six foot, quite skinny with a bandanna on his head, he was like Bruce Lee, doing roundhouse kicks and dropping people like flies. I found out later he was from Chesterfield and a local in the pub we'd been in. He didn't even know there'd been a football game on, he just thought his local pub was under attack and he would help this gang of nice lads to defend it. Thank fuck he was on our side – it was funny as hell, but it all added to the night's madness.

Finally I could hear a siren, which turned out to be an ambulance. At least someone had noticed there was a battle taking place on the main road through Chesterfield. Seconds later there was another siren and this time it was the police, but it was only two coppers and one of them was a policewoman. Fuck me, were they all on teabreak or what? Let me tell you now: if you're going to stage a robbery in Chesterfield, do it at 8pm on a Saturday. You could have spent half the money before the police get there.

As the coppers get out they can see the seriousness of the situation, they are radioing for more help when the policewoman gets hit on the head with a bottle which has come over from the Chesterfield side. This galvanises our lads even more. Police or not, you don't hit women. The lads steam into the area where the bottle came from, and the two coppers join in with battering all in front of us. My God, we have a proper little mob now: 35 taffies, a Chesterfield kung fu pisshead and two coppers!

By now, you could see the Chesterfield lot losing numbers from the back of the mob. Several of the main lads were still shouting and trying to keep things together, but you could tell they were well pissed-off that we'd more than held our own. They would never get a better chance to turn us over or get a prized scalp. Our lads were high-fiving it and hugging one another, comparing cuts and bruises and laughing, a lot of it from relief at coming out of this scrape more or less in one piece. The next thing going through my head was, *Oh fuck, CCTV. Who's going to get pulled?* It's funny, but I have been in some scrapes in the past and, even though you are aware of cameras, when things happen you just go for gold. Then, later, when you calm down you start to think, *Oh fuck.* This was one of those moments. I had to plan my story: "No, I wasn't smashing people over the head with this broom handle, I was just returning it to the nice man who'd thrown it down to me earlier. I was only rolling around on the floor with that lad because I thought he was having a fit and I was trying to save him from harming himself. Honest, Guv." You know the scenario.

Two ambulances had now turned up, seven or eight people were carted off to A and E. Luckily, none of them were ours. Apart from a few bruised hands and feet and a few cuts and scrapes, it was just like another day at the office for most of them. The police were now turning up in numbers and a bit embarrassed that they'd missed the action that had taken place under their noses. I should imagine a few awkward questions were asked about the post-match policing and intelligence that day. There were no arrests made of our lads, but I'm led to believe a few Chesterfield lads had early morning calls and quite a few were banned after the events of that night.

I was relieved later to find out that the lads who'd tried to get in the pub at the start of the night were some of theirs, looking for it. They had planned to slope in and, when it kicked off, to attack us from inside the pub as well as outside. It was a good plan but they came unstuck. Thank fuck that a few of my lads were a bit more switched on and less trusting than me. It could have wound up with a totally different result.

Some of the police, who had arrived by the dozen now that it was too late, bubbled us up and escorted us down the hill to the hotel. In all fairness they weren't too heavy with us. I think they could see from the numbers involved, and from the story given by the female police officer, that we were very much the injured party who were just defending ourselves and taking care of business. Even so, when we got to the hotel it was made clear to us that we would not be free to roam around Chesterfield again that night (or ever again, if they could help it). Mind you, half a dozen of the lads had soon formed an escape committee and, within the hour, they'd somehow managed to get out the back way through a toilet window and then jumped into a taxi to have a night on the lash in Mansfield. The rest of us just settled down for the night in the hotel bar, recounting the story and answering the many mobile phone calls we were getting off all the lads on their homeward bound coaches. One or two of the coaches wanted to turn around and come straight back up for round two, it didn't matter that they were now 140 miles away from Chesterfield. But our policy of never leaving a man down was proving true, even though we never really had a man down that night. They all felt robbed of a good square-up and, if we'd played Chesterfield the next year, we'd have had enough volunteers to fill three hotels. (LOL.)

I read in one of the local papers that the over-dramatic hotel manageress had described the hotel as like a hospital waiting room. Silly cow, she was a right drama queen and was trying to find any excuse possible to throw us and our bags out on the street. Short of a few grazed knuckles and the odd shiner, the place looked more like a typical Valleys pub on a good night. The major damage that we'd taken was from the paint. None of us had noticed at the time, but during all the commotion and missile salvos, some of the objects thrown were tins of pink paint that must have been in the skip. The next hour was spent seeing who had the most splashes over their shoes and clothes: anyone found with splashes on their backs was accused of running away from the trouble, even though in all fairness not one of them had taken a backward step. It was decided that everyone from that night's fracas would from there on be honourable members of the 'Pink Paint Posse'. Later on, for the crack, I had a load of business cards printed with the Pink Paint Posse logo and the letters V.C. printed in bold. This would now be known as the medal for 'Victory in Chesterfield'. It seems a bit childish now, but it all helped to bind these lads and all the others in our organisation even closer together. This was the first major test of a mixed Valleys bus and they'd passed with flying colours. There had been a lot of trust gained that night and people knew that if it came on top, even if the lads you were with weren't from your town, you could still count on them as if on one of your own.

Just to put the icing on the cake, when we woke up the following morning the same drama-queen manageress was on duty, and she was insisting that she was holding back a deposit that we'd given on a credit card to cover the damages in some of the rooms we'd booked. Well, keeping my fingers crossed and trusting the lads, I insisted that I accompany her around each of those rooms. It gave me great pleasure to find every room in good order, with not so much as a towel stolen or even a cup smashed. In fact, in some of the rooms the lads had even made the beds up (the soppy sods). Old habits and a smack off their mothers too many times in the past had served them well. One up for the Valley Rams, and the first time all weekend that I'd seen the drama queen stuck for words. They may know how to fight, but they also know how to behave when needs be. They're a great bunch, who in most cases I would trust with my life.

OLDHAM AWAY AND MAN UTD . . . OH WHAT A DAY!!!!!!
Oldham v Cardiff, 10th August 2002
Little Pete (CCFC): I was born and bred in a beautiful village on the outskirts of the wonderful city of Cardiff, called Taff's Well. I went to school in Caerphilly with my old infamous mate Dai Thomas. (I actually went to watch him have a trial for Cardiff when we were about 14, it was at Swindon and I even went on the youth teams bus to the game, sitting next to Scott Young.) I have had an intense love

affair with Cardiff City Football Club since I first went to watch them on my own, at the tender age of 12 in 1987.

As soon as I witnessed major violence at an away game at Bristol City, in about 1989, I was totally hooked on football violence. All I ever thought about was how I could become involved with that awesome fighting group of lads that I witnessed causing mayhem at Ashton Gate. Through hard work and getting involved in some crazy fights and situations over the years, I managed to work myself into the main firm of the Real Soul Crew, as I had now gained respect from some of the top older lads. The main lads who made me really welcome and look out for me at the time were Simmo, Lakey and Ginger Jones (Ely's finest and maddest).

I have followed Cardiff all over England, from the late 80's and then all through the 90's and the beginning of the year 2000. I've been banned since 2003, I was given a six-year ban and a six-month prison sentence for fighting with Plymouth's Central Element outside Cardiff Central station.

I first saw Annis at Walsall away in the 1987/88 season, I think it was, and then over the years I got talking to him and we became more friendly as time went on. When Annis rang me to ask if I would do a bit in his book, I was delighted to help him out as he's a well respected man in the football underworld and a true gent to go with it. I also know Annis is Cardiff through and through, and he was there through all the bad years.

It was our first game of the season and we had the long train journey up to Oldham. I had tried to arrange for about 40 of us to meet on Cardiff Central station, but only about 25 turned up. As is the norm when you try to organise a little firm, there are always a few who can't get out of bed because they have been out on the piss the night before. On our journey up, my best mate Christian mentioned United were at home to Boavista in a pre-season friendly! So obviously, mobile phones were used to get a United number in about five minutes. United were spoken to by P, so things were looking good for the day ahead. We were told United had about 25 to 30, but I will be honest, I thought they were lying just to trap us. But it turned out they were telling the truth, so I really respect them for that to this day, as they could easily have had 100-plus for all we knew.

We were drinking in the Wetherspoons pub near the station in Manchester and there were a good 100 Cardiff in there. So me and some of the lads spread the word that United wanted it before and after the Oldham game, me and my little crew of now exactly 18 solid, quality lads: Patsy, the two mad brothers Christian and Shaun Thomas, the Rawlings, Clayton, Chris Price, Scott from Carlisle, Goughy, Erickson, Bevon and Kirkby, Jimmy, Big Ginger, Mark Haynes and three North Wales boys whose names I don't know. We all stayed in the Wetherspoons pub, watching all the other Cardiff leaving heading for Oldham. Let's just say we were not fucking amused – they all make out they want it and here was their chance. I know who they are and so do they, but I won't name and shame them!!!

While we were still in the pub, United were now ringing and calling it on. I can't remember the name of the other train station in Manchester, but we all agreed to meet there in five minutes' time. As we were approaching the station we saw about 25, so I told all the lads to just keep walking towards them. But as soon as we saw the United firm, about 200 yards away, all the boys just ran straight at them and United turned and ran like fuck. At that time we didn't really know if they had the 25 lads, as they had said they would have, or whether there would be 225 (with the rest of their lads behind them), but we went straight into them without any hesitation at all. I couldn't believe we had just run United in their own city, it just seemed too easy. United's main lad then rang and said how disgusted he was with his firm running so easily, and that he would get more together to meet us after the Oldham game to make amends.

So after that little result we were bouncing, we couldn't believe what we had just done as that firm were part of United's main lads. So myself and the 18 gladiators got the next train to Oldham, where by now the game had already kicked off. We got into Oldham about 3.30, so P then rang Oldham's firm to see if they wanted to meet as well; they didn't sound too confident. They said to us to ring back in about ten minutes, so P did and they told him to go half a mile up the road. We were all on a high now, so we all marched up to the pub where they said they were. When we were about 50 yards away, we saw the curtains shutting along with the front door!!!!!! So P kept ringing and ringing Oldham's firm – but they would not answer their phones, surprise, surprise. The only reason I can think of as to why they didn't want it with us was because they had just heard we'd run United 30 minutes previously. Anyway, nothing happened at Oldham and I have heard many stories from other Cardiff lads over the years that Oldham have always hidden from them.

We then got escorted by five riot vans through an Asian area where we had some seriously strange, dodgy looks from the locals. The police put us all on a train out of Oldham and we were headed back to Manchester.

When we were all on the train to Manchester, P asked all 18 of the lads if they were ready and up for a meet with United, round two. They all said 100 per cent YES! So P said, "Are you all sure, as United could have loads more lads than earlier on in the day?" as there were still only of eighteen of us. "Fuck it, let's have a go, we only live once!" one of the lads said. United then said, "When you get into Manchester city centre, ring us and we will come to you." So we made our way to a pub at the bottom of the steps by the big triangle monument. P rang them and told them where we were and they said they would be there in ten minutes. I then told all the boys to be ready. I walked over to the pub and popped in to get a bottle of lager. Suddenly, Big Patsy came running in and grabbed me and said, "They are fucking here now!" So we ran out and saw United walking towards us at the top of the steps. Me and the rest of my real mental firm ran straight into United without even thinking again. When we went into them they still only had about 25, but they were all big lumps; they had a big lad at least six and a half feet tall, he was like a monster running into us, and Chris Price knocked him out with one of the best punches I have ever seen in my life. Scott from Carlisle had a bottle smashed into his face just above his eye and was bleeding heavily. Then fighting was just erupting everywhere for a solid two minutes proper, it was toe to toe, not your handbags. There were at least four or five United lads lying on the floor, as we had some serious big hitters amongst us, like Clayton, Christian Thomas, Chris Price, Erickson, Ginger and Patsy. We started to smash United everywhere and they were now starting to back off, quite a few of them even ran away.

When I looked around I saw Big Ginger smashing two half-caste boys in a shop doorway and they looked terrified. I then looked around again and I saw the six and a half foot monster getting his tongue pulled out of his throat by Scott from Carlisle. The Manc lad was in a serious condition. With that, Scott put him in a recovery position and shouted, "Call an ambulance!" We were gobsmacked and surprised that United had left one of their main lads knocked out and on his own. But we helped their lad and sorted him out. One of the United lads came back over to us, to see if he was okay, and I told him that he and his mates were total wankers for leaving him on his own. He told me to fuck off. With that, I hit him as hard as I could, then I hit him again and again until Big Ginger jumped on me and said, "Peter, he has had enough!" I turned around and shouted at Ginger, "I will decide when he has had enough!"

So that was it. The fight finished, a major result for our little firm. The usual police noises were now being heard, so we quickly made our way to a backstreet pub and all went straight into the toilets to clean ourselves up, as there was blood all over us. We then waited until the sirens had all died down and made our way back to Piccadilly station, where we then bumped into a couple of York City lads. They shit themselves when they saw the state of us and heard of what we'd just done in Manchester. On the way home, our phones didn't stop ringing until we got back to Cardiff. When we got back, we were met with a hero's welcome from some of our main players and doormen. At the end of the day, it was a major result for a small firm against one of the best in the country.

WE DIDN'T GO FOR SHOW

The following was sent by a well-known Barnsley lad who would like to remain anonymous.

Cardiff City v Barnsley, 8th February 2003

Barnsley Five-O: In the 2002/2003 season, a fixture cropped up that the Barnsley lads had been waiting for for a long time: Cardiff away. It also dropped on a special day for most of the lads in Barnsley, particularly the older heads. It was the anniversary of the death of a well-known and respected lad, Robert 'Gibbsy' Gibbs, who sadly passed away in February 2000.

The home game against Cardiff would be played in November 2002 and Cardiff had been in touch. A meet had been arranged in Wombwell, a village just outside Barnsley, with the main Soul Crew who were travelling up in two 50-seater coaches. By 9am we had 100 lads in a pub waiting for them to arrive, but unfortunately the Old Bill got wind of it, intercepted the Cardiff coaches and also shut down the pub our lads were in. Our mob headed back into Barnsley and the numbers swelled to 250 in The Room on Eldon Street. Rumours were doing the rounds that a large group of their boys had got into the town centre, so our lot tried to leave and confront them but riot police from all over Yorkshire blocked everyone in the pub. This didn't go down well with our lads and they attempted to smash their way out. The pub was completely wrecked as tables, bottles and stools were launched at the riot police; at one stage the pub was on fire, which forced the police to let everyone out. The mob headed through the streets, but the rumours of Cardiff in our town had been false and they were in fact held in a working men's club just outside the town centre, going nowhere.

The town centre was closed off to traffic for about an hour, as debris was cleared off the roads. After the match, Barnsley's numbers were massive. Once again it was mayhem, groups of Barnsley were all over the town, trying to get towards the train station and bus station. Fighting broke out with the police all over the town; the riot police weren't local, they had been drafted in from all over Yorkshire and they were up for it. The fighting with the police went on for around two hours, with running battles up and down the town well into the night. Cardiff were probably halfway home by this time, but it was just one of those days.

We were now looking forward to the away game at Cardiff. Leading up to the away fixture, the phones were red hot. Traditionally, every year, the lads would get together to meet up with Gibbsy's family and celebrate his life as he would have wanted, a good piss-up somewhere out of town or a decent day out at the football. These days usually ended up with everyone getting back to Barnsley in the early hours, normally with half of South Yorkshire police in tow.

As the day got nearer the numbers got bigger, as more realised it dropped on the day of 'Gibbsy's do'. Loads of the older end were up for it and some main faces were to be out for this one. The lads knew South Yorkshire Police would be wanting to spoil the fun so numbers were kept to a good 100-120.

The day of the game was an early start, 4.30-5am for most, as many minibuses and taxis were booked. The idea was to travel separately to Sheffield, get into the station and on the first available train at the last minute, so that everybody wasn't hanging about in Sheffield and attracting any unwanted attention from the Old Bill.

This plan worked fairly well and, by 7am, 120 good lads were on the train early doors. The lads had three carriages and, as soon as the train left the station, the booze was out. Halfway into the journey, the refreshments were in full flow and the lads were ready for whatever Cardiff had planned. The four-hour journey went fairly quickly and the plan was to get off the train at Newport, get taxis into Cardiff and head for their two main pubs at the time, Sam's Bar or the Philharmonic. Things were looking good, but as soon as the train reached Newport the platform was packed full with riot coppers. Everyone tried to get off but there was no chance, they wanted our lot straight into Cardiff where they could keep everyone on CCTV. Everyone was really pissed off by this time and thought it was game-over for the day. The coppers had even said they might stick us straight in the ground, which would have been a fucking disaster.

As the train pulled into Cardiff, a sea of Old Bill greeted us. They held everyone outside the station for about an hour, promising to get a pub open. As everyone was held, spotters from both sides were busy filming and taking notes of who was there and what they were wearing. A few lads were nicked for possession. As soon as it got to 10am, the Walkabout had finally agreed to open; everyone piled in there and everyone was at least now being served and having a beer, not being put straight into the ground.

Obviously our lot were now in Cardiff, and the Cardiff lads would get wind of it and hopefully put in an appearance. After an hour or so, more and more Cardiff lads drifted past; a few had chatted to a few of ours outside and they said they were turning out big.

Ten-15 minutes later the pub opposite started to empty. The Cardiff lads were trying to get at the Walkabout front door, a roar went up and our lot charged at the doors to get out. The Old Bill immediately pulled meat vans right up to the front doors, blocking the way out. They drew batons and CS gas, a few bottles and stools were thrown from both sides but the Old Bill kept control, although both mobs were trying their best to get at each other.

As the OB were still trying to force the Cardiff mob back, one of our lot stumbled on a fire escape that didn't have a padlock on. With a quick boot it was open and everyone piled out the backdoor. Most of our lot turned right, charging down the main street. Everyone knew most of the pubs would be full of their lads by now and anyone was fair game. About 20 of ours, who left the Walkabout last, went straight out into the car park at the back and bumped straight into about 20 of Cardiff's main lads. The timing was perfect, and as the Old Bill tried to round the other lot of ours up on the main street, it kicked off in the car park big-time. It was toe to toe for about five minutes, with each side giving as good as each other. One of our lads ended up with a broken collarbone. A Cardiff lad later said it had been their main faces, the Docks Boys.

The Old Bill were flapping like mad and it was kicking off down the main street, although many of the Cardiff lads in the pubs further down were caught unaware and couldn't believe where our lot had appeared from. Horses charged down the street towards us and eventually the Old Bill penned everyone in behind some scaffolding, with batons drawn and CS gas out.

As more Old Bill arrived, the streets were filling up with more Cardiff. Word had spread fast and they were trying to get at the Barnsley lot, only the sheer number of coppers kept both groups apart. They shut off the main street and ordered some buses to get everyone to the ground. Everyone was pissed off about this, as a couple of Cardiff lads had said they were going to ambush the escort on the way to the ground. With Cardiff in such big numbers, they could probably have done this by confusing the already stretched numbers of Old Bill.

As soon as they got our lot to the ground, everyone was herded straight in and we weren't happy. Luckily, they were serving ale and everyone carried on boozing right up until kick-off.

During the game a couple of attempts were made by both mobs to get at each other over the corner of the pitch, but the coppers soon put a stop to it. Halfway through the second half our lads decided to leave, charging down the stand towards the gate. The coppers weren't prepared and were flapping big-time. The stewards tried jamming the gate but the lads carried on; the coppers drew batons and gas and it kicked off. There were Old Bill on the deck, bins were thrown at them, a gate was ripped off and hurled at them, it was mayhem. The Cardiff lot were trying to get out as well. They weren't encountering as much resistance as ours, as most of the Old Bill were too busy trying to stop the lads smashing out of the ground. It looked like the Cardiff lot were trying to get out also, and had Cardiff managed to get behind the Old Bill, the police would have totally lost control and it would have been game-on.

More and more Old Bill arrived and finally shut the big iron gates. The coppers had kept both mobs apart by the skin of their teeth and had managed to drive the Cardiff lot back. The numbers of Cardiff outside the ground must have been 500-

plus, with a few barmies in with them. Even as the coppers tried to get our lads on buses, we were still charging through at the Cardiff lot, with the Old Bill only just managing to keep them apart again. A Cardiff lad later said their Old Bill had been "fighting for their fucking lives" behind the stand.

That day the lads had done as much as possible to get at it, and the lads that travelled didn't give a fuck how many Cardiff were there. Cardiff have a good reputation and can pull massive numbers, but a good mob of Barnsley had travelled and, unlike some, had gone for it. It wasn't just a show, all the lads who went knew the score and had taken it to one of the biggest firms in the country!

Jonathan Evans (CCFC): They were game before the game. They broke their bubble and went looking for it; not many firms come to Cardiff to do that. In the city centre we had to smash our way out of our pub to get at them; we followed them down the sidestreets, then hit them halfway down St Mary's Street. They did stand, but came unstuck. A few got KO'd. Myself and Rusty flew straight into them, it was a good little battle – they stood for fucking ages. Eventually, we backed them off after their front line got dropped, but they were still game. Even in the ground, they tried to burst out of their end. They battled toe to toe with our Old Bill, and many were later dawn-raided for it. So fair play to them: we never even knew they were coming.

"YOU WILL BE TREATED FIRMLY BUT FAIRLY"
Sheffield United v Cardiff City, 20th September 2003
Big Gwyn (CCFC): A couple of scrapes that I have got caught up in over recent years have been caused by police ineptitude or stubbornness, rather than a group of lads out looking for trouble. I will mention two of those that spring to mind, the first being Sheffield United away in the 2003/04 season.

Now, if you ask most football fans across the board who their least favourite football-related police forces are, then I would almost guarantee the Yorkshire and West Midlands forces would be in their top three, and this is partly why I use these two examples to highlight such events.

Part of our initial success at the Rams in helping to limit problems at games was discussion with away clubs and their police forces. You won't need me to tell you two of the forces who didn't want discussion with us – who the fuck did we think we were, offering some constructive discussion and teamwork to help things run with no problems? The reply we would get when trying to make contact would be, "Your fans, like all others, will be treated firmly but fairly," and we all know what that means. Firm is, "You will be met by officers in full riot gear, there will be no communication and you won't be told what's happening, other than hearing the odd shouted threat or order. You will be herded, pushed, shoved and goaded, and if you complain you'll be assaulted or arrested. Is that FAIR enough?"

The match at Sheffield saw us take 16 coachloads of Valley Rams up for the game. The only instruction we'd had was, "You will arrive in your coaches at 2pm, on the slip road/bridge at Junction whatever-it-was on the M1."

What we had planned to do was make our way up and stop for a meal and a drink in a small town called Chapeltown. We had used this town on a few occasions, and the three or four pubs and the British Legion club used to welcome us with open arms and ask us to call back whenever we could. We built up such a rapport with these businesses that we would tell them we were coming, give them the time and numbers, etc, and they would get in extra bar staff. For some games they even laid on a free buffet for us, it was good business all round for all parties.

On the day in question everything went to plan, until the police became involved. We had visited Chapeltown, had a great day out with no problems. Our coaches had loaded up and were en route to get to the rendezvous point at the allotted time. My coach was the third or fourth there; we were met by a load of police, told to stay on the coaches, and no other info was given. We waited ten minutes or so then started moving off, but little did I know that only eight coaches were allowed to travel and they were holding the last eight back in the lay-by. My phone started going, with all the reps off the other coaches asking me what was going on, so I phoned our Welsh Police FIO's (Football

Intelligence Officers). They came back to me, saying that the masterplan was to take our eight coaches in and bring the other eight in closely behind us. Not ideal for those stuck there in the lay-by, but just another example of the joys of being a City fan.

Anyway, our coaches got to the ground at around 2.30pm, and I was off and waiting for the next eight to arrive. But arrive they didn't, and I actually found out that they hadn't even moved, so basically they had been stuck there for 30 minutes or so. Twenty five to three, twenty to three, quarter to three, still no movement. I was bouncing by now, bawling out our FIO's – who, in all fairness, I had a good working relationship with – and they knew that I didn't just moan and stamp my feet for nothing, so they were doing the best they could to get our other coaches moving.

3pm came and still no sign. I got into the ground and then the phone started going mental. They had finally started moving our coaches in, but the match had already started and they were still ten minutes away. Then, from what I found out later, they stopped the coaches a mile or so from the ground and just sat there again. By now the lads on board had cracked, they could see the floodlights and were just stuck on these coaches like dummies, with no copper telling them what the hell was going on.

The doors open front and back and 400 lads jump off the coaches to start walking to the ground. Not looking to smash anything or anyone up, just wanting to get to a game they'd travelled 200 miles to see. This throws Yorkshire's finest into chaos – *What are these fans doing? Who do they think they are?* – and suddenly every copper within a ten-mile radius is heading for this mob of warlike hooligans (or frustrated football fans, depending which outlook you take).

Next thing, they are surrounded, bubbled up and marched to the ground (which is where they wanted to go anyway). From what I'm told by many sources, everyone in this escort is now seen as a criminal and fair game for the 'firm but fair' (my arse) approach. Several fans get arrested after asking why they are being hit with staffs.

Pandemonium! By the time these lads got into the ground, the place was bouncing and you could cut the atmosphere with a knife. (It's lucky they'd left the knives on the coaches. LOL.)

The game was a real cliffhanger and added to the tension. At the end of the game, part of me was dreading what might happen next. I get wound up like a coiled spring by certain police and certain policing methods, especially when common sense plays no part in events and you have some public school-educated knob sitting in his ivory tower, sending out orders and instructions to his officers on the frontline, having never ever been to a football match himself and having no personal knowledge of how things are, other than what he's read or been taught in a lecture.

How many times have you, as football fans, asked a copper why he was doing something mad and all he'd say was, "I know, but I'm just following orders"? In all fairness, not all coppers are knobs, just as all football fans aren't hooligans, but how they can work under such constraints sometimes is beyond me.

Now for those that have been to Bramall Lane, you will know how things work. You come out of the away end and the coaches are there waiting in the road for you. No problem, you might think, but for this match, possibly because of the tension that had been created, the police blocked each end of the road off to stop any Sheffield fans walking through.

It sounds straightforward and it should have been, but coming down onto this road at 90 degrees were a couple of sidestreets. Now this one particular street must have been a couple of hundred yards long, but at the furthest end you could see the Sheffield fans making their way down the adjacent road. Suddenly they must have had a rush of blood, they mobbed up and started running down the street to have a pop at the Cardiff fans; there were a couple of coppers mixed in with us, trying to get us on the coaches, and a couple more at the end of the street, but not enough to stop a couple of hundred Sheffield fans looking for a scalp.

Those Cardiff fans on the coaches were soon back off them, joining in with the others still milling around outside. To anyone who has been in this type of situation, body language and expression can tell you a million things. The Sheffield fans had broken through the handful of coppers at the top of the street and thought they would pour down on the Cardiff fans and scatter them. I could see ours grouping up, all excited for the scrap, and running up towards the Sheffield fans to meet them halfway. (Bless them, they must have thought they'd save them running too far.) You could see the approaching Sheffield fans slowing down and their faces showing the realisation that those in the front row were going to be the first to have it, rather than being the ones who could brag later that they had chased Cardiff everywhere. The next thing was the 'dancing' so synonymous with these sorts of scraps – you know, when people are bouncing on their feet side to side, arms widespread, saying, "Come on then!", blah, blah, blah.

Then, just as Sheffield were mid-dance, *bang!* Cardiff were straight into them. Now I did say earlier that I didn't want this piece to be the typical 'ten of us chased 50 of them and we never lose a fight,' etc, but this is how it is and what happened. In all fairness with regard to numbers, the 100-plus Sheffield fans who'd braved it were now being met by double or treble those numbers wanting to kick them back up the road. I don't want to glorify it but, unlike the Swansea comic that was written a few years back, why lie? There were hundreds there who know what happened and they would soon know if I was lying or exaggerating events.

Within less than a minute or so, the police had regrouped their numbers, swollen by dozens of the Robocops who had been stationed at each end of the main road, where nothing was happening. They'd put a couple of lines in between both sets of rival fans, who by now were nearer the top end of the street where the fight had now taken them. These coppers were now pushing the Cardiff fans back down the street and towards the coaches, but while this was going on the Sheffield fans were regrouping at the top of the street with what seemed like extra numbers from those fans still pouring out of the ground. Just as the Cardiff fans were within yards of the coaches, the Sheffield fans started making their way back down the street for round two.

Now, instead of leaving a line of coppers up that end of the street to stop such a thing happening again (which seems quite straightforward to a numbskull like me), all of the coppers were down with our lot. They didn't seem to have any plans to stop these Sheffield fans from coming down at us again, so if they weren't going to stop them there were 5-600 Cardiff loonies who were more than ready to.

Chaos prevailed. You now had a couple of rows of Robocops laying into Cardiff with everything they'd got. There was a mad few minutes when lads in t-shirts and jumpers stood toe-to-toe with coppers in suits of armour, who were hitting them with shields and staffs. I'll never forget seeing one copper helmetless (a real ginger head as well) who'd been standing down by the turnstiles in normal police outfit, rather than body armour. I could see him running in behind the Cardiff fans who were facing the other way, toe-to-toe and still bang at it with the riot cops.

Our ginger cop had lost the plot big-time, and he was lashing out with his staff, splitting heads for fun, and not just legitimate targets, so to speak, but lashing out at everything in reach. He'd gone too far into the crowd now for his own safety, and I could see two fists the size of cabbages smashing into his face. He fell backwards but, before he hit the floor, he must have been booted by a dozen or so different people, and not all of them the stereotypical lads that you'd expect. Lots of them had blood running down their heads, so no doubt these were some new friends he'd made earlier on his lone Charge of the Light Brigade.

It was hard to feel sorry for him, you don't want to see anyone badly hurt but this copper was a bad egg and out of control. It was frightening to see how much hatred was coming his way. Luckily for him, some of the Robocops had seen him go down and got to him before too much damage was done. Strangely, rather than making things worse, this seemed to bring some order to events and things started calming down. The police had finally worked out that if they got the Sheffield fans back up the street, then things would improve. And improve they did – mind you, a Dai's Taxis coach had to stay up there for a few hours after the game, parked outside casualty, waiting for several City fans to get stitched and bandaged up before returning home. We heard later that our ginger friend had a broken arm and quite a few lumps and bumps, so luckily it was nothing too serious, a good result for the police (not!) with their score of five injuries to one in their favour.

One of the few positives to come out of this debacle was a bit of communication about next year's game. The following year the police approached our club, asking them for some discussion about planning that year's game; they still wouldn't talk to us fans directly, but at least all parties could have some input. One of the things that forced this change was the realisation that their firm-but-fair approach may have wound up seeing someone killed. After the Hillsborough disaster from years earlier, I'm sure they realised their force could not take another enquiry and the findings it came up with.

One comment that came back to me from one of those meetings was one of their FIO's saying that he'd seen nothing like it before. He said that in his experience, when dealing with football fans, if you threatened a fan, saying you would be forced to draw your staff, then in most cases people would back off; those that didn't usually did when you actually did draw it. But, when dealing with Cardiff fans, he said none of these approaches worked and the more you hit them, the more people wanted to join in and fight you. I think this made them realise the firm-but-fair policy needed a back-up plan.

The following year, after listening to our input and asking us what could they do to limit the chances of trouble, we made several suggestions such as finding us somewhere to have a drink before the game en masse, not delaying us at rendezvous points unnecessarily, having some dialogue and communication, and not being met by coppers in riot gear, brimming with aggression.

That year's game saw them meet us at a roundabout on the M1; as each bus got there a friendly copper got on, welcomed everyone to Sheffield and hoped they'd have a good day. Each bus was then taken within seconds by a police bike into Rotherham, where they had basically given us the whole town for a drink and a meal. When the coaches arrived in Rotherham, they were met by small groups of coppers in shortsleeved shirts, smiling and showing you the way to the pubs, having a bit of banter, saying such and such a pub had the cheapest beer but it tasted like shite, and this other pub had the best barmaids. Fuck me, human beings in uniform! You could see our boys smiling and realising they might be treated properly if they behaved properly; at least they were giving us the chance.

Well, I won't bore you and dwell on the positives, but what a day! I must have had four or five phone calls from landlords thanking me and asking to pass it onto the fans, several of them saying it was the most profitable Saturday they'd had since they'd owned the pub.

The day passed with no arrests, no incidents, and can be summed up by a sight I thought I'd never see at Sheffield, when I noticed one of our Stone Islanded beauties sitting on a police motorbike with a police helmet on, arm around a copper's shoulders, both of them smiling broadly while his mate took a photograph. A slight difference from scenes witnessed a year earlier. In fact, things worked out so well that day that by half-time they had sent half the coppers home because there was no threat.

It seemed so simple to us, and worked so well, that other forces followed suit and things did start improving for a few seasons (West Midlands excepted).

VIII
A EUROPEAN TOUR

SIMMO's BATTLE BUS TO LIEGE, 15TH SEPTEMBER 1993

Simmo (CCFC): I know Annis and many other lads went over there – in fact, over 1,200 fans went, including about 500 lads, and they all probably have a tale to tell. So much went on over there, especially in the town of Liege.

On the day of the game we all met up at about 3am at the Foresters pub in Canton, Cardiff. It was a midweek night game in Belgium and we knew we had a long journey ahead of us. So by 4am we were off: 50 good lads, Beechie, Dolphy (RIP), Freddy (RIP), Ely Trendies, the Canton lads, and of course my wife Pam and my two lads, Lee and Jamaine, who were only young teenagers then.

It was 2pm by the time we arrived in Liege. Some of the lads were well pissed up but not pissed enough to not want to go to the first pub we saw, not far from the ground. We found a pub on a corner of the road to the ground and we made camp there. The lads gave the barmaids Ayatollah t-shirts to wear (Cardiff fans had adopted the image of Iranians banging their heads with their arms in a display of shared mourning and anguish, mimicking it on the terraces in a style often described as 'Doing the Ayatollah') and the banners with 'Cardiff City' on were put straight up. There were no problems for the first couple of hours, everyone was having a smoke and a dozen or more beers. Then we heard rumours that a couple of miles away in the town there had been some right battles, which we were to later hear about when over 200 Cardiff had been deported. We were all as sound as a pound in our corner pub: no Old Bill and we even had the barmaids having a right laugh with us, as they seemed to know their football. To top it all, two of the players who weren't playing on the night popped in, Nicky Richardson and Thomo.

Then a couple of locals started coming in; one had 'Hell Siders' on his back; no one said anything at first, but then more piled in, including a couple who started on Thomo because he was black. Beechie came over to me and Pam and said, "You'd better get your boys out of here," but they were going nowhere, even though they were still teenagers. One of our lads then saw the double-headed barmaids pass some knives to the Liege lads. That and the business with Thomo sent our lads steaming right into them. More and more came piling in, the next one who went past me had a full pint over his head. What a fucking waste! Eventually, we were all battling outside and each side gave as good as they got, until the Soul Crew cry went up and we got that little bit of extra go in us and had them going back towards the stadium.

Old Bill came from everywhere – there were loads of them, and I mean loads. Liege made a stand then and, as I went towards them, I got punched in the head by a copper who started chasing me with his baton. Pam was having none of that and was soon steaming into him and whacking him. She hasn't half got a good right on her, it was fucking mad! This went all the way down the road into a big car park, where the Liege lads just seemed to vanish. We walked all around the stadium looking for them – no such luck, just Old Bill, who'd eventually had enough and put all of us in the ground.

By kick-off, all the lads except the 200 who were deported were all telling their tales to us. In Brussels the night before, Cardiff had had a right off in the square with the local Turks, who pulled carving knives, etc, on them. Also, that last night in Liege, Cardiff had smashed the Hell Siders' pub up and ran about 40 of their lads out. That afternoon, the Docks Boys had fought the Old Bill for over an hour by the main train station and a water cannon was eventually used to calm it down. Fucking hell, everyone had a story!

As to the match, we got hammered 5-2 even though at first we were leading. It was totally peaceful in the ground, with just riot police facing us for the whole of the game.

There were no pubs open after the game and the Old Bill put hundreds of lads on buses and straight onto the trains out of Belgium. We had a bit of an off on the bridge, but the police soon had us on our bus and out of there. When Liege came to us, they brought over a hundred lads but our owner, Rick Wright, put them all up for the day in his Barry Butlin's camp, so we never saw them till they were in the ground. Liege had Arsenal in the next round, and I heard they made mincemeat of Arsenal when they went over there. As for us, we had the long journey home and we were going to Blackpool on Friday to see City play on Saturday, another long journey for the Battle Bus.

LIEGE '93 AWAY – 'THE NIGHTMARE'

Guff (PVM, CCFC): I was born (in 1968) and bred in Port Talbot. I've followed Cardiff since 1984 and still do, even though I now live in London and have settled down and married. I had brilliant parents who were always there for me, and took a keen interest in me regarding sport. I played rugby but, to be honest, it bored me and having it forced on me in school made me eventually give it up.

After a nightmare trip the year before to Vienna to watch City in the European Cup Winners Cup, we had stayed seven hours away in the Tryol and then got on a coach trip full of pensioners, etc. So we decided to go this time with the rest of the lads on the ferry, as we knew City would be taking loads.

Leaving Port Talbot on the Monday late afternoon, myself, Phil, Thugsy and Darren were going to meet the rest of the lads up in Victoria (London), so they set off earlier in the day to have a few drinks in Cardiff. We met up with Neath Punk, Huey, Tongy, Palmer and a few other older lads from Llanelli in the Shakespeare pub just outside of Victoria station, before boarding the train to Dover. Palmer already seemed on his way to being pissed, something which will play a major part in the tale later on. The train was packed and everyone was looking forward to this trip. At Dover we met up with Kevin from Bangor and Ger, who had been drinking in Dover all day.

Everyone carried on drinking throughout the crossing and, once arrived on foreign soil, everyone was carrying some mighty hangovers. Ger had pulled a girl on her way to visit her boyfriend in a Belgian prison for drugs, so Kev stayed with us to look for accommodation, etc. Once we arrived in Liege after another train journey, we all split up with the intention of finding digs for two nights; we soon found them after a short taxi ride just outside the city, chucked our bags in, showered, then we were back out. Myself, Kev and a few others found a small Belgian pub, where all of us and the owner sampled all the local beers. What a landlord he turned out to be, as he later drove us to the city centre with a merry head, all of us cramped into his car, seven in a five-seater.

All the City lads had gathered outside a small bar opposite the train station. Nearby, we'd settled down for a few drinks when we bumped into Palmer, who was on his own. After the other Port Talbot lads had gone just over the border to Holland, to get a few hours of the local coffee shops, etc, Palmer hung around with us all afternoon.

Early evening outside the train station, there were a lot of stories going around that there had already been some trouble during the day with their mob – Hell Side. Soon, this mob began to gather not so far away from the pub where the majority of City had gathered.

The Belgians had their typical look of the day: shell suits, mullets, etc. Me and a few others walked into the bar where there were a few of them drinking; when we entered, there was a total silence from them. They knew we were City without a doubt, but they continued to stare the other way. Shortly after leaving the bar, a few plastic tables and chairs were being thrown through the entrance. Then the Belgians just started giving the usual, "Come on!" behind the windows of the bar, which eventually got put through by us.

We returned to the original pub opposite the train station, which was packed full of City, including the Neath lads, and where by now Palmer was very much worse for wear. Because of his love of the whole punk scene, he stood out from the rest of the City mob. Suddenly, in through the doors came the local cavalry, all padded up and looking like they had a love of the local steroids – Euro Robocops. A few of us were dragged outside, and then they grabbed Palmer for no reason. The only thing he had done all day was drink like a fish. Seeing this, I decided to have a few 'words' with this local Old Bill.

After the short walk from our seats to the other end of the bar, where Palmer was now under cuffs, I started to try and explain to them that he had done nothing wrong, etc. With a very sly side whack from a baton-wielding, spotty, steroid twat to the side of my head, I was dragged outside and handcuffed to a waiting van where a line of muzzled police dogs were stood. The van was already full of Cardiff lads, some trying to get rid of their powder, etc, from their back pockets and one youngster getting stressed out, as this was his first time he had ever been arrested. Inside the pub, you could see Neath Punk, etc, really giving the police a hard time. I just wished we would get deported in the morning, just like the others from three years earlier when Wales were in Brussels.

We were driven at a fairly high speed through Liege, then met at the police station by a line of baton-wielding Old Bill, with each City lad dragged out of the van and beaten as they made their way through the police 'tunnel'. Me and Palmer were to be the last out and they seemed to reserve the best till last. We had a right pasting. Then we were placed face down on a stone-cold floor and threatened to be hosed down if we did not shut up about the abuse. Somehow we were separated from the others – there were around nine of us in total – and then they decided to put us in a cage, with no blanket, nothing. As you might expect, we had to piss in this cage as well.

It must have been the early hours by now. We were soon to meet our local friends, the police from South Wales. Mr Jeff Richards and a WPC asked us the usual questions – have you got a ticket for the game, etc – and we were then made to sign some forms. It was a stupid thing to do, but we just thought we would be deported at the worst.

With a massive headache and a severe black eye from the baton the night before, myself, Palmer and a guy from Barry

(Hedgehog) were now being taken to what we were told was the local court. My mouth was so dry, as we did not receive a drink at all but were just kept in tiny cells where you could only stand or sit (like you see in those prisoner of war camps of the 40's). There we were kept for around six hours, before finally seeing the local judge who would decide the next stage of our lives. But this turned out to be a pointless exercise as there was no translator, and we could only guess what he was saying.

They then forced us to sign more forms without an explanation; they kept pointing, "Sign here! Sign here!" We thought the judge might be letting us out. Around about 5pm, all three of us were put into another van which also included a few locals. It was at this time we found out there was no homeward bound journey for us, but a stay in the local jail – Lantin, about 30 minutes from Liege. All three of us said to each other, "Whatever happens, we must stick together." I must admit this was the first time I had a feeling of true fear without the buzz. Finally, we were put in a holding cell and then, one by one, asked to strip and change into the clothes of our Belgian friends: blue shirt, grey track bottoms with a thick blue stripe down the leg, not something which you could get in Woodie's at the time. When all three of us saw the doctor, Palmer told him he was an addict as he knew the medication for this would make him sleep. Mark and I knew nothing about this scam, as this was our first time inside. (Palmer had done a small bit of time regarding non-payments of fines or something like that.)

We were then placed in a lift to the fourth floor. The centre of the floor was the control room and on either side of the corridors were our cells. At the time, all the prisoners were out in the corridors and the sight of us drew them to the cage which separated them and us. Fuck me, all this was becoming a nightmare of nightmares! I would rather have faced a hundred Jacks on my own than stay in there.

Mark was taken to one side and me and Palmer were taken to the opposite corridor. *At least I won't be sharing with these Belgian twats,* I thought to myself, but we both feared a bit for Mark. We were then placed straight into a cell. There were continual stares through the small cell window the size of a letterbox. The night was the longest night, we just spent it getting used to the sounds as well as the smell. The toilet in the cell had no screen; until our second week there were no razors – fear of suicide, etc. But there was a pen and paper, with two stamps, so I started to write home.

Next morning was the start of the beginning of the usual shit: first hassle from the screws, then we had to meet the governor. We did not have a clue what he said to us, but he looked a horrible little twat. During the day I somehow managed to get a chance to use a phone. I phoned a mate from Port Talbot who told me that we'd been on both the national news and the local, it was front page of the *Western Mail* and *Evening Post. Shit,* I thought, *my parents must be worried sick.* Later, I found out that the press had been going around the local pubs for a story, etc. Thankfully, a friend of mine, Lyndi, who used to work in one of the pubs and was a Cardiff steward, told them where to go. I will always be grateful to him for this, as there were plenty of locals who would have slagged both of us off.

The days just continued with us not knowing what was going to happen. Overall, we went to court around seven times, those were the only times we were let out of our cell. Then we finally got let out of the cell after around two weeks for a bit of exercise in the yard, where we played football, something which Palmer took a little bit too far with his tackles. No way would we make any friends in this place. The three of us would share our cigarettes and we always looked out for each other. The trips to court were a long day, with the screws always looking for us to return their little digs or kicks while we were being led down to the holding cell before boarding the van to court. We got assigned a free lawyer, but she must have been younger than us and could hardly speak English. Each time we would return from court we would be a bit more down, without knowing anything about a trial date or release date.

I soon started getting letters from both family and friends; friends sent City posters and poppies for us to wear. We wore these poppies just to prove that we were all proud of who we were, Welsh and City. We started to get stronger and, believing there had to be an end to this, joked about an escape plan and I read a book about Colditz. Crazy ideas, I know, but it broke up the boredom. It's a strange book though to have in English in the prison library, along with their French novels, etc. The food wasn't too bad – steak, chips, meatballs – but somehow we were always last to be served, and always on Wednesday and Saturdays we were the last for the showers. They were always playing mind games with us, like our cell being turned over around four in the morning for a search. I wrote on our cell wall the amount of days I had been there, and I decorated it as well with small City and Wales flags, etc, that had been sent over, plus our own artwork.

After four weeks we got a black and white TV which could receive BBC1 and MTV. We were landed; life looked up a bit. I remember watching *Songs of Praise* on a Sunday and, being originally from the Rhondda, it did bring a tear to my eye. Crazy but true.

Finally, after around six weeks, we were told of a trial date. It would then be another two weeks after that when we would receive a sentence. Pre-trial, Palmer went to see the lawyer, but I could not be bothered anymore. I thought, *What a waste of time,* she had been shit so far. She told him that, with our charges, we could receive ten years, i.e. for AFFRAY, THREE ASSAULTS ON POLICE OFFICERS, CRIMINAL DAMAGE. Palmer also had a charge of holding a bottle with the threat to use it. When he told me about this, I did shit myself a bit but reminded myself that, if it did happen, we would only serve a third of that, but also promised myself I would learn French to improve our time there. I had become tougher, I don't know why, you just go one way or the other. Each night Palmer would receive his 'medication', which sometimes he would save up for a big one the next night. Once he took the liquid he would be out cold till the next morning. I would just write letters or watch the TV. The thing which did help our release was that Arsenal drew Liege after they beat Cardiff. We were told they feared our crazy fans would return with them, and they still had this hang-up about Heysel in the 80's with Liverpool. They really hated Brits in Belgium.

Finally, after eight weeks we got our sentence. Me and Palmer got some form of conditional discharge and Mark had everything dropped. What a relief! The nightmare was finally over. It was then we all had a real buzz – it was time to go home, after eight weeks. We were given a free ticket (THANKS FOR NOTHING) to Dover and were then told to get out of the country quickly. We all got drunk in Ostend and Palmer somehow managed to steal his trousers from jail and change into them on the ferry, which was not a wise thing to do . . .

With a sense of anger and the odd nightmare, I will always remember this time. Neath Punk was the first to phone me when I got back home, and I will always be thankful for the other Port Talbot and North Wales lads' letters, etc. I must admit it has calmed me down, so something positive came out of it. I kept the letters for a while, but threw them out to try to put the whole nightmare behind me. The local press were shit, still trying to stir things up, hassling my parents and their neighbours. I still try not to drink Stella, because I hate those Belgian twats to this day. But it has made me support the City even more – they were a great bunch of lads throughout, true friends.

After Liege, I admit I took a back seat. It was a mind-fuck to be in a foreign prison. But the rest of the lads continued going looking for it, including new younger lads Trev, Miffy, Petty and Webber (RIP), with Steve and Huey still making their mark. Today, like many other older heads, I just look forward to the game instead. I cannot afford to throw away what I have now: a great wife, Sharon, and a nice lifestyle. But the friendship remains strong – as do the memories of Brownhill's, sleeping in the reception the night before an away game with about 20 other lads, those were the days. I'm still addicted to watching Wales and the City Bluebirds.

IX

SOUTH COAST

PORTSMOUTH V CARDIFF CITY, 12TH MARCH 1983

Simon Williams (CCFC): I think we've both got a lot of respect for each other. The amount of trouble with the 6.57 lads was always big, as you have to rate Pompey as one of the top UK firms, especially after they got into our seats in Block A of our main Grandstand at Ninian Park and tried holding out for as long as they could.

Cardiff had massed under the stand and then poured into the seats. All hell broke loose and, as well as thick wooded seats being hurled at each other, Pompey were getting thrown over the adjoining wall into the enclosure below. This went on for no more than three or four minutes, though it was a nasty situation for the Pompey lads to be in, but fair play: they took it to us.

One of my best mates, Dai (Hooligan), was due to go behind the door the next day, and was using his final day of freedom to rid our seats of Pompey; as was another good mate of mine, called Willie, who was banging Pompey over the wall into the enclosure below.

Probably the biggest firm of Cardiff to travel to the South Coast happened during the season both clubs gained promotion from the old Division Three to the Second Division. The main mob of Cardiff gathered at Cardiff Central station to travel the three hours by train. Parsons was there, as if to marshal the troops and make sure everyone was present, correct and up for it, even down to the fact that he seemed to be inspecting what some people were wearing.

When we pulled into Portsmouth Harbour, everybody

imagined there would be hundreds of Pompey waiting, but there weren't. As 4-500 Cardiff piled off the train, they were looking for confrontation and started marching all over the city. Some then started blaming Parsons for messing up what they believed was going to be a meeting with Portsmouth's infamous 6.57 firm, and believed he'd got the station wrong. Whether this was true or not, I'm not too sure.

Eventually, after a pretty uneventful day so far, Cardiff's Soul Crew had reached Fratton Park. Cardiff must have had upwards of 4-5,000 out that day, and in those days it seemed as though 85-90% of Cardiff's away support were mad lads, always looking for a battle at every away ground in the country.

During the game there was a lot of scuffling with the local police, and major damage was caused to the famous 'Pompey Chimes' clock when a well-known chap named 'Freddie the Gargoyle' climbed up the main stanchions and grabbed the hands of the famous old clock and hung there till they snapped. Pompey, as you can imagine, went mental. As well as both sets of fans trying their hardest to get at each other inside the ground and pelting each other with anything they could throw, they couldn't wait for the final whistle to blow. As it did, the police tried holding Cardiff back in the ground, but they heaved and pushed their way out and the police lines broke. Hundreds of Cardiff met hundreds of Portsmouth outside and all hell broke loose, both firms going for each other and neither giving way. It took a massive effort from the police to keep both battling firms apart. All the way back to the station, mass disorder was taking place as well as mass destruction. I witnessed more than one vehicle lying on its roof, that's how bad things were becoming. As well as that, everything was raining through the air from both sides and many people were taking some nasty cuts to their heads and bodies. Both firms really wanted it and no matter how many police tried to keep us apart, the battles between us and them went on for a good half-hour.

Eventually, we got back to the station. Truth be told, the running battles all the way back were pretty even affairs, some of the events that day were pretty unbelievable to witness, especially the damage inside the old stadium. Back on the train, Cardiff were another point closer to their main aim: promotion back to the Second Division, and hopefully more meetings and days out like they had just experienced.

BRIGHTON V CARDIFF CITY, 5TH DECEMBER 2000

Mikey Dye (CCFC): Brighton was another tricky little trip, especially for a Tuesday night. There were nine of us on a hired minibus. We set off about noon and arrived about four hours later, finding a pub just on the outskirts. Baggers, Zub, Lucky Evans, GV, myself and a few others got the drinks in. After a few hours we left for the ground; we could see up ahead about 50 Cardiff being escorted by the police and about 20 Brighton giving them lip. We noticed this and sort of mingled with the Brighton lads. At first they were unaware of this. I noticed their main lad was a bit of a pie eater and we aptly named him Fatty. Zub and myself got right up close and said to him, "Here we are, big boy!" He was a bit stunned at this, and we all carried on walking to the ground.

As we got near, the main Cardiff lot turned right under their escort as ourselves and Brighton went left. Fatty realised we were still amongst them and shouted, "Come on, you Cardiff cunts!" It needed a good right hand to sort him out! All his lot were shaping up ready for the fight. *Fuck it!* I thought, and so did Zub, as we both laid into him at the same time. On cue, Brighton attacked; Lucky, Baggers and GV fought back. It was almost even numbers to start with, but being so near to their end they came out of everywhere and soon had us backing off, separating the two sets of supporters. We goaded them after it had settled, shouting, "What the fucking hell was that?" Fatty scurried off for a pie, also gaining a Lacoste watch which I lost in the fracas. But fair do's to Baggers – he claimed a Hugo Boss cap and said, "Never mind, Dyo, you can have this cap to replace your stolen watch." A £10 hat to replace my £100 watch. The thought was there, I guess!

X
SOUTH-WEST

NEWPORT COUNTY FULL ON

Kaged is a mate from the 80's who has always kept in touch with me. We had a right old time in the 80's and 'Kag' was on board for a lot of it. He was a game young lad, who took a couple of bad beatings for his bottle. He was a City fan through and through, and was one of those who would be on the long away trips on a Tuesday or Wednesday night to the Rochdales of this world. One thing about Kag is that he has an unbelievable memory, as you will see.

S. Kaged (CCFC): "Willie, Willie Anderson, Willie Anderson on the wing!" they all sung in their masculine voices when I first went to Ninian Park. 1974 was the year, flares were the fashion and bands like the Rubettes were in the charts. Bloody hell, we were a tasteless lot, weren't we?

I had already fallen in love with football, watching *Match of the Day* and *The Big Match* every Saturday and Sunday religiously. I could name all the players of all the teams in the First Division, parrot fashion. But actually going to Ninian Park introduced me to a different world, that day of 28th April 1974. Hearing the real roar when Gil Reece equalised against Orient was deafening, aggressive and real. For a six-year-old this was edgy stuff, and much more exciting than visits to the park or the zoo.

For the next few years I went to three or four games a season. I was aware that there were lads who went to the games only for the warfare. They were, of course, all bigger than me and just as hard as Dennis Waterman in *Minder*. I had seen the occasional outbreak of fighting as well, matches such as Chelsea '79, Stoke '79 and Tottenham '77 spring to mind, but I don't recall much about the specific incidents, I was too interested in the football.

Inexplicably, I was to be just as gripped by matters off the field in 1981. I was now 14 and able to attend games on my own. I had a school friend called Vincent, whose brother was a well known face at the football, and I used to overhear the conversations his older brother had with his mates. Let's just say that when they spoke about their plans to attend the games, they didn't dwell on the merits of playing the 4-4-2 system. They were preoccupied with 'christening' their Doc Marten boots.

Britain in the early 80's was a pretty depressing place to be, with the inner city riots and mass unemployment. There seemed to be a succession of personal and social upheavals that, for the average working man, took a long, long time to recover from. The song 'Ghost Town' by the Specials was influenced by both the Toxteth and Brixton riots, with the lines, "All the clubs are being closed down," and, "Bands won't play no more," talking about bands not being willing to play during the riots due to fear of being attacked. It summed up the nation's feelings.

That season I began going away, and the following season I didn't miss many. The first friendly of the 1982/83 season was at home to . . . wait for it, you guessed, Chelsea. I met the author of this book that day. He was sat outside the cafe that used to exist under the bridge by Ninian Park; we were due to play Millwall away and he was as excited as me to be making the trip. Not long after that season started, Annis moved to Bradford, so for obvious reasons his appearances at games became sporadic. But I still saw him at various home games and away games such as Lincoln, Huddersfield, Sheffield United, Doncaster, Preston, Wigan, Portsmouth, etc.

The next time I really came into contact with Annis was April 1984. By now he had moved back to South Wales and was living in Barry. In the early months of his return he ventured into Newport for a shopping trip with a friend of his (Little Col) and was promptly threatened. What happened that day was to be the catalyst to one of the most eventful times ever, as wars waged between the two cities and, for a group of 15-18-year-olds, things would never be the same again.

As in the early 80's, life and opportunities in Britain had certainly not progressed by 1984. This was the year of the miners' strike, Band Aid and Frankie Goes to Hollywood. Tommy Cooper died and I had a perm, wore pink and was 17 years old.

Wearing pink and having a perm, it was inevitable that I would hang around outside Olympus Sportswear on Queen Street in Cardiff and pose like a peacock, very majestic and with a touch of attitude. There were about 50 regulars from Canton, Ely, Splott and Grangetown mainly, and various other people would venture outside Olympus from a range of areas at different times.

Every mob has its own unique blend of personalities, and this one was no exception. Within our crew there was the full spectrum of types, from the flamboyant to the demure, from the repellent to the idealistic. Somehow, we managed to fit together in a kind of fragile alliance. One for all, and all for one. With one exception: Patrick boys, anyone wearing one of those stupid, awful cagoules was most definitely not welcome.

Most days were the same: we used to mess around, try and pull any girl who would have us, talk about clothes, walk around St David's shopping centre ten times in a day, anything to pass the time and not spend money as most of us were on a maximum of £30 per week. There were the occasional 'dust-ups' with the mods and whoever else took the liberty of walking down Queen Street in a group who happened to be our age. This was our street, our manor, we were untouchable. Then Newport started paying their uninvited, unwelcome visits. Let's put it this way: they didn't used to come to Cardiff to discuss the price of eggs.

Newport is a rough little ex-trading port 15 miles east from Cardiff, situated on the River Usk. The town itself is relatively small and therefore everyone seems to know everyone else's business. The suburbs of the city have grown outwards, mainly near the main roads, giving the suburban sprawl of the city an irregular, aggressive and somewhat ugly shape.

Newport – or as they call themselves in their own unique way, *kewenty* (county) – had a tight little firm of around 50-60 lads who were very loyal to each other. If Newport as a team had never existed and these lads had followed Cardiff in the 1940's, then together we would have given Adolf Hitler and his troops a run for their money.

Before I relay these events to you, I'd like to make a point. The series of events that took place in the spring of 1984 was extraordinary. Two sets of lads who hung around their local town centres fought a series of battles that caused chaos on a regular basis. None of these events happened at football games or grounds, as if this was the case it would have been a massacre by Cardiff. The advantage for Newport was that their town was smaller, therefore their mob was tighter. On regular Saturdays any stranger stood out like a beacon; it's like walking into a local pub, the connections are tighter and stronger. Whereas Cardiff was bigger, therefore it took longer to mob up and a mob coming out of a train station could have meant rugby, stag nights, lads out for the day, etc. Also, there were a lot of pubs in the vicinity of their train station, and therefore this attracted men of all ages who had no interest in football to become involved in what they saw as a free for all.

But the main point is that these events did not base themselves around football. It's easier for a group of lads from, say, Exeter to walk around Manchester rather than vice versa, as word would spread and every local would gang up ready for a pop. I just wish it had been at football as this would have been a mismatch.

My first encounter with our rivals from 15 miles east came on a Wednesday night in early April 1984. Cardiff had just had an amazing on and off the field encounter with Chelsea, and we were smarting from our city being totally overrun by our cockney invaders four days earlier. So we ventured to Newport, to sort what had happened in the aforementioned incident with Annis and Little Col.

We took the number 30 bus to Newport town centre – Annis, myself, Moorie, Dyo, Eugene, Chris B and a handful of others. Apparently, Newport knew we were coming, so we all agreed it was all-hands-on-deck as soon as we got there. But when we got to

Newport, nothing. After about 15 minutes of chasing any lad who was hanging about to suss what all the fuss was about, we soon became bored and made our way to the bus home. Unbeknownst to us, while we had been there we had whipped up a storm and every local was up for a bit of Cardiff blood. From the local pubs and down the alleys of the sidestreets they came, about 50 of them, all lashed up and ready to rumble. We were in trouble and backed off fast; in Newport bus station that night a few of us were given a bit of a slap. At first we were doing okay, but the sheer volume meant they overpowered us. We returned that night beaten but unbowed, and hell-bent on some sort of retribution.

That retribution came a fortnight later, over the Easter period, when Annis, Little Col, Bobby M, Tony G and me paid Newport a return visit. We drove up in a car one early evening and were ready for action. As we pulled into Newport and parked opposite the train station, there were about ten or so lads who were hanging around and did not take any notice of what was coming their way. As we got closer, one of these lads nodded as if he recognised us. I think he thought we were Newport. His face suddenly changed as we broke into a canter and he realised his little gang was in trouble.

Wallop! In went all of us; when something like this happens, you just hope you haven't picked out a black belt for your own personal duel. Fists flew and Newport were gone. One tall, thin lad was trying to make a stand and was screaming at his mates to come back and fight. We all went at him and he turned and ran – straight into a lamppost. We all fell about in hysterics. Yes, this was definitely a 'wish I had a camera' moment. We all returned home happy with our night's work.

The first Monday in May is known as May Day. It is the time of year when warmer weather begins and flowers and trees start to blossom. There is also another bank holiday at the end of May called the Whitsun bank holiday. It is said to be a time of love and romance, when people celebrate the coming of summer with lots of different customs that are expressions of joy and hope after a long winter.

If that's true, I don't know what the hell happened in May 1984. In 30-odd years of going to football matches, I have never been involved in so many incidents over such a short time. As well as trouble at the Brighton and Sheffield Wednesday away games, we also invaded Blackburn's end at Ewood Park; it was the usual crew: Mikey Dye (Dyo), Annis, Little Col, Mannings, Mallo, myself, etc. We actually scattered the whole end, about 20 of us, five minutes before kick-off. And oh yes! There was also the little matter of a further four incidents with Newport.

I was present at most of these events and will detail them in chronological order, with the facts as told or witnessed.

May 7th – Bank Holiday Monday 1984

At Cardiff Central train station, a few Cardiff fans were coming back from Barry Island. They were met by a group of a dozen or so Newport who caught them by surprise and chased them. Newport did not stay around and were attacked by a reorganised Cardiff on the train platform, while waiting for their return journey.

On returning to Cardiff after the 1-1 draw with Blackburn, this was the story that was reported to us. It was starting to become obvious that this was turning into more than just tit-for-tat one-upmanship.

Tuesday May 15th

While queuing to enter the under-18's Ritzy disco that night, about a dozen or so lads – including Tony G, Bear, Mallo, Eugene M, Moggy, Ivor and several others – decided to go with Annis and myself on a completely unplanned journey to Newport. This consisted of one car and one small train mob. We arrived at Newport around 8pm, and stood in a car park just outside the station to meet the carload of others. The first person we actually met was an old Newport lad called Dino, who was in a donkey jacket on his way home from work and riding a bicycle. He proceeded to ride into us waving a metal chain. This unnerved everyone, and we were waiting for what now seemed like an inevitable attack. We met the car full of Cardiff and, soon enough, Newport arrived. We were outnumbered that night and we were all kids, but everyone who was there did their bit; some

Cardiff were as young as 13, but everyone stood up to be counted. We charged at Newport, who ran; they came back and called us on, but we chased them again. This went on for about five minutes, with Cardiff coming out on top. No punches were thrown, as it was just a case of one group chasing another.

We made our way back to Cardiff and still made it to the Ritzy that night, and told all the other lads of the happenings 15 miles east. I felt like a giant.

Saturday May 19th – FA Cup Final Day 1984

Some Saturdays are just the same; nothing happens, just a repetition of previous Saturdays. But there are certain days that, right from the start, look, sound and feel different.

That Cup Final day, I had declined the invite to go to Wembley with the author for a look around, so I made my way into town with my then girlfriend, Vicky. She was a Scandinavian-looking girl who seemed older than her 16 years, with a blonde bob, curves and a healthy, pretty smile. As soon as I saw her, I realised she was the kind of girl I'd wanted to meet ever since I was old enough to. This was my first taste of that terrible thing, love in your teens. I thought I was the perfect catch, with my wedge, pink and yellow attire, gel, hairspray and Blue Stratos deodorant, and she was my prized possession. We ambled along at our usual leisurely pace into Cardiff town centre, where she would meet her friends and go for coffee and I would meet mine and we would act like something out of *The Wanderers*. We would then meet up about 5pm, catch the bus back to her house and meet up later in a park – or, if we were feeling brave, the pub – and be 16-year-olds for the night.

There are no two ways about it: when I was 16, I was a pretty cool (remember that word?) kid, or so I thought. Not in the 99th percentile of coolness, maybe, but definitely top third of the Cardiff Trendies. I knew the walk. I knew the talk. I had my own kinda . . . style. Vicky was part of that style, the perfect fashion accessory, a pretty and popular girlfriend.

This day, when we arrived in town, a local rogue called Greeky ran past us, chased by the police, and hid by a fruit barrow. On seeing he was safe, he asked if we wanted to buy the new Madness album, which was called *Keep Moving* (he had about seven copies under his arm), or a box of chocolates (he also had about four boxes under his arm). We refused. The sight of Greeky panicking with his arms full of stolen goods amused us greatly. He followed us back to Olympus and proceeded to ask everyone who was between the ages of 6-93 if they wanted to buy his goods. On arriving at Olympus, Vicky then left to meet her friends and do whatever girls do.

I had been outside Olympus about five minutes when a young kid called Dave from Grangetown plonked a complete case of Orange Fanta on the floor in front of us that he had stolen from some newsagent. Next, a few lads who were slightly older than me and were from my area were going to watch the Cup Final in a pub. *Wow!* I thought, *a pub, that'll be really grown up.* So I went with the slightly older lads to watch the game.

On arriving at the pub, it became immediately obvious that I hadn't a clue about drinking on a regular basis as they were not serving alcohol due to the time restrictions. I tried to call the bluff of the barman and told him that, the previous Saturday, I was in the same pub at the same time and they had served me that day. His reply of, "We close at 2pm every Saturday and we are only open today for the Cup Final," exposed me for the charlatan that I was and I became completely embarrassed.

We were in the pub about half an hour when someone came running in. "Newport are here!" That was enough for me to make my way to the central station. I noted that there must have been 40-50 hastily making their way to give this Newport lot a taste of real Cardiff. With a confident spring in my step, I was looking forward to this one.

On arriving at the station, it was obvious that whoever had run into the pub that day was correct. Newport were here, about 100 of them. By the time I was at the station, little one-on-ones had started. Newport were fast advancing. Moorie from Canton was first into them, he was holding his own too. Next, in went Subb, he actually flew into them almost feet first. At that moment I learned a little something about fear, and courage. If these two lads were brave enough to take life by the horns, maybe I could too.

Newport continued advancing. By now Moorie and Subb weren't faring so well, and Newport had by now gained momentum. I noticed that these weren't just kids – a big, fat, dark-haired lump of about 30 with a moustache was throwing his weight about. Still Newport advanced. Suddenly, I was right at the front with Tony G; a look of inevitability drew over our faces and we began to back off, but we were almost within touching distance.

I noticed two tall half-caste lads who had to be brothers, calling us on. They had picked us out and sensed blood. One made a charge into Tony on my left, who fought back and gave as good as he got. Me, I had my light blue Kappa polo shirt half over my head, exposing my back, and I was starting to get a beating. The next few seconds are a blur, but Tony was by now on the other side of me, getting a bit of a pasting from about four or five guys, he was trapped against the metal barrier outside Asteys Café and he was in trouble. I made probably the most pathetic attempt in the world to rescue him, I held my hand over my face and hunched my back ready for my anticipated further beating, looking like a girl protecting herself from a snowball, and made a feeble grab for Tony. Then *bang!* Someone caught me clean on the nose and it spread all over my face.

To my horror, there was more bad news as the police arrived and began to chase whatever Cardiff were left into the city centre. I ran along Westgate Street and into a department store called James Howells, out of the way of the police. I was in the shop a matter of 30 seconds and I bumped into Vicky. She gave me 'that look' and walked on; her friends were more sympathetic, and I was taken upstairs where the blood was washed off me in the middle of Circles Café.

After about half an hour, I left the café with Vicky and made my way to Olympus for the autopsy of that day. I slated a lot of Cardiff that afternoon, saw that Subb was okay apart from some scrapes, bought 'Automatic' by the Pointer Sisters and then left for home. That day there was no Little Col, Annis, Dexy or Richard E, etc, but fair play to Newport: they came down to us bigger than usual. Result to Newport.

May 26th – the following Saturday

I was in town early that day. I was walking past Boots in Queen Street when Gary from Rumney came running past. "Newport, Newport!" he said in a high-pitched, excited and energised tone. This time they were on Queen St, Cardiff's main thoroughfare. One lad from Ely called Jammo had already given them his own welcome of a table or chair from a nearby café over some Newport lad's head.

By the time Newport arrived outside Olympus, there was hardly any opposition. It was early and they'd caught us by surprise. Once again, this was the same lot as the previous week, grown men with moustaches. One of their lumps caught Cairnsy from Canton smack in the face; Cairnsy had a blond wedge and, when he was punched, his wedge haircut almost hit the floor. But *bang!* Fair play to Cairnsy, he hit him straight back and this stopped them in their tracks. Meanwhile, Little Col was having a one-to-one with someone twice his size and age, and was also giving as good as he got. I stood next to Little Col and noticed that a stray Newport lad had tried to sneak behind him and grab him; me and Subby pounced, Subb hit him with his brolley and he soon ran back into his mob.

The police then rounded their lot up and they were escorted back to Newport via Cardiff Central station. In the escort back they were attacked, as Cardiff by now had mobbed up as people arrived in the town centre. Although that week they made it onto Cardiff's main centre, I felt that Cardiff had fared better than previously as the small numbers stuck together and never took a step backwards. We gave them a better run for their money. Would a handful of Newport have done that to a fair-sized mob fronted by men twice their age? I doubt it.

May 1984, what a month! In a matter of weeks I had turned from a novice of a lad into a battle-scarred, experienced combatant. We started to realise that not everyone who stood outside Olympus was ready and willing to throw their fists about, not everyone had the courage of a lion and, when it came to it, there were not many screaming banshees among us. What this did was make Cardiff as a mob tighter.

We knew who we could trust and who was there to make up the numbers.

By the end of June 1984 we were drinking in pubs on Saturday afternoons, and the summer had set in. Vicky and I were still an item; I had an Ellesse polo shirt and Diadora Bjorn Borg trainers. Minor midweek incidents with little to nothing worth reporting occurred, but sure enough Newport made their way west.

As usual, word spread of their presence; by the time I arrived at the bus station, Cardiff were there en masse. Newport were hesitant of leaving the station and stayed in the foyer. Cardiff went at them, first about six of us and then, as more came, Newport fancied their chances less. Jammo and a few Ely went across to confront and beckon them on, and fists flew. Then it was the second charge, and they were ready to do the Canton mile, Newport were now getting picked off and were scattering. Then the police came in their dozens and we were all off to Dumfries Place, which would be the route the bus took.

We were now well and truly up for carnage. As we got to Dumfries Place the bus stopped, and a few of us had a couple of Newport out the windows by the scruffs of their necks, me included. When I felt someone grab me in a forearm lock, I was arrested. At 16/17, it had less to do with true heroism than with pure stupidity.

Earlier on that year I had been arrested at Portsmouth and fined £100, for running down the street and shouting. This time I was in real trouble. I thought I was going to be spending some time at Her Majesty's Pleasure. To my amazement, as this was not addressed as a football-related incident, I was only fined £25.

By the time the football season had arrived, there was great anticipation over the unknown. It's always exciting looking at the new fixtures when they are released and planning your trips, it's a real Pandora's box. The first game I made an effort to go to that season was at Newport, they were playing a friendly against West Brom on a Friday night in early August 1984, in torrential rain. About a dozen of us, including the usual lot – Annis, Mannings, Joseph, Moorie, etc – with an average age of about 18, made our way to Newport. We arrived in Newport late and, with the length of the walk from the station to the ground, we decided to catch a bus. On the bus were three very nervous Newport lads, avoiding eye contact and looking sheepish. As they numbered only three, nothing happened but a chat. This was a mistake, as when we alighted from the bus they led us to the back of the Newport end, and it emptied. We dozen were now stood at the top of some concrete steps and Newport were advancing up the stairs like a pack of swarming ants. We remained where we were until the advancing mob just overpowered us. Annis was demanding we stood, but we were being backed off and whacked everywhere. Eventually we were run. That chase through the backstreets of Newport was pretty scary, to say the least. We were chased into a Chinese takeaway, where we tried to hold the door shut. They tried unsuccessfully for some time to get in, until the police came and saved our bacon. It was a pretty scary night.

It was a risk going there that night, but if there's one thing every kid learns in growing up, it's that life is a series of risks. It's a cause and effect relationship: nothing ventured, nothing gained.

By the autumn of 1984, things quietened down on the Newport front due to the continual ad hoc midweek raids that Cardiff dished out. During that autumn, the author's nightclub was also near its completion. One afternoon, while I was actually working on Newport train station and had seen about ten lads make a midweek afternoon venture into Cardiff, I knew a few of the faces, one of whom was distinctive by his mop of curly hair. As this was way before the time of mobile phones, there was no way of informing anyone of our friends' pending visit to Cardiff. I had planned to finish my shift 2pm and head to Caesar's, where the decorating was in mid-process, and 'word up' the lads that the enemy were in town.

All my plans changed when I caught the train back to Cardiff. There, in the foyer of the station, were the ten Newport lads. I immediately spotted them and, as I was in British Rail uniform, I was able to walk through them, unnoticed, around the corner to Caesar's. Lying in wait in Caesar's were a few lads working at the decorating, as well as a few other faces – Annis, Tony G, C Beer,

Harris – who, on hearing the news, made haste around to Cardiff Central station and pounced. Newport did not know what hit them, they were immediately on their toes and hiding on the platform, where we all ended up picking them off. Priceless!

There are many, many more memories of that golden period when everything happened so fast and so often, and all for the first time. I guess magic doesn't last forever, no matter how much you wish it would.

MY FIRST AWAY GAME

Bristol Rovers v Cardiff City, 14th May 1983

Lee 'Tonto' Davies (CCFC): Growing up a few miles from Cardiff, I suppose it was inevitable I'd end up supporting the City. Some people's idea of supporting a club meant sitting at home with their football shirt on, waiting for the results on *Grandstand*. For me, it was all about being there, and besides, back then I'd never be seen dead in a City shirt.

I started going to home games in the early 80's with my mates from school. We'd jump the train to Cardiff and use our pocket money to get into Ninian Park. Maybe I'd buy a programme if my old man was flush that week. It was with these same mates that I experienced my first away game; it was Bristol Rovers and we'd already won promotion that season, so it promised to be good. I was still in school at the time, and I knew that if my old man knew where I was going he would have killed me. So I told him I was going swimming in Cardiff. I left the house early with my bathers rolled up in a towel, wedged them in a bush and I was off. I met up with my mates and we made our way to Cardiff; there were enough people on the train for us to be able to get all the way to Bristol without paying. We'd probably only been there about half an hour and we'd managed to buy some cheap cans of lager. We thought we were the business: drinking at an away game, probably acting like the pissed-up children that we were, it didn't take long to be spotted by the locals. It was just our luck that it happened to be a group of skinheads. One of the group approached us, he was a massive bloke (well, he looked massive to us – we were only kids) and he started bullying us, asking if we were Cardiff and taking the piss out of our accents. Then he tried to grab one of the boys. We shat ourselves and ran like scared sheep, dropping the last of our beer. I'd seen trouble before this game back at Ninian Park – small fights on the way to the ground, other fans trying to get onto the Bob Bank, Cardiff trying to get to the away end, pitch invasions and missiles thrown – but I'd never seen anything on this scale before. There were large-scale clashes involving dozens of rival fans, ambulances outside smashed-up pubs and what seemed like fighting in every part of the ground. I spent most of the game watching running battles between fans that hadn't gotten into the game, through a gap in the stands. I suppose I didn't feel threatened in Cardiff because of the familiar surroundings, but I did here and I didn't fancy the walk back to the station. I was pretty sure at this point that, if I got home in one piece, I'd never go to an away again.

Things change, and by the time I'd left school I was a regular, doing more away games than homes, probably because it was always a lot more fun at aways. It was about 1984, and it was around this time that I first met Annis. He was organising minibuses or cheap rail travel for the boys, which worked out great for me – cheap travel and safety in numbers. At this time the hooligan thing wasn't my scene, but when you travelled with this lot one basic rule was drilled into you from day one: don't run. So I used to try and stay at the back and let the boys do their thing, but even just being there and being able to read about it in the papers the next day, knowing I was part of it in even a small way, became a buzz. It didn't take long until I wanted more; being at the back wasn't enough. Back then I was never first in, but once it kicked off I couldn't help but get involved. From here on in it seemed like it would kick off at every ground we visited, either in small scuffles on the way to the ground, fighting at someone's end or proper toe-to-toe battles with other firms. That's right, 'other firms' – because by now I was part of the Soul Crew.

A FEW SANDWICHES SHORT OF A PICNIC

Neath Punk (CCFC): It was the summer of 1989, and we were all woken by the call of angels – or was it the tramps coughing and puking outside my room in Brownhill's hotel? This wasn't a football day, it was one of Annis's mystery trips. He got one of his paying guests called Nigel, a West Brom fan and a coach driver, to take us all on a trip to Western Super-Mare. Now Nigel, in my opinion, was a few sandwiches short of a picnic. He told us he was a bus driver and his wife was named Olive. I would have believed him, but he also said he was a brickie. I asked him, "Who for, fucking Lego?" but this was totally over his head, as he said, "No, I work for Wimpey." There was no beating this guy! But to be honest, he turned out to be a real gem.

It also turned out that he had a 33-seater bus, and he let us fill it full of lads and one girl called Helen from Lisvane. We also filled up with booze from the bar before Annis got there [*You bastards!* – Annis], because contrary to popular belief he's not tighter than asthma. So off we went to the shoplifter's paradise of Aust services, Bristol. Why the leather jacket shop man decided to go back to his van at 11am to get more stock (which he later needed) beggars belief. Rather than the usual stuff of pasties and crisps and the latest top-shelf magazine, the next thing I was seeing was a couple of our 18-year-old lads wearing full-length leather jackets in the middle of July, marching past the guy looking like a couple of SS stalwarts. It still tickles me to this day.

We arrived mid-morning and I swear the driver was more pissed than me. He finally parked up and probably hit two cars at the same time. With this, Annis, Darryl, myself, Martin (Cheltenham), Little Collin, Brownie, Chrissie Bear, Helen and various other beauts got off. We had only gone a few yards to the first pub when we set eyes on a big mob, and can you believe it? It was West Brom fans, about 50 in total; we found out later that they were on their main lad's stag do.

If you were a West Brom fan yourself, like the driver, the first thing you'd do would be to steam straight into them, saying, "Come on, you Baggie bastards!", wouldn't it? Well, our deranged driver, who'd rendered himself insane by this time with whatever he was on, did exactly that! We all steamed straight into them and, never mind *boing, boing,* we bounced them all down to the beach. I kid you not, they were running faster than the donkeys. They tried standing, to give them their dues, but it was a lost cause, especially when they were being steamed by one of their own. I dropped a lad on the beach and I was just about to give him a good wellying, when I thought, *Fuck it,* and walked away. Just as well, as the Old Bill arrived five seconds later, thank fuck, because all the lads were losing all sense of rhyme and reason and it was getting unnecessarily heavy. So we all scuttled off except the driver, who thankfully got nicked.

While walking back into town later, Little Collin was approached by a couple of kids who said, "Did you see the fighting, Uncle Collin?" To which he replied, "Wasn't it great? Did you see me? I was the first in." Priceless. (In all honesty, Collin worships his nephews and nieces. He gave them a couple of quid and told them to go and enjoy themselves.)

We all then went on a jolly; I've got to admit we were invincible in our own eyes, it sort of felt like a football day. Later on that day, we asked a couple of Old Bill what time they were letting our driver out. They said he would soon be dropped back by our bus and they didn't give a fuck who was driving, as long as we all fucked off back to Wales. Apparently, half of our group had just had a fight with a load of Wurzels from Bristol City, scattering the carrot crunchers everywhere.

In all my times of walking half a mile to a bus, nothing could have prepared me for what was about to happen. We were all on a high anyway, so what better than to nick a service bus and drive it back to our own one? What happened next goes with me to the grave among my top ten laughs. There was a bus parked outside the WSM depot, I'll never forget, it was one of those mini-town riders and the keys were in the ignition with the doors open. It looked like rain and a good two-minute walk to our bus, so of course we were going to nick it.

One of our lads, Chrissy B, had stolen a bus before and jumped in; with this, all except four of us got on. He then drove off while shouting, "Fares please!" with immaculate manoeuvring. A moment later, the driver came sprinting out of the depot shouting, "They've nicked my fucking bus and it's my first week in the job!" At that time, a grown man running up the road to see his pride and joy, his livelihood, disappearing before his very eyes and almost crying was fucking hilarious to us.

I have this picture in my mind still of us all singing, "We're all going on a summer holiday," while banging on the bus windows. At first we didn't pick anyone up until our crazy fucking driver, Chrissy, stopped and picked up this old geezer. He wasn't amused when we took a roundabout at 60mph with a police car up our arses; he was thrown from pillar to post as there was nowhere to sit, but at least we didn't charge the fucker. I wished him well as he staggered eventually off the bus (I've always been a sarcastic bastard).

How those highly trained motorway cops kept up with us I'll never know, because everyone knows you're a much better driver when you've had a few. When we finally ground to a halt, we legged it out of every possible exit, and guess what? The Old Bill only caught one of us, poor 16-year-old Helen. Once we got back to the bus, through about 30 people's gardens, we were met by the Old Bill and the real driver, who by now had a face like Hitler's gas bill. We were then escorted over the Severn Bridge.

I hear you shouting, "Please let there be more!" and if you're sitting comfortably, there is more. We decided to go to Newport, to smash Tutty, Adams and co, but firstly I must point out that Annis, Toddy and Darryl were not allowed in Newport because of a pending court case. We stopped off in Newport town centre; the above mentioned and the driver stayed on the bus, while the rest of us planned a surprise attack on their main pub on a Saturday night, knowing that all their main faces would be on show. The plan was to send two of our lads, Martin and Browny, into their pub, offer them out and then get chased back to where we were waiting at the bottom of the pedestrian walkways in the bus station. Well, it happened. We waited for about ten minutes and Newport County didn't disappoint, about 40 in all turned up, chasing our two over the bridge as planned, down the ramp and into our open loving arms. But the reason they had taken so long was that the two stupid twats had stood there and virtually let them get at them, but in a way maybe this helped bring them all down to us. We were straight into Newport's finest, like fucking madmen, then I noticed that two of our lot were trying to hold these fuckers back armed with a shopping trolley. Those were the days of no CCTV. I got hit in my leg with a big brick, but forget the nonsense of being in the wrong place at the wrong time, I was in the right place at the right time and fucking loving it. Unlike most rows, this was confined in a subway, which was no place for the weak, it was every man for himself.

I have no regrets whatsoever about that day, because I did to those what they were doing to me. The first County fucker who came within punching distance felt a brick right in the mush. What a connection! I've only made one like that twice since. It was goodnight Vienna and goodnight Newport and a very good night from me. Seeing a few of their mates horizontal soon had the rest of them running, and the night was ours.

The last 12 miles were great. All the lads on the bus who missed it wanted to know every detail, and cursed Jerky for getting them banned from the town centre and missing a tear-up with County. When we finally got back to our beloved Brownhill's there was a bit of good news. Annis asked us all to pay a pound each for Helen to come back by train from Western Super-Mare. It wasn't a problem, she took the rap, had nine points on her licence (which she hadn't even applied for yet), and when she arrived home at 12pm in the bar, she was given a hero's welcome because she was one of us.

BURBERRY, BRISTOL AND BULLSHIT

I've known Glenn and his family for many a year. Glenn does favour the casual look with all the latest designer labels, but he never was an out-and-out thug. Here he gives the true account of his wrongful arrest and court appearances. Glenn is the type that gets on with everyone he meets and is well liked by all the lads. In his own words, these are his experiences of being set up for something he never did and played no part in. Remember, it could happen to you!

Bristol City v Cardiff, 10th February 1990

Glenn V (CCFC): I had been to a few games here and there with some lads from school in the early 80's, but started going regularly to games home and away in 1985, just after leaving school. We were a really poor team at the time after consecutive relegations and we didn't have a great following, home or away. As we had low crowds, a lot of lads at the time got to know each other, seeing the same faces week in week out. I'd obviously heard of Annis, as he owned Caesar's nightclub in the centre of Cardiff. You heard stories, but I got to know a genuine, honest man who loved – and still loves – the City more than anyone I know. I've been with Annis home and away, he is a good laugh and a funny character.

I was going down with some lads from North Cardiff, met some others and it went from there. Football is a great way of building lifetime friendships. I started to drink with some lads in the Grand Vaults in Westgate Street, and we would go there before and after every home game. We called ourselves the BRAT boys, for some reason: British Rail Alcoholic Tribe, don't ask me why. We were lads from different areas of Cardiff and Penarth: Budgie (RIP), whom I was in school with and at 13 had a fullgrown beard, H (Partridge), Sully, Jenko and Elts from Penarth, Paul Simmo and numerous others. There were also a few other groups at the time, the Docks Boys, Booze Crew, Donut Mob, etc.

For Bristol City away, February 1989, I travelled up with Paddy from Llanishen whom I was friendly with at the time. The train to Bristol was always a short and unpleasant trip, not helped by the British Transport Police, who treat all football supporters like animals. Anyhow, the long walk to Ashton Gate was always with incident and there were a number of minor scuffles outside various pubs on the way. I remember coming up to the turnstiles and there were some naughty, ugly-looking Bristol who were looking for it, but they got moved on by the police. The game was tense as usual, and Bristol won 1-0 although it was a very poor spectacle. There was the usual hostile and intense atmosphere. As you would expect for a

February evening, it was getting dark and there was light rain. Near the end of the game I sat on a coach (Gray's of Tredegar) parked in the away area with Carter and Popeye from Llanishen, listening to the scores on the radio. We then got off the coach as the game had finished and I stood next to it talking to some other lads I knew, Wilburs and Ginger Simmo from Roath. We were about 15 or 20 yards away from the gate separating Cardiff from the Bristol supporters. At this point we could see the large gate between the turnstiles being rocked back and forth by the Cardiff fans trying to get through to the Bristol, and there were numerous items being thrown in both directions. There was a police van on the Bristol side, obviously filming (no CCTV in those days). It was at this stage that a few Cardiff lads climbed onto the turnstile roofs and began dismantling the walls, throwing down the debris so that others could use it as missiles to throw at the police and Bristol supporters. This went on for about ten minutes. Me, Wilburs and Simmo saw it all while leaning against a coach. When it all calmed down eventually, and the home fans had gone, we were let out to make the long walk back to Temple Meads. I chatted to a few people I knew, walking with a lad from Whitchurch, and could see Temple Meads in the distance. At this point three policemen came out of nowhere and jumped on me, pushing me against the wall. I had no idea what I'd done. They said I was being arrested for the turnstile incident and for hurling bricks, etc, at the police and the Bristol fans. I denied all connection with the incident. This was at 5.15pm. I was taken to a station and placed in a cell until 11.20pm, when I was eventually interviewed. I denied everything, as I couldn't believe I was in this situation. The main evidence was that I was wearing a Burberry scarf!

I was eventually released at 1am. Now, everyone in those days had a Burberry scarf, so it was not like I had a one-off Armani suit made especially for the occasion. The magistrate's date was set and I used a local solicitor whom my mother knew. On the first day, I think about eight were up as the pleas went in. Four pleaded guilty, including the lad on the roof from

Gabalfa, and four of us pleaded not guilty: myself, Paddy from Llanishen, one other lad and a young man called Anthony Rivers, often known as Lakey (author of the *Soul Crew* book), whom I got to know pretty well. The four who pleaded guilty did not have to return until sentencing, so it was just us four. I travelled to court on most occasions with Paddy and his father, a journey I got to know well as I went eight times to the magistrate's court. Then a Crown Court date was set. The only evidence from the police was the fact that I had this Burberry scarf. I had all the statements, etc, from the CPS and the police and they were very inconsistent. I also had a very poor videotape which contained footage from the police van on the other side of the fence. You could barely make anything out, so what little evidence they had wasn't even helped by the footage. As I've said, it was getting dark on the day of the match and it was raining. According to the police statements it was like a summer's day at lunchtime. The Crown Court hearing was set for two weeks. The jury was sworn in, and I said to my brief that I didn't want any Bristol City supporters on the case. I remember one lad put his hand up and had to leave the jury. The prosecution came first. At least ten of Avon and Somerset's finest gave a view of events which was totally incorrect, each saying how good visibility was and how it was such a nice day, the sun was beating down, etc. This went on for nine days, it was flakey to say the least. After the ninth day I think the judge had obviously heard enough garbage. Before we even had the chance to defend ourselves, the judge called a halt and the four of us were let off. The four who pleaded guilty got six months each. To say I was relieved would be an understatement. To have spent all this time going over to Bristol (a total of 17 times) for no reason at all was a joke. However, it was nice to get an apology from the police. (That last bit was a joke.) After this episode my mother, who had always held the police in high esteem, was no longer a supporter of them and has resented them ever since.

After this episode I stopped going down to the football for a few months and played Saturday footy, as it put me off a bit. If you can go through all this for doing nothing at all, what's it all about? However, the lure of live football, friends and drinking soon had me back on the terraces and I still attend regularly, home and away. Older and wiser though, I hope.

Mallo (CCFC): I will tell you about a few of my past trips as a youngster, with Bristol Wurzels being my 'bogie' trips:

Alongside Annis, Darryl, C Beer and Richard E, being the youngest I always wanted to be the first in, to show I was brave enough to run with them. On one occasion, at Bristol Rovers, in December 1982, we were in their stand and, as usual, up I got, wanting to be first in. Straight in I went, only to be confronted by a professional boxer. We were on the stairwell of their stand, having a standoff, when he started to throw 20 or so punches a second, he just rained punches into my head and face. I didn't know where I was, he was a fucking hard man who knocked the shit out of me. Annis and Richard E got me quickly out of there and dragged me down the stairs. Then we all walked along the pitch, back into the away end, to the usual clapping from the Cardiff fans for being at the other team's end. I was soon washing my face up and I instantly had two black eyes for my troubles.

On another Bristol trip, we were getting taken in a police escort from the train station when I decided to break escort with a few lads. When we got further up along the river, we got onto a footbridge where we ended up in a scuffle. All of a sudden I had blood pissing from my head. Matty (a lad from Cheltenham) dragged me away; I next remember waking up in an ambulance with Matty and some copper sat next to me. In the hospital I had stitches to my head; I had been slashed. The Old Bill wanted to take a statement from me, so me and Matty jumped out of the hospital window, stopped a car and told him to take us to the train station. We got onto the platform and I was swamped by OB. I forgot I still had a fuck-off bandage around my head, what a dead giveaway! Me and Matty still laugh about it to this day.

Another day out in Wurzel Land, at Bristol Rovers, I got stuck in their seats with a lad called Palmer. When it went off, just before the end of the game, we ended up on the pitch rowing with the home fans, who had waited until they'd grouped five times the number of us; we steamed into them and they backed off, but when they regrouped we had only one way out, and that was onto the pitch. Then the police came steaming into us; there was nowhere to go, we either had to face Old Bill or 100-plus home fans. The Old Bill option was taken and we both ended up getting nicked.

Encounter with Bristol City 2001

Mikey Dye (CCFC): In 2001, this fixture brought together two real enemies. It was a night game and our train mob was huge, I couldn't put numbers to it. Baggers, Lucky Evans and myself travelled by car, with Lucky driving. We never saw anything before the match, as we had a drink right by the suspension bridge. After the match, we left the ground and walked in what we thought was the right direction, but to our dismay it was leading us right into Bristol. We decided for safety reasons to turn around, heading back to the away end – safety in numbers. We could see our lot coming up the road behind us, although not many of 'em, then we heard a roar go up. It was Bristol's mob, charging around the corner looking really angry, and we were caught behind them. Cardiff retreated at first and Bristol were on top, with only a few Cardiff standing and fighting back. A shout went up from Cardiff and they stopped and turned. By now we were getting closer, fighting moved from one side of the road to the other, and before long Bristol were on their toes. Well, most of 'em anyway.

Myself, Lucky Evans and Baggers were amidst it now, and we had no choice but to get stuck in. I remember all too well hitting a Bristol fan and him hitting me back, then both of us getting caught by more fans of both sides. This was his chance. I heard a spraying sound as the fucker used pepper gas on me. I was all bent over and it went dark, my eyes stinging. Another punch landed on me and, as I looked up to fight back, I noticed it was a well-known Cardiff fan who could look after himself. He must have apologised a hundred times since. By now the fight had stopped and the police had taken control. My face was stinging and very red. My main concern now was to get away before the police picked me up. Baggers and Lucky, who also got slapped about, decided on getting me to a pub to clean up and start making our way home.

As far back as I can remember, the two Bristol teams have always come off second best when it comes to Cardiff. But I feel that in the last couple of years they've had a bit of revenge on us, but with bullying tactics. For example, on March 4th 2008 (my birthday), Annis, Justin, Penny, Craig, Peter M's stepson, my lad and myself travelled to Crystal Palace. It was a night match; as it was a Tuesday night there weren't many others going on, but one struck me straight away: Bristol City (who were at the top at the time) were playing at the Valley. We had a good drink on the way up and, before meeting up with Chelsea Pat, even bumped into eight Olympiakos travellers on the tube, getting ready for their match with Chelsea.

On arriving at Paddington, with only minutes to get the last train home at 11.30pm, we jogged to the train and just about made it. On board, it was full of the bully boys of Bristol City, who had been playing Charlton. With our six and their 150-odd, we knew we were in for a rough ride home. They were in our faces all the way back, giving Annis a right old time of it. If the Old Bill hadn't been on board, we would have been beaten and thrown off at Reading. We made it home unscathed, although at Temple Meads we were told to keep our heads down as they were likely to put the windows through. They never did though. (I think Annis gives a more detailed account in his life story book.)

About six weeks later we travelled to Burnley. Dan, James, my wife Nathalie and myself caught the 06.25 train out of Cardiff. While at the station, we noticed two young City fans and asked if they would like to join us on the journey. I now know these two lads as Dean and Pip, who I have a lot of time for, and boy, can they drink! Pip brought along eight bottles of Foster's Twist – he hated it! On every swig he would say, "Yuck!" We arrived in Burnley at 11.30 and consumed yet more ale before attending the game. We left with the score at 0-0 and headed for the station via the ale house, where the police entered the pub and advised us to drink up for our own safety. Dan and Jayo stayed till the end of the match. We were supposed to meet them in the pub, but the police had moved us on. (We'd already waited a while for them.) At 5.30 we rang to tell them what platform we were on, only to hear they were already on a train. I said, "You can't be, our train doesn't arrive till 17.45!" Then they realised they were on the wrong train and heading for Bradford!

We boarded our train and had to change at Preston and Birmingham, which took two hours. Our connecting train was the Leeds to Plymouth line. On checking the fixtures, I noticed that Bristol City were at Sheffield United. Funny thing, but this train housed not only 100 Bristol supporters but also our very own Dan and Jayo! Reunited!

As we had walked through the carriages, an oldish guy with a wurzel accent had made a suggestive remark to my wife. I heard this, so I went over and had words and he eventually apologised. This was the calm before the storm. We found seats and actually got chatting to some Bristol fans about how they'd got on, etc. On arriving at Cheltenham, Pip said to me, "Who the fuck were all them lads on the platform?" The problem was that we had to change trains yet again. I noticed 60-70 lads who were also Bristol, but must have caught the earlier train out of Sheffield. This was their mob – Stone Island United by the looks of it! They didn't seem bothered with us at first, and I don't think they noticed our crew. (There were only eight of us, including two kids and a lass.) They were at the other end of the platform. As we stood waiting for them to get on the train, two Bristol lads had got off next to us and one of them spat at my wife. I can tell you that she wasn't best pleased. She gave them a mouthful, and then I had yet more words! This frustrated the two lads, and they shouted to all the other Bristol fans as if to say, "Let's have 'em, it's fucking Cardiff!" They didn't come up the platform but actually boarded the train, walked up the coaches and got off again pretty close to us – maybe 40 of the twats in total. They surged forward and threw everything they could at us, the air was filled with flying bottles and beer cans that we had to dodge. The bottles broke and broken glass reigned supreme. We returned the favour with however much beer we had. (Only two cans, I think. If only Pip had some of his Foster's Twist left, I'm sure he'd have launched it!) This bought us about five seconds. My words to everyone were, "No one fucking run, just stand our ground!" Fair play to our lot, we didn't budge. Bristol got closer, giving it the "Come on, you Welsh cunts!", but we weren't going anywhere. If we had run they would have been in the driving seat with their sheer numbers. They got right in our faces yet we still weren't moving, just stepping back a bit to wait for the onslaught. I'd noticed by now that they were coming around the side of us, but still they never attacked. Then one of them got a bit brave and came charging in, smacking Pip; to which Pip responded with a hell of a punch. They stood off again; those to the side of me were wary, they were giving it the large one – "Come on then!" – but, being well outnumbered, it wasn't clever for us to make the first move. By now, more of them had got involved. We still stood firm and, on another attack from Bristol, more punches were exchanged. Our two new recruits, Dean and Pip, did us proud and there still wasn't a copper in sight. This could and should have been a walkover for them, although if the boot was on the other foot we would never have attacked eight of them under any circumstances.

Further up the platform, we could see the yellow jackets of the police. If I'm honest, it was a welcome sight. They got the bully boys from Bristol onto their train and it pulled off. We then boarded ours and headed for home. After this episode, I lost all respect for Bristol City. It's true what Bristol Rovers say about them – they're bullies! Respect to Dean and Pip for that night, and to my son and wife. Looking back, I wonder if this was some kind of revenge for all the years of beatings Bristol have taken.

THE CREAM OF DEVON

Con (CCFC): I could talk about my experiences at notorious grounds such as Stamford Bridge, the Den, Upton Park, Ayresome Park, St Andrew's or Elland Road. But I can hear people laughing when I make the confession that the scariest ground I've ever had the misfortune to visit is St James' Park,

Exeter. I've been there on four occasions to watch Cardiff City play Exeter City. When people mention Exeter, beautiful images of this leafy town full of character and ancient history are conjured up in most people's minds. Unfortunately, I am going to shatter that illusion. Images of unhinged fighting, broken bones and no-holds-barred thuggery collide inside my mind's eye.

November 16th 1985 – FA Cup, Exeter City v Cardiff City
In 1985, you didn't support Cardiff City for the joys on offer on the pitch. They were dark days for a club struggling on the verge of footballing oblivion. On May 11th 1985, we had been relegated from the old Second to the Third Division after losing 2-1 to Wimbledon at Plough Lane. The date lived long in my memory, as it was the same day as the fire at Bradford (more of which later). These were bleak times, with a clueless manager, Alan Durban, at the helm. We really did have the worst football team in history.

My first taste of Devon 'hospitality' was a first-round FA Cup tie. The Grecians had been promoted from the old Fourth Division to the Third, but as favourites we were still expected to win easily. In those days the FA Cup was still a massive draw, and most of Cardiff's major hooligans had made the journey to Devon. The trip had attracted a large crowd of eager City faces who'd expected to see us progress against the lowly opposition into the next round of the FA Cup. I was only 16 years old, totally green but up for whatever was on offer. At the time I was on a Youth Training Scheme at a government organisation, and in truth I also felt like I was on a YTS with the Soul Crew. I headed down to the Southwest with a large group of Grangetown casuals, including Mallo and Coxy – we were the youngest boys when we started on the scene in 1983. We reckoned it was the mighty Cardiff on the pitch against the minnows of Exeter and the mighty Soul Crew off of it. There was to be no giant-killing on or off the pitch – or so we thought.

As youngsters we were too young to be served in pubs, so we had to content ourselves with the alcoholic joys on offer at the local Tesco. We watched as all the older lads filled their gullets in Exeter's finest watering holes. For those who don't know, Exeter is a picturesque market town with leafy vistas popping up behind the many historic Tudor buildings. If you want tranquillity and serenity, you've picked the right place. Except when Cardiff City come to town, of course. As we walked cans in hand, the idyllic scene was shattered by what resembled a Wild West brawl. I saw a guy in a Rangers ski hat (contrary to popular belief, a lot of Cardiff fans in those days harboured loyalist sympathies); this was Jammo – a terrace legend who is worthy of a separate weighty tome – who was having to fight off three or four guys on his own. There was also Mark from Pontypridd, a granite-built British Army boxing champ and a Chelsea fan – who was having chunks of his hair pulled out by half a dozen guys. (Mark was one of only a few Valley boys who were members of the Soul Crew at the time. It was predominantly a Cardiff, Barry and Port Talbot affair.) There were literally hundreds of people fighting. This was way out of our league as innocent, 16-year-old Soul Crew youth trainees.

One of the boys, Maratzi, who was in the notorious B Troop from Llanrumney (a predecessor to the Soul Crew), had to be carried into a shop with a suspected broken leg, only for Exeter's Sly Crew to go in and give him another leathering before the ambulance arrived. Quite ironically, it was in a shoe store that he received this violent kicking. This ruck was so large and had spilled out so widely that the police were hard pressed to know where to begin to break it up. It had gone on for half an hour at least, but seemed like an eternity. Despite their lowly reputation both on and off the pitch, Exeter gave as good as they got. There was sporadic fighting all the way on the long walk from the town centre to St James' Park – a mile or two at least. This was a taste of things to come. If we thought it was going to get better as the afternoon progressed, we were wrong. The scenes unfolding were foreign to us. We were the mighty Cardiff City. It should be a stroll in the park, both on and off the pitch, against lowly Exeter. Shouldn't it?

On the pitch we weren't faring much better, going down 2-1 to a team fired up by the volatile crowd. The game itself will live long in the memory for three incidents: a last-minute penalty to

Exeter being stopped as Cardiff fans invaded the pitch; the goalposts being broken in the ensuing ruckus; and Cardiff City manager Alan Durban being attacked by his own fans, incensed by what they saw as a gutless capitulation. Make no mistake, this was a full-scale football riot.

After the match, the assembled Cardiff City hordes were gamely escorted from St James' Park to Exeter Central. As rioting was breaking out all around, the police were trying to manage the unmanageable, quell the unquellable and were having their ear turned by a large, blond-haired bloke, one of the poshest City hooligans I'd ever met. Simon Williams, who was to become a director at the club, was concerned less with the raw sights, smells and sounds around him than with retrieving the multi-coloured country-gent umbrella he'd mislaid in the melee. All we could hear was him repeating *ad infinitum* to any copper that would listen, "I say, have you seen a multi-coloured umbrella? I appear to have dropped it somewhere round here." It was as if Lord Charles had taken a wrong turn into the marching hordes of Babylon.

It's funny what you remember, but as an eyes-wide-open 16-year-old who had happened upon his first football riot, that stuck in my mind. It also gave us all a laugh, and broke up the palpable tension as we trekked our battered and bruised way to the station.

September 20th 1986
Division Four: Exeter City 0 Cardiff City 0

This season signalled a new low in the history of the football club. It was the first time we had ever been relegated to the old Fourth Division. Then manager Durban had been served his P45 in favour of fiery Scotsman Frankie Burrows – a no-nonsense ex-Swindon player who was a member of their famous 1969 team that beat Arsenal 3-1 at Wembley. Famous bedfellows that season were Wolves – who had plummeted from the old First Division to the Fourth. Another big fish in a small pond. Revenge was high on the agenda after the battle of St James' Park in the previous season. Two Transit vans full of Cardiff's finest included Annis, Dexy, Martyn Davies, Dixie, Dexy, Rich E and a group of well-up-for-it Barry boys. Also flying down to Devon in the back of the van was Boozer – a die-hard Millwall fan who, despite being from Cardiff, had a body which was a human gallery of Millwall tattoos. Despite also being a skinhead and thereby tarred with the racist brush, he'd famously launched an assault on a National Front march in Cardiff. While dispelling the lazy myth that all skinheads and football fans are fascists, he was still a headcase.

Once again the weather was warm, the scenery was stunning and, as we weaved our way down the M5 after making an obligatory stop-off in Taunton for a few Scrumpy Jacks, a few of the lads flung the doors open and hung their legs out of the bus. A risky manoeuvre, as one wrong move would have sent us bouncing down the motorway on our arses – easy roadkill for a passing truck! But when you're young and seemingly invincible, you don't measure risks to life or limb. On arriving in Exeter, thoughts of the previous season's events got the adrenalin pumping, mixed in with the West Country's finest cider. The sun was beaming a path from the sky as we parked up next to the town's towering cathedral – and a horde of sinners stepped out of the two battle buses. A huge police presence ensured that any pre-match rucks were kept to a minimum.

On entering the ground, it was completely different. Half a dozen of Cardiff's foremost fruitcakes decided to try and take the home end. Obviously, they hadn't been to Exeter the year before. At the front of the charge were Neath Punk (another one who could have a book penned in his honour) and Fulman (probably one of the hardest guys ever to grace the Ninian Park terraces – an absolute monster). Despite putting up a gallant battle, they were overrun. If Rourke's Drift had been transplanted to a leafy Devon town, it wouldn't have been too dissimilar to the scene unfolding before our eyes. Neath Punk (playing Michael Caine's role as Bromhead) bore the brunt of his gallant efforts in the face of overwhelming odds, escaping with a fractured cheekbone and several other broken bones. If there was a VC for attempting to take liberties he'd have been awarded it. (Anyway, he was used to living on the frontline, his home being just a few miles from Swansea!) The proceedings took another bizarre twist when City fans attempted to set fire to bushes at the back of the away terrace. Thankfully, a raging fire didn't take hold, just a few random flames.

This was mightily prescient, given that the next day's headlines would be full of stories of an arson attempt further north. That day, Leeds United would play Bradford City at the Odsal Stadium – an old rugby league ground. It was a Bradford home game, but their own ground, Valley Parade, was being rebuilt after the horrific fire that tore through it on May 11th 1985. Leeds fans set fire to a chip van and caused chaos at the Odsal. Luckily, no one was seriously injured and a fire didn't take hold at St James' Park. What did take hold was a lot of fighting at the end of the game with the Devonshire constabulary. *Mail* reporter Peter Walker, the ex-Glamorgan and England cricketer, famously described Cardiff City fans as terrace guerrilla warfare specialists. It may have been intended as an insult, but most of City's battle-hardened masses wore it as a badge of honour.

After a few minor skirmishes, we made it back to the Transit in one piece. It was such a beautiful sunny day and, after all the events on and off the pitch, we decided to stop off again in Taunton on the way back for a few more ciders. Dexy – who would become one of the first of a number of Soul Crew members to be charged with rioting, at Cardiff v Swansea in August of the following year, 1986 – nearly had the life knocked out of him at the pub in Taunton. He'd taken it upon himself to write 'CCFC' in a newly laid concrete floor that had taken workmen all day to lay under the sweltering sun, only to see their hard work spoiled. He was lucky to escape as the incensed navvies fronted up with shovels. The police vans turned up at just the right time to give us an escort out.

As an aside, the return game at Ninian Park on March 31st 1987 was famous for Exeter bringing the combined total of one away fan to Cardiff. Were they scared? Probably, but fair play to the guy, who stood there defiantly facing a barrage of abuse from the City ranks with his Exeter City flag draped over a Grange

End barrier. As you can imagine, chants of "Is that all you take away?" reverberated around the ground all afternoon.

April 2nd 1988 – Division Four: Exeter City 0 Cardiff City 2

It was our second season in the basement division, but we were now going up, finishing second only to Wolves – after famously beating them at Molineux 4-1, on February 6th 1988. That season we were taking huge numbers to every away game, a sizeable number of whom weren't there just for the on-pitch entertainment. Our now annual party at Exeter was guaranteed. A large crowd of us once again stopped off at Taunton, where we grouped up before heading off to our favourite Devon town. The trip was memorable for a fight breaking out between two Cardiff fans. At the time, outsiders weren't always welcomed by certain members of the Soul Crew. Mallo had taken exception to Matt – a half-American, Leeds-supporting fan from Cheltenham, who now resides in the States. We'd met Matt on our various travels around the UK, following our respective clubs, and he'd become something of a name when he jettisoned Leeds to become a fully paid-up City fan. He even decided to move to Cardiff to declare his love for the Bluebirds' cause. All hell broke loose as a lasting animosity between the two spilled over into the pub. A lot of the Soul Crew saw it as bullying by Mallo – picking on anyone younger than him.

The welcome was equally as hostile when we reached Devon. We were attacked from Exeter station all the way to the ground. Fair play to the Sly Crew, they were nothing but consistent. To underline their cheek, one guy walked towards me, went to shake my hand, headbutted me and ran off. We were in a small group and we had to battle our way to the ground. It was astonishing.

On arriving at St James' Park, we managed to get into the home end. Out of an act of bravado, and possibly sheer stupidity, we then found ourselves fighting our way out of their end as Rourke's Drift II took hold. All the sensible people were put on the football special from Exeter St James' station back to Exeter St David's. However, around 20 of us decided to walk back to Exeter Central, instead of travelling on the special train. At that age most us were neither sensible nor fully aware of just what we were letting ourselves in for. But we were bang up for a ruck – although, if we realised what awaited us a few hundred yards away, even youthful bravado and heavy-duty testosterone may have given way to commonsense.

It was as we reached the cathedral – in our youthfully misguided eyes, we were acting out some sort of eternal battle between good and evil – and rounded a corner that we were confronted by a huge mob of a couple of hundred Exeter baying for our blood. I was shaking like a leaf when they started to quicken their pace from a walk into a run, their faces full of anger and striding with a common purpose. It was then I heard Jammo utter the words that would go down in Soul Crew folklore: "Come on, Cardiff, this is where we make a name for ourselves!" I cannot describe the feeling of sheer terror as the Exeter horde tore towards us. Incredibly, as we faced up, it was as if the reputation of Cardiff, and the fact that we stood firm, rooted to the spot, had the effect of putting doubt in their minds. They couldn't quite believe we'd faced up to them. To be honest, neither could we. Seeing this show of defiance, Exeter thought twice, turned on their heels and ran. It was a retreat of biblical proportions, in the shadow of the cathedral. Call it divine intervention, but how we survived to tell that particular story I'll never know.

August 12th 2000 – Division Three: Exeter City 1 Cardiff City 2
It would be 12 years before I headed back to St James' Park. On my return the landscape both on and off the pitch couldn't have been more different. This was the very first match at the beginning of the Sam Hammam era. The day we played Exeter, on the opening day of the new 2000-2001 football season, the atmosphere around St James' Park resembled a carnival. Finally, a man with money – and lots of it – had come riding to Cardiff City's rescue. Or that's what we thought at the time. Nevertheless, in a place where I'd seen hooliganism at its very worst there was a party atmosphere. The promise of good times lying ahead was the perfect antidote to the edgy, foreboding place that Cardiff City had been in the 80's.

Cardiff City Football Club had reached a new chapter in its life and, just as the club had moved on, so had I.

PLYMOUTH V CARDIFF, 24TH SEPTEMBER 2002

Mikey Dye (CCFC): I organised my own coach for this one, as is the norm these days. It was a Tuesday night game, and Plymouth were game too. After stopping off just outside Plymouth, we had a rendezvous point with the local dibble, who would then take all the coaches in together to avoid trouble. How wrong they were. We arrived third in line behind two supporter's coaches run by Vince Alm, who does a tremendous job. As we pulled up near the car park at Home Park, the first coach stopped across the road. The Plymouth firm were egging on our supporter's coaches. They never banked on us at the back. Robbie spotted this and the rear door opened. Everyone piled off and Plymouth, having roughly the same numbers, soon had it on their toes, running to a nearby park. Cardiff pursued them. On reaching the park, they did take a stance against the eight Cardiff who had chased them the full distance. We were not stopping now, we were into 'em. Strange as it seems, most of the Plymouth fans ran again but the ones who stood took a hiding. We thought that was it, but as we got near the ground they regrouped, whereas we were all in twos and threes. They punched every City fan they came across. Arrests were made, but for some reason they were all Cardiff. Me and Lucky were nabbed and held till after the game. Then they released us and we made it back to the coach for home. Two weeks later, a summons for court was delivered. Fair play to Vince – he travelled down to court the second time as a witness, along with my mate CC, Annis's brother-in-law, Jamie, and my solicitor, Mojo. I got a Not Guilty, which was only fair as I didn't do anything. Good on our justice system for that one. To everyone who was there that night, well played, boys.

WE'VE GOT RESPECT FOR EACH OTHER

Danny (Plymouth Central Element): I met Annis in Brussels during the Euro2000 championships, outside a pub in the main square. There were about 30 Plymouth lads in Belgium at the time, but at this point it was just me and my mate Chris. I remember getting into conversation with a group of lads who turned out to be from Cardiff. Most clubs were represented and there were quite a few other small groups of Cardiff over there too. The ones we met were Annis, Dai Thomas, Moj, Flynny and another lad named Harvey, they had a Welsh flag with 'Cardiff City' on it. Through our previous encounters with Cardiff I had heard of Annis, but never had a face to put to the name. We stayed together for much of what turned out to be an eventful day and ended up in the same military prison before being deported. We kept in occasional contact after this and have come across each other at a couple of Plymouth v Cardiff games since then. In October 2008 I contacted Annis and, as we were chatting, he asked me if I would be happy to give an account for his new book. I was happy to oblige.

I was born in Plymouth in 1977, where I've spent my whole life. From the early age of four, I've had an affection for my local team and started attending every week. I have just finished my third ban and have been part of the scene in Plymouth for about 14 years. It was during the early 90's that I took an interest in what was happening off the pitch, and by 1994 I started drinking with known local faces and attending home games with them.

My first away game with the Element was at Exeter that season. One game that also occurred that season was a home fixture with Cardiff. I have asked a very close friend of mine, who has clear memories of that day and was a lot more active than me at the time, to give the Plymouth account of what happened.

Cardiff Home 1994 by Nick

I have been part of the Central Element since its coming together in 1985/86. After 23 years, several bans, arrests and the subsequent penalties that go with it, I am still involved in the scene in Plymouth.

Back in February 1994, Cardiff City were the visitors along with members of their much talked-about Soul Crew, who were highly regarded and respected within the football hooligan scene. There were not many mobile phones back then, but people who worked away from Plymouth and various lads in the know made sure that our firm, the Central Element, were aware that we were expecting a visit. Cardiff always bring a mob to Plymouth, and this day would certainly confirm this and cement our rivalry with them. We met early, as usual, and I remember being impressed with our numbers and 'up for it' attitude. Our mob numbered about 150, made up of lads of all ages, and we were spread between the Britannia pub and the social club across the road. These two venues were where we had been meeting since the days of drinking in the city centre had gone. They were very well sited due to the proximity of our ground, Home Park, and the fact that any visiting lads would always pass by them or near to them. Going between the two pubs and getting the info on Soul Crew sightings led us to believe that they were in a city centre pub called the Noah's Ark, and that they numbered about 40. The Noah's Ark pub used to be our main meeting place, what a pity we had not decided to go back and meet there on this occasion. A car full of our lads had agreed to drive down there and review the situation, and let the Cardiff lads know where we were drinking and the best way to get there undetected. If our mob that was spread over the two pubs had tried to go into the city centre, Old Bill and CCTV would have been all over us and it would have been game over. The car left, but returned no more than 15 minutes later. I remember seeing it speed up to our pub and, judging by the condition of it and the lack of windows, we knew something had happened. The news went round that Cardiff were in the Noah's Ark pub and, more to the point, were definitely up for it. It turned out that a few Cardiff were outside the pub having a drink as the car had pulled up. They'd clocked each other and, within seconds, the pub emptied and bottles and glasses were directed towards it.

I remember looking around our pub at this time and thinking all our main lads were out, and even more up for it than ever. We needed to know when Cardiff were going to leave the city centre and start making their way towards the ground. A few of our lads were sent out scouting and made their way to the train station, some to the nearby park, all prepared to report back on any sightings. At 2pm, word went round that Cardiff were on their way and they had been sighted halfway up Alma Road, the main road to the ground, still with no police presence. At this stage Cardiff had two routes they could have taken; one was through the park, the other was directly to the pubs. Due to this, a mob of ours of about 30 made their way into the park and the other 120 stayed in the pubs in case they arrived there. Within minutes, I remember looking out the window and seeing Cardiff 200 yards away, steaming towards us in the pub. The shout went up that they were here and things started to get serious. Bottles and glasses started flying from the pub into the nearing Cardiff mob, and there was a slight standoff when we were about 50 yards apart. There were only about two or three coppers around and, going by the look on their faces, they were not prepared to get involved until backup had arrived. At the front of our mob were some very game lads in their 30's, and they went straight into the Soul Crew, who in return were steaming into us, punching and kicking everything around. The traffic stopped and normal fans were staring at the brawl erupting around them. Shouts of, "Keep it together!" and smashing glass could be heard by all.

The first impressions of the Welsh were that they were certainly up for it, and I mean every single one of them. Plymouth were now all around the Soul Crew and everyone was trading punches; the 40 visiting lads were doing very well, bearing in mind they were heavily outnumbered, and at one stage they were even backing us off. There were a number of bodies from both sides dropping to the floor, but getting straight back up and into it again. The fighting just went on and on, and I remember thinking that this was one of the best offs that I had ever witnessed or been involved in. All of a sudden both firms seemed to split and a gap appeared. Give Cardiff their due: they had us at full stretch. The shout went up, "We are Central Element!" and at this point across the park came the 30 other Plymouth who had broken off before Cardiff had arrived. We steamed straight back into them from one side as did the other 30 from another. Cardiff were now well and truly on the back foot. The Old Bill, who were still short of numbers, were seen running around randomly hitting people with their batons. There had been lads getting out of cars in the traffic, leaving their kids and steaming in to have a go. Eventually, sirens in the distance could be heard approaching and both mobs backed off. Coppers piled out of riot vans en masse and within seconds the boys in blue were everywhere. Only a few lunatics from both sides were left fighting. Cardiff backed off into the park now as the Old Bill were pulling anyone they could get their hands on. Plymouth regrouped and tried one last attack, but by this time it was game over. Fighting stopped and the verbals started over the police lines. The Central Element mob, which now must have stood at about 200 lads, certainly knew that they had been in a battle. Both mobs started to clap and applaud each other, a sign of respect, as they were escorted away. The police could not understand that mentality and looked puzzled by this.

That was about it, we all made our way to the game. On reflection I would say that honours were even that afternoon. One of the other Soul Crew books tells their version of the incident and now we've had the opportunity to tell ours. A number of lads from both sides had been arrested that afternoon, and when the Cardiff lads came back to Plymouth for court hearings a few of our lads turned up and took them out for a drink as a sign of respect. Cheers, Cardiff – a top row and one that is still talked about amongst older heads to this day.

The following season gave me my first proper experience at football, the eye opener, the game that will stay with me forever, and it just happened to be the return fixture away at Cardiff. Although certain points of the day stand out, and probably will do for many years to come, many parts are still a blur. After speaking with some of our other lads and finding that their memories of the day were slightly clearer, I felt it was better to once again ask one of them to give his account.

Cardiff Away 1996
Cardiff has always been one of my top games. For some reason, there's always been a mutual respect between the two of us. For

a start, after Bristol City – even though it's about a 300-mile round trip – geographically they've usually been the nearest team to us with a firm worth bothering about. Exeter City can bang on all they like, but they've never been up to anything so far as I've ever made out, and as for Torquay, well . . .

Another thing with Cardiff which is similar to us is that they make an effort. We get somewhere, usually without getting picked up, and then have a scout around. It always amazes me when lads make the effort to go somewhere and then just sit in a pub until the police turn up. We've never been like that and neither have Cardiff. So I think another reason we rate each other is that we do what we can to make something happen. Although in the last five-six years it's got harder, with cameras and informants.

I've met a few of their lads over the years and they're pretty good. One thing that has pissed me off slightly though is the way that, in their books, they've put a couple of meetings with us across, so it's nice to be asked about a trip we made up to Ninian Park to get the story from our point of view.

One of my favourite trips there was in 1996. We took two vans up, around 30 of us, and got there a couple of hours before the kick-off. Old Bill were there, but we parked up and had a plan to get in the Ninian Park pub. The Ninian's not their main boozer, their firm tend to drink in the city centre or Canton, it's where their shirts and scarfers go and the odd lad having a beer before the game, but it's the nearest pub to the ground. The plan was to get in there, have a few beers, and get something on when they made it down that way to the game. Though most people know that Cardiff have got more than their share of civvies who'll have a row when it comes to it, and the pub had plenty of likely opponents if it went off.

What's quite funny about this is that back then hardly anybody had mobiles, so we were going on instinct and things that we'd learned and remembered from going up there before. Anyway, after our being there for a while, a few Soul Crew wandered in. One of them blatantly stood there counting heads, while the other two were just basically there as back-up.

I remember one of our lads (DK) asking who the fuck they were. "Soul Crew, mate. Is this all you've brought?" DK looked at me, and I have to say I had to give these three respect, but DK took exception, gave him a tidy right hand and put him down.

Obviously it went off pretty quick. A lot of our lads got into having it with door staff and scarfers, and about ten of us actually got outside. When we did, we realised we weren't going to get a result. I've heard all sorts of estimates about how many they had up the road, but it was at least 80-100, maybe more. They were into us pretty quick. To be fair, we were backing off right away. You hear stories about ten lads standing against that kind of number and giving it to them, and if you've been there and done that, fair enough. But I've never witnessed it, in 25 years of working against quality opposition.

In my opinion you do what you can to save a bit of face, but make sure you're fit enough to make a better show later in the day. During all the mayhem of flying bottles and kicks and punches, I'm sure both sides all stopped for a bit to let a mum get by with her pram, before it went off again. One of our boys (SM) got knocked over by a car. I don't know to this day if it was done on purpose or not.

Anyway, we backed off down the road and under the railway bridge, turning every now and then to exchange a couple of blows and save a bit of face. It died off then, because you get to the corner and turn down to the ground and, as the police were about and realising what was happening, Cardiff made their way back to the Ninian, where it was still going off with the rest of our lads. To be honest, I think the ones who got stuck in the pub came off worse than the ones who got out. We all have a laugh now about this, because everyone's got their own version of events. My brother and a couple of other lads even ended up on the railway lines, making their escape.

We all got together again in the ground and we had a chat about what to do. It was agreed that we couldn't just make our way home and pretend nothing had happened, so we did the old trick of leaving after the game, giving it 30 minutes and getting back into the town to hit one of their pubs. We did a bit of checking and found out we'd lost a couple of our lads to the hospital and the cells, but most of us were fine and up for a bit of revenge.

Back then, like I said earlier, you couldn't just call Lakey, or your Soul Crew contact number out of your mobile phonebook, to find out where they were. So we decided to drive back into the city centre, get a lad to stick his head in the pub doors and see if any Cardiff were in. We found one pretty quick, so we drove the vans down a street behind the pub, left two lads in the driving seat with the doors left open and went to work!

Basically, we just did as you'd expect. Straight through the front doors and into whoever was there. It was just one of those mad few minutes of high jinks. Punches thrown, tables and chairs turned over, a few glasses and bottles flying around. It was just a quick in and out, to let them know we weren't just taking what had happened earlier. We also take a lot of pride in putting one over on the police. There they were with all their 'intelligence', manpower and resources, and we still had two good offs without them anywhere to be seen!

Anyway, you know that when it's like that, and in a major city centre high street, that it can't carry on too long, or those blue lights are going to turn up.

So we make it back to the vans to get out of there. Job done! Everyone piles into the vans, and we start to head out of town. We're all laughing and buzzing with the adrenalin, feeling that we've done a nice job, then suddenly the van in front pulls over and they're waving us in. DK gets out of the front van and makes his way back to ours. "Is P on your van?" Quick checks reveal he's not. Obviously we've got to go back and see if he's around and make sure he's okay.

We turned around and drove to a car park which was close enough to the pub we'd just hit, so that a few of us could walk down and see if P was around. Me, my brother J, a friend called SH (who some of Cardiff know as Pinky) and a couple of others walked a couple of hundred yards down a sort of narrow backstreet, which brought us out more or less opposite the pub. Unfortunately, during this last 10-20 minutes, Cardiff had time to get the message out about what had happened, and they were mobbing up around the pub. We had a quick look about to see if we could see P anywhere. He wasn't, and in the meantime we got spotted by a few of their lads.

We started to walk back up the street to the car park, but pretty soon these few lads had put it about that we were back, and their firm were coming after us.

To be fair to them, it was nowhere near as many as they'd had earlier, probably around 30-40 lads. I told J, my younger brother, to run on and get the lads ready, and to get the vans out of the car park. My feeling was that this was a pretty fair row brewing. The numbers were near enough the same, the big problem was confusion.

Most of ours were sat in or stood around the vans, just having a can or smoking a fag, chatting about whatever, and I think that when J raced around the corner and started barking instructions, the message got lost. Instead of just the drivers getting the vans moved, and the rest of us getting stuck back into them, everyone started getting back into the vans.

If we could have just got back down the street it would have been a good toe-to-toe. Even if we were a bit outnumbered, the street was narrow enough that it wouldn't have made a difference. But it didn't happen, and it was the one part of the day when I think we let ourselves down.

Within seconds the Soul Crew were on the scene. The car park was on loose, stony ground, but a couple of us did try to make a go of it. I threw a few punches, caught a few back, and managed to get away up the road. The lads in the vans tried to drive out of the car park the wrong way, so they had to turn around and come back past their firm. By now they were all tooled up with rocks and stones, and as the vans came past they let loose. Every single side window and back window on both vans was put through. The drivers just had to keep their foot down and get away. Apparently it was a bit mad, although everyone says they remember laughing as they raced off down the road. There were a few cut up with flying glass, but nothing too serious.

I was stuck there now on my own. I decided to walk out of Cardiff on the main road, so that if our lot came back I'd get spotted, but I didn't have to go far, because after a few minutes I saw them up ahead.

Me and a couple of others had not got into either van, so they'd stopped, thinking they'd have to come back again, and a police car had pulled over to see what was going on. Needless to say, when he clocked the lads and the state of the vans he was calling for back-up. They sorted a couple of bikes and squad cars, and escorted us as far as the other side of the Severn Bridge to make sure we weren't coming back.

The three missing lads had all made their way to Cardiff station and got a train to Bristol and then on to Plymouth. It was good later, meeting up at home and finding out they were okay.

We had a couple of good moments on the way back. At one point we were in a traffic jam by Gordano Services near Bristol and a few Bristol City lads in a car asked what the fuck had happened. One of our main lads, PW, said, "We've been in Wales fighting the Welsh for England, where the fuck were you?" Even the City lads saw the funny side!

We all chipped the extra money in to cover the deposits on the vans, dropped them back at the rental place and went out for the Saturday night. On the Monday morning at about 8am I got a call from this shrieking voice down the line.

"What happened to the vans?"

"I don't know," I said. "What's up?"

"All the windows are smashed!" came the reply.

"Well, they were okay when I left them there," I said, and hung up. I don't know if he believed me but he never bothered calling back.

There's a story Lakey tells in the Soul Crew book about seeing us the following week in Manchester. A few of us went to the Oasis gig at Maine Road, and bumped into him and a few mates at Old Trafford earlier in the day (I think United were at home to Forest). Lakey's a fair guy, but in the book he says we thanked them for not using weapons. To put the record straight: time has probably clouded his memory, because that wasn't said. What *they had done was let a couple of our lads out of the Ninian when they could have hammered them, and we said ta for that.*

All in all though, they're good memories of a day out in South Wales.

As the 90's came to an end our mob was losing numbers. Many of the older lads had stopped going for one reason or another and a new generation was coming through. We might not have had the biggest numbers but the lads that were going could all be trusted. As a mob we would not only go to football together but we were drinking together on Saturday nights, and you could feel a real bond. We also started going to more England games, home and away, because Plymouth Argyle were in the bottom division, going nowhere. One trip I remember well was the away match at Cardiff in 2001. It was evidence that we might not have had many, but we were all up for it and ready to keep the name of the Central Element firmly within the hooligan scene.

Cardiff Away 2001

We all decided that the Cardiff game was a must. At first we had the usual, "Yeah, I will come," off everyone, but numbers dropped for one reason or another as the fixture came closer. So when the day arrived, and all we had was a 17-seater minibus and one car, we knew we were set for an interesting day. Despite us only having 22, it was a good set of lads and we knew we could all rely on each other. I'd only met one of the lads that came along, Les, eight hours before in a Plymouth nightclub. He seemed like a good lad who wanted to get involved in the scene, and so he also travelled with us on the minibus. Les has turned out to be one of my very best friends to this day.

The plan was to park the car and the van at Bristol Parkway train station and get the train in. The car arrived in Bristol probably 30 minutes before the van. They phoned us to say they'd arrived and that they were going to wait on the platform for us. As we were coming into Bristol on the minibus, we received another call from our five lads in the car. They were shouting down the phone, "Hurry up, it's going off!" It turned out that when they went on the platform there was another mob already there, numbering about 25-30. Sly as they were, they turned on our lads. It's believed that they were Rovers, waiting for a train to arrive, I can't remember who they were playing that day. Our van arrived just as this 30 were jumping in cabs, but that did not stop us chasing off a few tail-enders. You could tell by the look on their faces they were not expecting us 17 to turn up. The van had been parked next to a skip full of bricks, metal poles and wood, so you can imagine the array of weapons we had. Fancy 30 lads turning on five! No one likes bullies. It was then decided that, rather than hang around the train station, where the Old Bill were likely to turn up at any minute, we would get out of Bristol as fast as we could and cross the bridge to Wales by road.

We took the minibus straight into Cardiff and went for a drink in an area called Tiger Bay. This is where we stayed until about 2.15. We were getting calls from some of the Cardiff lads asking where we were, but due to the lack of numbers we were in no position to be marching around the city centre. Not only were they saying they had hundreds out, but their numbers were boosted by about ten Aston Villas lads, including Steven Fowler. We parked the minibus and car just behind the main car park, and then the 22 of us made the walk to the ground. As we were getting nearer to the turnstiles we could see large numbers of Cardiff queuing to get into the ground. They were probably numbering 100 if you added them all up, but on top of that were unknown numbers of Welsh who might not be lads but hate the English and are happy to take you on. We made the decision that we were not going to sneak into the ground unseen, and so we steamed straight into them. To be fair, they never saw us coming and a few Cardiff were floored before they even knew what was going on. It's what you might call the Element of surprise. Before they could regroup and come back at us, the Old Bill turned up and surrounded us with horses, dogs and riot shields. Cardiff were appearing from everywhere as our visit was announced. My banning order file suggests that 300-500 known Cardiff hooligans were congregated in the area. The Old Bill put us straight into the away end. Although heavily outnumbered, our attack on them was not taken well and you could feel the hostile atmosphere coming from the stand on the left throughout the game. I can't remember much of the game as we were all a bit intoxicated, but I can remember various objects being thrown at our stand by Cardiff supporters. I think it's funny how the stewards looked too scared to even ask them to stop.

About 70 minutes into the game, a Welsh copper with a fair few stripes on his arms congregated our 22 lads. He explained that if we did not leave the game now, they could not guarantee our safety, or our vehicles. Half the lads told him to fuck off and that, no matter what, we were staying to the end and would deal with the consequences. The other half had more realistic thoughts and were happy to leave. I remember the coppers telling a few of us that what had happened before the game was seen as a piss-take by a lot of people. You're not talking about a group of 50 or 60, but hundreds, if not a thousand. As the game neared its end we were forcibly removed by the police, to the disappointment of some and the relief of others. As they escorted us across the car park, half the fucking home stand must have tried leaving as well. I remember seeing the riot police fighting back Cardiff lads at three separate exit gates; once again, my banning order suggests they had 500. That was it for our day out on the vans, with a police escort back to England. It could quite easily have turned out differently. I imagine many other mobs of 20 would have taken the easy option and kept their heads down, but at least we made our stand. The day ended with a trip to Dawlish, where we were greeted by some of our rivals from Exeter and members of the Dawlish rugby team, another interesting event.

From 2001 the team started picking up results on the pitch, and the numbers of lads regularly attending home and away games started to swell quite heavily. We had achieved promotion and, as we started climbing the leagues, the fixtures became more interesting. During the 2002/03 season it was once again decided that Cardiff away was a must.

Cardiff Away 2003

It was a Friday night game and we decide to make a show of it. It turned out to be Cardiff's next home game following the visit they had from Barnsley. After our previous poor turnout of 22 lads, we managed to book and fill a 52-seater coach; add to that some cars and a few on the train and we managed to number 70. Not bad for a Friday night; if it had been a Saturday you could have added another 30-50 to this number. We decided to do what we had planned on our previous trip, which was to park in Bristol and get the train to Cardiff Central. We were greeted in Bristol Temple Meads train station by a couple of CSF, Bristol City hooligans who we reckon were scouting for Cardiff. They also promised us a reception on our return later that night. We boarded the train and got off at Newport for a drink while we waited for a couple more of ours to arrive. The drink was flowing around the pub nicely, added to which most lads were on the sniff, so there was a good, positive vibe coming from within the group.

The train we took eventually arrived in Cardiff Central at about 4pm. We had the usual welcoming committee from the police, but they seemed to just let us go where we wanted. We came out the station and headed straight towards the Prince of Wales pub. It was a busy Friday afternoon and there was a busy feel to the main street. All eyes were on us from the general public, as a group of 70 males walking around is not the norm. We still had some Old Bill with us, but not many. As we approached the Prince of Wales we saw a few lads stood outside on the phones, and all the lads at the front of our mob steamed right in. The lads at the door went back into the pub before any punches were exchanged and the law managed to put a line between us. Then no more than a handful of Cardiff attacked our mob from the rear, the lads at the back of our mob turned round and a small ruck took place. A couple of ours got nicked and a few on each side took slaps, but nothing too much. We then had the usual bubble from the police to contain us. To be honest, I thought Cardiff would have made more of an effort to come out of the pub; we were told they had 40 in there, but fair play to the five who attacked on their own at the rear.

While in the police bubble, I remember looking around and just feeling hate from all the locals. Not just lads, but everyone. There were lads on a building site opposite, giving it the big 'un; taxi drivers; even some of the police. You certainly got the feeling that we were not welcome.

The police quickly escorted us to an area adjacent to the railway station car park, where we were held for what seemed like ages. It was still three and a half hours before kick-off. We were kept there for an hour or so before being escorted to the ground. It's a fair walk to the ground but even so, we arrived about two hours before kick-off. We were the only ones in the ground, which was a bit weird. I normally get to the games a minute or two before they start, not 120 minutes. As the ground started to fill up, the usual atmosphere started to form in the stands on both our left and right. It was obvious that Cardiff were not happy with what we had done earlier in the day. I also imagine that there was a bit of a bad taste left from the recent visit of Barnsley, just a fortnight before.

After the game we were kept behind for about 30 minutes, for what we were told was our own safety. We attempted to break through the barriers a couple of times but to no success, just a few sore heads from police batons. You could see all the riot police and hear all the sirens outside of the ground, so it was clear Cardiff were up to something. After 30 minutes we did eventually get let out, but all the streets seemed pretty quiet. However, there were still a lot of sirens going on in the distance, you got the feeling that Cardiff were keeping the police very occupied not too far away. We were taken back to Cardiff Central where a special train had been organised for us. There was a little skirmish with a few Cardiff in the station, which led to four of ours being arrested. Then that was it, back to Bristol, where the CSF reception failed to materialise, and then back on the coach to Plymouth.

Most games with Cardiff always attract large mobs from both sides. Another game that stood out was our home fixture during the 2003/2004 season.

Cardiff Home 2003

I remember Cardiff bringing good numbers for a Tuesday night. Before the game we had met in a pub, and we were numbering about 80 as we made our way to the ground. On the way we had a couple of skirmishes with the law, but turned up in the ground without seeing many Cardiff. As it happened, Cardiff were being escorted in at the last minute by the police to avoid trouble. A few of us managed to get out of the ground and had a small battle with them on the grass by the Mayflower end. Our mob of 15-20 was mainly younger lads, and their mob that had just got off a coach numbered about 40. Hands up, they backed us off before the law ran in and separated it. It's a shame the bulk of our mob could not get out of the ground, as this would have made things much fairer. After this there seemed to be lots of fighting between twos and threes all over the place. It was fairly dark at the time, and no one seemed to know who was who, as everyone had split up. I heard afterwards of a couple of incidents where Plymouth lads had mistaken each other for Cardiff and ended up fighting.

After the game we had numbers of 200+, but the Old Bill had this well under control. Both mobs were kept apart by one of the heaviest police presences I have ever witnessed.

I was going to leave the story at this point, but me and a few of the other lads have just seen an account of a Cardiff v Plymouth game elsewhere in the book. It describes a very recent incident that occurred in Plymouth during the 2007/08 season. Some of the lads that were there just wanted to give their opinion on what happened that day. As this incident occurred fairly recently, names are going to be disguised. Also, it's just been found out that one of the young lads who had been getting more and more active was a paid informer for the law, so we just need to be a bit careful. Here is 'Mr S' to tell you about the incident as he saw it.

Cardiff Home 2007 by Mr S

One of my best mates had just been found dead the week before, and so we had a wake in Jumping Jacks, a pub we use in the city

centre. The lad was a really close friend, we used to travel
around the country doing unlicensed boxing together. Because of
his death and the fact we were playing Cardiff, we had a good
120+ older lads out. We had a couple of phone calls from Cardiff
telling us they were in different pubs in the town centre, but both
times it turned out to be false when our scouts turned up. I have
personally had a couple of incidents with Cardiff over the years
and always found them to be game, always with good numbers.
However, the problem in Plymouth now is the Old Bill are so on
top, nearly every one of them has a hand-held camera and you
don't even have to do much to get a banning order.

Anyway, my mate got a call just before 2pm to say there was a
mob of Cardiff lads in a pub on the outskirts of the city, in
Plympton. Plympton is one of the nicer suburbs, about six miles
from the town centre, although there would be limited police and
CCTV there. A few of the lads were up for getting a couple of
carloads to drive out and have a look. 'Mr G' asked me if I fancied
it; at first I said no, as I was not prepared to waste any more time
looking round for them, but the game was still an hour or so away
and so five of us drove up in a car. We had the rest of the pub on
standby; outside of the pub is a large taxi rank and so transport
would be easy for them if they were called upon.

It takes about 15 minutes to get there and so we went to the
Lord Louis pub, where we were told they were drinking. One of
the lads went inside – surprise, surprise, no one there. We called
the Plymouth lad who was in contact with Cardiff to find out
what was going on. The message came back that they were
definitely in Plympton but were not sure which pub they were in,
so we went for a drive all around. Just as we were about to give
up, 'Mr D' said there was one last pub to check. As we drove
past it we saw loads of lads on the front patio, leaning over the
railings, dressed in the usual CP, Stone Island, etc. I thought to
myself, That's Cardiff and there is not one copper to be seen. We
got straight onto the phone to call the lads back in the city
centre, telling them to come up in taxis. We parked the car up
about half a mile away and thought that by the time we walked
back the taxis should be arriving. Mr G was eager to get into

them a bit quickly, as we found ourselves getting nearer and nearer to them. I called the others up to see how long they would be, but they said that as they started leaving the pub the Old Bill had sealed it off and would not let anyone in or out. It seemed they knew something was up as everyone went to leave. At this time, we knew it was up to us five and we were now just 50 yards from the pub. One of the Cardiff lads clocked us and ran back into the pub to get the others. We agreed that we were likely to get done because they outnumbered us, and so we would just steam into them as we had nothing to lose. So that was it, four of us in our 30's and a youth lad walked up to the pub as what seemed like loads of Cardiff spilled out. I think they thought we were going to back off, but we kept walking towards them. We noticed that it was a younger mob, mainly early 20's. The lad who must have been their main lad walked towards me, and I asked him, "How many you got?" He replied, "Fourteen, how many more you got coming?" I said, "This is it,"and banged him right on the jaw with a left hook, knocking him right down and out. The other Cardiff seemed stunned at first and stood off for a moment. We took advantage of this, Mr G shouted, "Come on, you Welsh cunts!" and we steamed right in. With that, the Cardiff lads started lobbing bottles, glasses, ashtrays, whatever they could get their hands on. A bottle smashed against the side of Mr D's head and cut him open from his cheek to his ear; he was furious and, covered in blood, went back in for more. Mr G ran into a small group of them, knocking a few of them off balance, but took a bottle in the back of the neck for it. 'Mr O' grabbed one of the group and stuck him on his arse with a nut.

The main lad who I had hit first was still out for the count; at no stage did it cross any of our minds to kick him when he was down, it's not our style. Punches and kicks were traded for a bit longer and the whole thing just seemed to keep going on and on. If I have to be honest, it was probably only a minute but that's a long time in a situation like this. The fighting started to spread out from the pub onto the main road. Another standoff occurred as the five of us grouped up and Cardiff were all around us. Two of the five were covered in blood where they had been glassed, but the other three of us were unmarked. Even now we started to go back into them. Surely the 14 Cardiff must have thought, Fair play to them for keeping coming at us? Not one of our lads had even hit the deck and that's a fact, whereas a fair few of theirs had gone down. If at this point they had regrouped and steamed into us they would have probably battered us, but they didn't. Instead, one of them said, "Alright, lads, that's enough, Old Bill will be here any second, let's just all fuck off." So both groups backed off.

As we were making our way back to the car we thought, Result! We were buzzing. I'm not saying we did them but we gave as good as we got, and when it's five against 14 that's a result. I had a phone call the other day from Danny, telling me that in the Soul Crew book one of the Cardiff lads gives his account of the incident. This lad said things like, "Plymouth bit off more than they could chew and they were sent home with bruised egos." Come on, lads, I have always had respect for Cardiff and you normally tell it as it is. If it was the other way round and it was 14 TCE against five Soul Crew, we would hold our hands up to you and say fair play. We will call that one a stalemate, we are happy with that. Keep it real.

All real lads from Plymouth have nothing but respect for Cardiff, on their day they can match anyone. I don't agree with any club being number one or having the biggest mob, but Cardiff are certainly in with a group that can't be touched on their day.

XI

OUR BITTER ENEMY

Mikey Dye (CCFC): Cardiff have never claimed to be number one, and, truth be told, probably never will be. But we give it our best shot and we can come out on top – unlike the so-called Jack Army, who have never lost a battle, have they? My recollection of those bastards from down the road is that we would overrun them every game and take over, just like Chelsea did to us. We would terrorise them. In their *Book of Truth: The Jack Army*, they claim that their fixture would always land on an Easter Sunday, or when no trains ran. Well, we normally played down their place on New Year's Day, when there were no trains too, but would always fill the away end and normally the side enclosure. We can all remember when a Cardiff fan ran on the Vetch and started to fuck a plastic swan, which was sited on either penalty spot. Can anyone remember a Swansea fan running on to aid this poor swan? No! Those were the years when the Old Bill were not clued up, but we always travelled.

One year in the late 80's, Annis hired a coach and 50 of us young'uns went to Swansea leisure centre early and had a swim before the game (all of us paid, I think!), going into the pool with our bundies and boxer shorts on. How the fuck we dried off I will never know! We then walked along the Jacks' front and straight into their town centre. No Old Bill and no Jacks, as was usual in those days. By kick-off, our numbers had swelled to a few hundred and we were once again able to walk around with no Jacks in sight. The Old Bill eventually rounded us up. But where were you Jacks in the 80's? It started becoming a bore down in Gypo Land. I noticed the Jacks did turn up in small numbers throughout the late 90's and 00's, but the police always had a grip. Work it out for yourselves, boys . . .

Guff (PVM, CCFC): Getting back to our neighbours, of course everyone knows there's no love lost between us, but we would have at least some respect for them if they were more truthful about the 80's and 90's. They found it a hard enough battle just fighting Port Talbot and Neath lads, so how did they ever think they could do Cardiff on the whole, when Cardiff had ten times as many lads as them? Don't get me wrong, our firm from this area has taken some beatings from them and vice versa. But that's us, not Cardiff as a whole. I will tell a couple of tales of us and them which are honest accounts, no bullshit.

In and around March 1987, I was aged 19; 16 of us went over to Jackland on a Saturday when Cardiff didn't have a game. At that time we had no worries, nerves, etc, but when I think about it now it was suicidal. Even today our lads laugh about it. Taffy Anton, Clunis, Stavvy and some others arrived in Swansea around 2.45pm. We made our way down the high street, after already being clocked at the train station when we had got off, so there was no going back now. The Jacks were playing at home and word had spread all the way down to the Vetch. We were now down the Quadrant, which is famous as where they hang out; about 30-odd Jacks were there, the same ones who we regularly had trouble with either on our own turf or in Neath at night. Crazy as it seems now, as soon as we saw them we ran straight at them, with everyone a mirror image of each other, and ran them back into their shopping centre. This was happening on a sunny spring Saturday afternoon and in full view of all the Swansea shoppers. We then hung around for a while, until we heard sirens and went back via all the sidestreets to avoid being arrested.

Back at the train station we all stood outside, waiting to see if they would come back. We were thinking, *If only our other lads back home had been here today to witness this.* As we were going into the foyer of the train station, one of our lads looked back and said, "They're here." Not thinking, myself and the others went straight back outside, only to see the road totally full of them. It looked like half the North Bank had left the ground to come and find us. We were now in the middle of the station car park and were virtually surrounded on all sides. We had to show bottle, so we called the ones on at the front, slowly moving towards them, knowing we had no chance. Punches were thrown between the front line of them and us, then I was hit straight in the side of the face by a temporary bus stop sign. By now we had been going totally backwards and were being attacked by a load of angry wolves from all sides. This was vicious. We were still trying to fight back, but were knackered and relieved to hear sirens once again. The Old Bill came from everywhere, to our relief. The Jacks were gone and all that was left was us and the Old Bill, we quickly went and boarded the train back to Port Talbot. The Old Bill must have been pissed off with us by now. We were on our train and we couldn't believe they had gone on to another platform and were checking another train out, carriage by carriage. We spread out on ours, amongst the normal passengers.

The train left and all we could think about was that we had held our own and gone down to their area on a match day, kicked some arse and then stood and took what they had to offer in their big numbers. We'd once again gone down to our local enemy and had a good day's entertainment, now we were going to hit the pubs in Port Talbot and enjoy the evening talking about it.

We've had many battles with them over the years: Mumbles Road, the 'swim away' incident. We have been hurt by them but we were always outnumbered and we've held our own. They have never come into Port Talbot's drinking area and tried to take us on, in our own backyard.

Simmo (CCFC): I have known Annis for years and he asked me if I would write the following chapter. I am known to everyone as Simmo and I've also been a regular known face at Cardiff City for years. I'm not going to tell all the old war stories that other lads have written in this book, I was there for some but not all. The one thing that sticks in my throat is the total shit that was written in the Jacks book about the night in September 2003 when they came down to my local, the Exchange in Canton, and I'm glad that Annis has given me the chance to set the record straight.

It was a Saturday night in September 2003. We had played Forest at home that afternoon and the Jacks were meant to be playing at Mansfield, which was later to be postponed. On the Friday night the Exchange had over 150 lads out, expecting Forest to come down as we had heard a whisper, but as usual it was a lot of crap. On that Saturday afternoon in Canton alone we had well over 400 lads out for Forest. Nothing happened that day, but we started to hear the whispers again and this time the Jacks were meant to be stopping off on their way back from Mansfield. But over the last 30 years we must have heard it over a thousand times. That evening, up until about 8pm, we still had nearly 200 lads in the Exchange and, as we knew, the Jacks match had been called off. If they were going to come they would have by then. So over the next hour, most lads drifted into town or went home.

By 9pm my local was virtually empty of lads, and it was starting to fill up with some locals and a few of the ladies from the bingo next door. At approximately 9.30pm a group of about 15 lads marched in. I looked at them, went straight over and said, "Are you Forest or you on a stag do, lads?" With that, this Jack bastard said, "Come on, we're Jacks!" The next thing, bottles and glasses were flying back and forth. For the record, we had no more than seven lads including some locals. We managed to group together and force them back out of the pub; at no stage did my son or I get punched by any Jack. At the door we managed to hold them, but one of the Jacks was smashing our windows through. One of our lads just burst out the doors with a chair and ran into them, and with that we all steamed towards them. In the street there must have been over 25 of them and less than four of them stood. Some of them who stood took a pasting while their fellow Jacks just stood and watched, but from a distance. By this time, the Old Bill had arrived and whacked some of the lads that were with me. We had chased the Jacks as far as the old St David's Hospital, which is well over 300 yards away. By now they had virtually disappeared. I followed around the corner when I saw them piling into their two minibuses. Two of us walked over and just laughed at them, and with that the Old Bill sent us back.

What we can't understand is that the Jacks somehow think they had a victory. Yes, one of them got nicked for smashing a window, but me, my son and one of my mates got dawn-raided for it and not one other Jack was nicked for fighting.

I've seen the CCTV, and the Jacks had gone back three times before they decided to enter the pub, so they knew how few lads we had in their before they made their 'big entrance'. The fact is there were more bingo ladies in the pub than lads, but maybe that's why they came in. As we all know, CCTV doesn't lie, and it shows seven Cardiff and one chair chasing 25 Jacks. Ha ha, YOU JACK BASTARDS!!!

Annis Abraham Jnr. (CCFC): The following story is not about our battles with the Jacks, as I've already spoken about that in my autobiography, out later this year. No, this is more about how the hostility and hatred are still there, but also showing how times have really changed in the hooligan world. I've been to every derby match that has been played against the Jacks in the last 30 years; I've even gone down there when we have been banned. The first time, just as I was about to go through the turnstiles, I was collared by the Old Bill and told, "Not on this occasion, Annis." As I walked away from the ground there were lads from the Valleys standing outside, shouting to each other, "Everyone do the Ayatollah!" The other time, so many of us managed to get in that eventually 400 of us were put into the empty away end behind the goal.

I have also been there on many occasions when we've swamped the town centre and taken over virtually every pub. Well, I suppose those days are well and truly gone, but they were great days and any true, honest Jack should admit it. Cardiff in the 80's would well and truly take over Swansea.

When the fixture list came out for the 2008/09 season, every fan in Wales was looking for the fixture dates of the Cardiff v Jacks games. As it had been ten years since we had played them in the league, it would be interesting to go to their new stadium.

So we knew we had them away in November on a Sunday morning, and at home in April 2009. It was soon announced that they would both be bubble trips, but that didn't matter to the lads and fans from Cardiff as they were going no matter what. In the meantime, we had Birmingham, the Wurzels and Sheffield United to play.

Before the season had even started, there was trouble at Swindon away and Ajax at home in pre-season friendlies. At Doncaster away and Southampton at home, Cardiff fans were involved in scuffles and about 30 Southampton lads took a right pasting in the Grangetown suburbs of Cardiff.

On Saturday August 30th, I went up to Sheffield United with all the Bridgend lads, a great bunch of lads to be with. Yes, they like a good piss-up and have a good laugh at the same time, but they don't go looking for trouble. If trouble came their way, however, then man for man they would match any mob that is around today. A mate of mine, Dibs (Wayne Anderson), runs a coach to every away game from the Bridgend area and goes out of his way to pick me up. I'd started travelling with Dibs' lot in the last two seasons, for one because they are a good bunch of lads who don't backstab, and secondly, Dibs is a good friend of mine and I've always been good friends with the Bridgend lads over the years, through another lad called Jaffa (Alun Griffiths).

Anyway, back to Sheffield United away: we stopped off in Rotherham town centre on the way and, just after we'd got off the coach, we were greeted by hundreds of other Cardiff lads celebrating like we'd just won the cup. But in fact it had just been announced we had drawn the Jacks away in the third round of the Carling Cup. At first, the Old Bill thought they were going to be attacked, when everyone came running out of the pubs and they retreated onto the main road – until they were told by Simon Insole (our police spotter) that we were just celebrating drawing the Jacks in the cup. For the rest of the day and night that was all that was on everyone's minds, the main conversation of the day. There was trouble at Sheffield that day, mostly caused by their overzealous police force who seem to love whacking Cardiff fans with their batons, even though United's lads had put windows through on one of our buses. But that's a story for another day.

So for the next few weeks, all that was on everyone's lips was how many tickets were we going to get to go to Jackland. We all knew that the away end held 3,000. Different rumours were coming out of the club – yes, we could have the full allocation because it was the cup. Then, the next minute, it was being said that the police were against it; then they said they were staying out of it, and that the 500 officers that would be on duty for the game could handle whatever we brought down to Jackland. Then Sky TV wanted to televise it live, which gave the Jacks the chance to reduce our away support, as they said the car park at the away end could hold no more than 28 coaches due to Sky setting up on it. The Jacks at one point offered us 1,100 tickets, but eventually City agreed on 1,457. To me, we were sold short. The fans offered to take double-decker buses and the club then announced that the police were against it, but the police to this day insist it was the club. Yet again, will we ever know the truth?

So 1,457 tickets was the final allocation; they were like gold dust and this upset a lot of the Cardiff lads and fans. A number of lads did buy tickets in the Jack end, but they knew the days of showing themselves had gone – not because of fear of any of the Jacks, but of the courts and banning orders for just being in the wrong end.

The night before the game, my phone rang and it was Sam Hammam, who was ringing to wish us luck and said he wished he could be there himself. He was still in Lebanon and said he kept up to date with everything that was happening at the club. He reminded me that the cup and beating the Jacks weren't everything, but promotion to the Promised Land was more important. He finished off with his usual words of love to every Cardiff fan, and to my family; sometimes I wish he was still our chairman.

The day finally arrived and I drove down to Bryncethin near Bridgend, to a pub called the Royal Oak, with my brother-in-law, Jamie, and a good mate of mine, Simon. We got there nearly five hours before kick-off and, on arrival, nearly all the Bridgend lads were already down there, downing the ale as usual. Dibs had got a 70-odd seater bus, so it meant we had a good group of lads. We then had to go all the way back on ourselves to meet the other coaches at Ninian Park, where we were met by over 60 Old Bill including some of our spotters, and the usual videocameras were in full swing. I thought to myself, *What's the point of all this?*, as we were 40-odd miles from Jackland and yet the police were already in our faces. They were going to travel down with us to make sure no one accidentally took the wrong turning. Ours was the last coach to arrive as usual, so we were the last to leave Ninian Park.

Soon we were back on the motorway, 28 coaches all in a line, holding the M4 virtually at a stand-still. The chants soon went up as we passed Bridgend, the place we originally left from. The buzz on the coach was unbelievable, and the slow 40mph journey was broken up by laughter and cheers when a Valley lad got on top of one of the coaches and sat himself down as it moved along the motorway. As we passed through the outskirts of Port Talbot and Neath there were some amazing sights. Only a few miles from Jackland, many houses had Cardiff flags hanging out their windows and on the bridges above us, on the motorway, banners were hanging with 'Cardiff City' and 'Bluebirds' on them. It was a sight to be seen. Cars drove past, hooting their horns and people cheered us on as they passed. I will repeat: this was on the doorstep of Jackland and 30-odd miles from the heart of Cardiff.

The journey went quick, until we were taken past the outskirts of Jackland, into a quiet trading estate. Yet again, as we were one of the last coaches to pull in it meant that we would be at least an hour waiting by the side of the road, as the police took about eight coaches at a time to the Liberty Stadium.

The problem for us was that there wasn't even a toilet on the coach and tempers soon started to flare up as the lads asked for a piss, only to be refused time and time again by the Old Bill. Every coach had at least five Old Bill standing outside the door in the middle of an empty trading estate – what was that all about? If you ask me, that's how trouble can soon start. We were all sweating as the air conditioning never worked (thanks, Dibs), and the driver was told the doors had to be kept shut. Asylum seekers would have been treated better, but, just as tempers were about to boil over, a sergeant saw this and allowed us, one at a time, to have a piss by the side of the coach. Hooray, common sense prevailed!

Eventually, we were off to finish our last few miles of the trip. As we passed any man and his dog, up went the chant: "You Jack bastards!" We were all getting phone calls saying that the first few coaches had been attacked by flares and rockets. As we drove nearer the ground, on the right-hand side by some trees it looked like there were maybe 600 Jacks, all being kept back by riot police, dogs and horses. The Jacks looked a mixture of all sorts, from lads to hundreds of kids and even women shouting abuse. Well, you can imagine the noise on our coaches. We were eventually put into a specially erected steel caged area (built in the last two weeks prior to the match, especially for us). As we got off, I looked around me and, besides our coach, you had Big Sam, Ketty and Mogs' coach full of monsters, Mac's lot, and even the Ely Trendies had brought their own coach, led by my old mate Mikey Dye. Everyone tried to stand outside, but the police with cameras in our faces had opened double doors to the stadium; no turnstiles were used, we were just pushed in, tickets weren't even checked.

Once inside, the bar was absolutely packed. I was shocked to see them selling alcohol, as at most places we go to alcohol is banned to Cardiff fans, yet Swansea, of all clubs, were allowing us to drink. They must be desperate for money.

Jamie and I went upstairs to have a look. We had been here once before a few seasons ago, to see Wales play their first ever match at the Liberty Stadium. About 100 of us had travelled down there in cars that evening, and we never saw a Jack lad all the way to the ground or in the ground all night. The crowd had been a paltry 10,000 for the first ever Welsh game in the Jack stadium; there wasn't any kind of atmosphere, full stop. Anyway, back to the day's events: as we entered the seats I was stunned; there was just an arena of hate all around us and virtually the whole ground was just pointing and singing songs of hatred against us, from pensioners and women to school kids, they were all doing the stupid 'swim away'. One idiot even had the full costume on with a rubber ring around him. The hatred in their faces was unbelievable – and yes, we hate them, but they're not the be all and end all. But you could see by their actions how much they hated us. It was jealousy maybe – we are the capital, all the money comes to Cardiff, everyone has heard of Cardiff throughout the world and even Cardiff's lads, the Soul Crew, are known throughout Europe. But what is Swansea known for? Not once did the crowd stop for breath; I've been to their old ground, the Vetch Field, and yes, the north bank had been loud and always had a mouth at us, but this was different. All three sides of the ground were filled with sheer hatred.

The police had positioned themselves so that we could not move left or right or enter the seats down below; there were three lines of police and stewards betweens us and rows of empty seats, on top of which had been placed black sheets. How times have changed, none of this would have happened ten years ago. As the match started, the atmosphere got worse and their fans seemed to go into overdrive with their hate-filled songs. They actually managed to drown our singing which, to be fair, I've virtually never witnessed before. I suppose there were 15,500 of them and only 1,400 of us. The atmosphere reminded me of when we played Leeds in the great giant-killing FA Cup win at Ninian Park, but this time the roles were reversed.

What I did notice was that the Jacks never had hundreds of lads, as most were just kids on either side of us. On the left-hand side I noticed Ledley getting continually abused by Toozey and his 40 cronies, sat in the front rows by the halfway line. Well done to Ledley – the more stick they gave him, the more he kissed his badge.

To the right of us the Jacks had no more than 100 lads, probably only 50 good ones at that, but hundreds of wannabe kid fighters. I knew that, if there had been a proper outbreak of trouble, then at least 400 amongst the Cardiff contingent were proper old-school game lads.

For most of the first half there was just abuse going back and forth and the odd coin and piece of rubbish thrown at our players as they took the throw-ins. We had played well for the first 20 minutes, but from the moment Swansea scored the game went downhill. The longer the game went on, the more it looked like they would score again. At half-time and 1-0 down, I went under the stand. The bars were packed once again, everyone was wound up and we felt like we were in a prison camp.

During the second half, a lot of our lads just stayed down in the bar. Our end got quieter and quieter, as we were continually drowned out every time we even tried to sing. So most gave up – just like our team, you could say. In the last ten minutes a lot of our younger Cardiff lads tried to push through the police lines, only to be quickly sent flying back. For the whole game the police had cameras in our faces.

While the game had been going on, about 100 lads who follow Cardiff had sat themselves down in Port Talbot, waiting to see if any Jacks came back after the game. They had originally wanted to meet in Neath, nearer Jackland, but every pub had been banned from showing the match and all of the lads' pubs had been closed down for the night. Five vanloads of Old Bill sat there all evening, monitoring the Neath and Port Talbot lads.

When the final whistle was blown, I really felt that the Jacks had deserved to win as their players had more desire for it than ours. It felt like our team never really bothered to turn up on the night, maybe Dave Jones hadn't wound them up enough as to what the game meant to us. We were then told we had to remain in our seats for 30 minutes. Well, for the next 30 minutes thousands of Jacks stayed in theirs as well, taunting us. At one stage a group of 30 older Cardiff nearly got over to them. The Jacks on the right fought with the police for about ten minutes to get to us, but the ones on the left just sang their stupid song. The police just let them stay in the stadium, it would never have happened at Ninian Park in the year 2008. But Toozey's little firm had already left the stadium by now.

The Old Bill had moved in closer to us, virtually not letting us breathe. We were sitting ducks with missiles continually flying our way, but the Old Bill were more concerned with watching us. So Cardiff decided to try and leave, and everyone steamed out the back. A few lads from the Rhondda managed to get up a fire exit left open by the Old Bill when they had dragged a fan out; a small charge occurred up the stairs, with the Jacks retreating, but the Old Bill soon got to the area.

As I stood in the coach car park a hail of stones and bottles rained down on us, just like in the ground. Cardiff fans had had enough of it, and it wasn't just the lads – everyone near the fences tried to tear the fencing down. It did come down by the Sky TV lorries, but this only led to the main steel cages, which got the Old Bill steaming towards the Cardiff fans. For a good 40 minutes Cardiff refused to go onto the coaches, and at one stage a lot of Cardiff fans decided to sit down on the floor as we were totally surrounded by Old Bill and steel cages. They eventually forced the Cardiff fans onto the coaches. While this had been going on (I've seen the videos on ITV Wales and on the net), about 800 Jacks, mainly kids, had running battles with the police, which later led to 20 getting their mugs in the local papers.

Finally, the coaches were on their way. I thought we might be one of the first out as we were one of the last in, but we were about eighth and, as we came out, hundreds of Jacks tried to attack the first two coaches. Everyone tried to get out the fire doors but, as the coaches drove out, the police in their dozens were having to run by the side of each, while the rest of the police were chasing the Jacks back into their slums. Rockets and flares were fired once again by them.

The journey home was fast and the Old Bill let us go straight back to Bridgend (hooray!). The Jacks never did go back to Port Talbot or Neath.

All in all, I have to say that, even though not a punch was thrown between either side, the Jacks had got the message over to us: they hate us with a vengeance and are jealous as fuck of us. What this did show was that the hatred has never gone away and that – if it wasn't for the CCTV, the Old Bill's hand-held cameras, black plastic sheets across rows of empty seats between us, a steel compound put up just for us, no freedom of movement outside the ground, every single supporter vetted before they got a ticket, then bubbled in and surrounded by massed ranks of Old Bill, after weeks of police intelligence gathering – there would have been fighting all over the ground and probably at every street corner. The 80's feelings are still there amongst the fans and have never really gone away. If it wasn't for this mass operation by the police, then a guaranteed riot would have occurred.

I've written just a short account of our league game down there. We were once again in our usual bubble, but this time the lads had to get up at 6am and report to Ninian Park for 7.30am, for a journey by car that would haven taken only 40 minutes.

The league game at the Liberty Stadium, at 11.15 am on Sunday November 30th 2008, had a larger police presence again and the atmosphere wasn't as bad, but the day still had its incidents. Cardiff were allowed a couple more hundred fans this time; the Jacks did their 'Swim Away' again, including one of their players, Pratley – when he scored in the nineteenth minute, he ran past the Cardiff fans doing the Swim Away with his hands. You could say that was inciting violence in itself – but oh, my mistake, it's alright, he's a player and can get away with it. Maybe that's why his name is 'Pratley'.

Trundle and Tate got away with wearing t-shirts in the Millennium Stadium with derogatory comments on them, and holding a Welsh flag up with 'Fuck off Cardiff' on it. Are they all obsessed with us or what? At the end of the game the Jacks did their pretend charge at the police, while a lone Cardiff fan stood next to them doing the Ayatollah and got smacked a bit, falling down the seats into the arms of one of our spotters – probably the highlight of the day. The good news is that he was put back in the Cardiff end. After the game, the Jack kids did their usual stone throwing and then it was off home after a great match, ending 2-2.

XII

IS THE HOOLIGAN SCENE DEAD?

SOUL CREW, 2009/10 SEASON

Annis Abraham Jnr. (CCFC): The hooligan scene went quite quiet really, since the riots and arrests with Stoke in 2000. The fan base has changed too. At the beginning of the two previous seasons we played FC Twente and Ajax. There was quite a bit of violence at both these home games and it resulted in about 20-30 arrests.

During the actual season 2009/2010 we had moved into a new stadium, and the Soul Crew had gone off the scene really. The police were virtually on top of it all. The club started introducing memberships and, if you wanted to attend any away games, the police would check them, similar to what Milwall were doing years before. If the police okayed it then the club would sell you a ticket. Every game we went to was all-ticket and a lot of games were restricted. Our allocation was less than any other clubs for away games. Not only had they got on top with the arrests, I think we also had the highest number of fan bans at any club.

A lot of our Valley fans can't be bothered with tickets, they just prefer to turn up on the day and pay on the gate. That's how the Soul Crew used to work. They were never organised. Cardiff fans were used to paying on the gate, but times have changed and it doesn't happen anymore. As we have gone up through the leagues, the club has become stricter on the fans.

PRE-SEASON FRIENDLIES: SWINDON AWAY AND CELTIC HOME

So, this season I thought all the violence was dead with Cardiff. We had Swindon away in the first pre-season friendly. I travelled to the game in the car, but a lot of other fans travelled on the train. I just went for a quiet drink, but when I got there in the morning I heard rumours of groups of 60-70 Swindon fans attacking groups of 10-20 Cardiff fans. The last two seasons we'd been to Swindon there had actually been no trouble, so it was all very low-key with the police. But Swindon fans were getting away with murder.

It was Swindon's youth mob. There were a few older guys but about 70 youth. (The last time I heard of Swindon having that many was 12-14 years ago in the FA Cup.) Apparently, they were having a right go at a few Cardiff, but our fans had stood their ground, although they did catch a few offguard and Cardiff took a few slaps that morning.

I walked the the ground with about nine other Cardiff fans and didn't see any trouble. When we entered the stadium, there was no real evidence of any police, though normally when you go away with Cardiff there are loads of police everywhere. Then, the next minute, I couldn't believe it! Inside the stadium, some young Swindon fans jumped over the segregation area and started running at our Cardiff support. That was a first for a team to do. But some of the Ant Hill Mob jumped in and started fighting, they're not actually part of the Soul Crew but have got their own separate section. One Swindon steward nearly got his finger bitten off! The police were called into the ground and threw about 30 of the Ant Hill Mob out.

Apparently, as the match was going on there were a few running battles. There have since been 24 Cardiff fans and 19 Swindon fans arrested for the trouble at this match, Cardiff had gone to Swindon's pub and had a big off with them while the match was going on. Anyway, the game finished and as we left the ground there were police everywhere, I could hear lots of sirens. By the time we got back to the train station, the Swindon fans had split themselves into groups of 30 and 40, and then they'd attacked Cardiff in the pubs and down the main streets, but by now the police had taken control. We stayed and had a few drinks with some of the Cardiff fans, some then left, and we got in the car and drove home.

Later on, about 7.30pm, some of the Ant Hill Mob went back into the town centre. About 30 of them had a toe-to-toe battle with 70 Swindon fans and they've all been arrested for it now. That was the first game of the season, so it shows that the hooligan scene isn't dead.

I have personally moved on from these days, but I will talk about what's gone on in the past. You think it's all dead, but with Cardiff it never dies. As some fans are banned, new ones seem to just appear on the scene.

We had Celtic at home next – the mighty Celtic – to celebrate the opening of our new stadium. Cardiff fans have mixed views of Celtic fans. You've got the Welsh fans who think we should be independent, like Celtic fans, and you've got the Welsh people who are against Celtic and what they believe in. So I just went along with my four-year-old daughter to watch the game. Apparently, Celtic fans were walking through the streets, shouting, "Fuck the army, fuck the British army!" Inside the stadium, I couldn't believe it! A few Celtic fans had managed to get an IRA flag in. My mate Warren Feeney plays for Cardiff and Northern Ireland, he was warming up before the game and was amazed that they'd managed to get the IRA flag into the ground; in Scotland they would have been arrested straight away. I also heard that, outside the ground, Celtic fans had picked on a few of our young casuals and at the Ninian Park pub there had been a few 'handbags'. I left the match and went home thinking nothing of it. I found out later that around 20 Celtic fans were outside the Ninian Park pub singing IRA songs. They met around the same number of Cardiff fans and there was a two-three minute battle before the police arrived. A few Celtic got put on their backsides, they took quite a slapping from Cardiff! A few of our fans were arrested and ended up with five-year bans. So, in just two pre-season friendlies, we ended up with about 40 arrests. The 2009/10 season had started with a bang!

NEWCASTLE V CARDIFF CITY, 5TH FEBRUARY 2010

Like I said, I've moved on from the old days but a lot of the youngsters have started coming through now. Newcastle was the big game that everyone had planned for. I hadn't been there since 1980. I remember going there as a 15-year-old and the streets were full of graffiti reading, 'West Ham will die' and 'Cockneys are dead.' Apparently they had a big thing for West Ham in the 80's. It was quite frightening down the back of St James Park with all those mad Geordies around. A few Cardiff fans had dressed in donkey jackets to look a bit like them at the time. Gary and Dave Bennett, the Bennett brothers, were playing for us back then and we lost 2-1 that day. There was a crowd of only 14,000 in the Newcastle end. Everyone talks about them being a massive club, but the crowds weren't huge back then!

Anyway, the Newcastle game was in 2010 and the police were terrified. Leeds were playing at Hartlepool; Sunderland were at home to Wigan. These were all on the Saturday, so the game was to be played on the Friday night before. It didn't deter anyone from going though. I flew up to Newcastle with my mate Cheggers. We got a train from Newcastle airport to the town centre and there were hundreds of Cardiff fans everywhere. Over 3,000 travelled for a Friday night game, which I think was brilliant. All the pubs were packed and the atmosphere was amazing! The police were keeping it low-key and there wasn't a Newcastle fan in sight. It was just a great pre-match build-up. There were guys in their 30's and 40's in every pub, we just treated it as a day on the laugh. You had some of the old-school Soul Crew faces there, but there was no trouble at all. The lads in their 50's were there, they were all there. No one left the pubs en masse and I was in a group of eight of us.

As we got closer to the ground I saw a few Newcastle fans, but again there was no trouble and still a great atmosphere. As I've said, there are usually a lot of police when Cardiff play away, but the place was virtually free of them. As we got nearer to the ground, there were about four or five different pubs in the close vicinity. As the group of us got closer to the stadium we noticed some Newcastle fans across the road, known as the Gremlins. They were staring at us and I was thinking, *Oh, 'ere we go!* They were a mixture of guys aged between 20 and 45.

I remember one of them shouting, "Fuck your Soul Crew!" We all looked at each other and just started laughing. Next thing you knew, bottles were flying towards us. We weren't looking for trouble but they started chanting and shouting at us. There was a Sheffield Wednesday fan with us named Sam, he was going out with a Cardiff girl; they all started laying into Sam so we jumped in to help him. I'll be honest, we got absolutely annihilated. There were 40 or 50 of them but only eight of us. I'll never forget them looking at me and saying, "There's their top lad!" They all started coming at me, a few bottles were thrown straight at me, and then from all sides Cheggers, Carl and myself and the other lads just took a bit of a pasting.

The pubs had started emptying and the police turned up as we arrived outside St James Park. As Cheggers and myself were walking past the supporters' shop we were jumped again. I've moved well and truly on from the past that gave me a reputation, so I try not to get involved, but maybe I was a target because I've written the books, I don't know. I was trying to collect my comp match tickets from Warren Feeney. The police grabbed me and Cheggers and I said, "What you on about? There were six onto one of us!" They checked the CCTV and it came over the radio that we'd been attacked. As we made our way into the ground I noticed Simon Insole, one of our own police spotters, and he asked, "I heard you had a bit of trouble, Annis?" I just said, "Yes, the usual problems because of who I am." Simon's always been fair and straight to the Cardiff lads in my book.

It all reminded me of Old Trafford. As you walked into the ground you had Newcastle queuing up, Cardiff fans, Newcastle, Cardiff, and it was all going off! Everyone was running into each other like in the 80's. I thought we'd left all of this behind us. There were police horses rushing around everywhere and non-stop fighting.

Inside the stadium we were 3-0 down after about seven minutes. We were losing but the Cardiff fans were singing. Everyone I bumped into had taken a bit of a beating. There were lots of cut faces and they'd all been attacked. Apparently, the Gremlins had made this their biggest game for years, their 'Big One', whereas Cardiff fans had gone up there for a day on the piss. We were out enjoying ourselves and they were out trying to make a name for themselves. The Newcastle fans didn't attack the pubs with 200-300 Cardiff fans, they attacked groups of eight-ten on their way to the ground. They took the piss, if I'm honest. I'd even say it was bullying, as we were caught offguard enjoying a few drinks.

We lost the game 5-1, totally outplayed. After the match Cardiff fans were hell-bent on revenge, but the police were there ready. All the pubs were closed. Cheggers, Carl and myself decided to make our way to the bar we were in before the match. I was approached by a lad, who came over to me and shook my hand. "Alright, Annis?"

I thought he must have been from the Valleys because he seemed to know me by name. It turns out that he was one of the Shrewsbury EBF who had just jumped a Cardiff lad called Christian and his mate. The Shrewsbury fans have a bit of an alliance with Newcastle going back to the 80's. So that shows you how Newcastle had gone en masse. We made our way back into town and groups of Newcastle fans were stood by the police, while 700-800 Cardiff fans were marching through the town centre looking for revenge. We thought that was the end of it as we began drinking in the bars, but Newcastle apparently started up again on small groups of Cardiff fans. I left early on Saturday morning as I was unable to stay the weekend up there, due to family commitments.

When you tell people about what happened, they say, "Newcastle?" I say, "They were naughty in the 80's and they were naughty again in 2010. They can say they had a result, but Cardiff and the Soul Crew were there just for a day out and we took a bit of a hammering. So it's not dead and buried like people think. There are fans of teams that will turn out just for the 'big ones'."

CHELSEA V CARDIFF CITY – FA CUP, 13TH FEBRUARY 2010

Within a week we had Chelsea away in the cup, the team that all Cardiff dream of. Apart from West Ham, Spurs and Millwall, I think Chelsea also dreamed of playing us. Cardiff were rubbing their hands together and so were they. My old mate Pat Dolan rang me and said, "Look, Annis, me and you are the best mates of all time but I think it's best I stay in the house for this one. I love Cardiff and I love Chelsea."

I've never known so many Chelsea fans think of Cardiff as their dream of dreams. It's also the same for Cardiff fans. Before the Newcastle game it was the cup draw, and I received about 40-50 texts from people saying they couldn't believe it! Chelsea were my second team in the 80's, as well as little Bury from where my mother is from. I've been to many Chelsea games and I've got lots of friends there too. I felt that Chelsea fans were very similar to Cardiff's, but from the year 2000 onwards they had become a different type of fan.

For the game with Cardiff, all the old firm Chelsea would be turning up. Surely the police would know this? There was no way you could let these two sets of fans mix together. Surely they could see the writing was on the wall for this one? They gave us 6,000 tickets but we could have sold 10,000. When you give Cardiff 6,000 tickets they are going to get into the wrong hands. It doesn't matter whether you are a member or not, people are going to pass them on. There were probably a lot of fans that didn't want to go because of the anticipated violence, so they were happy to sell them on. Also, because it was London, a lot of banned fans travelled. The logistics of London as an area means you have a loophole around the banning order restrictions, and as long as the banned person stayed a certain distance away from Stamford Bridge they were free to travel to other parts of the city, quite a few putting themselves up in Shepherd's Bush for the day.

The police made it a 12.30pm kick-off, shutting all the pubs before the game. I think the whole of the West London police must have been there. Before the game, Chelsea tried bullyboy tactics. Like I've said, Cardiff have never been organised and have never pinpointed people. Cardiff fans knew this was the 'big one' and knew it would be the Chelsea of old. You name them they'd be there, all the names of the past, all the major faces of Chelsea and Cardiff were going to be at this one. It would be a real nightmare game for the police.

Cardiff fans were arriving in groups of 20, 30 and 40. They were all rushing to get to the ground as the traffic was making everyone run late. Chelsea fans were hanging around in their hundreds on the streets of Fulham Broadway. They were trying to use bullyboy tactics, calling Cardiff on, and Cardiff were just laughing at them. The police were pushing Cardiff on and there were lots of handbags before the game, with Chelsea doing the most of the mouthing. Chelsea tried to put the fear into Cardiff, using the old exaggerated cockney voices to intimidate. They didn't realise that Cardiff have grown up since those days. They aren't kids anymore.

Chelsea probably were the governors in those days, but the Cardiff lads were now older and more active. Cardiff had no fear for this fixture – no fear whatsoever. They actually believed they could turn Chelsea over. They knew Chelsea would be big, but nobody thought, *Oh God, it's Chelsea!*

Inside the ground the atmosphere was like a library with the Chelsea fans. It wasn't like the days I remembered, with the noise and the roars in the West and East Stands, and fights breaking out everywhere. The Cardiff fans didn't stop singing. It was a good game and the team tried their best, but they were never going to outclass a team like Chelsea. We got well defeated on the day, 4-1.

Can you believe it? They let both sets of fans out at exactly the same time. Surely the police should have known better? Even our spotter said he asked them to keep Cardiff in the ground for half an hour after the game.

On the way out of the ground you had 6,000 Cardiff fans, and out of those you'd probably got 1000-2000 looking for trouble or trying to arrange it. As Cardiff came out onto the streets there were around 700 Chelsea, all the old faces and names from the past. The fans from the Valleys have no fear of the police, so Cardiff just went straight through the lines. Nobody was going to stop them, and the Chelsea faces were dumbstruck with shock and horror. They thought they were going to bounce around and torment Cardiff, but while Chelsea were doing all this Cardiff just came forward. In the end it was more like Cardiff fighting the Metropolitan Police than Chelsea. It went on for quite a few minutes.

As this was going on, Chelsea apparently had a massive mob along the King's Road as well, including a lot of the old faces. About 100 of Cardiff's younger lads, aged between 18 and 30, went off alone down the lanes and had a toe-to-toe head on with about 150 Chelsea old heads, just like it was in the 80's. One of our spotters said, "I've been a police spotter for 15 years and that was full on!" He said he'd feared for his life. "For four or five minutes it was horrific. I've never seen so much violence. Nobody was giving way. Chelsea and Cardiff were going at each other and beyond – way beyond!" Chelsea also showed that when it really matters they can still pull big numbers of all their old heads.

And where could all this be seen taking place? On CCTV, of course. When the police turned up there were just bodies all over the floor. Both sets of fans said, "Nobody ran and nobody backed down." They also said it was some of the worst violence they'd been involved in for many a year.

Cardiff had a few battles with faces from the past: you had your infamous well known old-school Chelsea firm. They'd all turned out for this one, and I think you'll find a few of them had broken noses and were knocked around a bit.

What Cardiff couldn't understand is why there were 20 of the Wolves firm there outside the ground with Chelsea. And what were five Stoke faces doing with them? Ten-15 QPR? Actually, the ones who did have a go at Cardiff outside were Wolves and QPR. Cardiff were shocked, because they were by themselves and couldn't understand why Chelsea needed all these others. Apparently, they were mates of mates and people from all over London had come to have a look at what was going on. But did Chelsea really need all of them?

It brought back memories of the 80's. Since then, on Sky TV and the BBC they have been asking the public to name about 40-50 photos they have of Cardiff and Chelsea fans. They are expecting 50-60 Cardiff to be raided and I don't know how many Chelsea, but up to now about 30-odd Chelsea have been raided. The police have now said it's going to be one of the biggest operations ever. By the end of the 2009/10 season there will also be the biggest number of Cardiff fans banned ever. So it lived up to its name: Chelsea versus Cardiff. I think it brought back lots of memories for many people.

So, is the hooligan scene dead? No, it's not. But it's not happening every week. And that's really the story of Chelsea/Cardiff.

There's never been any organisation with Cardiff, but nobody was ever going to stop it. It doesn't matter how many police are there, if two sets of fans want each other it's very hard to stop it.

CONCLUSION

Even though our team for most of the last 30-40 years was shit, nearly always in the lower leagues and for years in the 'dungeon league' (old Division Four), off the field the Soul Crew were always in the Premier League.

The lads who wrote their stories carry it in their blood, although it's now officially over due to banning orders, police intelligence and CCTV. But they will never take it out of them totally, as it was such a big part of their lives. We get looked upon as major criminals, but I would have rather have mixed with them than with paedophiles, rapists, murderers, robbers and drug dealers.

Personally, I don't think anyone can really say that they had the best all-time firm, though on our day we all felt we were the best from Barnsley to Chelsea. If the right lads met the right lads on that day, fair enough. But most of the time, for some reason or other, the Old Bill had got there first and stopped one mob, or half of the other team's firm was split up and depleted.

But, no matter what other people say outside football, at the time you felt you were fighting on behalf of your club. Unless people really have been there, they will never understand the buzz that there was at that time. I am not saying that fighting at a football match is right, but most lads have a fight when they're growing up; some continue it as they get older, others move on, like myself. In the 70's and 80's it was the in-thing at football; others got involved later, in the 90's or even lately. But what I do guarantee is that, in every town in this country, there are street gangs causing ten times more trouble than a football lad.

These lads have been named, shamed and lost their jobs in the past, all for a fight at a football match against a like-minded lad. They then have to sign on at a police station, hand their passports in and prove when they are going on a holiday for the next three to ten years, some of them for just sticking two fingers up or being drunk at a football ground. I am not totally blaming the police for this, as they are acting out orders from our government, but millions of pounds have been spent on cracking down on so-called football hooligans. There are times when it has got well out of control, like the Cardiff v Swansea games where hundreds of police are needed, as I've shown in my story 'Our Bitter Enemy'. But week in week out, thousands are still spent on the everyday match and fans are treated worse than animals, with no rights at all.

I have been involved in pubs and clubs for 20-odd years, I've seen fights which make a football fight look like a playground scrap in an infants school. When the offenders are nicked, they are given respect, bailed and back in court for a £50 fine, or most of the time cautioned and told, "Don't do it again." Brownhill's has been mentioned by a lot of the lads – and yes, a lot of football lads used to drink in the pub in the late 80's, but so did a lot of other people. It was known as a football pub and in the three years that I worked there, we had one glass inside smashed by a football lad, who apologised. We had no doormen on football days and up to 400 lads would frequent the premises. On rugby days we had six doormen, and at the end of the day we had the drainpipes pulled off the walls outside, pictures and lights pulled off the walls inside and the toilets totally flooded. When a fight occurs between rugby fans, we're told that it's all just high spirits. The papers forget to tell you that, on rugby days now, every train back up to the Valleys has to have numerous police for the safety of the normal public, and that in the last few years, when rugby teams have been abroad on tour, there have been bars wrecked by the teams and a number of rapes have been alleged.

At the end of the day, all we football fans are saying is treat us the same as everybody else is treated in Britain. Most police forces treat Cardiff fans like scum. Yes, we've been naughty boys and have fought battles with like-minded lads, but we haven't murdered anyone. What goes a long way in this world is RESPECT. If they treated lads with more respect, the police would find they got it returned. We've had two main police spotters assigned to Cardiff, who have managed over the last decade to gain respect from some of our worst nutters and our main lads, because they haven't stabbed them in the back and they have also tried to stop other police forces from going over-the-top on our fans. Yes, they're police and they have a job to do, but they have been fair and have treated us like human beings. I just wish that the government and the rest of the police up and down the country realised we're not the main criminals. (Players themselves actually behave worse than us – but I forgot, they're not fans, they're celebrities.)

Times have really changed for Cardiff, probably more than for any other team's fans in Britain. All our big games are bubbles, the club and the police vet every person who travels on the coaches, and we don't receive our match ticket till our arrival at the ground. Swansea, Bristol City, Bristol Rovers, Birmingham City, Millwall, Leeds, Wolves and West Ham away are all bubble games for our fans. Yet look at Millwall v Leeds, Swansea v Birmingham, Wolves v Swansea, etc – no restrictions. So the days out and the big occasions are over for Cardiff fans.

Most of the lads that I know have totally moved on, grown up, got families like myself and look back on it as part of growing up. This book is not saying, "Yes, it's right what we did," it's saying it happened, it's not a lie, but did anyone else get hurt other than football lads? A great percentage of these lads still love and follow their clubs week in, week out, and most have no interest at all in fighting nowadays.

What is good now is that a lot of lads from the 70's, 80's and 90's all have a lot of respect for each other, and even turn up at each other's events – e.g. Boro lads went to an event held in Hull to raise money for nine Hull City lads' families while they were in prison. This actually happens all over the country.

I moved on from all this over ten years ago. As far as I am concerned, my wife and children are the reasons for that, they come first. They are what I live for. But I've never touched drugs/raped/burgled/attacked people for no reason. My vice was being one of the lads at football, against like-minded persons. But we all eventually move on, and I certainly have. People who fight at football nowadays must be mad: CCTV, signing at police stations, heavy prison sentences, passports taken off you, and for what? Punching a like-minded football lad. The sentences are crazy, it's just not worth it.

If you have a fight in a nightclub or in the city centre on the weekend, you get either a slap on the wrist or at most an £80 fine. Yet a football fan gets jail for the same thing. On 31st March 2010, three Cardiff fans got 14 months in prison for a fight with like-minded Southampton fans, where no one got hurt. How can they get that sentence when a burglar gets bound over to keep the peace for a year, or a drug dealer gets eight months for selling something that can ruin or even kill people?

At the end of the day, the memories of the 70's, 80's and 90's will always live with me.

Annis Abraham Jnr.

PUBLISHED OCTOBER 2010, £8.99.
THE NEW AUTOBIOGRAPHY OF ANNIS ABRAHAM JNR.

I LEFT MY HEART IN NINIAN PARK

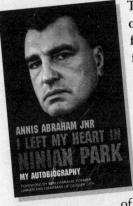

This is the extraordinary account of one man's relationship with his football club. Annis Abraham Jnr. first saw Cardiff City play at their Ninian Park ground in 1973; since then he has visited almost every ground in the Football League to witness his beloved team's triumphs and tragedies.

This personal memoir of the beautiful game is also a chronicle of its times, the passion of Cardiff's huge active following often spilling over into mayhem off the pitch. The author gives a full and honest account of his own life as one of the boys, both with the Cardiff fraternity and their notorious 'firm', the Soul Crew, who mixed it with every other rival firm back in the days when hooliganism was rife.

Abraham also chronicles how some of the hardcore fans have risen up through the hierarchies – whether muscling their way into big-time crime or the boardroom. Most controversially, the Welsh football fan reveals how he was thrust into the media spotlight by damaging allegations of hooliganism in a *Panorama* special.

On the other side of the terraces, *I Left My Heart in Ninian Park* details Abraham's personal relationship with Cardiff City FC's two most controversial chairmen – Sam Hammam and Peter Risdale – in an autobiography that will amuse, amaze and entertain anyone with even a passing interest in Britain's football culture.